THE ART OF EDITING

Now in its 12th edition, this core text is the most comprehensive and widely used textbook on editing in journalism.

Thoroughly revised and updated to incorporate more online and multimedia formats, this hands-on guide offers a detailed overview of the full process of journalistic editing, exploring both the "micro" aspects of the craft, such as style, spelling and grammar, and "macro" aspects, including ethics and legality. Recognizing the pronounced global shift toward online multimedia, the authors continue to stress the importance of taking the best techniques learned in print and broadcast editing and applying them to online journalism. This new edition also includes an in-depth discussion of the role editors and journalists can play in recapturing the public's trust in the news media. Additional chapters examine how to edit for maximum visual impact and how to edit across media platforms, teaching students how to create a polished product that is grounded in the best practices of journalism.

The Art of Editing, 12th edition, remains an essential resource for students of journalism across all media and levels interested in editing, design and media writing, as well as for professionals seeking to refine and refresh their skill set.

Accompanying online features include instructor PowerPoints and student exercises.

Brian S. Brooks has served as editor-in-chief of the *Columbia Missourian* and as the top editor of the European edition of *Stars and Stripes*, the U.S. military newspaper in Europe and the Middle East. He served as a faculty member and administrator at the Missouri School of Journalism for 38 years, the last ten of those as associate dean for undergraduate studies. He continues to work part-time for the school. Brooks served as deputy director or director of the Dow Jones News Fund internship program at Missouri for more than 40 years. He is the co-author of four journalism textbooks and is a member of the Missouri Press Association's Newspaper Hall of Fame.

James L. Pinson has worked for newspapers in Missouri, Colorado and Michigan and holds a doctorate in journalism from the Missouri School of Journalism, where he taught for six years. He later taught for 25 years in the journalism program at Eastern Michigan University, where he is now a professor emeritus, and for 13 summers in the Dow Jones News Fund's internship program. In addition to this book, he and Brian S. Brooks are also co-authors of *Working With Words: A Handbook for Media Writers and Editors*, along with Jean Gaddy Wilson.

THE ART OF EDITING
in the Age of Convergence

12th edition

Brian S. Brooks and
James L. Pinson

Routledge
Taylor & Francis Group

NEW YORK AND LONDON

Cover image: © Orbon Alija / Getty Images

Twelfth edition published 2022
by Routledge
605 Third Avenue, New York, NY 10158

and by Routledge
2 Park Square, Milton Park, Abingdon, Oxon, OX14 4RN

Routledge is an imprint of the Taylor & Francis Group, an informa business

© 2022 Taylor & Francis

The right of Brian S. Brooks and James L. Pinson to be identified as authors of this
work has been asserted in accordance with sections 77 and 78 of the Copyright,
Designs and Patents Act 1988.

First edition published 1971
Eleventh edition published by Routledge 2018

Library of Congress Cataloging-in-Publication Data
Names: Brooks, Brian S., author. | Pinson, James L., author.
Title: The art of editing : in the age of convergence / Brian S. Brooks
    and James L. Pinson.
Description: 12th edition. | London ; New York : Routledge, 2022. |
    Includes bibliographical references and index.
Identifiers: LCCN 2021035920 | ISBN 9780367820138 (hardback) |
    ISBN 9780367820107 (paperback) | ISBN 9781003011422 (ebook)
Subjects: LCSH: Journalism—Editing. | Copy editing.
Classification: LCC PN4778 .B3 2022 | DDC 070.4/1—dc23
LC record available at https://lccn.loc.gov/2021035920

ISBN: 9780367820138 (hbk)
ISBN: 9780367820107 (pbk)
ISBN: 9781003011422 (ebk)

DOI: 10.4324/9781003011422

Typeset in Futura
by Apex CoVantage, LLC

Access the Support Material: Routledge.com/9780367820107

CONTENTS

Preface   vii

 1 The Evolution of Editing   1
 2 Journalism's Credibility Problem   16
 3 The Editing Process   43
 4 Macro Editing for the Big Picture   79
 5 Macro Editing for Legality, Ethics and Propriety   114
 6 Micro Editing for Grammar and Usage   166
 7 Micro Editing for Style, Spelling and Tightening   196
 8 Holistic Editing: Integrating the Macro and the Micro   220
 9 Edit Yourself   275
10 Writing Headlines, Titles, Captions and Blurbs   285
11 Using Photos, Graphics and Type   314

Glossary   347
Index   359

PREFACE

New to This Edition

It's common knowledge that changes in the media industry have been accelerating for two decades or more, and that it's no longer enough for students to train merely as print or broadcast editors. Editors, like reporters, must be well-acquainted with the skills needed in both media while also acquiring familiarity with all things web-related.

This book is designed to help students find their first jobs as editors and perform well when they do. But it is also designed as a refresher and update for professional editors and a guide for reporters who want to improve their writing and increase their chances of finding a better job, doing well at it and ultimately advancing through the ranks.

With that in mind, *The Art of Editing*, long the leading editing text in the country, in this 12th edition again has been thoroughly updated. We continue to instruct in the basics of editing—in far more detail than any competitor— while also preparing users in the fundamentals of multimedia journalism.

The fundamentals of editing first developed in print are at the heart of what all editors still do, but you also will find ample references here to online media—with a stress on both similarities and differences when writing and editing for newspapers, magazines, newsletters, books, radio, television, the web and mobile media, as well as public relations.

Perhaps the most notable change in this edition is a complete rewrite of the first three chapters to stress the enormous challenge journalists face in recapturing the public's trust. Survey after survey shows that people simply don't have trust in the accuracy of news they read in newspapers and magazines, watch on television or hear on radio. They also are skeptical of what they read or watch online, although they are turning to that medium at a rapid pace. In this edition, we pay far more attention to that problem and suggest some ways that journalists might redefine the concept of objectivity and move to recapture readers' and viewers' trust.

In Chapter 3, we roll together information on editing for various media— magazines, radio, television and the web—that earlier appeared in separate chapters. That's desirable because all editors now need the skills taught in those chapters.

Another new element in this edition is Chapter 9, an entirely new chapter focused on self-editing. In today's world, the redundant editing that once dominated in print editing has often disappeared as newspapers and magazines cut employees to protect the bottom line. Sadly, editors are often the first to go. That means writers must pay more attention than ever to turning in copy that is both clean and correct. Chapter 9 is designed to help you do just that.

In this edition, we also added more advice on what we call *holistic editing*, which improves both the speed of editing and the chances of improving accuracy while doing it. We provide specific guidance for reporters writing almost 30 kinds of stories (and for editors reviewing their work).

As we publish this edition, we find journalism students are often naturally concerned about the job market. While it's true that many newspapers have downsized and a few have disappeared in the past decade, many still employ more journalists in their market than all the radio and television stations combined. And, of course, the World Wide Web has opened thousands of new jobs for aspiring journalists.

Interestingly, at the University of Missouri, where both of us once worked and one still does, we noted an interesting anomaly during a survey that attempted to determine where former students were working three years after graduation. Surprisingly, the highest placement rate was among those who graduated with an interest in newspapers. How can that be when newspapers are reducing the size of their staffs? Simple: Because of the bad publicity regarding the future viability of newspapers, fewer students are majoring in newspaper journalism. Those who do have little trouble finding jobs in that labor-intensive industry. We've also seen increasing employment prospects for our students in cable television, the online and mobile media world, and public relations.

So, our advice is not to shy away from seeking a job at a newspaper or other media company if that appeals to you. Just understand that as a journalist today, you will have to become a multimedia journalist, equally at home in writing and editing for the web as for print.

Of course, the changes in journalism are being driven by the changing patterns in news consumption. Fewer and fewer people read newspapers and watch local television each year, but more and more consume news on the internet. Much of that is on social media, so we've seen media companies go from only delivering news in their own original medium to adding a web page, then their own mobile app, and now also distributing via social media platforms such as Twitter and Facebook.

That means it's no longer adequate for a student to view himself or herself as a "newspaper reporter" or a "magazine editor" or even a "television reporter." Today, for example, a newspaper reporter must be able not only to write for print but also to take still photographs, operate a video camera and edit the resulting video, produce a podcast, and write differently for the outlet's web page, blogs and social media. Today's magazine editor also is likely to be producing audio and video for the web. A television or radio reporter also must be able to produce varied content for the web, and the stories written for the website may be more akin to print stories than to those written for broadcast.

In short, we live in the Age of Convergence, as the title of this book suggests. Being a journalist today requires understanding not only traditional writing and editing for print but also writing for the web, producing and editing audio and video, and learning how social media can be used to drive traffic to news websites. New ways of receiving news, particularly over mobile phones, promise to continue changing the industry in ways heretofore unimagined.

The editing skills taught here are still those honed for decades at the nation's best newspapers, magazines and broadcast stations. Those skills— updated to include online media—are still in great demand throughout the media industry. As a result, in this edition, we place more stress than ever on how those skills apply to editing for the web.

Convergence is fundamental to what's happening in the industry. Although that means many things to many people, we define *convergence* here as cooperative ventures or cross-media skills development among some combination of print, radio, television and the web. Put simply, there is a growing demand for multimedia reporters and editors who can edit for print, produce audio and video, and cope with the nuances of the web.

Through all the turmoil and change, one constant remains: Those who can edit, and edit well, have no trouble finding jobs. If the market for newspaper reporters is difficult, the market for editors of all kinds is not. That's because good editors remain hard to find, and they are still in great demand.

As in past editions, we stress the importance of editing as an art. We say that because in editing, unlike in the sciences, there often is no one right way to do things. The best editors learn the principles of editing and then adapt them to the demands of their jobs. As in previous editions, we have included numerous examples of editors' successes and failures as illustrations of how to edit and how not to edit. We have taken examples, both good and bad, from newspapers, magazines, radio and television stations, and websites from coast to coast. Through them, we learn.

Journalism is an interesting, stimulating and exciting profession. Editing, in turn, is a vital part of journalism, whether delivered in print, through broadcast or on the web. Newspapers, magazines, radio and television stations, and websites would not be nearly so good without editors as they are with them. They can be superb with top-flight editors. We hope this book inspires many of you to become just that.

The excitement of producing the news is universal, and it is a process in which editors are full partners. Still, it is difficult for any book to capture the excitement of editing because the beginner must first master the intricacies of the editor's art. Attention to detail is of primary importance to the editor, and we believe this book—especially this newest edition—attends to that detail more thoroughly than any other. We hope we have done so as interestingly and as concisely as possible.

Those of you who are attentive to detail will note one deviation from Associated Press style, which the book generally follows. We have adopted the book publisher's convention of italicizing newspaper, magazine and book titles.

With the previous edition, we made the move to the prestigious academic publishing imprint Routledge, part of the Taylor and Francis group. Our new editors are terrific, and like all good writers we are grateful for their careful attention to detail. They provide the inspiration and careful editing all authors need, including—maybe especially!—authors of a copy-editing text. For this edition, our excellent editors were Elizabeth Cox and Priscille Biehlma.

We also would like to thank Taylor Pinson, a reporter at WEMU-FM in Ypsilanti, MI, for his suggestions on broadcasting and for his sample radio script, for which we further want to thank WEMU's general manager, Molly Motherwell, for permission to include. We also want to thank Randy Reeves, former news director of KOMU-TV in Columbia, Missouri, for providing and giving permission for the sample television script.

Through the continual updating and streamlining of this book as the world of editing has changed, one axiom holds true: Editing is an art no matter where or by whom it is practiced. To those who will accept the challenge of careful and thoughtful editing, we dedicate this book.

Brian S. Brooks
James L. Pinson

1 THE EVOLUTION OF EDITING

The Editor's Role Changes

Oh, how editing has changed! Since this book's first edition, published in 1971, hundreds, if not thousands, of editing jobs have disappeared from U.S. newspaper newsrooms. Indeed, many of the publications on which those editors worked have vanished, too. And the sharp decline in the number of editors at newspapers has been accompanied by a decline in the number of editors at magazines, television stations and networks, albeit in much lower numbers.

Why has this happened? Quite simply, it's the result of technology providing new and more efficient ways to deliver the news, most obviously through the internet, which in turn has reduced the income of the traditional media. Companies simply can't charge as much for internet ads as they did for

DOI: 10.4324/9781003011422-1

newspaper and magazine ads. It's the same sort of technological revolution that occurred when airplanes derailed trains as the primary means of passenger movement. Airplanes made us more mobile in less time, just as the internet makes news faster and less expensive to deliver.

In the U.S., the overwhelming majority of media operations are commercial, and their financial model, long based on print and broadcast advertising, has been severely undercut. Further, the World Wide Web allows news to be transmitted at a much lower cost—in terms of both personnel and production—than is the case with more traditional media. In short, the financial model that served us well for centuries has been broken. The problem, of course, is that news is expensive to gather and produce, and lower ad rates on the web make it much more difficult to pay the bills and make a profit.

Newspaper copy editors often were the first victims—except at top-notch publications like *The New York Times*, the *Washington Post* and *The Wall Street Journal*. Those publications, unlike so many others in this country, still have the circulations and advertising appeal to afford multiple levels of editing. The reporter writes the story, the assigning editor edits it, then a copy editor gives it another edit. That's the way most newspapers functioned until they quit making money by the bucketful. Now, at most newspapers there is only one editor to tackle a story rather than the two or more who once did. At many websites and small newspapers, there often is no editor other than the writer.

Career editors and teachers of editing, like the authors of this book, lament the decline in editing nationwide and its negative effect on publications and television news programming. Errors abound in big-city dailies, small-town weeklies, magazines and on television. And while there are far fewer editors than in the past, there is no turning back. We find ourselves in an era in which profits have declined to the point that hundreds of publications have shuttered their doors and most traditional media operations have reduced the size of their staffs. Sadly, too often editors—particularly copy editors—seem to be the first eliminated.

Why is the reduction in the number of editors alarming? Quite simply, it's editors who correct spelling and grammar, find and correct errors in fact, make fuzzy writing more readable, and, perhaps most important to the publication, keep libelous material out of the news. With fewer editors to review a story, chances of all those things occurring increases.

Sadly, returning to the good old days isn't in the cards. The hope that traditional media outlets like newspapers will suddenly find a new source of revenue is slim. Many print publications, in particular, now find themselves in survival mode because of their high costs of production and distribution. Most are attempting to reinvent themselves as internet-based websites as their traditional sources of revenue sink lower each year. In the newspaper business, for example, there is now a strong movement to the internet and emphasis on publishing news on the web first, then in print. That would have been unthinkable 30 years ago. And jobs in those media continue to decline because web publishing simply does not create the income that print once did.

Given the presence of fewer and fewer editors, **self-editing** is now more important than ever. The reporter who produces clean, concise copy becomes a coveted and valuable member of the staff. As a result, this edition of *The Art of Editing* gives an increasing amount of attention to those who would not only write but also edit. Writing is important, of course, but editing also is important to communicate well.

The Rise of the Reporter-Editor

The best reporters have always submitted copy that was not only meticulously reported and written but also meticulously edited. Many reporters, however, *needed* editors to help them revise tortured prose and make it presentable. Yet today, many journalists have no one at all to edit their copy before it is broadcast, printed or placed online. Nowhere is that more true than at websites. Thus, those seeking jobs at the websites of local newspapers and magazines, or even much larger national or international sites, need strong skills in all areas of journalistic practice, including reporting, writing, editing, photography, audio and video production, and likely even design of a page or website.

Figure 1.1 A reporter interviews a news source at the scene of a local festival. Back at the office, the reporter may well write a web story first, then one for print. Both reporters and editors must understand the differences in presenting news in print and online.

Photo by Christopher Parks.

"Some of the old-time reporters at newspapers simply could not hold a job in the current environment," one former newspaper editor said. "When I was a city editor, I had a reporter who wrote every story in chronological order. He reported a City Council meeting chronologically, not with the most important information first. It had to be heavily edited—even rewritten."

Indeed, that reporter would have a difficult time adjusting to today's news environment, where a reporter is expected to gather the news, write it, edit it, engage with consumers on social media, and often even create graphics, audio and video pieces. The job of a journalist is much more complex than it was in years past, when roles of reporters, editors, photographers, graphic artists, and audio and video experts were clearly delineated—and separated. Oh, and today's journalist often writes headlines and photo captions, too.

Similarly, broadcast journalists find themselves writing newspaper-like stories for the web because their TV scripts don't work well on websites. Not every story merits a video, and without those, the scripts alone are not explanatory. Rewriting will likely be needed. These journalists, too, must learn about writing headlines for the web and how to use social media. In other words, **the skill set needed to succeed in journalism has grown significantly.** In every area of today's journalism, skills in audio and video editing, web production and use of social media are essential.

Readers Choose Their News

The way news is produced and consumed also has changed. For generations, news was produced and distributed in assembly-line fashion. Reporters gathered and wrote it, editors edited it, and publishers produced and distributed it in print or broadcast form to mass audiences. It was a one-to-many model born in the Industrial Revolution.

Editors in that environment served as **gatekeepers**. They decided when to open the gate, allowing information to flow to the public. Editors had total control over what was published or broadcast. They determined which stories were *newsworthy*—those they deemed useful, relevant or interesting to their audiences. Editors controlled the gate, and consumers got only what editors gave them.

Editors also controlled the **play** a story received. Was it newsworthy enough for page 1, where almost everyone would notice it, or should it be relegated to a brief on page 37, where few would read it? Did it make the cover of *Time,* or did it not make the magazine at all? Did it warrant top billing on the evening newscast, or was it left to the local newspaper?

Editors were powerful. They called all the shots.

Today, that is far from true. The internet and wireless devices (mobile phones and tablet computers) allow users to *choose* what news they want to consume from multiple providers—some traditional and some not—and from digital databases of information vastly larger than the content of the nation's largest newspaper or a 24-hour-a-day cable-television news channel. In this more egalitarian environment, the one-to-many model disappears, and the user takes control.

Consumers now have almost unlimited access to millions of daily news items on the internet. Simply download a computer or smartphone application to give you only the news you want from the sources you prefer. Increasingly, that software, not an editor, serves as the gatekeeper. The consumer, not the editor, has control of the flow of information.

Obviously, not everyone consumes news this way. Editors still serve as gatekeepers at newspapers and magazines, and in radio and television newsrooms. Editors still choose what to put on the front page of news websites. Editors still edit newsletters, corporate magazines and even advertisements. But an ever-increasing percentage of the world's population is discovering that it doesn't need editors to get information.

Editors, then, are faced with a changing environment. No longer are their roles as gatekeepers and *agenda setters* guaranteed. In today's changing media environment, these roles must be earned. Consumers must trust editors to give them what they need to know to be productive citizens. Consumers must perceive value in the editor as gatekeeper and agenda setter. Consumers must perceive a need to have editors help them sort through the sea of information now at their fingertips.

Earning that trust won't be easy. Each time a newspaper makes a mistake or a television station ignores real news in favor of the sensational, public confidence in the news media erodes. Each time a cable news network passes off editorializing as news, the credibility of that medium among thoughtful consumers erodes a bit more.

Editors cannot afford to be arrogant. They must earn the public's trust by making good judgments and presenting the news fairly and accurately. If they fail to do that, their influence will continue to diminish. Thus, the best path editors can follow is this one: **Practice good journalism grounded in the fundamentals of truth and accuracy.** In the end, this is the only way to earn the public's trust.

The Changing Media Environment

While the role of the editor is changing, it is doing so in consort with the changing nature of the media. Consider these realities:

- Newspapers continue to reach a smaller segment of the general population each year. While the population continues to grow, newspaper circulation declines. But when print circulation is combined with unique website page views, the total number of people reached each day by newspaper companies is actually increasing, and they remain the best and most thorough source of local news in most communities.

- Many newspapers are still marginally profitable, but often that's true only because of a print monopoly. In almost every city across the nation, print circulation is declining, and in most there is only one newspaper. Newspaper advertising is plummeting.

- Broadcast television audiences have been fragmented by the growth of competition. Networks such as Fox and The CW have added local stations in many markets, and the proliferation of cable-television channels—particularly 24-hour news channels such as CNBC, MSNBC, Fox News Channel and CNN—have added to audience erosion.

- Except for public broadcasting and all-news stations in a few major markets, radio isn't much of a player in North American news. Many stations air network news or read news items from local newspapers, but few local stations employ news reporters. Talk radio, however, is quite influential. Huge audiences get their "news," no matter how slanted, from conservative commentators like the late Rush Limbaugh, Sean Hannity and Glenn Beck. They counter what they and their listeners see as liberal biases in the mainstream media.

- Arguably, the best news found on American radio is produced by National Public Radio, which has affiliates nationwide. Indeed, in cities that have lost their newspapers, public radio may be the only good source of local news. Satellite radio and the internet have allowed subscribers to listen not only to public radio news but also to foreign news services such as the BBC and CBC, and to channels devoted to 24-hour coverage of traffic and weather for the nation's main metro areas.

- Magazines, for the most part, reach targeted audiences that are widely dispersed, often making them unsuitable for local advertising. Production costs are high, and postal rates, on which many depend for distribution, inch ever higher.

Thus, the traditional media, while still profitable, often find their profit margins challenged by forces largely beyond their control. But make no mistake about it: **The existing media, while challenged, are not all dying.** To illustrate:

- Many media companies (with the exception of newspapers) typically operate on profit margins around 12% of gross income, down from around 25% less than 20 years ago. That's still a healthy margin, surpassing that of many other industries. Even extraordinarily profitable industries such as oil don't have profit margins like that. Each year, for example, ExxonMobil earns about 10% of its revenue in profits.

- Most magazines, while not necessarily news oriented in the traditional sense, attract advertisers because of the appealing demographics of their audiences. If an advertiser wants to reach computer users, *PC Magazine* or *Macworld* will do the job, either in print or online.

- Most local broadcast stations are thriving, even as the traditional networks—NBC, CBS, ABC and Fox—have been hurt by **audience fragmentation**, a result of the explosion in the number of cable, satellite and streaming networks. Targeted cable-television outlets such as The Food Channel and ESPN do a great job of delivering the target audiences advertisers crave.
- All-news and talk-radio stations, found mostly in large metropolitan areas, are doing well financially.

The Media Converge

Traditional media have found new ways to compete. A buzzword in the media industry these days is **convergence**, and traditional media are exploring many forms of it. So, what is convergence? It's defined in many ways, but possibly the best definition yet offered is this one:

> Convergence is the practice of sharing and cross-promoting content from a variety of media through newsroom collaborations and outside partnerships.

The U.S. Telecommunications Act of 1996 made convergence possible because it relaxed ownership regulations on television and radio, and made it possible for stations to collaborate with print counterparts.

Cultural differences among the media can cause problems when media converge. When television first came along, many of its early newscasters came from the newspaper industry. Edward R. Murrow and Walter Cronkite brought with them the demanding ethical and reporting standards of the newspaper industry. But over the years, television developed a new set of standards driven more by what is visually pleasing than by traditional news values as practiced by newspapers.

Cultural differences aside, convergence makes sense, and it has happened nationwide. Among the traditional media, television and the internet remain the unquestioned leaders in providing the American public with today's news headlines. Newspapers and magazines can provide depth and understanding. But the internet can offer even greater depth than newspapers and interactivity unmatched by either print or television. The reality is that U.S. media have already converged—most have websites that combine print, still photographs, audio, video and web links. That's accomplished either internally or through partnerships with other media companies. **The merging or collaboration of disparate media makes sense for a changing world in which the consumer sets the terms for the consumption of news.**

The goal of forward-thinking media companies is to give consumers the news and information they want in whatever form they prefer. An increasing number, it seems, prefer web-based news delivered to mobile devices such as smartphones and tablet computers.

So, convergence is not dependent on cross-ownership of media companies or collaborative agreements. Some companies merge. Some collaborate. Some do it all themselves if they have the resources to do so. Newspaper companies have added audio, video and interactive graphics to their websites. Television stations have added newspaper-like stories and still photographs to theirs. And almost all of them are delivering news to mobile phones and tablets.

Clearly, convergence is here to stay. What we are witnessing is nothing less than a technology-driven revolution in the way news is produced and consumed. And none of that is necessarily dependent on common ownership.

In converged newsrooms, journalists have found they must learn about a medium other than the one in which they were originally trained. A television reporter might be asked to write a newspaper story and headline, or a headline for the web, and he or she must be able to do so. A newspaper reporter might be asked to produce a **podcast** or take along a digital recorder to get a sound bite of a news event for a website or radio station. And many, while not required to cross quite so dramatically into a new field, must at least have enough knowledge of the strengths of various media to know how best to tell a story in a multimedia environment. This is the world of the editor in the age of convergence.

Journalists may train in one medium, go to work upon graduation in another, and at some point change to a third or fourth career, depending on job opportunities at the time. Today's best journalism schools recognize that and prepare students well in cross-media skills. Today's journalists should view themselves not as television reporters or newspaper editors but as news specialists comfortable with working in a variety of settings—on the internet, at a magazine, in television and perhaps even in the related fields of public relations and advertising. Media companies realize the importance of giving consumers news and advertising information whenever and however it's wanted. That, in the end, is what convergence is all about.

It could also be said that convergence has clarified the descriptions of what editors in various media do down to three things they all have in common:

- **Some editors select the news and highlight it** (and the volume on websites is vastly increased from what appeared in traditional media).
- **Some editors cut and add information.**
- **Some editors are focused more minutely on changing a completed work to improve it**, much as writers edit their own work to try to improve it.

Today, almost all editing jobs fall into one of those three categories. So, despite the title an editor may have, at least 90% of today's editing functions can be summed up in one or more of those three.

The Changing Nature of News

If editing is changing, so is the nature of news itself. Editors no longer are the sole arbiters of what news is and what it isn't. As we said earlier in this chapter, consumers increasingly decide that for themselves. Traditionally, editors defined news as information having one or more (usually more) of these qualities:

- **Audience.** Readers of *The New York Times* are more likely to be interested in urban renewal than those of a local paper in Cedar City, Utah.
- **Impact.** The number of people involved in or affected by an event, as well as the emotional depth of an audience's reaction, helps to determine whether it is news.
- **Proximity.** Things that happen nearby are often more interesting than things that happen far away.
- **Timeliness.** Something that just happened is likely more interesting than something that happened last week or last year.
- **Prominence.** People like to read about famous, wealthy or powerful people, so entertainer Taylor Swift is more interesting than someone of whom few people have heard.
- **Novelty.** Something that is unusual or the first, the largest or the greatest is news.
- **Conflict.** People are drawn to read about conflict between people, states and nations.

A briefer way of saying it is that editors have defined news based on how *relevant*—that is, how *useful* or *interesting*—they think readers, listeners or viewers are likely to find it.

Today, however, consumers are defining news for themselves. If a website has appealing content, some viewers will find their news there, no matter how reliable or unreliable that site may be. And web entrepreneurs are carving out markets to take advantage of this reality.

Traditional media have done little, for example, to cover the recruiting of high school athletes for college football and basketball teams. Today, national websites, including Rivals (www.rivals.com) and 247 Sports (247sports.com), provide reporters who collect that information and distribute it online to an audience with a seemingly insatiable appetite for sports. The related forums on these networks help spread both news and rumor.

The reality is that much of the information provided by these specialized internet services is timely and reliable. On the reader forums, however, much of it is not. Consumers don't seem to care. Whether fact or fiction, to them it is news—rumors included.

How Changes in News Are Changing Us

In an effort to take a snapshot of changing news-consumption patterns, the Pew Research Center, centerpiece of the Pew Charitable Trusts' initiative to stimulate citizen involvement in community issues, conducted a landmark study it called *The Modern News Consumer*. It showed just how much news-consumption patterns had shifted from the heyday of newspapers. As Pew said in the introduction to its report:

> Wave after wave of digital innovation has introduced a new set of influences on the public's news habits. Social media, messaging apps, texts and emails provide a constant stream of news from people we're close to as well as total strangers. News stories can now come piecemeal, as links or shares, putting less emphasis on the publisher. And, hyper levels of immediacy and mobility can create an expectation that the news will come to us whether we look for it or not.

As Pew pointed out, news remains an important part of public life:

> More than seven-in-ten U.S. adults follow national or local news somewhat or very closely—65% follow international news with the same regularity. Fully 81% of Americans get at least some of this news through websites, apps or social networking sites. And, this digital news intake is increasingly mobile. Among those who get news both on desktop computers and mobile devices, more than half [now] prefer mobile.

In this digital news environment, the role of friends and family is amplified, but Americans still reveal strong ties to news organizations. The data also reinforce how, despite the dramatic changes witnessed over the previous decade, the digital news era was still very much in its adolescence.

Among the many interesting insights into changing news-consumption patterns are these Pew findings:

- Only about 20% of U.S. adults report that they often get news from printed newspapers. That varies widely by generation—only 5% of those 18 to 29 often get news from newspapers while 48% of those 65 and older do so.
- Despite the growth of the web, apps and social media, television continues to be the most widely used news medium. Fifty-seven percent of Americans often get TV-based news, either from local television (46%), cable (31%), network (30%) or some combination of the three.

The web is the second most common way of consuming news, followed by radio and print, which follow far behind.

- Television's lead is somewhat fragile because of demographics. While those aged 50 to 64 (72%) and 65 and older (85%) often get news on television, far smaller shares of younger adults do so (45% of those 30 to 49 and 27% of those 18 to 29).
- Television's staying power over print is buttressed by the fact that Americans who prefer to watch news still choose television while most of those who prefer to read the news have migrated online.
- Within the digital realm, mobile news consumption is rising rapidly. The portion of Americans ever to get news on a mobile device went from 54% to 72% in recent years and continues to climb.
- Online news consumers are more likely to get news from professional news outlets than from friends or family, but they are just as likely to think each provides relevant news. When asked about trust and accuracy, however, local and national news organizations were considered more trustworthy than news passed along from family and friends. And news from social media, which by definition often comes from family and friends, ranked as the least trustworthy.

If those findings are troublesome for the media companies that supply the news, there are some positives, too. Three-fourths of Americans believe that news organizations keep political leaders in line, even while believing that the news media are biased.

Credibility and the Media

At the heart of the media–public relationship is the question of credibility. And make no mistake about it: The obvious and blatant bias of cable-television news networks contributes greatly to the perception that the news is slanted. So, too, does the increasingly common practice at newspapers and magazines of allowing the writer's opinion to seep into news stories. **The loss of credibility is an unfortunate byproduct of allowing journalists and personalities more "voice" in their television stories, and the increasing penchant on the written side to produce narrative journalism in an effort to make the news more readable.** To the public, a lot of that looks like bias.

Much of cable "news" is indeed entertainment and not news at all. There is often no pretense that the network strives for anything close to objectivity, fairness or balance. Entertainers with little or no news background masquerade as journalists. Viewers watch the network that most closely aligns with their political views and simply don't get anything resembling a balanced view of news events or issues. That, in turn, has led to the increasing political polarization we see in this country.

What are the reasons for this bias? We have three possible answers:

- Journalists often have big egos and enjoy spouting their opinions about what they already think more than doing actual legwork only to discover they might be wrong.
- News outlets are trying to stay alive by finding a market niche— conservatives mainly for Fox, hard-core liberals for MSNBC and more moderate liberals and nonpartisans for CNN. Gaining that market niche means telling that audience what it wants to hear, not necessarily the best possible version of the truth.
- More and more journalists don't think **objectivity** is possible and don't even attempt to achieve it. And yet they ignore the fact that scientists and juries make honest attempts to get at the truth without preconceptions. True, absolute objectivity is elusive, but replacing it with slanted or one-sided reporting is far from a good solution.

For many years, newspapers and magazines, and even television, reported the news with every attempt to achieve what journalists called objectivity. If one politician, for example, voiced a viewpoint, another with the opposite viewpoint was sought out to "balance" the story. What most journalists now recognize is that true objectivity is almost impossible to achieve. Indeed, attempts to provide such objectivity often led to distortions of the very news they sought to balance. If, for example, it is objectively possible to show that the Holocaust was real, it's folly for a news organization to balance a story by finding a Holocaust denier for each person who is convinced it occurred. That would merely distort what most know is the truth.

Bill Kovach and Tom Rosenstiel, in their widely acclaimed book *The Elements of Journalism*, argue that the kind of phony objectivity journalists historically embraced is not only elusive but also can actually distort. They argue that journalists should instead practice objectivity of *method*, employing something quite similar to the scientific method that scientists employ. Like a scientist, it's permissible for a journalist to have a hypothesis about what the story will ultimately reveal, but it's also necessary for the journalist to change or alter the intended story approach if the reporting shows the original hypothesis was in error.

As for the print media, we're not opposed to narrative writing; indeed, it *does* make newspapers and magazines more enjoyable to read. But employing the practice comes at a price—and that price is often a decrease in perceived credibility. When readers can detect the writer's viewpoint, which often occurs in such writing, the result is often decreased credibility, particularly if the reader does not share the writer's viewpoint.

As a result of the changing media environment, it's only natural that consumers' view of journalistic credibility would decline. But ultimately, journalism is an art, not a science, and at every point in its production and delivery there are opportunities for the writer's or broadcaster's viewpoint to appear and for credibility to suffer as a result. There is no easy answer about how to solve that problem. Journalism is created by humans, and human fallibility is real.

More mundane issues, such as spelling and grammar errors, also affect the credibility of the news, according to a recent Pew study. More than a third of newspaper readers surveyed said they see mistakes more than once a week and 21% reported seeing them almost daily. "It seems like the paper's gotten sloppier in the last 10 years," said one focus group respondent. It probably has. Declining revenues have led many newspaper companies to cut staffing—particularly on copy desks, where such mistakes are supposed to be detected and corrected.

Pew also found that more than 80% of Americans believe that sensational stories get lots of news coverage simply because they are exciting, not because they are important. Further, 78% believe the media are biased. The same percentage believes powerful figures in society are able to influence a newspaper or broadcast station to "spike or spin" a story.

When asked which medium was the worst offender in the realm of bias, 42% said television, and 23% said newspapers. That's sad when television is overwhelmingly seen as the dominant source of national and world news.

Skepticism about the veracity of the media is not new. Unfortunately, the media reinforce doubts about their credibility when they refuse to admit errors, when the names of people and places are misspelled, when grammatical mistakes abound and when hoaxes of one type or another are uncovered.

Editors concerned about their credibility have tried to find ways to convince the public that newspapers, magazines and television are in fact reliable. These range from simple steps, such as the attempt to reduce annoying grammatical and typographical errors, to elaborate schemes designed to check the accuracy of reporters' work.

To enhance the image of newspapers, today's editors readily admit errors. Some newspapers run a daily notice, prominently displayed, inviting and encouraging readers to call attention to errors in the paper. Some editors regularly conduct accuracy checks of the newspaper's locally written news stories. A clipping of the story is mailed to the source along with a brief query on the accuracy of facts in the story and headline. Another editor invites people involved in controversy to present amplifying statements when they believe their positions have not been fully or fairly represented. Television stations tend to be far less candid in admitting mistakes, although there are exceptions.

More balance in opinion is evident in the use of syndicated columnists whose opinions differ from those of the newspaper's editorials and in expanded letters-to-the-editor columns. Some newspapers are using **ombudsmen** to hear readers' complaints. More are providing reader-service columns to identify newspapers with readers' personal concerns. More attention is also being given to internal criticism in employee publications or at staff conferences.

Broadcast stations are making similar efforts to increase their credibility. Many stations now provide email addresses for viewers to contact their news directors. Listeners and viewers are encouraged to write with questions or complaints. Still, some studies show that the public considers television news more credible than print news. The reason? It's easier to believe what you can see and hear. Few serious journalists would agree with that. In many U.S. markets, the newspaper staff is much larger than all the television news staffs in town put together, and fact-checking is much more rigorous in the print media.

Even websites are trying to improve their credibility by allowing online comments following stories and on Twitter and Facebook feeds. We'll tackle the problem of media credibility in much more detail in Chapter 2, but it's important to recognize it here. It's real, and it's a serious problem.

Editors Are Still Important—And in Demand

As noted earlier in this chapter, convergence is creating a demand for a new type of editor, one as capable of handling a magazine or newspaper story as editing video and the words that accompany it. The demand for those cross-trained in various media is growing daily. This, too, adds to the demand for editors.

Editing jobs are plentiful enough, in fact, companies are often willing to pay editors a higher salary than writers. Some of the nation's largest newspapers pay a differential to copy editors as a means of enticing journalists to work at the few copy desks that remain.

The variety of skills editors must master and the large range of news with which they must be up to date keep their work varied and interesting. Rather than being specialists on a narrow beat, they are generalists, and the skills good editors have developed make them prime candidates for promotion in their organizations.

And, while the demand for newspaper copy editors has plummeted, editors are still in high demand at websites. Indeed, most jobs there involve editing first and other skills secondarily. That's true whether they work for local media companies' websites or national websites.

The Art of Editing

In the first edition of this book, we described editing as an art, no matter where or by whom it is practiced. That axiom remains true today. Although media may change, the role of the editor remains clear: Provide timely and accurate information in the best form possible.

This edition of *The Art of Editing* has been extensively revised to reflect the dramatic changes occurring in the media industry. **It's worth remembering that despite the unsettled nature of the industry, there is no chance that editing jobs will disappear. Indeed, the number**

of career opportunities for talented editors seems to grow each year, particularly at websites. But those being hired are not just editors; they are multimedia journalists.

The skills that can be acquired from this text will help you edit and perform well as a multimedia journalist, whether that occurs in the mass media, in corporate media or in the related fields of advertising and public relations. Not everyone is an artist, and not everyone can be an editor. Those who learn here can be both.

Suggested Websites

American Copy Editors Society: www.copydesk.org
Columbia Journalism Review: www.cjr.org
Dow Jones News Fund: newsfund.org
News Leaders Association: www.newsleaders.org
News Media Alliance: www.newsmediaalliance.org
Nielsen Media: www.nielsen.com
Pew Center for Civic Journalism: www.pewcenter.org
The Poynter Institute: www.poynter.org

Suggested Readings

Gant, Scott. *We're All Journalists Now.* New York: Free Press, 2011.

Kolodzy, Janet. *Practicing Convergence Journalism: An Introduction to Cross-Media Storytelling.* New York: Taylor & Francis, 2013.

Kovach, Bill and Tom Rosenstiel. *The Elements of Journalism: What Newspeople Should Know and the Public Should Expect.* New York: Three Rivers Press, 2014.

Mathison, David. *Be the Media: How to Create and Accelerate Your Message . . . Your Way.* New Hyde Park, NY: Natural E creative group, 2009.

Meyer, Phillip. *The Vanishing Newspaper: Saving Journalism in the Information Age.* Columbia, MO: University of Missouri Press, 2009.

Mindich, David T.Z. *Tuned Out: Why Americans Under 40 Don't Follow the News.* New York: Oxford University Press, 2005

The Missouri Group: Brian S. Brooks, Daryl R. Moen and Beverly J. Horvit. *News Reporting and Writing*, 13th edition. Boston/New York: Bedford/St. Martin's, 2020.

2 JOURNALISM'S CREDIBILITY PROBLEM

The Harris Poll has been tracking Americans' trust of institutions since 1966. Trust in the media has declined overall during those years but moves upward or downward from time to time. Its poll in July 2020 reported:

> Americans are voracious consumers of news but tend to favor news sources that support their own political ideology. During these tumultuous times, Americans are checking the news more often and turning more to

DOI: 10.4324/9781003011422-2

24-hour news outlets. Americans access news for over an hour each day (77 minutes per day, on average). The main sources for news are TV (53%), 24-hour channels (43%) and social media. Fox News is the most watched news outlet among Republicans (57%), while Democrats watch CNN the most (52%).

(https://magazine.medill.northwestern.edu/wp-content/uploads/2020/07/NUQ-Trust-in-U.S.-Media-Report_09July2020.pdf)

Despite the fact party affiliation is a big factor in their news outlets of choice, Americans—88%, Harris found—think reporting should be impartial and completely neutral, but many say journalists are partisan instead. Still, 75% say it's OK for journalists to express a point of view as long as they make clear it's their own opinion.

Harris also found that 58% of Americans think the media report fake news. Yet 55% of the public trust the news media anyway. There's an even stronger distrust of social media—67%—yet 42% still get their news there each week, including 54% of Millennials and 62% of Gen Z. Still, 82% say they're concerned about distinguishing fake news from reality on the internet.

Another landmark 2020 study of 20,000 Americans found that hope for objective media is fading rapidly. The study, sponsored by Gallup and the Knight Foundation, found that:

- **Seventy-three percent of respondents said they see too much bias in news that is supposed to be objective. That's up from 65% in 2017.**
- **More than 80% say they worry that inaccuracies in stories are intentional because the reporter misrepresented facts (54%) or made them up (28%).**
- Political polarization affects this. **Seventy-one percent of Republicans strongly distrust the media, while only 22% of Democrats do. Fifty-two percent of independents also distrust the media.**
- Most see the media as under political attack. **Seventy percent of Democrats believe those attacks are unjustified, while 61% of Republicans say they are.**
- **While Americans generally blame the media for our strong political division, 80% think the media could bring people together.**
- Americans feel overwhelmed by the amount of news available, the speed with which it's transmitted and the vast number of news sources available. And clearly, many of them are unable or unwilling to distinguish between reliable and unreliable news sources. Instead, they simply gravitate to those with which they agree.

Other studies have found that at a time when media are fighting to stay in business, they're alienating many potential audience members. Often, public perception is that the media don't represent their views, are biased or unfair, and are sensationalist. This leads to a feeling among many that the press needs to be regulated to ensure journalists act in a socially responsible way. The problem is that would transfer control of the media to politicians by letting them decide what is or isn't socially responsible or even true, and Democrats and Republicans have very different ideas about those things. Such government control could spell the end of a free press and result in people being systemically more distrustful of the media.

What Undermines Media Credibility?

Bias (Particularly Political Bias)

We think this is the biggest criticism of journalism today, so we'll mainly focus on partisanship in this chapter and advocate a new form of objectivism in place of the activism. But the press is also credibly accused of bias in regard to race, gender, sexual orientation, religion, social and economic class, and so on. All news must be selected by someone, and people disagree on what is fair, important or true. But we should carefully listen to such criticisms and try to do a better job as much as humanly possible.

We'll mention here a related criticism: that political bias often results in journalists being too adversarial, perhaps most famous is CNN's Jim Acosta at White House press conferences during the Trump administration before being given an anchor job. Others would argue that many of Trump's actions were so outrageous that *someone* in the press needed to confront the administration, and Acosta did.

The old journalism maxims that "A newspaper's function is to report the news and raise hell," and "A journalist should comfort the afflicted and afflict the comforted" both have a built-in credibility gap. Of course, many people won't always like what you say if you say something they don't want to hear because it conflicts with their own biases. But you wouldn't want a newspaper in the South in the 1950s just to reflect the community's positive attitudes about segregation—it wouldn't have been doing its job. As Ben Franklin said, "If all printers were determined not to print anything till they were sure it would offend nobody, there would be very little printed." Journalists must find a solution for both appealing to and maintaining an audience without merely distorting the proof and pandering to them. We'll propose later in this chapter a new version of objectivity as a possible answer.

Media credibility is generally at an all-time low, and actual or perceived bias in the news is at least partially to blame. Harsh criticisms of proud institutions like *The New York Times*, *The Wall Street Journal* and the *Washington Post* are commonplace. Political conservatives bash the *Times* and *Post* for their left-wing slant in both news and opinion pieces, and liberals criticize *Journal* news coverage and its right-wing editorials in particular. The cable-television networks are reviled by millions as liberals denounce Fox News Channel and conservatives trash CNN and MSNBC. Clearly, our polarized politics play a major role in such criticism.

More than a third of U.S. citizens (42%) say television is biased. Most of that negativity is usually caused by the cable networks, not by the mainstream television networks or local television stations, although conservatives have had particular grudges against CBS going back to the Dan Rather years and more recently against NBC. But cable networks regularly go from more-or-less legitimate news programs into talk-show and opinion mode—think of Rachel Maddow on MSNBC and Sean Hannity on Fox News Channel opposite each other in the same prime time slot each weeknight—without differentiating between news and opinion. It's little wonder that when people watch MSNBC, CNN or Fox News Channel they find it almost impossible to tell the difference between fact and opinion.

Newspapers have less of a problem with this because they have historically confined opinion to the editorial page, in most cases, or clearly labeled "commentary" pieces as just that if published on news pages. Still, 23% of newspaper readers see bias in their local papers. Sometimes this is because newspapers, too, are more often mixing opinion into news stories, even at *The New York Times*. But this perceived bias may also be from readers failing to distinguish between clearly marked news versus opinion pages.

Most journalists have been found in decades worth of studies to be mainly liberal (80 to 90% or more) on both party identification and position on issues. By contrast, according to Pew Research in October 2020: "49% of *all* registered voters either identify as Democrats or lean to the party, while 44% identify as Republicans or lean to the GOP" (www.pewresearch.org/fact-tank/2020/10/26/what-the-2020-electorate-looks-like-by-party-race-and-ethnicity-age-education-and-religion/).

Some observers on the left have suggested the reason journalists are so liberal is that they are more informed than the general public by the nature of their work. The problem with that hypothesis is that most students who major in journalism tend to be liberal, even more so than working journalists. The field attracts more people on the left, just as business schools seem to attract more on the right. But most journalists definitely lean more to the left than the public as a whole in our experience and in decades worth of studies, and that contributes to the vastly different views of journalism as expressed by Democrats and Republicans. Here are a few thoughts on why journalists are mainly liberal:

- Journalists, even in high school and college, are people who want to see the nation become a better place for all to live. They abhor the fact that so many people are poor, and they believe the political system is stacked in favor of the wealthiest among us.

- Journalists themselves are not particularly well-paid, so they tend to support things that help the poor—welfare, Social Security, Medicare, Medicaid, a minimum-wage increase and similar programs.
- Those motivated primarily by money don't go into journalism. Instead, they choose professions like medicine, engineering and business, where the earning potential is arguably quite higher, at least initially. But, while financial standing is important, what many forget is that high-paying jobs can be found in almost any profession, including journalism. We've seen a few former students become millionaires only a year or two out of college.

Whatever their politics, though, we think that other than in opinion pieces, journalists should write in such a way that their political views should never be apparent—especially in "fact checks." If expressing your own political views or crusading for them are foremost in your mind, you should go into politics yourself, work for a candidate or cause as a PR person, or become an honest political commentator. If you choose to stick with writing news, before submitting your story to your editor, reread it to make sure you have not inserted language that would reveal your political leanings.

It's easy to blame the media for bias, but at least some blame rests with news consumers themselves. Far too many of them are more than willing to read or view even the extreme news outlets that support their biases while ignoring more objective media or failing to balance views from their favorite news source with news from the opposite end of the political spectrum. Indeed, many Americans are happy to consume biased news, even to the point of reading fringe publications and websites like the far-right InfoWars and the far-left Wonkette. It's rather simple to see where those publications stand just by reading a couple of headlines:

Infowars: **Arizona Rep. Paul Gosar: Child Trafficking and the Deep State Are Real, 'Systemic Racism' is a Hoax**
Wonkette: **Oh, Sarah Palin, How We've Missed Your Crazy Talking, Dumbass Self**

Readers who flock to such sites aren't getting real news. Instead, they are consuming propaganda that reinforces and inflames their existing biases.

Where, then, are readers and viewers to go if they want to make sure the news they are getting is accurate and relatively biased? We provide our opinion of news source positions left, center and right in Chapter 4. For other opinions, a number of websites, including allsides.com and MediaBiasChart.com, try

to provide guidance. While not perfect—and the authors of this text disagree with a number of their rankings and sometimes with each other, as well—a check with one, and preferably more than one, is useful in helping you judge the reliability of a site.

MediaBiasChart.com, for example, regularly updates a chart that shows its opinion of the level of media outlets' reliability, from best to worst, and political bias, from left to right. At the top center of the chart are what it finds to be the most accurate and unbiased news sources—the Associated Press, Reuters, Agence France-Presse and Bloomberg. Of those, the Associated Press has by far the largest U.S. readership, and we'd point Americans to that source if they want the best and most unbiased news.

Close behind in the top tier of accurate media operations that lean to the political center are three major television networks, ABC, CBS and NBC; National Public Radio; Newsy; the Weather Channel; the Public Broadcasting System; *Newsweek* magazine; Politico; *The Financial Times; The Guardian; USA Today;* The Hill; HuffPost; Vox; and *Forbes.* Also in this group are the CNN website (but not the television network), *The New York Times,* the *Washington Post* and *The Wall Street Journal.* While the *Times, Post* and *Journal* are frequent targets of critics from the opposite side of the political spectrum, most would rate their journalism as among the best in the world. But clearly, one can sometimes find political bias, if only subtle, in their news columns. They also can be criticized on some occasions based on what they do and do not cover.

CNN television is in MediaBiasChart's next tier as is *The Washington Times.* These are rated as offering complex analysis or a mix of factual reporting and analysis with CNN tilting to the left and the *Times* to the right. MSNBC and Fox News Channel both are rated lower in accuracy and are seen as prone to opinion with a high variation of reliability.

American media outside the top ratings tier, especially—and we'd add even inside it, as well—should be read or viewed skeptically with an eye out for bias. You should also be skeptical of such evaluation sites, as well as fact-check sites, by comparing their rankings against each other and deciding for yourself which you find most trustworthy.

Interestingly, local media outlets almost always rate higher with the public than national outlets. Surveys show that most citizens believe their local newspaper or television station makes a serious effort to get it right, at least on local news.

Nonetheless, bias in media, ranging from subtle to extreme, remains a huge problem in American media. But bias isn't the only reason media credibility is questioned. Here are some others:

Sensationalism

The public has been losing faith in journalism, many critics say on all political sides, because the media are increasingly

seen as businesses interested more in saying what will make money than the truth, and many journalists are seen as interested more in saying what will further their career (a big, sensational scoop or acclaim from fellow journalists) than the truth. So, related to the charge that the media distort the news to appeal to a certain market niche is that of sensationalizing the news to expand the audience and make more money. This can be done in overstating stories, stressing celebrity and scandal, and providing less straight coverage about real issues in the news. Some of the pressures in journalism for sensationalism include:

- News values of prominence, oddity and conflict promote sensationalism.
- Pressure for journalists to make a big name with a dramatic scoop.
- Pressure from bottom-line managers to bring in a bigger audience to sell more ads and make more money. So, news gets pushed into entertainment and is dumbed down to reach the lowest common denominator. For example, (4–7 second) soundbites and yelling debate shows. Even presidential debates are just joint press conferences that stress soundbite comebacks, digs at opponents and image over substance.
- Or, the outlet decides to rebrand itself politically, and journalists are encouraged to stress a desired niche audience, often appealing to a single political viewpoint.

Arguments offered in defense of increasing sensationalism include:

- The public WANTS to be entertained. Why shouldn't news both instruct and entertain? Isn't that why we have features, sports and news you can use?
- The public thinks we pick stories that are most sensational when often we reject such stories or run them reluctantly because we know what a backlash they create.

Beyond bias and sensationalism, there are other criticisms often heard about journalism:

Too Much Bad News

Sensationalism leads us to a related charge: that we stress negative news just to bring in higher ratings and make more money. A motto in TV news is even "If it bleeds, it leads." But throughout history, the public has tended to blame the messenger for the existence of any bad news, even important and truthful bad news. Journalists are constantly asked, though: Why don't we publish more good news? Why are we so negative? Doesn't too much bad news depress people, increase anxiety, bring conflict? At least one study has found the public thinks news actually harms race relations rather than bringing us together.

Journalists answer these questions often by saying they're not responsible for all the wrongs in the world. "We just report the news—we don't make it. If you don't want to know about these things, then you're just burying your head in the sand." But journalists should acknowledge that we are responsible in the sense that although we may not have made the events that are the news, we are sometimes the gatekeepers who made the choices about what the news is. The question is: Why do we make the choices we do?

Still, most consumers of news look for stories that make them feel good, such as stories that confirm their own prejudices. Journalists should look for stories that tell us the truth about whatever's going on, not just what they or their audiences want to hear.

Perhaps bad news is newsworthy in America because we are generally optimistic about progress and bad news catches our eye as an exception—it has oddity and conflict value. In a market economy, with news a commodity to be sold, bad news makes people more interested in more news. And exposure of bad news helps improve the world by calling attention to problems to fix.

It's interesting, though, that many journalists look down on "soft news" almost as much as they look down on advertising and think only "hard news" is serious. As a profession, we seem to be biased against good news.

Fake News

We hear a lot these days about fake news, but much of what's labeled that way really falls into this category: "I don't agree with it, so it must be fake news." Often, that's the case when you hear a politician (left or right) decrying fake news. A lot of truthful news is labeled false by politicians who seek to discredit media reports with which they disagree. Unfortunately, it often works.

Actual fake news is simply any "news" that's not true. It's "journalism" that departs from the objective news model and tries to establish as fact something that simply is false. We'll discuss fake news further in Chapter 4, but for now here are some key points:

There's a long history of fake news in journalism—it's not something Democrats invented to describe Fox News or Trump invented to describe mainstream liberal media.

- In the Colonial Press Era (1492–1776), Samuel Adams' *Journal of Correspondence* made up a lot of stories about British atrocities designed to inflame sentiment for the Revolution.
- In the Party Press Era (1781–1833), James Callender, angry that Thomas Jefferson had not given him a commission, reported that Jefferson kept a "Congo harem." Even if it's true he was the father of the

children of his slave Sally Hemings, his dead wife's half-sister—there's no evidence of Jefferson having a whole "harem" of slave women.

- In the Penny Press Era (1833–1861), a famous astronomer had seen through a powerful telescope people on the moon who were dressed like Quakers.
- In the Yellow Journalism Era (1883–1900), fake news stories in papers owned by William Randolph Hearst and Joseph Pulitzer sparked the Spanish-American War. They claimed that Spain had sunk the battleship Maine, but later evidence showed an exploding boiler may have blown up the ship.

Today, some fringe news sites push far-out conspiracy theories they believe or even try deliberately to mislead the public into thinking that something false or misleading is indeed true to fit their agenda—an attempt to convey *disinformation,* much as the media in communist nations regularly do.

Media outlets should not knowingly publish or broadcast something that's false. But even some of the best publications, broadcast and cable outlets, as well as websites, make mistakes and allow their personal biases to slip into stories or affect what events are covered and not covered. News is produced by humans, and humans are not infallible. When they do make mistakes, they should publish or broadcast corrections, something many seem to be less willing to do. Lately, we've seen fewer and fewer corrections or apologies of even major flubs, and we think that only adds to the distrust of journalism.

News media should beware of getting taken in by hoaxes. Through the years, the number of hoaxes that have made their way into newspapers and onto television is lengthy. A few examples:

- A 1994 hoax claimed that Microsoft had acquired the Roman Catholic Church. It is considered to be the first hoax to reach a large audience on the internet.
- A hoax claimed in the early 1970s that Paul McCartney of the Beatles was dead. A later hoax claimed Apple founder Steve Jobs was dead. Jobs later died, but at the time the hoax appeared he was alive, and Apple stock briefly plunged with the "news."
- In 2004, a television program fooled contestants into believing that they were training to become space tourists at a Russian space academy.

Often, careless reporting and nonexistent fact verification result in hoaxes appearing. One type of hoax that has occurred repeatedly is when newspapers receive obituary information, then publish obits without verifying that the individuals are indeed dead. Now, most newspapers insist on receiving such information directly from the mortuary to ensure this doesn't happen. **When hoaxes of this type appear, media outlets that carry them lose credibility with their audiences.**

Mistakes (Even Minor Ones)

Journalists are generalists, not specialists in their knowledge. They're usually doing stories about things on which they're not experts and are relying on sources whom they may misunderstand or who may be spinning to them. Most people don't read most stories in a newspaper but rather those in which they're most interested. Often, then, the readers know more about the subject than the journalists and notice mistakes the journalists didn't. But journalists should do everything possible to research their stories thoroughly and honestly and make multiple checks on their accuracy before going to print, on air or on the web.

Media have always made mistakes, many of them caused by deadline pressure. Management decisions to trim the number of editors also have levied a toll on readers' and viewers' perception of media accuracy. That, in turn, hurts credibility. Errors seem to be much more common than in the past, and many of them are the result of a decline in editing. The problems discussed earlier are obvious concerns, but so are more mundane issues such as bad grammar, and misspelled and misused words.

Then there are the hoaxes even respected outlets sometimes fall for. Mainstream media sometimes publish false information, which often is the result of carelessness or a failure to conduct original research into something they pick up on the internet. For example:

- A fake news story saying that columnist Paul Krugman of *The New York Times* had filed for bankruptcy wound up on Boston.com through an automated third-party service that fed the site. Verifying the veracity of that would have been quite simple.
- Similarly, the *Washington Post* fell for a fake news story that Sarah Palin, the former Republican vice presidential candidate, had taken a job with Al-Jazeera. Again, verification would have been simple if someone had actually attempted to check it.

Why are mainstream media so easily duped? One reason is that many of the fake news sites have names that sound legitimate—Empire News, National Report and World News Daily Report. A reporter who does not recognize those for what they are can be easily duped. Understanding the true nature of legitimate-sounding websites is important, and verifying the information—from more than one source—is essential. No good reporter would simply pick up something from one of those sites and repeat it. Nor would a good editor.

Arrogance and Insensitivity

Journalists are often accused of being too arrogant at press conferences and too insensitive by asking victims of tragedies, "How does it feel?" There are individual journalists we might think are obnoxious, but we also think part of the problem may be the way movies, TV and books present journalists—almost always as uncaring, obnoxious people shouting out questions in a pack. Those of us who have spent years working as journalists know that most of our colleagues have actually been caring, good people.

To this criticism we should also point out that **studies have found the public does like and trust individual journalists, especially local ones or national ones at outlets that agree with their own political views.** The recent Harris poll we cited earlier found that although only 55% of Americans trust the news media as an institution, 67% respect journalists.

Return of the Party Press and Yellow Journalism

When the American Revolution ended in 1783, the country had a mere 35 newspapers, but by 1833, it had about 1,200. That explosion of interest in news occurred as our political process matured and sparked the creation of parties, which in turn funded newspapers that would push their ideas into the public arena.

As our newfound freedom flourished, it became common for political patronage, often in the form of government printing contracts, to fund almost the entire income of a newspaper during a time when circulation and advertising revenue was meager. In turn, the newspaper staked out a clearly partisan position in support of its main source of revenue. Historians call that the Party Press Era of American journalism, when political partisanship ruled the press.

News content in that era was made up largely of political news and interpretation, and slinging abuse toward opposing parties was both common and expected. Newspapering was something of a free-for-all, and that was intentional, as expressed in the First Amendment's provision of "freedom of the press." James Madison, the main author of both the U.S. Constitution and our Bill of Rights, included press freedom in the same amendment as religious freedom. **Just as the founders abhorred the idea of a single state religion, they also abhorred the idea of an official government-mandated version of the "truth" about current events that all newspapers must publish. Instead, they favored what eventually became called the "marketplace of ideas."**

"Marketplace" in that phrase is usually written as one word, but it was two when first written by U.S. Supreme Court Justice William O. Douglas in a dissenting opinion in a case in 1953. His wording owed a lot to an earlier Supreme Court Justice, Oliver Wendell Holmes, in a previous dissenting opinion in 1919:

> The ultimate good desired is better reached by free trade in ideas—that the best test of truth is the power of the thought to get itself accepted in the competition of the market.

And even earlier than that, 17th-century English poet John Milton expressed a similar idea in his essay arguing for freedom of the press, "Areopagitica." The thought was, and is, that it's best to allow multiple ideas to be expressed and that in the end the best of those will prevail.

The idea of a free and unfettered press wasn't uniformly popular, though, and there were efforts to control what some considered to be the messy situation it had created. Our second president, John Adams, signed the Sedition Act of 1798, which made criticism of the federal government illegal. His political opponent and successor, Thomas Jefferson, let the law, which to continue had to be renewed, expire. Jefferson believed strongly that there was no need for a Sedition Act and that a vibrant press could hold government accountable for its actions. Jefferson famously wrote in a letter in 1787 to Edward Carrington:

> The basis of our government's being the opinion of the people, the very first object should be to keep that right; and were it left to me to decide whether we should have a government without newspapers or newspapers without a government, I should not hesitate a moment to prefer the latter.

Clearly, Adams feared the press more than government, and Jefferson feared government more than the press.

After the Party Press Era, newspapers entered the Penny Press Era that lasted until the Civil War. During the Penny Press Era, newspapers continued to editorialize about politics, but there was a movement toward selling news more through sensationalism that appealed across political lines than through narrower partisanship. Newspapers became less partisan politically, so you could say that in that sense, oddly, their sensationalism was more objective. Partisanship never completely disappeared, though, and was stressed again in the years around the Civil War, especially along North-South lines. But eventually sensationalism strongly returned during the Yellow Journalism Era, followed again by a resurgence of stress on political activism during the Muckraking Era.

By the 1920s, a third major model of American journalism had begun at *The New York Times* with a new stress on "objectivity" rather than the previous models of partisanship

or sensationalism. The *Times'* definition of journalism, at the beginning, though, was not what we later came to think objectivity represented.

It was not so much in the early days a fact-based model rather than an activist or entertainment model. Instead, according to sociologist Michael Schudson's book, *Discovering the News* (Basic Books, 1978, the classic history of objective journalism), it began as trying to appeal both to the upper class and middle class by offering a model of news that presented the consensus of the elites. It was the conventional wisdom aimed at selling newspapers by flattering the more privileged while offending no one. That formula led it to becoming generally recognized as the greatest of America's newspapers in the 20th century—the "newspaper of record."

The New York Times, though, leaned left even in those days, with favorable coverage of the 1917 Russian Revolution ushering in communism, then a Pulitzer in 1932 for articles by Walter Duranty defending Soviet dictator Josef Stalin. Generally, though, **The New York Times seemed less partisan than most newspapers and its style more informative than sensational compared to its competition. Over time, the public came to think of its brand of "objective journalism" as the gold standard for journalism—more of a fact-based, information-oriented journalism rather than partisanship or sensationalism.**

Today, we're living through a second Party Press Era combined with a second Yellow Journalism Era—blatant partisanship combined with sensationalism. This is probably most evident in the coverage of cable television's 24-hour news channels. It started with the 1987 repeal by President Ronald Reagan's Federal Communications Commission of the 1949 so-called "Fairness Doctrine," which had required broadcasters to counter any partisan view with the opposite side (see Chapter 5).

With the Fairness Doctrine repealed, Rush Limbaugh was the first to become hugely popular by creating a talk show free to express political views unfettered. He thought conservative views were underrepresented in the media, and he was now able to say what he wanted without stations being required to hire a liberal to counter him. When an early caller unaware of the change in law called his show to express dismay that he could legally freely present what she saw as one-sided views without "equal time," Limbaugh famously responded, "I don't need equal time—I AM equal time." His show led to the rise of conservative talk radio, which has become a huge market niche. Liberal talk radio shows have often been tried but have so far never become as successful as conservative talk radio.

Limbaugh's success with radio and then with books led him to be host from 1992 to 1996 of a syndicated TV show produced by former Reagan aide Roger Ailes. The same year Limbaugh's TV show ended, Fox News Channel was created (1996), and owner Rupert Murdoch hired Ailes to be its CEO. Ailes realized Limbaugh's success had tapped a huge—maybe the biggest—underserved market niche, conservatives. Somewhat less than half of the public considered themselves conservatives, and Ailes rapidly brought FNC the largest audience in cable news, often even beating network news in audience share.

Sixteen years earlier, CNN, the original cable news network, had opened in 1980, at first following in the footsteps of the print press and mainstream television, and sought to maintain "objectivity," as then defined, in its news reporting. It established itself for years as the cable news standard like *The New York Times* in print, leaning center left politically. But following the success of FNC on the right and MSNBC to the left, it eventually added more news talk shows and opinionated hosts and began to drift further left.

MSNBC had begun in 1996, the same year as FNC, and like CNN, began as a relatively nonpartisan news source, even with both liberal and conservative hosts. Its main calling card originally was trying to create with its partner Microsoft a new journalism combining cable news with the newly growing internet. But as everyone in journalism soon combined cable, broadcast or print news with online sites, Microsoft began divesting itself from the channel in 2005 and was out of MSNBC's website by 2012.

MSNBC then found a new purpose by revamping its programming to be a liberal-progressive counterpart to FNC. Eventually, though, it's had to split that left-leaning audience niche with CNN, as well, limiting its market share in comparison to FNC, which for many years had the conservative market niche to itself. Recently, FNC has been facing much smaller competition for the conservative niche from BlazeTV, Newsmax, One America News Network, The First and perhaps more by the time you read this.

All three of the major cable networks—FNC, CNN and MSNBC—are owned by corporations, not by a party, as many newspapers were in the late 1700s and early 1800s, but Americans drifted toward one or the other based on political beliefs just as in the Party Press days. Today, many consider left-leaning CNN a mouthpiece for Democrats and right-leaning Fox a mouthpiece for Republicans. Then there is MSNBC, which leans even farther left that CNN.

Most media and political observers will tell you the creation of the cable news networks has been a direct cause of the increased political polarization we see in the U.S. today, and the situation is unlikely to improve anytime soon. Indeed, the Second Party Press Era seems to be very much alive. We can hope that the marketplace of ideas will lead us to adoption of the *best* ideas, but will that happen? Most people simply get their news only from sources that *affirm* their political views, rather than *inform* them, as former U.S. House member Harold Ford Jr., D-Tenn., has said. In other words, most only pay attention to news outlets skewed to their own political bias. Few Americans are bothering to hear alternative political views—like a jury that hears the prosecution's case and reaches a verdict without listening to the defense. **This partisanship is**

then amplified even more by social media, where the non-face-to-face environment seems to encourage many people to respond, especially to an unknown friend of a friend, with hateful name calling. By now, probably many of you have been called a liar because some person who doesn't know you hadn't heard about a news story you referred to that wasn't reported in that person's partisan news outlet. Separate news in separate media have created separate warring realities.

The Demise of Objectivity and Credibility

The first edition of this book was published in 1971 (by previous authors), and the 50-plus years since then have brought the greatest upheaval in the journalism industry since Johannes Gutenberg invented movable type in 1439. Much has been written about the continuing demise of newspapers, and there's no doubt that has been traumatic for newspaper companies and those closely wedded to print. The primary cause of newspapers' demise is clear: The web has created a faster and less expensive way to deliver the news while also providing virtually unlimited capacity. That, in turn, has had a severe detrimental effect on newspaper companies' bottom lines.

That same problem also affects magazines, television and other media to a lesser—but still significant—extent. But **as severe as the financial problems of the mainstream media may be, a far more challenging problem to journalism as a whole is the sharp decline in credibility. Most newspapers may well disappear as media continue to change, but journalism's survival does not depend on being delivered in any particular medium. The real problem is not preserving newspapers but restoring credibility so that people will want to pay attention to news. The key to that is providing journalism people trust.**

As noted earlier, partisan publications in the U.S. date back to the early days of the republic. In most big cities, it was easy to find a newspaper that agreed with one's political perspective. So, there's nothing new about the trust issue: One trusted the publications he or she agreed with and distrusted the publications of the opposition party. But more recently, for most of the 20th century, mainstream media tried to be objective in the sense of presenting information factually and fairly, offering opinions directly from spokespeople of both sides rather than the reporter's opinion. Journalistic opinions were ideally seen only on the editorial page, and journalists could be fired for taking political stands either on or off the job.

Although today it's easy to spot bias in the print media, both in language used and the stories newspapers choose to cover or not cover, bias is arguably much worse on cable-television news networks. We've already discussed how that came to be. And, **as media have become more partisan,**

their credibility has taken a deep dive. People who agree with an outlet's political stance become more wedded to it because of the appeal to their own bias, but others are turned off. Polls now show that although the public trusts outlets that tell them what they want to hear, their trust in journalism in general is much lower as they see the growing partisanship, at least of outlets whose viewpoint is different from their own. Local newspapers are especially vulnerable to this trend. In the days of multiple newspapers in most cities, you could just buy the one that appealed to your political party, but today, when few communities have more than one newspaper and an increasing number none at all, ignoring half of your audience is a recipe for disaster.

Political discourse is currently the most divisive topic that news outlets tackle, so news media could try harder to focus more than they already do on regular departments of nonpartisan appeal, such as well-written features, news you can use, and, in the case of local media, interesting stories about local history. But the problem is much bigger than providing more reason to read, listen to or watch a news outlet other than non-political stories, and we're not suggesting focusing only on "fluff" and an end to covering politics. Far from it. Instead, we suggest a close examination of what objectivity means and how it can be accomplished when covering even the most divisive topics. We think a new kind of objectivity is needed to replace the current stress on partisanship and sensationalism if we want to restore the public trust in journalism.

A good start at restoring credibility with a wider audience would be stricter separation between straight news and commentary than even in the past. The news section of a newspaper or news show or site should be factual, not judgmental. If the "facts" differ based on political views, then all sides should be presented fairly—preferably even side-by-side as some websites already do. The commentary section in a news outlet that seeks wider appeal than a partisan audience should provide the best available opinions from multiple sides and perspectives. Commentary even in partisan outlets should be as true to the evidence as a scientific report—that is, honestly reviewing the evidence and presenting the best case based on that rather than activist spin.

But we think a more comprehensive answer is that it's time to reassess the old principles of objective journalism we've discussed in previous editions of this book. We've said the principles of objectivity that journalism schools have long taught students boil down to four things:

- Be factual.
- Be neutral.
- Be fair.
- Be impersonal in style (in hard-news stories).

You can find similar lists in other books. David T.Z. Mindich, for example, in his book *Just the Facts: How "Objectivity" Came to Define American Journalism* (New York University Press, 1998) offers these five principles:

- Detachment.
- Nonpartisanship.
- The inverted pyramid.
- Facticity.
- Balance.

We're suggesting the answer to the problems of advocacy journalism is to re-examine these old principles of "objective journalism" honestly, and we're suggesting a new form of objectivity that strives for truth not defined by matching a pre-ordained bias based on loyalty to a partisan viewpoint. Fact checks, for example, would be honest fact checks, not ones that defined anything by the journalist's or outlet's own views as true in advance and anything contradicting them as a lie. That just doesn't work, and it's misleading.

We think such a redefinition is necessary if we want to restore credibility in the media. But many need to be persuaded that objectivity is even possible. Most journalists today don't think so. And beyond that, many outside the field are the product of college classes teaching Postmodernist Critical Theory's view that objectivity, like reason, science and even math are really just vestiges of white male Western privilege and no more truthful than anything else. They even seriously argue that 2 plus 2 can equal 5, just as Big Brother did in George Orwell's 1984. But if you argue objectivity, reason, science and math are unique to one race and gender, how is that not an attack on the capabilities and achievements of Blacks and women, for example, in science, technology, math, as well as the fields of history and journalism?

So, let's start with the current attack on objectivity itself and offer possible answers to the critics.

Objectivity Re-examined

Here's how we got to this point when the dominant idea seems to be: Objectivity is impossible, so we might as well just agitate for our favorite political cause. Or, as Karl Marx wrote (and his tombstone reads): "The philosophers have only *interpreted* the world, in various ways. The point, however, is to *change* it."

To begin at the beginning, it's said that the ancient Greek sophist Gorgias of Leontium (483–375 B.C.) wrote a book that advocated three theses:

- That nothing exists.
- That even if it did, we couldn't know it.
- That even if we could know it, we couldn't communicate it.

Gorgias, who was also the title character of Plato's dialogue "Gorgias," was one of the first known skeptics in philosophy. He actually preceded by a hundred years or so Pyrrho of Ellis (about 360–270 B.C.), who is generally considered to be the father of skepticism. And yet Gorgias' ideas have a strangely contemporary significance for journalists because these same three points are echoed again and again in attacks on the idea of "objective journalism." They're also, incidentally, the same as the most common attacks on reason, science and objectivity that have come from the Postmodernist Critical Theory proponents since the 1960s, which have taken over many academic departments on college campuses and are now spreading throughout the culture (see Helen Pluckrose and James Lindsay's book *Cynical Theories*, Pitchstone Publishing, 2020).

Such attacks are as apt to come these days from practitioners of journalism as from the field's outside critics. Many deny that journalistic objectivity, or any kind of objectivity, is possible at all. Many who deny objectivity embrace a journalism of personal involvement or/and advocacy. Others who deny objectivity is possible say it's nonetheless an ideal for which to strive despite its unattainability.

But mainly, until the recent trend of activist journalism, journalists have practiced a methodology they tended to call "objective"—even when they denied objectivity is in theory possible. **A close examination of this traditional method of objectivity will reveal, however, that its practices aimed at producing reports that conform to a public or vocational consensus, something like the original meaning of objectivity invented at *The New York Times*, rather than ones that attempted to correspond to facts.**

More than 50 years ago, John DeMott of the journalism department at Temple University gave a speech that clearly identified three essential ideas assumed if we're to consider the possibility of objective journalism:

> Every vocation or occupational calling relies upon certain basic assumptions about the nature of reality . . . Journalism is no exception, obviously. We assume these things:
>
> - First, that there is such a thing as objective reality . . . existing independent of our own individual existence.
> - Second, that such reality . . . can be comprehended—somehow—by a human mind.
> - Third, that comprehension or understanding of objective reality . . . can be communicated from one human mind to another.

Reject any one of the three assumptions he cites—the exact opposite of the positions taken by Gorgias and today's "Critical Theorists"—and then journalism, objective or not, becomes impossible. Even activist journalism. For if there's no reality, then on what does a journalist propose to report? If there is no way to know reality, then what's gained by attempts at news gathering or activism? If we cannot communicate, then why bother to publish or broadcast a news item or try to persuade people to action?

But when journalists, like Critical Theorists, deny the possibility of objectivity, it never occurs to them that they are out on a limb. Such opponents contradict themselves because to argue for their own position, they must tacitly assume there's a reality they're describing, that it can be known because they think they know what they're saying is true, and they're communicating their views in a way meant to be reasonable even while denying reason and communication are even possible. They are usually unaware of what Gorgias said long ago or De Mott said more recently, or important philosophers, scientists and historians have said in the past about objectivity. Objectivity, after all, is not a concern merely of journalism. If there is no reality, or we can know nothing, or it's impossible to communicate, then the impossibility of objective journalism is among the least of the problems humanity faces.

Even when journalists try to defend objectivity, they usually ignore the arguments that have gone before, in effect ignoring the tree from which the limb they sit on grew. They are tacitly assuming the limb could stand on its own without the support of a larger branch, a trunk and roots. Meanwhile, those who deny journalistic objectivity is possible use arguments that implicitly deny the limb on which they stand even exists.

For example, they forget that in denying objectivity is possible to humans, they are also denying the possibility of it in any human endeavor—including science, something few journalists would attack as nonobjective: "Follow the science!"

But when journalists discuss the "impossibility" of objectivity, they seldom reveal any awareness of the discussion on the topic carried out in science, history and the other social sciences for at least the past 200 years, much less any understanding of relevant philosophical concepts of metaphysics (the nature of reality) and epistemology (how we know what we think we know). The only philosophical arguments they're likely to have heard on the subject are those coming from the Postmodernists.

Perhaps sociologist Gaye Tuchman is right that "Processing news leaves no time for reflexive epistemological examination." But even after the daily deadline rush is over, journalists seldom probe the deeper issues underlying and making possible journalistic objectivity.

Journalists need to understand better the philosophic underpinnings of their field and the relevant groundwork already laid in other fields. In integrating such knowledge, they may also find they can learn to do their jobs better.

Judging by their criticisms of the press, many members of the general public seem to assume, however, that objective journalism is possible and preferable—they just don't think they're getting it from the media. They often say they suspect the media of actively pushing a liberal agenda rather than being objective. Meanwhile, critics on the left, such as Ben Bagdikian, A.J. Leibling and Herbert J. Altschull, agree the press isn't objective but contend it presents news from an establishment, big business perspective.

Redefining "Objectivity"

We're not the first to say "objective journalism" needs to be rehabilitated and redefined. In Chapter 1, we briefly discussed how Bill Kovach and Tom Rosenstiel in their book, *The Elements of Journalism*, called for the media to redefine "objectivity." For a good part of the previous century, journalists tried to be objective by writing about both sides of controversial issues and refraining from expressing their own opinion in news stories. As a result, reporting was considered "balanced." Unfortunately, in some cases that tended to distort the news rather than clarify it. Journalists were merely repeating the opinions of those on opposite sides of an issue rather than helping their audience determine which argument was correct. Sometimes, one side of the argument was so lacking in truth that it was potentially misleading even to report it—as though, for example, the arguments of segregationists had equal merit to those of integrationists.

Kovach and Rosenstiel argued that this approach should be replaced with *objectivity of method*, which, if properly practiced, gets us closer to the truth. They likened it to the scientific methods researchers use to seek the truth. But this newer approach has its own problems, most notably that the truth is not always easily determined. That's particularly true when journalists are under deadline pressure. Scientists, after all, sometimes take years to reach a decision.

To ensure that some measure of objectivity is achieved, in addition to objectivity of method we need a diverse array of editors who are alert to this problem and can help us avoid it. That's also why it's desirable to have multiple editors reviewing stories. Each brings a different perspective and helps to ensure that the story is not only true but free of personal bias, even subtle bias.

So, we'd argue that reporters and editors need to adopt a new approach to achieving objectivity, one rooted in the use of objective methodology, of newsroom diversity (of race and gender, yes, but also political viewpoints) and of more redundant editing by additional editors. Reporters should do their best to determine the truth and be transparent in how they arrived at it. Further, a diverse set of editors needs to ensure that this happens in every story. **In other words, take a position as close to the truth as you can possibly get, but make every attempt to be correct and support your position with facts.** And to increase transparency, it's desirable—sometimes even necessary—to explain to your readers or viewers how the conclusion was reached.

The Lost Meaning of Objectivity

We have found no better brief explanation of the creation, evolution and application of the term "objectivity" in journalism than this by the Project for Excellence in Journalism in 2003. Notice that it echoes the call for a more scientific journalism made in *The Elements of Journalism*. It also echoes our own in this regard going back to 1996.

> Perhaps because the discipline of verification is so personal and so haphazardly communicated, it is also part of one of the great confusions of journalism—the concept of objectivity. The original meaning of this idea is now thoroughly misunderstood, and by and large lost.
>
> When the concept originally evolved, it was not meant to imply that journalists were free of bias. Quite the contrary. The term began to appear as part of journalism after the turn of the century, particularly in the 1920s, out of a growing recognition that journalists were full of bias, often unconsciously. Objectivity called for journalists to develop a consistent method of testing information—a transparent approach to evidence—precisely so that personal and cultural biases would not undermine the accuracy of their work.
>
> In the latter part of the 19th century, journalists talked about something called realism rather than objectivity. This was the idea that if reporters simply dug out the facts and ordered them together, truth would reveal itself rather naturally. Realism emerged at a time when journalism was separating from political party affiliations and becoming more accurate. It coincided with the invention of what journalists call the inverted pyramid, in which a journalist lines the facts up from the most important to the least important, thinking it helps audiences understand things naturally.
>
> At the beginning of the 20th century, however, some journalists began to worry about the naïveté of realism. In part, reporters and editors were becoming more aware of the rise of propaganda and the role of press agents. At a time when Freud was developing his theories of the unconscious and painters like Picasso were experimenting with Cubism, journalists were also developing a greater recognition of human subjectivity. In 1919, Walter Lippmann and Charles Merz, an associate editor for the *New York World*, wrote an influential and scathing account of how cultural blinders had distorted *The New York Times'* coverage of the Russian Revolution. "In the large, the news about Russia is a case of seeing not what was, but what men wished to see," they wrote. Lippmann and others began to look for ways for the individual journalist "to remain

clear and free of his irrational, his unexamined, his unacknowl-edged prejudgments in observing, understanding and presenting the news."

Journalism, Lippmann declared, was being practiced by "untrained accidental witnesses." Good intentions, or what some might call "honest efforts" by journalists, were not enough. Faith in the rugged individualism of the tough reporter, what Lippmann called the "cyni-cism of the trade," was also not enough. Nor were some of the new innovations of the times, like bylines, or columnists.

The solution, Lippmann argued, was for journalists to acquire more of "the scientific spirit . . . There is but one kind of unity possible in a world as diverse as ours. It is unity of method, rather than aim; the unity of disci-plined experiment." Lippmann meant by this that journalism should aspire to "a common intellectual method and a common area of valid fact." To begin, Lippmann thought, the fledgling field of journalist education should be transformed from "trade schools designed to fit men for higher salaries in the existing structure." **Instead, the field should make its cornerstone the study of evidence and verification.**

Although this was an era of faith in science, Lippmann had few illusions. "It does not matter that the news is not susceptible of math-ematical statement. In fact, just because news is complex and slip-pery, good reporting requires the exercise of the highest scientific virtues.

In the original concept, in other words, the method is objective, not the journalist. The key was in the discipline of the craft, not the aim.

The point has some important implications. One is that the impartial voice employed by many news organizations, that famil-iar, supposedly neutral style of newswriting, is not a fundamental principle of journalism. Rather, it is an often-helpful device news organizations use to highlight that they are trying to produce some-thing obtained by objective methods. The second implication is that this neutral voice, without a discipline of verification, creates a veneer covering something hollow. Journalists who select sources to express what is really their own point of view, and then use the neutral voice to make it seem objective, are engaged in a form of deception. This damages the credibility of the whole profession by making it seem unprincipled, dishonest and biased. This is an important caution in an age when the standards of the press are so in doubt.

Reporters have gone on to refine the concept Lippmann had in mind, but usually only privately, and in the name of technique or reporting routines rather than journalism's larger purpose. The notion of an objective method of reporting exists in pieces, handed down by word of mouth from reporter to reporter. Developmental psychologist William Damon at Stanford, for instance, has identified various "strategies" journalists have developed to verify reporting. Damon asked his interviewees where they learned these concepts. Overwhelmingly the answer was: by trial and error and on my own or from a friend. Rarely did journalists report learning them in journalism school or from their editors. Many useful books have been written. The group calling itself Investigative Reporters and Editors, for instance, has tried to develop a methodology for how to use public records, read documents, and produce Freedom of Information Act requests.

By and large, however, these informal strategies have not been pulled together into the widely understood discipline that Lippmann and others imagined. There is nothing approaching standard rules of evidence, as in the law, or an agreed-upon method of observation, as in the conduct of scientific experiments.

Nor have older conventions of verification been expanded to match the new forms of journalism. Although journalism may have developed various techniques and conventions for determining facts, it has done less to develop a system for testing the reliability of journalistic interpretation.

(Used with the permission of the Project for
Excellence in Journalism)

What Would the "New Objectivity" We Propose Mean in Practice?

What does all this mean for working journalists? The first of the following five answers may sound merely theoretical, but by asserting the possibility of real objectivity (something many people deny), it forms the grounding for the more obviously practical points that follow:

1. **Journalistic objectivity does not require that you be either an omniscient god nor that you magically present information without using your mind to help you select what's relevant.**

Journalistic objectivity is not precluded by the fact that you are a finite being with human senses, a mind, a self, a specific background, education and experience. If it were, no knowledge of any kind would ever be possible to human beings, including the statement that no knowledge is possible.

Instead, objectivity begins with acknowledging these so-called "limitations" and working with them. Knowledge is always, by its nature, contextual. That is, knowledge is always of something with a specific nature as understood by a being with a specific nature.

Journalistic objectivity doesn't require you to avoid selecting facts, to include the entire universe of facts or to be the final word. These would be impossible demands much harder than we place on scientific reports, which most of us nonetheless accept as objective. Facts are not self-evident—they must be selected. But such selection does not inherently invalidate a report's objectivity.

2. Stick to the facts of reality.

That should be interpreted to mean: Strive to report truth (a correspondence to the facts of reality), not merely consensus (a correspondence to a perceived social agreement). That people once thought the world flat was consensus—it did not make the world flat in fact. Some journalists today confuse the two.

You may make predictions based on extrapolations from the facts without invalidating your report's objectivity.

3. Strive for neutrality, but don't confuse that with either lack of a viewpoint or accepting any perceived consensus as neutral.

The traditional version of objective journalism boiled down mainly to not making any judgments or reaching any conclusions. What we propose instead is that any judgments made or conclusions reached are achieved without prejudice or bias and should be based on the evidence available at the time.

Journalists are by their nature interested in current events and tend to have definite political views. That doesn't mean you can't be objective. You may—just as a scientist does—have a hypothesis going into the research. **The real difference between this and advocacy journalism is that if you want to be objective, you should be like a scientist in looking at the evidence honestly and open-mindedly, and be willing to admit you're wrong if the facts lead there.** Buddha said the path to enlightenment is non-attachment—not seeing only what you want to see. Remain open to the facts, even if what you discover goes against what you'd prefer to believe or what would be easier, more dramatic or safer to write.

In 1938, Curtis D. MacDougall published a classic journalism text called *Interpretative Reporting*. He thought that more was needed than the kind of objective journalism taught in journalism schools then. He argued that journalists should provide more context and background to help readers understand the news. We have no problem with that. We even think it's a good idea as long as it's fact-based rather than meant to push a preconceived partisan-formed view.

We say you may supply background and interpretation in addition to raw facts to make a story understandable. Instead of invalidating the story's objectivity, doing this may actually sometimes enhance it by preventing misunderstandings.

You may express value judgments without necessarily invalidating your report's objectivity. Expressing value judgments may be objective or not, depending on the values expressed. Although this may sound odd at first, some values are more objective than others. This idea goes back to Aristotle, who disagreed with all those who say today you can't get from IS (facts of reality) to SHOULD (moral values). Aristotle's solution was that the nature of humanity requires certain actions and traits for people to live well as people: things like work, honesty, fairness to others, and so on. Although many seem to think you can get a better life by thinking only of yourself and to hell with others, things like being a parasite on others, stealing and treating others without respect make life worse for all of us, not better. And, in fact, they also rob the person who acts that way from living the life of their full potential. Values are acknowledgments of such principles (see Mortimer J. Adler's book *Aristotle for Everybody*, Macmillan, 1978).

You may present an honest evaluation of the evidence or list unanswered relevant questions without violating neutrality. In fact, it may be more objective to do so than to remain silent and leave false impressions. When you analyze data, you may—just as a scientist does—point out flaws in methodology. It may even be necessary sometimes to come clean and be self-critical about personal limitations or affiliations that may have affected, even unknowingly, the completeness or neutrality of the piece, especially if they help the audience decide how much trust to place in an account. Scientists do this regularly in their reports.

But journalists—as opposed to commentators—should no more try to be advocates than should scientists. It's not enough to leave objectivity entirely to the realm of being open to criticism from others. Rather, the journalist's own attempt at disinterestedness combined with making all the data available for criticism are what together make up an objective methodology. That is what objectivity should be about—in science, history or journalism.

4. **Remember that the idea that fairness entails giving equal weight to all sides can result in the unfairness of legitimizing and elevating positions that lack evidence or that present morally reprehensible positions. In other words, fairness as currently interpreted by journalists may in fact be unfair—to the readers and to the truth.**

The injunction to be fair should instead be understood as being open to new evidence and reasonable alternatives, of which the journalist must be the judge, just as the journalist must always decide which facts should be selected as relevant to the presentation.

There can be objective standards for fairness, as we pointed out when discussing Aristotle's approach to values. Such standards would focus not only on being fair to the people in the story but also especially on the validity of an argument and its fit with the evidence rather than whether it was one of the two most popular views.

5. Understand the deeper meaning behind an impersonal style. The idea that an impersonal style necessarily shows objectivity confuses the window dressing with the real goods.

A personal style is not necessarily nonobjective. Your writing need not sound like everyone else's in order to be objective. The demand that the words of reporters sound as though any other reporter had written them does not inherently guarantee real objectivity. And, in fact, such uniformity, were it possible, would probably be an enemy of "real" objectivity.

That doesn't mean, though, that it would be better necessarily to strive for a personal, more "creative" style in straight news reports—any more than that would be appropriate, for example, in written instructions for assembling a bike. But in certain kinds of stories, such as features and opinion pieces, a more creative, entertaining but honest style is an asset.

Narrative writing is a related issue that has become increasingly popular in U.S. newspapers in the past few decades. These are longer news articles written with descriptive adjectives and the drama employed by top storytellers. Without question, they make reading the news much more interesting.

But a key component of narrative writing includes plenty of observations by the reporter—some innocuous like the color of a subject's dress, the diplomas on the wall of another—and some more prejudicial such as obvious disdain for the views of a politician. The nature of such writing requires writers to inject their observations. It makes for good reading, but to the reader it's evident that the reporter is adding personal opinion. And when reading the news, as opposed to features, that's not what most readers want.

We appreciate narrative writing, and we think it has an important place in journalism. But again, we also think it's better reserved for the features section rather than the hard-news pages. If, however, it appears on those pages, which is often the case, a note from the editor might explain why the reporter was given such license.

(Portions of this chapter have been edited from James L. Pinson's 1996 doctoral dissertation on objective journalism and are printed here with permission of the author, who is the copyright holder.)

Suggested Websites

Gallup and Knight Foundation: https://knightfoundation.org/reports/american-views-2020-trust-media-and-democracy/

Harris Poll: https://magazine.medill.northwestern.edu/wp-content/uploads/2020/07/NUQ-Trust-in-U.S.-Media-Report_09July2020.pdf

Pew Research Center: www.pewresearch.org/fact-tank/2020/10/26/what-the-2020-electorate-looks-like-by-party-race-and-ethnicity-age-education-and-religion/

Suggested Readings

Adler, Mortimer J. *Aristotle for Everybody: Difficult Thought Made Easy.* New York: Macmillan, 1978.

Lichter, S. Robert. "Consistently Liberal: But Does It Matter?" *Forbes Media Critic.* Fall 1996, 26–39.

Mindich, David T.Z. *Just the Facts: How "Objectivity" Came to Define American Journalism.* New York: New York University Press, 1998.

Pinson, James Leland. *Objective Journalism and Ayn Rand's Philosophy of Objectivism.* Doctoral Dissertation at University of Missouri-Columbia, 1996.

Pluckrose, Helen, and James Lindsay. *Cynical Theories: How Activist Scholarship Made Everything About Race, Gender, and Identity – And Why This Harms Everybody.* Durham, NC: Pitchstone Publishing, 2020.

Schiller, Dan. *Objectivity and the News: The Public and the Rise of Commercial Journalism.* Philadelphia: University of Pennsylvania Press, 1981.

Schudson, Michael. *Discovering the News: A Social History of American Newspapers.* New York: Basic Books, 1978.

3 THE EDITING PROCESS

The Philosophy of Editing

This book focuses on the skills of editing, but learning those skills without a thorough understanding of the philosophy of editing would be like learning to hit a baseball without knowing why hitting is important. In editing, it is important to know not only *when* a change in copy should be made but also *why* that change should be made.

Good editing depends on the exercise of good judgment. For that reason, it is an art, not a science. To be sure, in some aspects of editing—accuracy, grammar and spelling, for example—there are right and wrong answers, as is often the case in science. But editing also involves discretion—knowing when to use which word, when to change a word or

DOI: 10.4324/9781003011422-3

two for clarity and when to leave a passage as the writer has written it. Making the right decisions in such cases is clearly an art.

Anywhere words are communicated—in any medium—editing skills are important. Editing skills are needed in media operations, of course, but also in corporate communication, in advertising and public relations, in broadcasting, at online sites, in newsletter and book publishing and in the briefs attorneys write for courts. That's why law schools love to admit journalism graduates. They have already learned how to write clearly and simply. In this chapter, after stressing the basic editing skills that apply to all forms of written and spoken communication, we include information to highlight differences where those exist.

Editors search for errors and inaccuracies, and prune the useless, the unnecessary qualifiers and the redundancies. They add movement to the story by substituting active verbs for passive ones, specifics for generalities. They keep sentences short so readers, listeners or viewers can grasp one idea at a time and still not suffer from writing that reads like a first-grade text.

Editors are detectives who incessantly search stories for clues about how to transform mediocre articles into great—or at least better—ones. The legendary Carr Van Anda of *The New York Times* studied ocean charts and astronomical formulas to find missing links in a story. Few editors today would correct a math error Einstein made in a speech, as Van Anda once famously did, but if they are willing, they can probe, question, authenticate and exercise their powers of deduction.

Experience tells us that:

- Editors make stories better, regardless of the medium—print, broadcast or online. The best printed publications, the best broadcast stations and networks, and the best online sites have editors who fine-tune stories to make them accurate, clearer and easier to understand.
- Editors often save a news outlet from egregious errors that could result in misinformation or even a costly libel suit being directed at their company.
- Yes, occasionally editors foul a story that was completely understandable as written. It's rare that this happens, but when it does **overediting** is often the problem. So, if the writer's work makes sense, it's often better to leave it as written unless a change makes it demonstrably better.

The greatest danger in today's media environment, however, is not overediting. A much greater danger is the possibility of printing, broadcasting or posting online a story that has not been edited at all. So, the skill of self-editing is becoming increasingly important.

In a perfect world, no journalist would be in the position of publishing or broadcasting a story that has not been edited by another human. But cutbacks in the number of editors at some media often makes that impossible. Magazines and newspapers historically had **redundant editing**—multiple layers of editing—to rely upon, which increased the likelihood that a story would be accurate, clear and concise. Sadly, today we see fewer and fewer layers of editing at most media operations, but particularly at newspapers and websites, and as a result the product can suffer.

What Makes a Good Editor?

Some who enter journalism learn quickly that chasing fire engines and covering courts is not their passion. Some find that asking tough questions of news sources is uncomfortable. For those who discover that reporting is not a desirable career path, choosing the editor's lifestyle may be more appealing. The best editors typically have:

- A passion for, and detailed knowledge of, grammar, spelling, style, punctuation, usage and tightening wordy copy.
- A love of good writing and the ability to see the potential in a piece, then the skill to help bring it out—or the good sense to know when to leave it alone.

Figure 3.1 Some copy editors print out longer, more complicated stories and use traditional editing symbols to mark the paper copy before fixing it on the computer. This can help them spot inconsistencies in longer stories, but most editing is done only on computers.

Photo by Christopher Parks.

- Knowledge of graphics processes and typefaces; the creativity to see photo, illustration and graphics possibilities; knowledge of good design; knowledge of editing sound and video for broadcast or websites; and, these days, knowledge of web and mobile content creation.
- An interest in everything and a broad grasp of news. One wouldn't want to play a game of trivia against a good editor.
- Knowledge of enough mathematics and accounting to calculate percentages and to read budgets and see whether they add up.
- A grasp of legal, ethical and taste considerations.
- Skepticism that raises doubt in everything and the fortitude to check it. They also need a librarian's ability to find the best sources in print or on the web to check facts.
- A mind that lets them see embarrassing double meanings before they are published or broadcast. Evidently, a "nice" person missed this headline: **Republicans turned off by size of Obama's package.**
- Enough self-confidence to know how to improve even veteran reporters' copy but enough maturity not to rewrite everything into the editor's own style, a classic form of overediting.
- The ability to handle people—whether freelance writers or staff members, sources or subscribers.
- Sound business and management skills.
- A clear vision of the news organization's purpose, its personality, and the audience and advertisers to whom it appeals.
- At a specialty publication, such as a business magazine or a specialty website, a working knowledge of the subject matter covered.
- A strong sense of responsibility. "The buck stops here," read President Harry Truman's desk sign.
- A willingness to work anonymously behind a desk for eight hours a day. For many young journalists, this is a tough hurdle.

Here are some suggestions for developing as an editor and making yourself more valuable to your employer:

- **Embrace the editing process.** Understand that editing almost invariably makes the product better.
- **Embrace the coaching process.** Take criticism of your work not as something personal but as an opportunity to improve.
- **Find peers to respect and emulate.** Almost every news department has role models for you to follow.
- **Watch what the pros do and how they do it.** Similarly, avoid the bad habits of the worst.
- **Seek advice.** Don't come across as a know-it-all. Show your editors that you are willing to grow professionally and improve your skills.

- **Don't be seen as a complainer.** Remember that no workplace is perfect. Keep your complaints to yourself, or complain directly to your supervisor, not to the entire news department.
- **Work hard.** People advance to higher positions in the news business, or almost *any* business for that matter, when they outwork and outperform their peers.
- **Adhere to the highest standards of ethics.** If you see a co-worker take ethical shortcuts, quietly report that to your boss. Never, ever take an ethical shortcut yourself. (See Chapter 5.)
- **Adhere to the highest standards of excellence.** Practice good journalism in every story, no matter how long or how short.
- **Never be satisfied with your work.** You can always get better.
- **Stay informed.** Read newspapers and news websites daily. Read news magazines and books on history, politics and economics. Listen to National Public Radio's news or talk-radio programs while you commute. Watch local and network TV news, Sunday-morning news talk shows and cable news programming. Try to read, listen to or watch news from a variety of outlets with different political perspectives, not just those that reflect your own views. Take a look at foreign sources, as well, for added perspective.
- **Join ACES, the Society for Editing** (www.aceseditors.org). Its conferences, website and publications are invaluable sources of information, and it offers scholarships to college students interested in editing. Some schools have student chapters.
- **Compare your print and online headlines with those found in competitors.** Look for fresh approaches. Keep an eye open for useful headline synonyms.
- **Learn to write effective web headlines that draw traffic to a website and print headlines that attract readers' attention.** (See Chapter 10.)
- **Learn what information typically needs to be in particular kinds of stories, what order that information generally takes and which errors usually crop up.** Leaving an obvious question about a story unanswered is frustrating for consumers. (See Chapter 8.)
- **Keep notes on things you have to look up or useful tips you learn from your editor, your news organization's attorney or other staff members.** Many of these items crop up on a regular basis, and referring back to your notes can save precious time. Notecards are a useful way to organize these.
- **Ask your supervisor to give you feedback about your strengths and weaknesses, and what you can do to improve.** Many companies are not helpful with this, so occasionally you must ask for critiques.

The Basics of Editing

Over the years, journalism teachers have come up with various useful outlines for describing what editors look for in copy. In this book, we've used the common convention of dividing editors' text-editing duties into the *macro* and *micro*. Macro errors are big-picture items such as missing information that is critical to understanding the story. Micro errors are the more routine errors such as misspelled words and bad grammar. We'll cover those more in later chapters.

Another useful approach was suggested by Don Ranly, a professor emeritus at the Missouri School of Journalism and a widely sought speaker in professional-editing circles. He refers to "The Seven C's Plus One"—that's eight, but Ranly argues most people can't remember more than seven things at once. Ranly says writers and editors should make sure copy is *correct, concise, consistent, complete, clear, coherent, creative* and *concrete*.

Here, we offer another approach, one focusing on the Three R's of Copy Editing: making sure writing is *reader-centered, readable* and *right*. This model can easily be applied to non-print media by substituting the word *reader* with *listener, viewer* or *audience member* and changing *readable* to *listenable* or *watchable*.

Is the Story Reader-Centered?

Editors have to approach their job as though they are the readers', listeners' and viewers' advocates, making sure stories serve their interests, needs and time.

Is the Story Audience-Focused?

- Has the writer kept foremost in mind what the audience wants and needs?
- People's time is limited. If the story isn't interesting—if it isn't informative and fresh—then what's the point of running it? Do I care to read 20 column inches of typeset matter about it or watch a video 10 minutes long? If not, how much? Then that's how long the story should be.
- Is the topic important to our readers or viewers? Does it clearly show consumers why they should care? If the story could have an *impact* on the audience, does the writer take that angle instead of something else? If there doesn't seem to be any major impact, does the writer at least focus on whatever in the story would be of *most* interest to the audience? Does the story answer the question, "So what?"
- News is people acting and reacting, as the late Jessica Savitch, a former anchor at NBC News, once said. Does the story focus on how the news affects the *people* involved, or does it focus on a thing?
- Is the tone appropriate for this story?

Did the Writer Focus on the Latest?

- Does the writer focus on the latest news rather than on old news? If this is a **second-day story**, does it have a second-day lead, or did the reporter lead with yesterday's news?
- Does the writer take a fresh, creative approach to the story? Does the reader, listener or viewer learn something new? Or will he or she think this sounds like a story read many times before? Does the lead grab a person's attention? Are the lead and story angle fresh or hackneyed? Does the writing sound honest?
- Does the writer apply relevant news-writing formulas — intelligently as opposed to slavishly?
- Does the writer offer original, concrete details, quotations, examples and comparisons that lend color, authenticity and clarity? Does the story appeal to the senses or just seem abstract? Is the overuse of adjectives and adverbs avoided? Are specific nouns and verbs used instead? Are the details concrete? Or does the story contain clichés of wording or of vision that make it seem tired and dishonest?
- If the story is a feature as opposed to a hard-news story, does the writer use an appealing, personal voice but one that does not detract focus from the subject and inappropriately draw too much attention to itself?
- If this is a hard-news story, was the writer careful not to editorialize or insert his or her own personality and value judgments?

Is the Story Readable?

Editors need to make sure readers will be able to understand what's being said.

Is the Story Clear?

- Is the main point of the story clear? Does every sentence grow from the main point and point back to it? Are the words and sentences simple to understand? Would it sound natural and conversational if read aloud? Do I understand better after reading the story, or am I left confused or apathetic? (If anything is unclear to you, ask the writer or that writer's editor. Don't guess.)
- Does the story answer any questions and concerns the audience would likely have? (Examples: What does the story mean by a "sizable crowd"? One hundred people? A thousand? If there's a community blood shortage, where can you go to give blood, and what types are needed most? If a jogger had a heart attack while running, did the jogger have a history of heart disease?)
- Have loose ends been tied up? Are any intriguing angles introduced then dropped without explanation? Are all first references to someone or something complete?

- Is it clear who is saying each quotation or paraphrase in the story?
- Are all unfamiliar terms explained? Has jargon been avoided wherever possible and defined where unavoidable? Are all words used precisely and correctly? (*Admitted, anxious, bureaucrat, claimed* and *refuted* all have specific meanings that may not be intended by the writer who uses them but are likely to be inferred by a reader.)
- Is the story arranged in the most logical manner? Does it seem well-organized?
- Does it flow well? Are the transitions between sentences and ideas good ones? Is the pacing good? Do sentence lengths vary?
- Are rhetorical techniques such as metaphors, analogies and images used to illustrate the meaning? Are examples given? Are comparisons made?
- Are there possibilities here to tell the story better with graphics so it will be more appealing and understandable to the reader? Would the reader benefit from a photo, illustration, chart, summary box, blurb or second headline deck to make the meaning clearer and the story more interesting? Do the audio and video clips complement the text? If editing a print story for online or mobile media, would an audio or video clip add value?

Is the Story Concise?

- Does the story need to be this long? Is its news value worth this length?
- Is anything in the story irrelevant?
- Has the writer avoided redundancies, clichés, unnecessary use of passive voice and other windy phrases that add uninformative bulk to a story?
- Can any paragraph be said in a sentence, any sentence in a **clause**, any clause in a phrase, any phrase in a word, or any word in a shorter, simpler word? (For more specific hints on tightening, see Chapter 7.)
- Are too many examples or quotations used?
- Does each quotation say something either unique or important enough to quote?
- Can quotations be shortened? Can partial quotes be used? Can quotations be succinctly paraphrased without loss of impact?
- If the story goes off on a lengthy tangent, can that part be turned into a sidebar?

Is the Story Right?

Editors need to make sure stories are correct in all ways, big and small—all the way from being accurate, ethical and legally safe to being correct in spelling, grammar and punctuation.

Is it Accurate, Objective, Legal, Ethical, Tasteful and Sensitive?

- Are there any inconsistencies within the story, in matters of facts, style, viewpoint, verb tense or tone?
- Is anything inconsistent between this story and previous stories?
- Have you checked that facts and quotations are accurate?
- Have you checked the math? (Examples: ages against the birth and death dates in obits, percentages and totals in budget stories, vote ratios in election stories.)
- Have you checked names and addresses of local people?
- Have you checked when a story says *today* whether it means the day it was written or the day of publication?
- Does the writing sound honest, or is its credibility undercut with refutable logic, sloppy writing or clichés (such as with a lead that says "Christmas came early for . . .")?
- Is the story objective? Is it factual, neutral, fair and, if hard news, impersonal in style? Does it avoid mind-reading attributions like *believes, feels, hopes* and *thinks*?
- Does the story avoid any statements that might bring a lawsuit?
- Is the story ethical and in good taste? If someone is accused of or criticized for something, does he or she get a chance to reply? Are all sides given? Were enough people interviewed.

Obviously, many of these issues will not arise in every story you edit. Nevertheless, these are the matters you should be prepared to tackle whenever they surface.

Editing the Story

Now, let's delve into the editing process itself. Most experienced editors suggest that the process be divided into three distinct steps:

- Read the story.
- Edit it thoroughly.
- Reread the story and make any final corrections.

Editors too often skip the first step or abbreviate it by scanning the story for the gist of the news. To do so may be a mistake because intelligent editing decisions cannot be made unless the editor understands the purpose of the story and the style in which it is written. Occasionally, for example, a story is intentionally written with a suspenseful ending. If the editor starts hacking away at the story without understanding that, time is wasted and the piece can be ruined. That understanding is developed with a quick but thorough initial reading.

Some editors try to skip the third step, too. They do so at the risk of missing errors they should have detected the first time or those they introduced during editing. **Few sins are greater than to introduce an error during editing.** The more times a story is read, the more likely errors will be detected.

Unfortunately, deadline pressure sometimes dictates that the first or third steps, or both, be skipped. When this is done, it becomes increasingly important for the editor to do a thorough job the first time through the story.

To illustrate the editing process, let's see how one newspaper copy editor edited the story shown in Figure 3.2 on the vote to delay the construction of new student apartments in a downtown area. The editor began by making changes in the lead to conform to Associated Press style, which most U.S. media companies follow. "City Council" should be uppercased when referring to a specific one, and 5–1 is the correct style for reporting votes. The "on" in front of Monday also is superfluous.

AS WRITTEN

The city council voted 5 to 1 on Monday to delay a vote on approving the construction of new student apartments in downtown Columbia until the impact of the construction can be assessed.

The council acted at just the second meeting since a new mayor and two new council members were elected. All promised during their heated campaigns to place a moratorium on controversial downtown construction, particularly student housing.

Opponents of additional apartment buildings in the area bounded by Broadway and Elm, Fifth and Tenth Streets have argued that additional housing would harm the city's outdated water and sewer infrastructure in the area and increase crime.

"We need to know the ramifications of overburdening the water and sewer systems in the area," Mayor Bob Gould said. "Let's do an assessment of the infrastructure before allowing any more construction."

Six new apartment buildings with a total of 347 apartments have been built in the area in the past four years.

"The whole character of downtown has changed as a result," said Sixth Ward Councilwoman Barbara Osher. "And we've seen a spike in crime down there with more people living in the area."

Councilman Roger Valdez disagreed vehemently.

"To suggest that college students contribute to crime disproportionately is nothing less than insulting," he said.

The area in question boarders the university campus and because of that is an attractive housing location for students.

AS EDITED

The City Council voted 5-1 Monday to delay a vote on approving the construction of new student apartments in downtown Columbia until the impact of the construction can be assessed.

The council acted at just the second meeting since a new mayor and two new council members were elected. All promised during their campaigns to place a moratorium on controversial downtown construction, particularly student housing.

Opponents of additional apartment buildings in the area bounded by Broadway and Elm, Fifth and Tenth streets have argued that additional housing would harm the city's outdated water and sewer infrastructure in the area and increase crime.

"We need to know the ramifications of overburdening the water and sewer systems in the area," Mayor Bob Gould said. "Let's do an assessment of the infrastructure before allowing any more construction."

Six apartment buildings with 347 apartments have been built in the area in the past four years.

"The whole character of downtown has changed as a result," said Sixth Ward Councilwoman Barbara Osher. "And we've seen a spike in crime down there with more people living in the area."

Councilman Roger Valdez disagreed.

"To suggest that college students contribute to crime disproportionately is nothing less than insulting," he said.

The area in question borders the university campus and because of that is an attractive housing location for students.

City Council (uppercase) is AP style when referring to a specific one. 5-1 is AP style for votes and the "on" before Monday is not needed.

To describe their campaigns as "heated" without explanation is editorializing.

"Streets" should be lowercase per AP style for pluralizations.

If they were built in the last four years, they obviously are "new," and therefore that word is not needed. "A total of" also is unnecessary.

"Vehemently" amounts to an editorial assessment and should be deleted.

"Borders" not "boarders"

Figure 3.2 Good editing is often subtle but nonetheless important.

Words that can be viewed as editorializing also surface in the story. In the second paragraph, what one person considers a "heated" campaign might be quite mundane to another. That's particularly true if, as in this case, the writer never explains why the campaign may have been "heated." And in the next-to-last paragraph, "vehemently" is another subjective word used by the writer without justification. What one person considers "vehement" another may not.

Another AP style error surfaces in the third paragraph. AP calls for lower-casing *streets* after compounds such as "Ninth and Elm streets." The same rule applies for other pluralizations, including *Tennessee and Kentucky legis-latures* and *Atlantic and Pacific oceans.*

In the fourth paragraph, the editor reduced wordiness. "Six new apart-ment buildings with a total of 347 apartments have been built in the area in the past four years" was improved by deleting "new" and "a total of." Neither was necessary.

Overall, the story was fairly clean and straightforward, so the editor let the writing style stand. **Again, one of the worst things an editor can do is overedit.** Much more detail on the editing process may be found in later chapters, but what we've covered so far gives us a basic understanding of the editing process.

Differences in Editing by Media Type

We've covered the basics of editing that are true across all forms of media, and we'll do more of that in detail as we progress through this book. For now, though, let's take a step back and consider how editing varies from newspapers to magazines to online sites to radio to television and finally to newsletters and books.

Newspapers

Newspapers are the oldest news medium in America and the world still used today, and the basics of editing were developed there. Indeed, the editing concepts presented earlier in this chapter are based on those of newspaper editing, which evolved over the last three or four centuries. News magazines arrived and slightly changed editing conventions, but editors of those publi-cations mimicked newspaper practices and changed them only slightly.

The real changes in editing began with the arrival of radio. Radio writers and editors found it desirable to edit differently for the spoken word than for the written word. Television, which added video, changed those practices even more. Then, when the web arrived and began to mature, editors in that medium were forced to learn not only the conventions of print editing but also those of audio and video editing. The web was an entirely different medium that required a convergent approach. Editors had to learn how to edit in *any* medium.

Technological advancements also brought us desktop, portable and tablet computers as well as mobile telephones. All are now used to consume news, and those, too, have altered how news is both edited and consumed.

Before we describe how editing for those newer media differs from editing for newspapers, let's tackle one editing issue that is done most commonly there—editing wire copy.

Editing Wire Copy

Newspapers contain a lot of edited wire copy. To be sure, radio, television and websites also carry information from the wires, but much of it is run exactly as received other than cutting the length. At newspapers, editors are encouraged to hone and improve what comes from the Associated Press and other services. With rare exception, only at newspapers are reports from various wire services regularly molded into an entirely new story.

News from the wire services plays different roles in the various media. For radio, television and online media, breaking news provided by the wires remains a staple of the daily news report. For newspapers, which usually get second crack at wire stories after the web and broadcast media have used them, offering greater depth and interpretation have become more important.

The wire stores favored by newspapers today are those that expand on the bare-bones reports provided by radio and television. To be sure, newspapers still contain plenty of basic wire stories, but, increasingly, these are short summaries confined to roundup columns. The mission of newspapers is to interpret, to explain and to amplify. That's true of local news, too, but the trend is particularly noticeable in the wire report.

Newspapers seldom have the opportunity to beat the electronic media to a wire story or even a local one, except at its online site where it can publish almost instantly, often before scheduled broadcast news shows. These realities for print led to the **"web-first" strategy** at newspapers. News is placed online when it breaks, then the print edition follows by providing more analytical stories and headlines that stress the latest developments since the original story broke. All this is tacit recognition of the fact that the various media have different strengths. The broadcast and online media excel at delivering the news with speed, but the print edition of a newspaper has the time and space to provide analysis and insight. So, too, do websites.

The dominant wire service in the U.S. is the Associated Press, a cooperative owned by member newspapers and broadcast stations. Privately owned United Press International, once a major competitor, shriveled into a minor player after going through a series of bankruptcies and ownership changes during the past 50 years. Today, UPI's main presence in the U.S. is in some radio newsrooms.

The decline of UPI opened the door to the U.S. market for British-owned Reuters, French-owned Agence France-Presse and other foreign-based services. Major U.S. newspapers often subscribe to such services, which provide excellent alternatives to AP for international news at affordable rates. Increasingly, the major foreign services cover U.S. news as well.

Another source of wire news is the so-called supplemental wire services—syndicates and news services formed by major metropolitan newspapers, alliances of such papers or a newspaper group. Such services make it possible for a newspaper in Danville, Illinois, to carry a major investigative piece from *The New York Times* on the same day the *Times* itself carries the story.

News is visual as well as written, so the wire services and syndicates often handle pictures and graphics in addition to text. The AP operates AP GraphicsBank, which allows clients to download ready-to-use graphics and photos. Today, wire photos are processed in digital form rather than with conventional photo-processing techniques. Information graphics—maps, charts and graphs—also can be delivered directly to computers.

How the Wires Operate

Stories delivered by a wire service come from several sources:

- **Copy may be developed by the agency's own large staff of reporters, feature writers, analysts, columnists and photographers.** Other wire service staffers rewrite from any source available—smaller papers, research reports and other publications.
- **Stories from the service's subscribers may be circulated.** Newspapers and broadcast stations contracting with a wire service agree to make their own news files available to the service, providing electronic versions of broadcasts or stories.
- **Stringers or correspondents in communities where there is no bureau can submit stories.** These newspaper reporters are called **stringers** because of the old practice of paying **correspondents** for their strings of stories by the number of column inches.
- **Exchanges of stories may be made with other news agencies, such as foreign agencies.**

Traditionally, the wire services have opened the news cycle with a news **budget** or digest that indicates to editors the dozen or more top national and international stories that were in hand or were developing. Today's wire editors may get a four- or five-line abstract of the complete offering—foreign, national, regional and state—directly to the media outlet's computer. From these abstracts or from computer directories, editors select the stories they think would interest their readers. Then, they retrieve these stories directly from the newspaper's computer.

Budgets and Priorities

The wire services operate on 12-hour time cycles—PMs for afternoon papers, AMs for morning papers. The broadcast wire is separate, but major broadcast networks and stations also take the newspaper wire, which is more complete. The cycles often overlap so that stories breaking near the cycle change are offered to both cycles, or stories early in one cycle are picked up as stories late in the other cycle.

Wire editors have two considerations in selecting wire copy for publication—the significance of the stories and the space allotted for wire copy. If space is tight, fewer wire stories are used, and heavier trims may be made on those that are used.

Budget stories usually, but not necessarily, get top priority. When stories listed on the budget arrive, they are indicated by BUDGET, BJT or SKED, together with the length in words. If such stories are developing or are likely to have additional or new material, the editor may wait before assigning them to editors and concentrate first on stories that will stand. The wire service will typically notify wire editors when a recap is coming, and then deliver a complete new story.

Editors always have more wire stories than they can use. This is true no matter the medium because all media run under space or time constraints. *The New York Times* slogan may be "all the news that's fit to print," but the truth is a paper can only print all the news that fits. On larger dailies using all the wires from the AP and several supplementals, the number of stories available is astounding. To help handle the large amount of copy, the computers are set to recognize the different headings on wire stories and sort them according to categories like state, national, world, Washington, features and so on. But editors still have much more to choose from than can be run.

Wire Editing Peculiarities

Editing wire stories isn't that different from editing local ones, but a few peculiarities apply to wire news. **First, a wire story, unlike most locally written news, usually carries a dateline, which indicates the city of the story's origin:**

OVERLAND   PARK,   Kan.   (AP)—An   apparent   good Samaritan . . .

The city of origin is in capital letters, and the state or nation is in uppercase and lowercase letters. At most newspapers, style calls for the dateline to be followed by the wire service logotype in parentheses and a dash. The paragraph indention comes before the dateline, not at the start of the first paragraph.

Stories that contain material from more than one location are called **undated stories**. They carry no dateline but a credit line for the wire service:

By The Associated Press
Islamic extremists said today . . .

Stories compiled from accounts supplied by more than one wire service may carry a combined credit line at the top, but a more specific list of wire sources should appear at the end:

From our wire services
LA PAZ, Bolivia—Mountain climbers tried today to reach the wreckage . . .
At the end of the story:
The Associated Press and The New York Times News Service contributed to this story.

Combining stories this way often provides a newspaper's readers with a better story or more information than could be obtained from one wire service. Good newspapers make a habit of doing this often.

If you use other wire services in addition to the AP, as many newspapers do, be on the lookout for differences between the styles of those services and AP. Usually, there won't be many. But once you've identified the differences and know what to look for, you can be faster and more complete in fixing the style in the stories to be more consistent. For example, *The New York Times* capitalizes *federal, government* and *administration,* contrary to AP style. The *Times* also writes *3rd* rather than *III* behind a name.

Two points should be kept in mind as you edit wire copy:

- **The wire isn't sacred.** The AP has a deserved reputation for accuracy, impartiality and speed of delivery. It also makes errors, sometimes colossal ones. Other services do, too.
- **No wire service tailors copy for a particular newspaper. You have to do that yourself.** Abundant details are included, but most stories are constructed so that papers may use the full account or trim sharply and still have the gist of the report. Local angles may also be inserted.

Wire stories often use the word *here* to refer to the city included in the dateline. If the editor has removed the dateline during the editing process, the city must be inserted in the text.

Wire services typically use Eastern time in their stories. Some newspapers outside the Eastern time zone prefer to convert these times by subtracting one hour for Central time, two for Mountain or three for Pacific. When this is done, if the dateline remains on the story, it will be necessary to use phrases such as "3 p.m. St. Louis time" or "1 p.m. PDT" in the text.

Wire Stories Versus Local Stories

Editing Wire Stories

- They usually take much less time to edit than local copy, but they still have errors. Don't trust them too much.
- You usually can cut more from them, and you don't get complaints from the reporter.
- Many newspapers don't use bylines for wire stories unless the story is significantly longer than the average one or an investigative piece.
- Don't be afraid to call or email the wire service with queries, time permitting.
- Don't automatically assume that because you received a rewrite that you need to replace a story already on the page. Often, the rewrites contain only additional quotations or minor details. But you need to check them.
- Look for missed angles. Sometimes, the wires bury much more interesting angles than what they lead with, so move up the better ones, especially local angles.

Cutting Wire Stories

Given the limited space in many newspapers, editors usually try to run local stories fully and make cuts in wire stories. One thing you'll be called on to do is to cut wire-service stories—often to turn 18-inch stories into 3-inch briefs.

Remember, though, that if the story is written in the inverted pyramid, the most basic of all writing styles, the most important 3 inches are at the top. If it's not in inverted-pyramid form—if it's a feature, commentary or analysis—it should not be chopped. Don't even waste your time trying. Just point it out to your supervising editor, who probably was misled about its content by a poorly written budget summary.

Here's what to do when told to chop a wire story to a brief:

- Scan it to make sure it's in the inverted-pyramid form.
- Thoroughly edit the first four or five paragraphs, then ask yourself whether anything would be left up in the air if the remainder were cut.

- Scan the rest of the story to make sure a better detail is not buried, or that the first few paragraphs were not misleading.
- If necessary, move material up. If not, chop at that point.
- Measure the story, then tighten to the exact fit.

Magazines

What comes to mind when we think of the term *magazine* are the big consumer magazines found on newsstands. Examples include *Time, Sports Illustrated, Cosmopolitan* and *O.* If the only magazines you know are those you see on the newsstands, look in the annual *Writer's Market,* easily found in library reference sections and even in mall bookstores, which lists 4,000 to 5,000 magazines. There are more specialty magazines, and they often make great places to start work—or carve out a career:

- **Corporate communications publications.** These are primarily magazines providing information to employees of large companies, but there also are business publications aimed at distributors and customers. These publications often hire people with degrees in journalism, public relations, technical writing or English, and they tend to pay more than newspaper jobs at the same level.
- **Trade publications.** These are specialized publications aimed at people in a particular field, such as farming, auto manufacturing or plumbing.
- **Association publications.** These are magazines published by associations of various kinds, such as trade groups. For example, members of the Fraternity Communications Association publish more than 100 titles.
- **Government and nonprofit organizations' publications.** Municipal, county, state and national governments all have their own publications, as do hospitals, colleges and various nonprofit organizations, such as churches. Examples include *Missouri Conservationist* and *Arizona Highways.*
- **Special-interest publications.** These range from *Maximum PC* to *Golf,* from *Simply Sewing* to *This Old House.* For almost any possible hobby, there is a magazine or two—sometimes more.
- **Newsletters of various kinds.** This is the fastest-growing category of all print publications. Schools, hospitals, public utilities and credit unions often have their own. Then there are the financial, political and other special-interest newsletters.

There are far more writing and editing jobs available in far more places than you ever imagined—many of them at places

you never thought of as media outlets, like auto companies, hospitals and professional associations. In addition, if you have special knowledge in some field—perhaps because you grew up on a farm or in a certain religion or you have certain hobbies or interests—you may have just the right combination, with your writing or editing talent, to fit into a niche publication—and face far less competition for the job.

Smaller publications are especially interested in people who have skills in several or all of these areas: writing, editing, photography and graphics, desktop publishing and web editing. **If you want to work eventually for a big consumer magazine in a city like New York, these small publications are where you get your experience.** The big consumer magazines seldom hire students right out of college, except as a gofer. And the best bet for jobs in consumer magazines? You guessed it: editing.

Although the total number of magazines published in the U.S. depends on what you count, and different sources report different counts, here are some figures that help give a picture:

- The National Directory of Magazines lists more than 20,000.
- Some say there are 800 to 1,200 consumer magazines in the U.S. Of these, only about 200 are seen on most newsstands. But others put the number higher, including one source that says more than 7,000 consumer magazines have websites.
- Some magazines are published only on the web. These, which are sometimes called **webzines**, include *Salon, Slate* and *Politico*.
- Experts suggest there may be about 12,000 specialty magazines.
- There may be about 13,000 PR magazines and newsletters.
- By the time you add in industry and association magazines, there are perhaps 50,000 magazines total, says one source, more than all other media combined.
- In addition, there are the virtually uncountable number of blogs and **e-zines**—small magazines on the internet—and **zines**—privately printed, small-run magazines.

The advice given earlier in this book—such as using the Three R's of Copy Editing—applies just as much to magazines and newsletters as to newspapers. But there are differences:

- **Magazines have fewer deadlines, so everyone has more time to work on an issue.** Magazine articles at the largest magazines are edited more heavily than the average newspaper story. This attention to detail often makes magazine writing more polished and refined than in newspaper stories, which often must be hammered out on tight deadlines. Such high standards don't always exist, however, at small magazines and newsletters. When one editor does everything—writing, editing and design—there is little opportunity, if any, for additional sets of eyes to challenge and improve the content.

- **Magazines usually have longer (and often better-written) articles that tend to be features, and therefore more personal and opinionated.** How-to articles, top-10 lists and celebrity interviews are often key sellers touted on the cover, but what appeals to many writers about magazines is the chance to produce longer, more involved, more personal articles of high quality.
- **Readers expect more from a magazine than a newspaper.** Readers expect longer, more entertaining articles, better photos, better design and higher-quality paper. Most throw away the newspaper after one day, but they keep the magazine around the house longer. **In the end, the main difference between magazine and newspaper editing is that while most U.S. newspapers follow AP style, most magazines write and use their own stylebooks.**

Websites

When the World Wide Web arrived in 1994, newspapers and broadcast stations began putting their content online. Their efforts reminded veteran journalists of the early days of television, when, absent knowledge of how to use the strengths of that medium, newscasts amounted to nothing more than a reporter reading the news on camera. Similarly, early efforts to put news online amounted to little more than making the text of stories available on the web. As the internet has evolved, online journalism has become more and more sophisticated, and so have editors' views of what they are doing.

Good web editors now understand that most stories—at least major stories—should not appear on the web exactly as they might appear in print. Such stories often should be broken into pieces so that a main story is accompanied by sidebars. Those stories also should take advantage of the web's ability to deliver photos, audio, video and graphics— perhaps even interactive graphics—to take full advantage of the medium's capabilities. Dumping print stories onto the web may be acceptable for brief stories, although even then the headlines often must be rewritten to allow search engines to find them.

Layers and Links

Increasingly, journalists recognize that writing and editing for the online media differ from writing and editing for the traditional media. And, while space is virtually unlimited in the online media, there is an increasing awareness that long, unrelieved blocks of text inhibit reading rather than promote it. **Increasingly, web stories are layered, usually with these parts:**

- **The headline or title.**
- **A one-sentence tease, or lead.**
- **The first page or a quick summary of what happened, not unlike a short radio or television story.**
- **Accompanying visuals, usually photos or graphics.**
- **Accompanying audio and video, if any.**
- **The in-depth report, often broken with subheads.**
- **Links to related material.**

Layering and links make editing for the online media different. **Layering** makes it simple for readers to consume as little, or as much, as they want. **Links** provide access to incredible depth that far exceeds what newspapers or magazines can offer. Indeed, rich links can provide web consumers with all they could want to know about the subject. As many have observed, the internet is the world's largest library. Links to both internal and external sources of information let the online editor take advantage of that.

Editors have at their command all the necessary information to tell the story in the best way possible. But the online editor has to be a jack-of-all-trades. At a newspaper, magazine, or radio or television station, the work of assembling the various parts of a story usually is parceled out to reporters, graphic artists, photographers, videographers or editors. In an online newsroom, one person may well handle most or all of these functions. Thus, the online journalist is a multimedia journalist.

There is no single way to produce a story for online publication. Although traditional newspaper and magazine writing formulas often work in the online newsroom, there may be better ways. A quick story may lend itself to the classic newspaper inverted-pyramid writing style, a staple of quick-hitting news websites. A more complex one may require links to audio, video and still photos with multiple layers of text. Major projects may require complex forms of storytelling.

Online journalism is multimedia journalism. Thus, the journalist is required to select the best medium—text, graphics, photos, audio or video—in which the story should be told. Almost without exception, the best way to tell any story is with a combination of these.

Differences Between Online and Traditional News Audiences

Online audiences are much more easily targetable by outlets and advertisers than newspapers or broadcast stations—even more, perhaps than magazines. Although small, targeted audiences may be too small to sustain other media, they are large enough to warrant attention from websites.

Online readers differ from those in the traditional news audience. They tend to be younger, and they are attracted by the web's often-informal language and the intimacy and interaction afforded by electronic mail and bulletin boards. Web readers feel more like participants in an online community than consumers of a product. Today's news consumers want to talk back to the providers of their news, and they want to participate in discussions about the events of the day. With access to email, blogs, bulletin boards and chat rooms, they form communities to argue about and discuss the issues of the day. In comparison, the traditional media, with their one-way form of communication, seem to some to be preachy and arrogant.

The objectivity and authoritative tone of the traditional newspaper, so valued by editors, clearly is not preferred by online consumers. Indeed, these consumers may value just as highly the opinion or approach of a fellow online consumer. Thus, if newspapers, magazines, radio and television stations, and other traditional media are to succeed online, they must rethink the way they relate to their customers.

To be sure, there still is a need on the web for the authoritative services provided by the traditional media. But much of the online business opportunity for newspapers and broadcast stations probably lies in providing news based around interactive forums in which readers talk with reporters and editors as well as each other. In the process, web-based news becomes something quite different from what's offered in the traditional media. According to Scott Whiteside, the retired general manager of the *Atlanta Journal-Constitution*, news sites on the web are increasingly likely to:

- Publish massive amounts of information that has little to do with "news" or broad public issues.
- Adopt the point of view of the groups being covered.
- Provide content for services dedicated solely to selling.
- Provide access to numerous services independent of the newspaper brand, services that may appeal to people who don't like newspapers.
- Cede a certain amount of editorial control to the readers themselves.

In the minds of traditional journalists, some of these issues are problematic because they challenge the norms of traditional newsroom values and ethics, as well as objectivity. For example, a real journalist, they argue, would not be associated with "advertorial" copy. Nor would a real journalist adopt a point of view in a typical news story or cede a portion of editorial control to the reader. Yet, it is clear that online journalism is challenging these older standards. Notes one editor: "Alternative newspapers and topic-specific magazines have been doing some of those things for years, and in the process they have built loyal audiences. They also have built credibility with their audiences that the mainstream media too often lack."

The idea of relaxing traditional newsroom standards to accommodate the demands and expectations of the online media makes many older journalists uncomfortable. This briefly sparked a movement to divorce online operations from traditional newsrooms. Those who did that argued that the values of the newspaper or broadcast newsroom often clash with what's needed to succeed in the online marketplace. In their view, what the online marketplace needed, and demanded, was smaller, focused staffs uninhibited by the agendas of their parent organizations.

Today, most media organizations have found this approach to be counterproductive. Online operations must become central to the organization's focus, and to separate online operations from the traditional newsroom is increasingly viewed as a mistake.

Still, to many traditional journalists, adaptation to the online culture smacks of a major relaxation of journalistic standards and ethics. Why, they argue, should a reporter be forced to blog and answer readers' questions? To others, doing that is nothing more than adaptation to the realities of a changing marketplace. But one thing is certain: **In a medium that permits readers to become active participants, attempts to shut them out and retain the "we-know-best" attitude, historically so prevalent at newspapers and news magazines, is doomed to failure.**

Some innovative editors are adapting well to the new realities. Minnesota Public Radio embraced the concept of citizen participation in the news-gathering process by creating a database of 150,000 or so experts on all sorts of topics it calls the Public Insight Network. When something important happens, MPR finds it easy to tap the expertise of people willing to talk publicly about the event or problem.

Online media, then, require reporters and editors who are willing to engage the public in ways that promote interactivity rather than those who are deeply rooted in the traditions of one-way communication. That's not to say that reporters should be asked to write stories for advertising sections. They shouldn't be. But in today's world, it's increasingly common for reporters to be tasked with maintaining blogs and communicating on them with readers or with responding to comments about their stories online. The environment has changed, and journalists must adapt to it. News-oriented websites must do that while also attempting to improve their credibility.

Online Journalism and Credibility

Simply engaging readers—or even experts—is not enough. In today's media environment, readers must be convinced that

what they read or hear is accurate. It's no longer enough just to report what a candidate for president claimed. The veracity of what he or she said must be checked. Websites such as FactCheck.org and Politifact.org attempt to do just that, and media outlets nationwide are embracing the reports of those organizations and creating their own fact-checking operations. That effort, combined with open, unfettered online discussion sites, help to engage readers while improving credibility.

These changes in journalism standards brought about by the nature of online media are also affecting other media. Broadcast news operations have also increasingly rejected the idea of credibility through striving for objectivity in coverage, for example, replacing it with blatant partisanship to appeal to a targeted ideologically partisan niche audience. This is also carrying over more and more to newspaper journalists, as well, and has long existed in politically oriented news magazines. We see this trend as understandable from a marketing standpoint but dangerous to the public trust in journalism, as more people find the news media less and less credible as a whole, even though they may trust outlets that appeal to their own biases.

Like their print or broadcast counterparts, online editors must be careful to use information only from reliable sources. But an added danger of online journalism is providing web links to unreliable sources. Stan Ketterer, a journalist and journalism educator, suggests that editors evaluate information on the internet by following the same journalistic practices they use for assessing the credibility and accuracy of any information. He developed these guidelines:

- Before using information from a website, verify it with the source. There are exceptions to this rule. Information from a highly credible government site like the Census Bureau is probably OK. And perhaps one source must suffice on a breaking story because of time constraints. An editor must clear all exceptions.
- If you have any doubts about the accuracy of the information and you cannot reach the source, find a second source. When in doubt, omit the information.
- In most cases, information taken directly from the web and used in a story must be attributed. You can use the name of the copyright holder or government agency in the attribution—for example, "according to the EPA" or "EPA figures show." If you cannot verify the information, attribute unverified information to the web page, such as, "according to the Voice of America's site on the World Wide Web." Consult your editor before using unverified information.
- Check the extension on the site's internet address to get clues as to the nature of the organization and the likely slant of the information. The most common extensions used in the U.S. are .gov (government), .edu (education), .com (commercial), .mil (military), .org (nonprofit organization) and .net (internet service provider). Most of the government

and military sites have credible and accurate information. In many cases, you can take the information directly from the site and attribute it to the organization. If college and university sites have source documents, such as the U.S. Constitution, attribute the information to the source document. But beware. Personal home pages of students often have .edu extensions, and the information on them is not always credible.

- Do not use information from a personal home page without contacting the person and without the permission of an editor.
- In almost all cases, do not use information from the home pages of commercial and nonprofit organizations without verification. Verify and attribute all information on these pages.
- Check the date when the page was last updated. The date generally appears at the bottom of the first page of the site. Although a recent date does not ensure that the information is current, it does indicate that the organization is paying close attention to the site. If no date appears, if the site has not been updated for a while or if it was created some time ago, do not use the information unless you verify it with the source.

As Ketterer notes, using the web as a source of information is no riskier than using books, magazines or other printed material, provided one uses common sense. He also cautions editors to remember that material on the web is subject to copyright laws. With some exceptions, there is no problem linking to a website. But taking copyrighted material and placing it on your own site is clearly a copyright violation.

Finally, we need to note that online sites—as well as traditional media—now pump massive amounts of information directly to mobile phones. Millions of consumers have access to fourth- and fifth-generation (4G and 5G) mobile phones that permit news and other information—including video—to be delivered with ease.

Broadcast

Most of the techniques for editing in newspapers and magazines apply as well to news on radio and television (see Figure 3.3). Those responsible for news copy for any medium must have good news judgment, a feeling for the audience and the ability to handle the language. But broadcast writers and editors have to be more concise and also make their words work with audio and video.

Broadcast news should be written and edited so newscasters can read it conversationally, sound natural to listeners and not be misunderstood. So, read your story out loud to detect any potential problems with it before it goes on the air. Broadcast news must be so simple that listeners can immediately grasp its meaning. The

Figure 3.3 Television and radio journalists need to master many of the same skills as print journalists, but also video and audio editing of recorded and live broadcasts. Of course, with the growth of newspaper and magazine websites, the skill sets are increasingly overlapping.

Photo by Christopher Parks.

language must be so forceful that even casual listeners will feel compelled to give the story their full attention.

A reader's eyes may on occasion deceive, but not to the extent that the listener's ears deceive. A reader who misses a point can go over the material again. A listener who misses a point likely has lost it completely. For example, radio and TV news manuals caution against inserting information that separates subject and predicate. So, if the copy reads, "The Community of Christ, a break-off group from the Mormon Church, has ordained women for decades," many listeners will be left with the false impression that the Mormon Church ordains women.

Broadcast copy should talk. It uses contractions and, often, sentence fragments. It is rhythmic because speech is rhythmic. The best broadcast copy teems with simple active verbs that produce images for the listener.

The present tense (The president says) or the present-perfect tense (The president has said) creates immediacy and freshness in good broadcast copy and helps eliminate repetition of the word *today*. As an example:

A winter storm has covered the Atlantic seaboard—from Virginia to Maine—with up to 20 inches of snow. Gale-force winds have piled up

6-foot drifts in Virginia, bringing traffic there and in West Virginia to a virtual halt. The storm has closed schools in six states. Trains and buses are running hours late. Pennsylvania and Massachusetts have called out huge snow-clearing forces.

A broadcast news story should sound warm and intimate, and be more personal than a newspaper story. The refreshing, conversational style of broadcast news writing has many virtues that all news writers might study. Broadcast writing stresses plain talk. The newspaper reporter may want to echo a speaker's words, even in an indirect quote: "The city manager said his plan will effect a cost reduction at the local government level." Broadcast style calls for simple words: "The city manager said his plan will save money for the city."

The lead on the broadcast story should function like a newspaper headline to attract readers and let them know what's to come. First, give a capsule of the news item, then the details:

The New York stock market took a sharp loss after backing away from an early rise. Trading was active. Volume was 15-million-950-thousand shares compared with 16-million-740-thousand Friday.

The newscast should be arranged using transitions that help listeners shift gears. Such transitions should be made with ideas and skillful organization of facts and not with crutch words or catch phrases. One of the most overused transitions in broadcast copy is *in other news*. It often seems to be used inappropriately to make sudden, jarring transitions between a tragic story and one that's lighter, even humorous.

The broadcast story should complement, not merely repeat, what's obvious from any accompanying sound clips or video.

Sources of Copy

Written copy for the broadcast newsroom comes from local reporters and news-gathering associations. Some radio and television stations subscribe to a newspaper news service as well as to the broadcast newswire. This provides a greater number and variety of stories.

Some local stations broadcast the news in the form they receive it from the news agency. But most broadcast news is edited by trained reporters who know how to tailor the news for a specific audience. Almost all wire copy is rewritten before it is assembled for broadcast and sometimes from newscast to newscast to give listeners some variety.

| NewsCenter 8 Slug **arrest** | |
| Newscast **6** Date **9/1** Writer **mm** | Length: **:28** |

`moc:`	Columbia police have
	charged a Moberly
	man with last week's
	robbery of the Boone
`ENG  :22`	County Bank.
`ENG  :00- :22`	An eyewitness
`Cassette E-100`	identified 23-year
`Cut 1 Cued`	old Rober Wilson of
`VOICEOVER`	Moberly as the man
	who took almost
	10-thousand dollars
	from the bank
`Key: File Tape`	Friday afternoon.
`     (:05-:10)`	Acting on a tip,
	police took Wilson
	into custody this
	morning in downtown
	Columbia.
	(more)

| NewsCenter 8 Slug **arrest ADD** | |
| Newscast **6** Date **9/1** Writer **mm** | Length: -- |

`tape rolling for` `VOICEOVER`	Wilson denies
	committing the robbery,
	but remains in jail
	under 50-thousand
	dollar bond.
	These bank photographs
	show the robber
	escaping with the
	money bag under
	his arm.
`back to moc:`	Police say they
	also want to question
	Wilson about a series
	of burglaries in the
	county over the past
	year.

Figure 3.4 This television script indicates the use of voiceover while video rolls on the screen after the anchor introduces the story. The announcer's one-sentence summary ends the story.

Courtesy of KOMU-TV, Columbia, MO.

Broadcast Style

There are almost as many copy formats and scripting styles as there are broadcast newsrooms. Most broadcast stations triple-space their scripts, but formatting and terminology varies. In one newsroom, the script designation voiceover, or VO, might mean that a newscaster is reading over video, while in another newsroom, voiceover might mean that the reporter's recorded voice is running with video. Adapt to the way things are done at the broadcast station where you get an internship or job, just as you would at other news organizations.

Figure 3.4 is a typical script from KOMU-TV in Columbia, Missouri. It is from a 6 o'clock newscast devoted to local news. The robbery arrest story calls for the newscaster to read it all, but after a few lines, the picture will change from the newscaster's face to video illustrating the story. Figure 3.5 is a typical radio script from WEMU-FM in Ypsilanti, Michigan. It's the second version of what was basically the same story to be used during the local segment in two National Public Radio news shows, one morning, one afternoon. The story includes a sound clip to be played by the board operator after the anchor introduces it.

All editing of broadcast copy is done with ease of reading for the newscaster in mind. For example, for television, the teleprompter copy should average only four words a line so the newscaster's eyes do not have to travel noticeable distances back and forth across the page. The teleprompter works by beaming a picture of the script to a monitor mounted on the studio camera, so the newscaster can read the script while appearing conversational and pleasant. There is no need to refer to notes or a script, but newscasters have them in case the teleprompter fails.

All paper copy should be triple-spaced in capital and lower-case letters. If a letter correction is to be made in a word, the word should be scratched out and the correct word substituted in printed letters. If word changes are made within sentences, the editor should read aloud the edited version to make sure the revised form sounds right. If the copy requires excessive editing, corrections should be made and a new copy printed before it is submitted to a newscaster. No hyphens should be used to break words from one line to the next.

News editors put each story on a separate sheet. This lets them rearrange the items or delete an item if time runs short. A few briefs tacked near the end of the newscast help fill leftover time.

Properly edited broadcast copy also should include pronunciation aids when necessary. The most common dilemma for newscasters is place names, many of which get different pronunciations in different regions. No newscaster should confuse the pronunciation of Palace of Versailles (vehr-SIGH) in France with the town of Versailles (vur-SALES) in Missouri. The editor should add the phonetic spelling to the script, and the newscaster may underline the word on his or her copy as a reminder.

The wire services provide a pronunciation list of foreign words and names appearing in the day's report. The guide is given in phonetic spelling (*Gabon—Gabone*) or by rhyme (*Blough—rhymes with how*).

Some commonly mispronounced words include:

acclimated	heinous	prerogative
advertisement	inclement	prescription
Antarctica	incomparable	prostate
Arctic	lambaste	recluse
Boise	libel	recur
bologna	machinations	sherbet
cavalry	Mackinac	short-lived
comparable	mischievous	tenet
debacle	Morse code	utmost
envelope	NASA	verbiage
extraordinary	nuclear	wash
February	ordnance	whet
harass	preferable	zoolog

For advice on most of these and more, see www.alphadictionary.com/articles/mispronounced_words.html

Phonetic Spelling System Used by Wire Services

A	like the *a* in cat	OW	like the *ow* in cow
AH	like the *a* in arm	U	like the *u* in put
AW	like the *a* in talk	UH	like the *u* in but
AY	like the *a* in ace	K	like the *c* in cat
EE	like the *ee* in feel	KH	guttural
EH	like the *ai* in air	S	like the *c* in cease
EW	like the *ew* in few	Z	like the *s* in disease
IGH	like the *i* in tin	ZH	like the *g* in rouge
IH	like the *i* in time	J	like the *g* in George
OH	like the *o* in go	SH	like the *ch* in machine
OO	like the *oo* in pool	CH	like the *ch* in catch

Broadcast style differs from newspaper style in several respects. In the following section, we summarize the most notable differences.

Abbreviations

No abbreviations should be used in radio or TV news copy with these exceptions:

- Common usage: *Dr. Smith, Mrs. Jones, St. Paul*
- Names or organizations widely known by their initials: *U-N, F-B-I, G-O-P* (but *AFL-CIO*)
- Acronyms: *NATO*
- Time designations: *A-M, P-M*
- Academic degrees: *P-H-D*

Punctuation

To indicate a pause where the newscaster can catch a breath, the dash or a series of dots is preferable to a comma:

The House plans to give the 11-billion-500-million dollar measure a final vote on Tuesday . . . and the Senate is expected to follow suit.

The hyphen is used instead of the period in initials: *F-B-I.* The period is retained, however, in initials in a name: *J.D. Smith.* All combined words should have the hyphen: *co-worker, semi-annual.* (Spelling should also use the form easiest to pronounce: *employee.*)

Contractions are more widely used in broadcast copy to achieve a conversational tone. Common contractions—*isn't, doesn't, it's, they're*—may be used in both direct and indirect quotes. Good broadcast writers, however, avoid contractions when they want to stress verbs, especially the negative: "*She does not choose to run*" instead of "*She doesn't choose to run.*"

Quotation Marks

Don't read quotation marks into the script—"quote" and "end of quote." Instead, indicate the speaker's words by phrases such as "*and these are his words,*" "*what she called,*" "*he put it in these words.*"

Figures

Don't start a story with a number. By the time the listener hears what the number pertains to, it may be forgotten. This is different from print and online media, where the number is read rather than heard.

4-21   Verdict Voicer   TAP

Local civil rights activists are praising the conviction of former Minneapolis Police Officer Derek Chauvin.
We get the details from WEMU's Taylor Pinson.

Verdict0421-1 :33

Chauvin was found guilty of all charges in the murder of George Floyd. Trische Duckworth, the Founder of Survivors Speak, says she's grateful for the verdict and thinks this is a catalyst to change unlike any she's seen before.

"I believe that just witnessing his murder before all of our eyes ignited something in a lot of us. And we all see the need for change."

Duckworth says this is only the beginning and more still needs to be done to address racial justice and policing.

4-21   Verdict 2   TAP

Civil rights activists gathered in front of the Washtenaw County Sheriff's Office Tuesday to show their support for the conviction of former Minneapolis Police Officer Derek Chauvin.
Chauvin was found guilty of all charges in the murder of George Floyd. Trische Duckworth, The Founder of Survivors Speak, attended the rally and says she is grateful for the verdict, but more still needs to be done.

Verdict0421-2 :09 *"We need to see more of this. Not just for police, but for prosecutors and judges and everyone that violates and harms our black and brown people."*

Duckworth says she hopes this will serve as a catalyst to change like she's never seen before.

Figure 3.5 This sample radio news script demonstrates a lead-in to be spoken by the anchor followed by the reporter's words, including a short clip spoken as a cut-in from a news source interviewed. At the top, "4-21" means the story was for April 21. "Verdict" is the name of the story. "Voicer" indicates the story had a lead-in spoken by the anchor to a report voiced by the reporter. "TAP" are the initials of the reporter. "Verdict0421-1" is the name of the clip on the computer for the anchor to pull up and play, with the "-1" the version of the story, since multiple versions were prepared. The ":33" indicates the time of the story—a typical length for such reports. The name "Trische" could be read as either Trish or Tricia, so would have had a pronunciation written behind in parentheses had the story been written to be read by the anchor rather than the reporter. Verdict 2 is a variation on the same story for another hour of the newscast.

Courtesy of WEMU-FM, Ypsilanti, Michigan.

Be aware that numbers can be easily misheard in broadcast copy. *"A million"* may sound like *"8 million."* No confusion results if *"one million"* is used. Likewise, *"Police are looking for a man 50 to 60 years of age"* could sound like *"52"* to the listener. It should read, *"Police are looking for a man between 50 and 60 years old."* **In most copy, round numbers or approximations mean as much as specific figures.** *"Almost a mile"* rather than *"5,200 feet,"* *"about half"* rather than *"48.2%"* and *"just under 2%"* rather than *"1.9%"* are clearer to the listener.

An exception is voting results, especially when the margin is close. These should be written *"100-to-95 vote"* rather than *"100–95 vote."* The writer or editor can help the listener follow statistics or vote tallies by inserting phrases such as *"in the closest race"* and *"in a landslide victory."*

Here are some additional style rules for figures:

- **Fractions and decimals should be spelled out**: *one and seven-eighths* (not *1⅞*), *five-tenths* (not *0.5*).
- **Numbers under 10 and over 999 are spelled out and hyphenated**: *one, two, two-thousand, 11-billion-500-million, 15-hundred* (rather than *one-thousand-500*), *one-and-a-half million dollars* (never *$1.5 million*).
- **When two numbers occur together in a sentence, the smaller number should be spelled out**: *twelve 20-ton trucks.*
- **Any figure beginning a sentence should be spelled out.**
- **Figures are used for time of day** (*4:30 this afternoon*), **in all market stories and in sports scores and statistics** (*65-to-59, 5-foot-5*). If results of horse races or track meets appear in the body of the story, the winning times should be spelled out: *two minutes, nine and three-tenths seconds* (rather than *2:9.3*).
- **In dates and addresses, the -st, -rd, -th and -nd are included**: *July 20th, West 83rd Street.*
- **Figures are used for years**: *2021.*

Titles and Names

The identification or title usually precedes the name: *Secretary of Defense Lloyd J. Austin III.* Some titles are impossible to place before the name, such as: *The vice president of the Society for the Preservation and Encouragement of Barbershop Quartet Singing, Joe Doe.* Use *"Vice President Joe Doe of the Society for the Preservation and Encouragement of Barbershop Quartet Singing."* Use *"Police Chief Don Vendel"* rather than *"Chief of Police Don Vendel."*

Likewise, the attribution to the person making a statement should come before the rest of the sentence: *Russian leader Vladimir Putin said . . .*

Some radio and TV newsrooms insist that the president should never be referred to by his last name alone. It would be *President Biden, the president* or *Mr. Biden.*

Broadcast copy seldom includes middle initials and ages of persons in the news. Of course, some initials are well-known parts of names and should be included: *Richard M. Nixon.*

Ages may be omitted unless the age is significant to the story: *"A 12-year-old boy—Mitchell Smith—was crowned winner."* Ages usually appear in local copy to aid in identification. Place the age close to the name. Do not say, *"A 24-year-old university student died in a two-car collision today. He was Bill Armstrong."* Use *"A university student died in a two-car collision today. He was 24-year-old Bill Armstrong."*

When several proper names appear in the same story, it is better to repeat the names than to rely on pronouns unless the antecedent is obvious. Also, repeat the names rather than use *the former, the latter* or *respectively.*

Places

The dateline of a wire story may be used as an introduction or a transition: *In Miami.* Or the location may be noted elsewhere in the lead: *The Green Bay Packers and the Chicago Bears meet in Chicago tonight in the annual charity football game.*

Broadcasters don't use street addresses routinely in stories as newspaper reporters often do.

Time Angle

In a newspaper wire story almost everything happens today, but broadcast copy breaks up the day into its parts: *this morning, early tonight, just a few hours ago, at noon today.* The technique gives the listener a feeling of urgency in the news. Specific time should be translated for the time zone of the station's location: *That will be 2:30 Mountain Time.*

Use mainly the present and present-perfect tenses:

> Searchers have found the wreckage of a twin-engine Air Force plane in Puerto Rico and continue to look for the bodies of six of the aircraft's eight crewmen. Authorities confirm that the plane, missing since Saturday, crashed atop a peak 25 miles southeast of San Juan.

If past tense must be used, add the time element after the verb: *Sen. Bernie Sanders of Vermont paid a visit Thursday to . . .*

Newsletters and Books

There also are many editing jobs available at newsletters. These typically fall into one of two categories:

- Corporate publications.
- Special-interest publications.

Corporate newsletters typically target employees, customers or both. They can be in printed form or online. Special-interest publications often are directed to people with certain shared interests like investing. Many in that category have large subscription prices because of the proprietary information they convey that customers want. Editing at newsletters is basically the same as editing at newspapers or magazines, although the subject matter will almost certainly be more narrowly focused.

And, of course, the many book-publishing companies employ editors, too. Most U.S. book publishers use the *Chicago Manual of Style* for most works unless there is good reason to use something different. This book, for example, follows AP style (with a few exceptions) because it addresses the media industry.

Self-Editing

We mentioned earlier that cutbacks in editing positions throughout the media industry have reduced the amount of **redundant editing**. That's a problem because almost *any* news story can be improved to make it easier to understand and more factually correct. As the number of editors has been reduced, redundant editing becomes more unlikely. That, in turn, results in an increase in misspellings, grammar errors, factual errors and fuzzy, muddled prose.

Newspapers, in particular, have been hard hit, but they are not alone. Magazines, other than the largest and richest ones, have similar problems, and broadcast stations have never been known for outstanding editing. All the websites of those traditional media outlets also suffer, as do many websites with no ties at all to traditional media. Grammar errors, in particular, are commonplace in the broadcast media and in print, broadcast and online advertising, both national and local. So, it's fair to state that the best editing today occurs only at the best magazines and newspapers, and only at the top-of-the-line book companies. The primary cause of that is the decline in redundant editing.

We're unlikely to see a reverse in that trend anytime soon, which means that young people entering the media industry must learn to edit their own copy. Often, if your story is going to be edited at all, you're the one who will have to do it. The problem with that, of course, is that it's far too easy to overlook a mistake in something you have written. You know what it was supposed to say, and you know what you meant, but will the reader or listener understand it?

Any good writer will go through a story for a second or third time before submitting it, when time permits, but even then it's likely that errors will be missed and that passages will remain fuzzy to the reader. A second set of eyes on your work is *always* desirable, even if it's increasingly unlikely that will happen.

Here are suggestions on how to edit your own copy:

- **Take a break if time permits.** Deadlines may sometimes make this impossible, but if you have time to walk away for lunch or a 10-minute break before submitting your story, do so. That will allow you to clear your thoughts a bit and approach the story with renewed vigor when you return.
- **Print out your story and read it.** If the consumer will read the story in text form, putting it on paper is sometimes more effective than merely reading it on a computer screen. It's a good way to find things you missed.
- **Read your story aloud.** Just as broadcasters simplify their stories before reading them on air, print and online writers will benefit from discovering their own fuzzy writing by hearing it spoken.
- **Edit line-by-line.** Editors make more mistakes when they skim through copy at high speed. Slow down and be deliberate in your editing.
- **Pay attention to grammar, syntax and style.** Good grammar and syntax make any article more readable. Observing style rules avoids annoying inconsistences within your story and across your publishing or broadcast platform.
- **Look for forms of passive voice.** Active voice always makes a story more forceful and removes doubt about who is doing the acting. Writing in the passive voice is less direct and forces the reader to guess.
- **Study in detail the most critical functions of the editor.** We cannot emphasize enough how important it is to commit to memory as much as possible of Chapters 4–8 of this text. The points made there are those most vital to becoming a good editor. There's also a small book, *Edit Yourself* by Bruce Ross-Larson, that should be the constant companion of anyone who regularly self-edits.
- **Reread your story.** Then reread it again. The more times you read through a story, the more mistakes you will find and correct. The last read should be focused on reading as a top-flight proofreader might check your story.

While self-editing may be a poor second choice to editing by another, it's possible to train yourself to be meticulously careful. And remember, any time you can find a colleague who has enough time to read your story, ask that person to do so and offer to return the favor. A second set of eyes on a story always improves it.

Suggested Websites

ACES: The Society for Editing: https://aceseditors.org/
The Associated Press: www.ap.org
British Broadcasting Corporation: www.bbc.co.uk
Cable News Network: www.cnn.com
ESPN: www.espn.go.com
Ezine Universe: http://new-list.com
Magazine Publishers of America: www.magazine.org
Most Mispronounced Words in English: www.alphadictionary.com/articles/
    mispronounced_words.html
National Association of Broadcasters: www.nab.org
The New York Times: www.nytimes.com
Newsletter Access: www.newsletteraccess.com
News Media Alliance: www.naa.org
Poynter Institute: www.poynter.org
Radio and Television Digital News Association: www.rtnda.org
Society for News Design: www.snd.org

Suggested Readings

The Associated Press Stylebook. Latest edition. New York: The Associated Press. (There's a section called "Broadcast" at the back.)
Apfelbaum, Sue, and Juliette Cezzar. *Designing the Editorial Experience: A Primer for Print, Web and Mobile*. Beverly, MA: Rockport Publishers, 2015.
Banks, Beverly, Jean Ruggles and Kathleen McGullam, Eds. *Oxbridge Directory of Newsletters 2014*. New York: Oxbridge Communications, 2014.
Benson, Christopher D. and Charles F. Whitaker, *Magazine Writing*. New York: Routledge, 2014.
Carroll, Brian. *Writing and Editing for Digital Media*, New York: Routledge, 2017.
Dotson, Bob. *Make It Memorable: Writing and Packaging TV News with Style*. Lanham, Maryland: Rowman & Littlefield, 2016.
Folio. The magazine about the magazine industry.
Harrower, Tim. *The Newspaper Designer's Handbook*. New York: McGraw Hill, 2012.
Ross-Larson, Bruce. *Edit Yourself*. New York: W.W. Norton & Co., 1996.
Williams, Andy. *WordPress for Beginners 2019: A Visual Step-by-Step Guide to Mastering WordPress*. Dr. Andy Williams, 2018.
Williams, Robin. *The Non-Designer's Design Book*, 4th edition. Berkeley, CA: Peachpit Press (Pearson), 2014.

4 MACRO EDITING FOR THE BIG PICTURE

Macro Editing: The Overview

Editors often speak of macro editing and micro editing. Macro editing is big-picture editing and includes:

- Making sure stories are worth running.
- Making sure stories have good leads, are organized and flow well.
- Making sure stories don't leave unanswered questions.
- Making sure stories are accurate.
- Making sure stories are objective.
- Making sure stories are legal, ethical, tasteful and sensitive to the audience.

DOI: 10.4324/9781003011422-4

In this chapter, we'll look at all of these except the last item, then we'll devote Chapter 5 to law, ethics, taste and sensitivity.

Micro editing is editing with an eye toward the details and includes:

- Making sure the grammar and usage are correct.
- Making sure abbreviations, capitalization, numbers and punctuation conform to the publication's, website's or station's stylebook.
- Making sure words are spelled correctly and that there aren't any typos.
- Making sure the copy is tightly written so it doesn't waste the audience's time and conforms to space or time limits.

We'll look at grammar and usage in Chapter 6; examine style, spelling and tightening in Chapter 7; and then, in Chapter 8, we'll show how to combine macro and micro editing into a holistic-editing approach.

Making Sure Stories Are Worth Running

As explained in Chapter 3, the first of the Three R's of Copy Editing is to make sure the story is reader-centered, if you're editing for print or print-based web, or listener- or viewer-centered if you're editing for radio or television or audio- or visual-based web stories.

To be worth the time, a story should focus on something your audience either wants to know or needs to know. It should also be told in a way that makes it new, that comes across as fresh rather than stale. To know whether a story contains information that's wanted or needed by your audience, you first should get to know your audience. Readership studies can help you do that, but so can something as simple as talking regularly with readers.

The stories that mean the most to media consumers usually directly affect their lives in some way. Examples include money-related items, such as tax cuts or college-tuition increases; information that has an impact on daily life, like road closings and weather; and stories that have an emotional effect, such as human-interest features, obituaries of close friends or family members, and crime and terrorism stories.

Of course, not all stories have a direct impact on your audience, so the next strongest stories are those about a topic that interests them. A story about a popular celebrity or a science-page story about a new theory concerning dinosaurs may not have much impact on the way readers live, but both will be well-read or closely watched items that day.

If the story seems to have neither the potential for audience impact nor interest, before killing it the editor should check whether the reporter focused the story on people. When reporters forget the broadcast maxim that "news is people," it's easy to make a potentially good story boring. If the story is focused on a thing—say, the widening of a street—ask the reporter to refocus it on the reactions of people affected, such as those who live there and will now have bedrooms 10 feet from the traffic.

But sometimes, reporters turn in a nonstory—a story that seems pointless and not worth running. Perhaps the story has been written from a press release about something that would better be handled by an advertisement. Perhaps the story is out of date, or it advances an event too far in the future to run at this time. Sometimes, a story is handed in that just plain leaves you asking: "So what? Why would anyone care?"

In such a case, if you're the **assigning editor**—the city editor, sports editor, features editor or other editor to whom the reporter answers directly—the solution is to kill the story. Of course, if you think the point of the story is unclear and that you might have missed something newsworthy, check with the reporter. If you're a copy editor, point out the problem to the copy-desk chief, who may want to speak with the assigning editor about it.

But if a story is worthwhile, as most are, how long should it be? Both the assigning editor and the editor designing the page or website, or the person editing the broadcast, should ask themselves two questions:

- How much will our audience care about this story?
- How much of the available space or time is this story worth compared with the other stories we want to run?

Try to answer these questions in terms of inches in a publication or website, or seconds or minutes in broadcast. For example, at a particular newspaper, briefs might be 3 inches, short stories typically 8, medium stories 12 to 18, and longer stories typically no more than 30. Likewise, at a broadcast station, brief items might be 10 seconds, medium ones 30 and longer ones two to three minutes, depending on how long the newscast runs.

Answering these questions will help give the reporter guidance as to how much to write or determine how much the editor must trim. **A rule of thumb for editors, though, is that when even good stories must be trimmed, cut wire-service stories first, allowing local stories to run as completely as possible.**

Making Sure Stories Have Good Leads

Writing or editing **hard-news stories** is somewhat different from writing or editing **soft-news**, or **feature**, **stories**. Their **leads** are different, and so is the structure of the rest of the story, but they do have certain things in common.

Rules for Both Hard-News and Soft-News (or Feature) Leads

The lead of a story is its most important element because the lead's quality may determine whether the reader is hooked or turns away. Keep these rules in mind as you are writing or editing:

Keep the lead short and simple. Don't jam too many facts or figures into the lead. A lead sentence normally isn't more than about 20 words. Don't believe the myth that you need to cram *who, what, when, where, why* and *how* all into the lead.

Most problems arise when reporters try to pack too much into the lead. Either delete unnecessary details, or move minor ones to later paragraphs.

Wordy: The former girlfriend of a man who came forward to say he actually killed a local bartender for which another man is on trial said her boyfriend couldn't have done it because she was with him that night in a motel when the killing occurred.

Short and Simple: A man who says he actually committed the murder for which another man is on trial was contradicted in court Monday by his former girlfriend.

Wordy: A Springfield exotic dancer was arrested and charged with indecent exposure last night, officers George Smith and Henry Brown said Monday.

Short and Simple: A Springfield exotic dancer was arrested and charged with indecent exposure last night, police said Monday. (We don't need the officers' names in the lead.)

Wordy: Former Assistant Secretary of State for Latin American Affairs Lincoln Gordon said today . . .

Short and Simple: A former U.S. diplomat said today . . . (The title is too long, and why should this man receive an immediate-ID lead, since few people will have ever heard of him?)

Avoid clichéd leads. We'll discuss this more in relation to soft-news leads, but they can also sometimes be a problem in hard-news leads. Examples:

Quick action by two alert police officers was credited with saving the life of . . .

Police and volunteers staged a massive search today for a man who . . .

To keep the writing fresh for your audience, remember: If you've seen or heard this lead before, send it back for a rewrite.

Make sure the lead actually says something definite. The lead should state a thesis—a definite statement—not merely announce a topic.

Vague Topic: A Springfield College researcher spoke on campus about cancer Thursday night.

Definite Thesis: A Springfield College researcher told a campus audience Thursday night that new evidence suggests second-hand smoke may not pose as big of a cancer risk as previously thought.

Intensity Density

Intensity density is a term we coined to name a practical concept that can be applied to words, audios and visuals, whether in newspapers, magazines and newsletters, books, websites, radio, television, film—even music, video games, advertising and term papers.

The concept is simple: **Audiences value a media product more if they find more things to like about it in a given space or time.** To give a few examples, you'll find a television sitcom funnier the more laughs you get in the space of half an hour, an action movie more involving the more action there is within any 10 minutes, a rock radio station more listenable the more hits played per hour, or a textbook more appealing the less it wastes your time with a lot of fluff between the points worth remembering.

Likewise, television ads and music videos use fast-paced cuts to keep your attention; teachers grade term papers higher that have more original ideas or interesting examples or clever phrasings per page; poetry readers value poems more that have more meaningful lines; and music listeners like songs with interesting **hooks**—whether interesting lyrics (especially in a chorus), a rhythmic groove, a memorable vocal phrasing or an instrumental part.

So, readers find publications more interesting that have more stories, headlines, photos and graphics of interest per page. Audiences also find broadcast outlets and websites more appealing if there are more items of interest in the time or space they have available. **Make sure that any media product you edit has lots of hooks in a given space or time to grab the audience and make people take notice.**

Don't waste your audience's time. As an editor on a fictional television drama told a reporter: "This is a morning newspaper—don't put the readers back to sleep!"

So, get the unnecessary words out of stories, making them as intensely useful and interesting as possible. Then, use the space saved to get your **story count** up—more quality stories in each edition. And while you're at it, remember if you're editing a print or web publication that readers look first at the big type and at photos and graphics. So, try to get more important information into more headlines, second decks, blurbs and captions, and try to get more graphic elements—photos, illustrations, charts, boxes and bullet lists—on each page.

Is there an upper limit to intensity density? Yes. You can't have a series of mountains without valleys between, and if a page is too full of graphic elements, it can become too busy and distracting. Likewise, it's possible for an article or book to become so full of ideas, readers have little time to pause and digest them, so the writing becomes too dense, too hard to fathom. This is where the idea of editing as an art comes in again: You have to use your own judgment. But pumping up the intensity is often what's needed.

A Comparison of Hard and Soft News

Hard-news stories are meant primarily to inform. **Soft-news**, or **feature**, **stories** are meant to entertain while informing, or even to entertain without informing, as in the case of humor columns and some human-interest stories. As a result, a feature story often intentionally aims for the emotions. Human interest alone is enough to justify a feature story, although a **news peg**—a timely, newsworthy event on which to base the story—should be used whenever possible.

A **hard-news story** is an article that focuses on presenting the news in a no-nonsense, straightforward, get-to-the-gist-right-away manner. A hard-news story is meant to be the more objective of the two in the sense that the writer should step back and keep out his or her own opinions and not draw attention to the writer's personality by instead keeping the style of writing more impersonal and less obviously creative.

Unlike hard-news writers, feature writers tend to be more successful the more personal their literary style. So, features tend to have an individual voice—figures of speech and personal observations—that lend them a sense of liveliness, color and personality when compared to the relatively impersonal, give-'em-the-bottom-line approach of hard-news stories. The feature story sometimes conveys a sense of the author's immersion in the lives and events covered, a stark contrast to the objective distance between news reporter and what's being reported.

Reporters and editors need to keep these distinctions in mind when deciding which approach should be taken in writing or editing any given story. With some stories, you just want to present the facts straightforwardly. With other stories, you want to throw in some entertainment with the relaying of information.

How do you know which kind of story you're editing? Look for other clues, such as whether the story is in present tense (typical of features) or past tense (typical of hard-news stories), and whether the story has a feature ending or just trails off like a hard-news story.

Remember these common stylistic differences between features and hard-news stories:

- Features are usually written in present tense, hard news in past tense. When it comes to attribution, then, features typically use *says* rather than *said*.

- Features sometimes address the reader or viewer directly as *you*.
- Depending on local style, features may refer to people in the stories on second and subsequent references by their first names rather than their last, as is standard for hard-news stories.
- Feature stories may be written in first person if the author is important to the story. But "I" should not be used gratuitously. If first-person pronouns can be left out, they should be.

Sometimes, reporters combine the feature and news approaches by starting with a feature-style lead atop a hard-news account. This mixed approach is used when a story is primarily informational and about a recent event, so a hard-news approach overall is best, but one brief, dramatic anecdote stands out as too good to pass up in setting the stage. Increasingly, reporters are taking the mixed approach, beginning hard-news stories with feature-style leads that dramatically introduce the story rather than immediately give the bottom line. These stories can usually be cut from the bottom to fit available space, but make sure you're not ruining a feature-style ending.

Don't start a lead with a time, day, place, quotation or question. Otherwise, every local story might start with "Today in Springfield . . ." or with a quotation or question, like a freshman term paper.

Don't editorialize in a lead with value judgments or unattributed paraphrases.

> *Unattributed Lead:* All Delawareans over 45 should be vaccinated now against Asian flu. (Without attribution, it sounds as though the reporter is editorializing.)

Don't hype the story more than it's actually worth. A good lead must be straightforward and capture the flavor of the story. But no matter how well-written, the lead is no good if it misleads the reader into thinking the story is better than it really is.

Don't bury the lead or miss the real story. For example, a wire-service follow-up to a story about a mass killing in a restaurant the previous day began with the condition of the surviving victims. But at the end of the story, the reporter mentioned that the killer, who had died in the attack, had tried calling a local mental-health hotline the morning of the rampage, according to his wife, and had received a recording that because of funding cuts, callers had to make an appointment. The hotline funding cut should have been the lead.

Don't lead with old news. Lead with the latest, up-to-the-minute news, not yesterday's.

The Hard-News Lead

Often called an **inverted-pyramid story**, hard news is written in the order of most to least important facts and usually has a bottom-line lead that tells the main news in the first paragraph.

The hard-news lead sentence is typically in the order of first who, then what—although sometimes these are reversed, especially when covering speeches and public meetings.

There are two ways of writing the *who*:

1. If the person is well-known to your audience or appears often in the news, then an **immediate-ID lead** is used. The person's name appears in the first paragraph, sometimes after a descriptive title. Examples:

   City Council President James Smith . . .
   Rapper Snoop Dogg . . .

2. If the person is not well-known to your audience, a **delayed-ID lead** is used. A brief label for the person is used in the lead, with the person's name stated usually at the start of the second paragraph. Example:

   A Gainesville man was in critical condition Tuesday after he was knocked off his bicycle by a truck.
   Paul Rodriquez was riding . . .

The lead next tells *what* the who did or *what happened* to the who. The *what* could be one thing or several things. If several things happened, only the most important might be mentioned in the lead, with the others perhaps appearing later in the story. Or the different things that happened might all be mentioned in the lead—preferably in the order of most to least important—or summarized if they all have something in common.

If time, day and place appear in the lead, they typically appear after, not before, the who and the what. If all three are used, they should appear in the order of time-day-place. *Time* comes first in the *time-day-place order*, but events are usually described as taking place *Wednesday night* or *Friday morning* or *this afternoon* when exact time is unnecessary. Newspapers usually do not use *yesterday* or *tomorrow*, but *today* or *tonight* are fine when referring to the day of publication or broadcast. If important, the exact time of day will appear later in the story (for instance, the moment of an earthquake). For more rules about the *time-day-place* order, see the style section of Chapter 7.

If a hard-news lead doesn't follow this typical order—*who-what* or *what-who*, then *time-day-place* (time being optional)—try to figure out if the lead achieves more the way it is. If it doesn't, it's probably better to use the traditional ordering as the story is introduced. When beginners fail to follow this order, it's usually because they just don't know what they're doing. When professionals switch things around, they usually have a valid reason.

The Soft-News (Feature) Lead

Some journalists deride features or soft news as mere *fluff pieces*, and newsrooms may have an unofficial pecking order that places reporters on the government and crime beats at the top and feature writers at the bottom. The hard-news reporters are assumed to be better at news gathering, the feature writers at writing. This is an unfortunate view, and the best journalists are good at both.

· Hard-news stories tend to have more sense of **timeliness** than features, despite the fact that hard news is written in the past tense and features in the present tense. The sense of immediacy in hard news comes from the focus on reporting up-to-date accounts of who did what or what happened to whom. Feature writing, at its best, is more creative, literary, entertaining and emotionally involving than hard-news stories.

The poet Ezra Pound's definition of literature as "news that *stays* news" is an apt description of good feature writing. Good feature writing, in other words, may be more time*less* than time*ly*.

So, **features tend to be less timely (such as how-to articles) than hard news. They also are more opinionated (such as columns or reviews) and more focused on personality (such as personality profiles) rather than hard news.** And sometimes, a feature will supplement a news story with a behind-the-scenes, colorful account of the news.

Features come in many varieties, but essentially a feature story is a piece of nonfiction writing that uses fiction techniques. It has character and monologue, if not dialogue. A feature can have a locale that sets the mood, a colorful description that is sometimes symbolic, a narrative plot with foreshadowing and flashbacks, and sometimes even author's asides.

Feature stories tend to have a beginning, a middle and an end rather than the inverted-pyramid organization of hard-news stories. The beginning of the article, however, is seldom the chronological beginning of the story behind it. Features often begin *in medias res* (as they say in literature classes)—in the middle of things, at a dramatic moment. The first paragraph is not usually a bottom-line lead, as in a hard-news story, but a more emotionally gripping sample to interest readers in what follows.

A feature story uses a **soft lead**. Instead of getting to the bottom line of *who-what* and *time-day-place* in the first sentence, a soft lead starts with description, dialogue, character, anecdote or personal address to the reader. All except the last provide a sample rather than a summary of what will follow. The personal address is the exception: "You may want to take an umbrella today because the National Weather Service predicts thunderstorms this afternoon."

The purpose of the soft-news lead is to seduce the reader or viewer into the story. The bottom line, or summary, or **nut graf**, usually appears a few paragraphs into the story.

Feature leads often use the immediate-ID form of identifying the *who* in the story—that is, using a person's name in the lead—even when the person is not famous. So, when you're editing a story and see an immediate ID in the lead, either the person is well-known to local readers, or this should be the soft lead of a feature. The situation gets more problematic when a reporter uses the mixed approach with a soft lead on a hard-news story.

The main problem to look for in soft leads is the cliché lead. Understand that there's a difference between clichés and the hard-news and feature formulas examined here. Formulas represent a genre and permit creative variations. Clichés are particular phrases or approaches that are repeated non-creatively. So, for example, a sonata is a musical genre with a general formula that defines it. But a specific phrase stolen from another musical work and repeated often in various songs is a cliché.

Feature leads are one of the biggest sources of clichés in journalism. Many cliché leads start with a quotation, a question, one word or a dictionary definition. Others include: "What a difference a day makes," "It's official," "First the good news, then the bad," "Rain couldn't dampen the spirits of . . .," "Christmas came early for . . . ." **Because rewriting leads is a major revision, copy editors should draw cliché leads to the attention of the copy-desk chief or the writer rather than change them on their own. If you're editing your own writing, then revise the lead yourself.**

Making Sure Stories Are Organized and Flow Well

Here are six steps to making sure stories are well-organized and flow well:

1. **Look at the lead, and determine whether this is a hard-news story or a feature.**

   Remember, in a mixed approach, a story may start out with a feature lead but turn into a hard-news story.

   If the story has a hard-news lead, check for the typical order of *who, what, time, day* and *place* in the lead. If this order isn't followed, is there a logical reason? *What* or *why* are sometimes better ways to start, and *time, day* or *place* often aren't needed. But it's almost always a bad idea to start a story with *time, day* or *place*.

   If you've determined that this is a hard-news story, verify that the story follows the inverted-pyramid structure of most to least important. If anything lower in the story is more important than something higher, move it up. If anything seems irrelevant to the story, delete it.

   If you've determined this is a feature story, check to see whether the lead pulls you into the story. Is it hackneyed or dull or misleading? Did the writer get to the bottom line within a few paragraphs so that you soon knew the "so what"?

If the story has a feature lead, make sure there's a **nut graf**—a paragraph summarizing the bottom line—soon after the lead. If not, readers will have a hard time figuring out the point of the story.

After checking the feature lead, look to the end of the story to see whether there's a definite sense of conclusion, such as a return to the beginning or a dramatic statement or quotation. If so, make sure you don't cut the ending if you need to trim the story for space. If there's no sense of conclusion to the story, then this is either a hard-news story with a feature lead (and you could trim from the end if needed) or the story reads like a feature but needs a better ending.

2. **Notice whether the lead is an immediate-ID or delayed-ID one.** If a delayed-ID lead is used, verify that the person is named soon, usually at the start of the second paragraph. If an immediate-ID lead begins the story, verify that the person is well-known to your audience or in the news often, or that this is a feature lead in which immediate-ID is appropriate for everyone.

3. **Look at whether the story contains quotes.** If the story doesn't have quotes, does it need them? If it is short enough, the story may not need them, but stories 8 inches or more typically *do* have direct quotes.

   If there are quotations in the story, does the writer get to the first quote within the first two to five paragraphs? If not, consider moving up the quote that best summarizes the story or is most dramatic.

   Is it always clear who's speaking in a quote? Is a name provided at the beginning of a quote every time the speaker changes? Are all paraphrases attributed so they aren't confused with the reporter making a pronouncement?

   Does the story effectively use the **seesaw technique**? Statements made and facts presented by the reporter should seesaw back and forth with a quotation or other evidence to back them. Does the length of the statements and quotations vary so the technique doesn't become too sing-song to readers?

4. **Look for the basic details that must be answered in this kind of story and in this one in particular.** In other words, what questions would a reader expect to have answered in this story?

   Next, which of these questions is the most important to answer first? Which second and so on? Now, verify the story is organized in the most logical, coherent manner. Does it stick to the subject and explore it completely, or does it ramble off on irrelevant or illogical tangents that should either be cut or made into sidebars?

5. **Ask whether along the way each step in the story is clear.** Are the words and sentences simple to understand? Are all unfamiliar terms explained? Has jargon been avoided wherever possible

and defined where unavoidable? If anything is ambiguous, ask the reporter what it means—don't guess. Here are some additional questions to help you seek clarity:

- Is the main point of the story apparent? Does every point and every sentence grow from it and point to it?
- Do sentences vary in length so that the story doesn't sound too choppy?
- Are transitions clear—between sentences and between points in the story?
- Is the full name provided each time a new source in the story is first introduced and an explanation provided of who the person is?
- Are all words used precisely and correctly? (*Admitted, anxious, bureaucrat, claimed* and *refuted* all have specific meanings that may not be intended by the writer but are likely to be inferred by a reader.)
- Have you checked when a story says *today* whether it means the day it was written or the day of publication?
- Are rhetorical techniques such as metaphors, analogies and images used to illustrate the meaning? Are examples given? Does the writer make comparisons? (When a writer makes a statement such as "The room was large," always ask yourself: Compared with what?)
- Does this story need a photo, illustration, chart, summary box, blurb or second deck to make the meaning clearer?

6. **Ask whether the story moves along at a good pace.** Are points raised given an appropriate depth of treatment before new ones are introduced? Do sentence lengths and structure also vary in an appropriate manner? Is the tone appropriate for this story, and are there any violations of that tone? Does the story hold your interest, or do you get bogged down in irrelevant details?

Special Problems of Editing Features

Monitoring the organization and flow of a feature story poses additional issues to editing hard-news stories. For one thing, features are often longer and typically require more time to edit, and the headlines are expected to be more creative. Still, don't use these facts to sit on a feature too long, or you might miss deadline.

Be on the alert for material you could quickly pull out to a sidebar or that would make good graphic possibilities, and pass along the suggestion to the copy-desk chief. Examples include a box with the *time-day-place* of an event, a locator map with directions to a place described in the story, or a list of materials for a do-it-yourself project.

When editing a feature story, you'll often be dealing with more elements than with hard-news stories—photographs,

artwork, sidebars and blurbs—and you'll need to make sure these elements all work together. Here are some hints:

- **Make sure the various elements agree—especially on spelling of names.**
- **Make sure your headline doesn't conflict with what the photo portrays or what the photo caption says.**
- **Use all your big type to get across information to readers just scanning the page—maybe they'll even stop to read the story.**

A feature story should have a definite sense of conclusion. If it doesn't, either it was intended as a mixed-approach story—a hard-news story with a feature lead—or the reporter failed to come up with an ending. If the latter, look for something already in the story that would make a good ending. If you don't see anything appropriate, send it back to the reporter.

The two most common types of endings for features are:

- **The ending ties back to the beginning.**
- **A dramatic quote or statement.** This is often used either to summarize the implication of the story in a catchy phrase or image or to point to future implications.

The worst kind of feature ending is one that resorts to a cliché like "but one thing's certain" or "only time will tell," both of which most commonly appear in broadcast.

Give the reporter of a feature story more freedom to be personal than you would if it were a hard-news story. But feature writers shouldn't abuse this freedom by needlessly involving themselves in a story when they aren't the story. And just like news writers, feature writers should not fall into telling the story through the use of modifiers like *controversial* rather than giving the details so readers can see for themselves that the subject is controversial.

Headlines are expected to be more creative on features than typical hard-news stories, so put more effort into these. Try to make feature heads not just tell the story, but sell it as well.

Making Sure Stories Don't Waste the Audience's Time

Stories in newspapers and magazines often have to be trimmed to fit space requirements, and broadcast stories to fit time constraints. Web stories may be trimmed also because it's thought you tend to lose readers the more they have to scroll down. But in addition to the reasons of space and time constraints, stories should be trimmed simply not to waste the audience's time with unnecessary wordiness.

Trimming Hard News Stories

Because the inverted-pyramid order of hard-news stories puts the most important details before the least important, trimming a hard-news story to fit a given space is relatively easy: **Cut from the end, taking out information the reporter deemed the least important.**

Sometimes, though, reporters mess up and bury an important detail later in the story, lower down than less important ones. If you, as editor, see this, you should move the more important detail higher in the story, where it belongs.

Trimming a Feature Story

Unlike an inverted-pyramid story, a feature shouldn't be cut from the bottom. When a feature is too long and you have to make it fit, instead of cutting from the bottom, tighten it from the middle. Take out the weakest points, or extra anecdotes, quotations, facts or details. Then, when the length is close, tighten wordy passages or delete lengthy, uncommon words.

Making Sure Stories Don't Leave Unanswered Questions

Don't leave out details the audience would like to know. This occurs when writers or editors fail to see that the story would naturally raise certain questions in a reader's mind.

People in the audience for news in any medium want to feel they're getting at least the gist of the story—the most important details—and as much more of the story as time or space permits. For newspapers and magazines, especially, the ability to provide details is the great advantage print has over broadcast media. The web can provide more details, as well, although web readers are often more in a hurry, with many reading on a smartphone.

But whether people are getting their news from newspapers, magazines, radio, television or websites, they *are* bothered when something about a story strikes them as incomplete and leaves them with unanswered questions.

Here are some cases where the absence of vital information would leave readers confused:

- A congressman was censured for ethics violations, but the writer didn't tell readers to which party he belonged. (Republicans often criticize the media for not giving a party affiliation in such cases for Democrats, or burying it deep in the story, whereas it would be prominent, they say, in a story about a Republican.)
- A scuba diver stayed underwater for 31 hours and spent much of his time reading a paperback book. The reporter did not explain what kept the pages from disintegrating. (The paper was on glossy stock.)
- A judge reversed his own conviction of a union leader for breach of the peace. The reversal was described as based on "new evidence," but the writer failed to tell readers what this new evidence was.

- A story contained the clause "where family income is below federal poverty levels" but didn't tell readers what the poverty level is by federal standards.

Checklist for Unanswered Questions

- Who will read this story, and what will they want to know about the subject?
- What would have to be in any story on this subject for it to be complete?
- Are there any questions a reader would likely ask about this particular story?
- Are any intriguing angles introduced, then dropped without explanation?
- Are all first references to a person or organization complete?

Making Sure Stories Are Accurate

Of all the editor's duties, editing for accuracy is one of the most important. A news outlet that is inaccurate soon loses its credibility and, ultimately, its audience.

Good reporting, of course, is the key ingredient in ensuring accuracy. But all who edit the story share that responsibility. Assigning editors ensure accuracy by questioning the reporter about the information and the means by which it was gathered, and copy editors ensure accuracy by checking verifiable facts.

Newspapers, broadcast stations and websites, with their much tighter deadlines, seldom have the luxury of being able to check every fact. Instead, they depend more on their reporters to get it right. It's especially important, then, that editors at newspapers, broadcast stations and websites have a heavy dose of suspicion to help them decide when to question a reporter or take the time to look up something that doesn't sound right.

Common Kinds of Inaccuracies

Look out for inconsistencies within a story. These could include different spellings of a name or statements that contradict something else in the story. Watch for figures that don't add up—such as percentages in a survey that don't add up to 100, figures in a budget story that don't match the total, votes that don't tally with the number cast, or ages that contradict birth and death dates in an obituary.

Here are a few examples:

The United Way on Monday awarded $23,000 in supplemental funds to three agencies. . . . The additional funds will go to the Boy Scouts, $11,000; the Girl Scouts, $9,000; and the Salvation Army, $4,000.

Tanglewood Barn Theater ended its regular season with a bang in its production of "Wonderful Town" Wednesday night. . . . [Last paragraph] The show will be repeated at 8:15 p.m. through Sunday.

Sara La Grange, 94, Lincoln, died Sept. 10, 2019, at home after an illness of several months. Mrs. La Grange was born in Omaha on Dec. 21, 1925, to the late John and Mary La Grange.

One inconsistency in the last example is that Mrs. La Grange likely did not have the same maiden and married names. Therefore, her parents' surname is probably wrong here. A second inconsistency is that if she was born in September 1925 and died several months before her birthday in 2019, she was not 94 years old but 93.

Look out for inconsistencies with previous stories or information you've heard or read elsewhere or can check out. Many protesters, politicians, bloggers and even some journalists make statements that "the rich don't pay their fair share of taxes." Although what a "fair share" should be is something people can reasonably debate, the amount of money that Americans in different tax brackets actually pay in income taxes is not—that's a matter of public record. And yet, few journalists bother to look up those figures and put the claims to the test. In fact, IRS records show that even with tax loopholes, wealthier Americans as a whole not only pay the vast majority of taxes but also have higher tax rates. Whether they are paying their "fair share" is another matter.

What to Check for Accuracy

- Check spelling of local names.
- Check spelling of other names.
- Check local addresses. With criminal suspects who move often, you may have to trust the police blotter.
- Check unfamiliar place names.
- Check spellings and whether words are two words, one word or hyphenated, first in *The AP Stylebook*, second in *Webster's New World College Dictionary*, then in *Webster's Third New International Dictionary*, taking the answer from the first one of those you find it in, but checking them in that order. If a compound word is not listed, make it two words as a verb or noun, hyphenated as an adjective.
- Check well-known quotations in *Bartlett's Quotations*, if possible. Online sites are useful, but you'll find many misquotations online, as well. Paul F. Boller Jr. and John George's book *They Never Said It* is handy for spotting famous misquotations.
- Check facts and figures against recent stories in the news outlet's morgue files (collection of old stories) or online. Jan Harold Brunvand's books are useful for spotting "urban legends" masquerading as news stories.

According to Internal Revenue statistics for the year 2009, the last one available at the time when Occupy Wall Street first made its claims in 2011 about the wealthy not paying "their fair share," the wealthiest 1% of Americans paid 36.73% of all income taxes. The wealthiest 5% paid 58.66%, the top 10% paid 70.47%, the top 25% paid 87.30%, and the top 50% paid 97.75%. The bottom 50% of wage earners paid only 2.25%.

Not only were those earning more paying a higher percentage of the total, they also paid a higher rate on wages earned than those who made less. In fact, almost half of Americans paid no net income tax. But the journalistic failure to check the facts left many Americans with the false impression that the rich actually paid less than the poor. That said, it's also true that some rich people manage to pay little or no taxes at all because of deductions. All of that should be explained for a full understanding.

Check out inconsistencies and possibly misleading claims, and explain and evaluate them without bias. That's part of a journalist's job.

Beware of unwarranted superlatives. When reporters write that something is the "first," "only," "biggest," "best," "most," "the largest" or "a record," good editors question the statement.

For example, when a shooter killed 49 and wounded 53 more in June 2016 in an Orlando, Fla., gay dance club, the media labeled it "the worst mass shooting in American history." As many pointed out on social media, though, between 150 and 300 Native Americans were killed by the military at the Wounded Knee Massacre in 1890, and 76 were killed by the government at the siege on the Branch Davidians' Waco, Texas, compound in 1993. And between 30 and 300, depending on sources, died in the 1921 Tulsa Massacre in Oklahoma of black residents.

Journalists should have learned from their coverage of the Columbine Massacre in 1999, in which two high school students in Littleton, Colorado, opened fire on their classmates, which prompted a number of media mistakes like these:

- *The New York Times* wrote: "It was the largest death toll in an act of terrorism at one of the nation's schools."
- Reuters wrote: "The country's worst school massacre in Littleton, Colorado. . . ."
- United Press International wrote: "The worst school massacre in U.S. history."

Unfortunately, all of them were wrong. At Columbine, 12 students, a teacher and the two gunmen died. But on May 18, 1927, 45 people, including 18 elementary students, were killed by a series of dynamite explosions at a school in Bath, Mich. Because it happened so long before, most reporters knew nothing about it. All superlatives should be checked, and if they cannot be verified, they should be hedged with wording like "thought to be."

Beware of common false quotations. Many common quotations that writers know and repeat turn out to be misstated or misattributed:

- According to the Bible, it's not money that is the root of all evil but "the love of money."
- Ralph Waldo Emerson did not say, "Consistency is the hobgoblin of little minds," but "A foolish consistency is the hobgoblin of little minds."
- Voltaire did not say, "I may not agree with what you say, but I will defend to the death your right to say it." That was traced back to Evelyn Beatrice Hall, who wrote in her biography of Voltaire, "I disapprove of what you say, but I will defend to the death your right to say it," which was a sentiment she thought Voltaire would support.
- George Santayana did not say, "Those who ignore history are doomed to repeat it." It's often attributed to him, but no one's ever actually been able to find it in his writings.
- Benjamin Disraeli is often cited, including by Twain, as saying, "There are lies, damned lies and statistics." There's no evidence Disraeli ever actually said that.

Beware of common "facts" that aren't. As with common quotations, many widely known "facts" that writers repeat turn out to be wrong:

- Washington did not have wooden teeth—they were ivory. (And the teeth of slaves?)
- The Gettysburg Address was not written on the back of an envelope.
- Witches were not burned in Salem—they were hanged.
- St. Bernard dogs never carried casks of brandy in Switzerland.
- It's the Smithsonian *Institution* in Washington, not the Smithsonian *Institute*. And by the way, it maintains, despite mention to the contrary in various articles, that it does not have bank robber John Dillinger's pickled penis preserved in a medical exhibit. See: www.snopes.com/ risque/penile/dillinger.asp

Beware of news that isn't, such as hoaxes and urban legends. Virtually every newspaper, magazine and broadcast station has been victimized at one time or another by a hoax. **Hoaxes** often start with a press release or when an individual calls or stops by a publication or station, claiming to be someone he or she is not. Good reporters should verify the identity of anyone they do not know.

The importance of following this rule is clear in the case of a hoax perpetrated on the *Star Tribune,* published in the twin cities of Minneapolis and St. Paul. The *Star Tribune* ran an eight-paragraph story quoting Richard L. Thomas, president of First Chicago Corp., a large bank holding company, as saying his company was interested in purchasing troubled First Bank Systems of Minneapolis for $20 to $22 a share. That day, First Bank stock jumped sharply higher—before First Chicago issued a statement denying that Thomas had talked to the Minneapolis paper. The whole story, it turned out, was a hoax.

But these days, an even more common source of hoax stories is social media. Many people are getting their news primarily from Facebook and Twitter, for example. They find interesting information in their daily feed—often from politically biased sources that skew to their own views—and believe the propaganda memes.

Many more don't recognize the name of the source when it's a satire news site and take it seriously, even ones as well-known as The Onion and The Babylon Bee. For a list and brief discussion of some of the more widely cited satire sites, see the list of top 100 satire websites at https://blog.feedspot.com/satire_blogs/

In addition, you can find various lists online of what the creators of the list consider "fake news." One of the longest lists (176 entries as of 2020) is provided at www.dailydot.com/debug/fake-news-sites-list-facebook/, but the introduction to it is blatantly anti-Trump so you may want to take into account possible political bias. In addition to checking such lists, if any news source is suspicious to you, either as satire or fake news, look it up on the web and look at the site itself and reviews of it.

An example of one likely hoax is the hilarious "Instruction and Advice for the Young Bride," from a Methodist pastor's wife, about the honeymoon night. It makes its rounds on the internet every so often and speaks to the common perception of how far sexual mores haves changed during the past 100-plus years. Snopes.com reprints and evaluates this one at www.snopes.com/weddings/newlywed/advice.asp.

By the way, Snopes is a prime source for checking out hoax stories and urban legends that make the rounds on social media and too often end up in legitimate news outlets after journalists take them seriously without checking them out. Snopes is at www.snopes.com. (Note: Snopes has also faced criticism for sometimes fact-checking satire sites like the Babylon Bee, when it thinks pieces might be confused with real news.)

Urban legends are really modern folklore—stories that get repeated as factual but that really didn't happen. The internet has made the problem even worse. Two of the more famous examples include the story of the woman who dried her poodle in the microwave oven and the story of the poisonous exotic snake found in either the imported coat or the basket somebody bought at Walmart. Another especially funny one is the bricklayer story that makes the rounds periodically. You can read one version of it at www.darwinawards.com/legends/legends1998-08.html.

A good rule to apply is that if you ever edit a story that sounds too good to be true, it probably is—especially when the story doesn't supply details such as names and direct quotes from the people supposedly involved.

Beware of news stories or "facts" and figures originating from potentially biased sources. We're not saying that information from a source with an ax to grind is always deceptive or wrong, just that it bears extra skepticism. Often, they can be useful to make sure you're understanding the actual views of an issue from multiple sides, especially views that aren't your own. Otherwise, it's easy for all of us not to recognize our own stereotypes of other political and religious positions, for example, and not grasp what people from other sides actually think.

- **Polls funded by politicians or political action groups.** Often, these are push polls—polls consisting of biased questions aimed at influencing the public perception rather than measuring it. Not only are the questions often biased—"Do you oppose fighting terrorists in Afghanistan or do you support the American troops?"—but also the polls are often conducted of people on mailing lists known to have contributed to a particular side's causes or candidates in the past. The results, then, when either of those things has happened, are utterly unscientific and biased.

- **Reports by researchers funded by industries with a vested interest.** Journalists should be suspicious of studies funded by a group with a vested interest. We might well wonder whether the money didn't buy the desired results. But we should not assume that simply challenging the funding of one side's research in itself proves the other side to be right. And we should be even-handed when running stories about how funding may compromise truth and ask how much funding and from whom did the other side get?

- **Information originating on blogs and websites lacking gatekeeping checks and balances.** Obviously, there have been times the mainstream media, with their multiple layers of editors, have gotten it wrong, and websites or blogs without editorial staff got it right or broke important news first.

  For example, CBS aired documents attacking George W. Bush's military record that were later roundly discredited by littlegreenfoot balls.com, which showed that the documents were produced using Microsoft Word, not a typewriter of the period. CBS anchorman Dan Rather eventually lost his job over the matter.

  Generally speaking, however, because anyone can start a website that says anything, it's wise to be more skeptical of information originating from unknown sources or those without a proven track record of accuracy. This is especially true of websites and blogs known to have an agenda other than the impartial weighing and reporting of facts.

- **Criticism from "media watchdog" groups with political agendas.** Again, we're not saying that criticisms stated by media watchdog groups are always deceptive or wrong. As in a courtroom, the give and take of charges and countercharges can be part of the debate that leads to the truth.

But too many journalists and their audience assume media watchdog groups have no political leanings of their own. Among those leaning left are Fairness and Accuracy in Reporting, Mediamatters and Project Censored. Among those on the right are Accuracy in Media and the Media Research Center. Again, this is not to say that their reports aren't interesting criticism, but the critics themselves need to be viewed critically.

Beware of imprecise words or phrases that make a statement inaccurate or misleading. A common source of incorrect writing is the imprecise phrase or word. Legal terms can pose an especially dangerous problem. For example, in some states, *driving while intoxicated* differs from *driving while under the influence of alcohol.* The first is more serious, so if you don't know the local legal difference, using the wrong one could result in a lawsuit for libel.

Another example:

> The U.S. Supreme Court did not ban prayers in school. The court banned the requirement that children pray any particular prayer and the writing by public authorities of a required prayer. The decision had to do with public schools. It did not interfere with required prayers in church-operated schools.

Beware of numbers that don't check out mathematically. Numbers add specifics and credibility to a story, and they should make the story more understandable. But sometimes, numbers are inaccurate, confusing or misleading, and the editor needs to correct the situation.

Here's some general advice for editing numbers in a story:

- **Review AP style on numbers.** Basically, spell out zero through nine, then go to Arabic numerals. Know the exceptions, as outlined in *The AP Stylebook.*
- **Don't clutter a lead with numbers.** Nothing is duller than a lead full of numbers.
- **Cite sources for any statistics.** We don't mean footnotes as in a term paper, but name the person or organization that provided them.
- **Double-check all math.** For example, an advocate for the homeless was reported as saying 45 homeless people die in America each second. Do the math. In one minute, that would be 2,700 people; in one hour, 162,000; in one day, 3,888,000; and in one year, that would be 1,419,120,000—far more than the estimated 330 million population of the U.S.

- **Round off large numbers.** In the previous example, if the statistic had been accurate, it would be better to report 1,419,120,000 as more than 1.4 billion.
- **Don't assume numbers always explain themselves.** Relate the significance of numbers by putting them in context and in terms people can understand. For example, in a story about an upcoming election over a millage increase in property taxes to fund a new high school, explain how much property taxes would increase on an average-value home in your community.
- **Watch inclusive numbers and numerical comparisons**:

  - Insist on this style: *$5 million* to *$7 million*, not *$5 to $7 million*.
  - Odds should not be written as *3 million to 1* but as *1 in 3 million*.
  - *Five times as much as* is not the same thing as *five times more than*. Five times as much as $50 would be $250. But five times more than $50 would be $300 — $50 plus five times $50.

Where Editors Create Mistakes

Editors are most likely to create mistakes when editing quotations, rewriting copy, or writing headlines, blurbs and captions.

Quotations

Don't turn paraphrases into quotations. Don't insert quotation marks unless you have good reason to suspect the words are a direct quotation. An open or closing quotation mark without the opposite on the other end is the obvious clue it might have been intended as an actual quotation. Even then, check with the reporter about where the quotation begins and ends rather than guessing.

Don't doctor quotes to make them read better. If a quotation is weak, consider cutting it completely, tightly paraphrasing it (remembering to remove the quotation marks) or using partial quotes (quoting key phrases, paraphrasing the rest). Quotation marks are a contract with the reader that these are the exact words someone used, so the safest policy is *don't fix quotes.*

That said, though, even the strictest editors have no problem editing out *uh* and *er* and false starts of sentences. Many, if not most, editors would even go a step further and say it's OK to correct minor grammatical errors that needlessly make someone—especially an average person—look foolish. There is, after all, a difference between spoken and written English.

But clearly, it's not a good idea for journalists to reshape entire sentences like a speechwriter would revise text, spicing up a speaker's original words. This is dishonest in a news story, even when it captures the spirit of the speaker's point. Revising quotes also introduces the likelihood that speakers will be misunderstood and their point distorted in print media, thus damaging the news outlet's credibility and opening the possibility of a lawsuit.

Guidelines for Specific Number-Editing Situations

Percentages

- Appear in stories on budgets, economy, taxes, sports, etc.
- To calculate: Divide the part by the whole, then move the decimal point two places to the right.
- Be aware of how differences in wording affect the accuracy of percentages. For example, all the following statements are true even though the percentage changes:

1. Five is 50% of 10.
2. Ten is 200% of five.
3. Ten is 100% more than five.
4. Five percent is 5 percentage points less than 10%.
5. Ten percent is 5 percentage points more than 5%.

Average Versus Median

- Many uses, such as stories on educational testing.
- To calculate an *average* or an *arithmetic mean*: Add a list of numbers, then divide by the number of numbers you added.
- To find the *median*: List all the numbers from largest to smallest, then find (1) the number in the middle, or (2) if there is an even number of numbers in the list, the average of the two middle numbers.

Per Capita Rates

- Appear in stories on budgets, economy, crime and suicide rates, etc.
- *Per capita* is Latin for "by heads."
- To calculate: Divide the total amount spent by the population it will be spent on.

See also pages 225–227 on numbers in finance stories.

Rewrite

Know when not to rewrite. Many editing desks have the explicit policy that they are not rewrite desks. Send major rewrites back to the assigning editor. Don't rewrite perfectly fine stories the way you would have done them. "If it ain't broke, don't fix it."

You may rewrite for smaller problems, of course, such as when a passage is unclear. But realize you may have misunderstood it. So, check back with the reporter or the assigning editor to verify that your revision is accurate. If necessary, call the source.

Be careful when writing headlines, captions and blurbs. Reporters and their sources often complain that the story was correct but the headline, blurb or picture caption was inaccurate. Follow these tips:

- Verify that you have accurately summarized the story in the headline and not distorted it to attract readers or to fit a headline count.
- Make sure blurbs accurately summarize the story. When using a quotation in your blurb, use it word for word, and make sure it will not be misleading or out of context.
- Be certain that facts and spellings of names in headlines, blurbs and captions are consistent with those in the story.

Making Sure Stories Are Objective

Objectivity in journalism typically refers to being factual, neutral, fair and impersonal in style. Those characteristics apply most specifically to hard-news stories, rather than features or opinion pieces. But more broadly, in any kind of story, even opinion pieces, journalists should be honest about the facts, and neutral and fair by not letting their own biases and opinions color the truth.

Be factual. Stick to things that are provable as opposed to opinions, guesses, rumors and predictions. Ask yourself:

- Does the story stick to facts?
- Has the writer avoided all speculation of his or her own, confining any speculation only to quotes or paraphrases from others?
- Has the writer avoided attributions that might imply mind reading, such as saying that someone *believes, doubts, feels, hopes* or *thinks* something rather than sticking to what the source *said*?
- Has the writer avoided predicting that a suspect will be arraigned or convicted? If the person is released without being charged or found guilty, the suspect might have grounds for a libel suit if the story predicted otherwise.

Be neutral. The writer should not editorialize or intrude his or her own value judgments in a hard-news story. Ask yourself:

- Has the writer avoided all speculation and opinions of his or her own, confining any speculation and opinions only to quotes or paraphrases from others?
- Was the writer careful to avoid verbs of attribution that might inadvertently express an opinion, such as *claimed* (implies disbelief) or *refuted* (means successfully answered)?
- Has the writer avoided saying anything that may disparage or offend someone on the basis of race, sex, religion or ethnic background?

- Did the writer avoid the following modifiers or similar words that betray an opinion?

alleged (adj.)	exciting	respected
allegedly	falsely claimed	sadly
amazing	fittingly	shocking
arch-conservative	good	spectacular
arch-liberal	honestly	still
astounding	important	stunning
awful	inevitable	successfully
bad	insurmountable	tragic
best	interesting	troubling
bizarre	ironically	ultra-conservative
certainly	luckily	ultra-liberal
complex	mysterious	undoubtedly
controversial	obviously	unique
crucial	perfectly	unprecedented
definitely	poignant	unquestionably
disturbing	positively	unusual
dramatic	predictably	very
effectively	quagmire	wonderful
evil	radical	worst

Be fair. Make sure the story represents all sides as evenly as possible.

- Are all sides given? Were enough people interviewed to get the full picture?
- If someone is accused of or criticized for something, does he or she get a chance to reply?
- Is the story legal and ethical?

Be impersonal in style in hard-news stories. A unique, creative voice is for personal essays and fiction, not hard news. Ask yourself:

- If this is a hard-news story, has the writer avoided intruding his or her own personality into the story?
- If this is a feature, such as a review or column, does the personality of the writing contribute to the story or merely distract from the subject?

Can Journalism Ever be Objective?

That depends on what you mean by "objective." Even if it's not possible, it may be that it's something useful for which to strive. Others say we should just be upfront about our biases.

Some Meanings

Philosophy. Objectivity is seen as impossible because people are not God. We're limited by our human senses and brains, plus our backgrounds—including culture, race, sex and social-economic class—our experiences, our education and so on.

Problem: If objectivity is defined as impossible to humans, it's not a useful, practical idea.

Law. You want in judges or juries people who can hear both sides in an open-minded way and reach a just and fair verdict. In the case of the jury, attorneys increasingly want someone who at least hasn't reached an opinion in advance and who preferably never heard of the case.

Science. It's perfectly acceptable for the scientist to have an opinion in advance—that's where hypotheses come from. But the scientist then tries to prove his or her opinion wrong in an honest test. Like the judge or jury, the scientist should reach a conclusion in an open-minded, honest way.

History. Similar to journalism, this field has historically seen objectivity as a goal, but, like journalism, has increasingly questioned it.

Objective Journalism

- Arose as a new business model to sell papers, not from philosophical conviction.
- Developed at *The New York Times* in the early 20th century as a kind of consensus of views of the elites in power—based more on class and status quo than political partisanship.
- The basic characteristics of objectivity in journalism—being factual, neutral, fair and impersonal in writing style—are all humanly possible. But some question whether true objectivity is possible in journalism, if, as philosophers say, it's not possible for humans at all. But what about adopting something like the idea of objectivity as practiced in science? Scientists often state their conclusions, but they do so only after investigating a hypothesis in an open-minded, critical way despite their own opinion at the start and then explaining how they arrived at those conclusions. Couldn't a similar approach work for journalism? Or for journalists to act like referees in sports, making calls honestly?

Sports broadcasters seem to be able to do this—why not other journalists? See more about this in Chapter 2.

Problems with the Definition of Objectivity in Journalism

- Determining what's a fact. People on different sides of an issue often disagree on what's factual.
- Neutrality is ultimately not necessary to being objective, if by that is meant always giving equal weight to falsehood and never reaching a verdict. In science and law, for example, the evidence is weighed as to how strong it is and a decision reached.
- Fairness to "both sides" may make evil a moral equivalent of the true and good. And the idea of only two sides tends to exclude views beyond the main two. Think instead of neutrality and fairness as examining all sides of an issue with honesty and open-mindedness.
- An impersonal style impersonates objectivity—it really isn't objective or necessary to it.

Objectivity at Partisan Outlets

- Some say the answer is not to try to be objective. Be upfront about your biases, and let the free market provide the diversity of views from which people can choose. In other words, this view says go ahead and be a crusader, if you like, and try to change the world for the better as you see it.
- Another view, taken by the authors of *The Elements of Journalism*, for example, is that a journalist's primary obligation is to the facts, not our wishes or loyalty to groups to which we belong. This could apply to journalism regardless of model—persuasion, entertainment or information—and offers a niche as trusted arbiter.
- We think there's value in both ideas but would add that even partisan journalists or outlets should not pander by outright lying, spinning reports contrary to the facts or not covering important news even if it hurts their side.

Instead, keep in mind who your partisan audience is and what their interests are and look honestly into stories that interest them, rather than censoring potential bad news to their viewpoint.

For example, instead of banning the story that came out days before the 2020 presidential election that the FBI was examining Democratic candidate Joe Biden's son Hunter's laptop, liberal-audience-oriented National Public Radio should have called the FBI to see whether that was true and also interviewed the computer shop repairman who turned it over to the FBI. At least some of the audience probably knew about the story from other sources, and refusing to cover it could have damaged NPR's credibility with the audience. Many probably would have liked to know whether it was true and what it meant to Joe Biden's chances.

Pros and Cons of a Partisan Press

PROS

1. It's clearer what the journalist actually thinks—it's more honest for not being partisanship disguising itself as objectivity.
2. It's more entertaining as people present one side in more extreme ways that will make the choir cheer them on for going after the bastards on the other side.
3. The audience is more loyal to a news source that tells them what they want to hear rather than acknowledging another side.

CONS

1. It's usually less honest in the sense of trying to get at the facts as opposed to presenting a PR case for one side.
2. With the press spinning one way or the other, no one's trying to examine the situation with an open mind.
3. People tend to just pay attention to the media that express their own ideological views, so there's no common culture where you're really getting both sides from the horse's mouth. When other views are presented, it's more likely to be a strawman, comic-book stereotype rather than who opponents really are and what they're saying.
4. Journalistic credibility is damaged.

How to Get at the Truth

- Don't trust everything you see or hear.
- Be aware of the viewpoint and track record of the source.
- Consciously avoid news from only one source or even one side—seek a variety.
- Especially pay attention to outlets with views different from your own.
- Look at some foreign sources, too, such as the BBC and CBC broadcasts or foreign news outlets online.
- Look for topics of real importance, not just ones of interest to you.

- Check out particularly important "facts" that are the most crucial to your own viewpoint to make sure they are true rather than just assume they are.
- Take a look at media criticism—professional journals and websites, media watchdog groups, shows like *On the Media* on NPR (and podcast) *MediaBuzz* on FNC, talk radio and books of media criticism, such as those by Bernard Goldberg (on the right) or by Project Censored (on the left).
- Know the political orientations, if any, of commonly cited news outlets, media critics and think tanks. We've tried to be fair in our lists below but recognize some people will disagree on at least some of our classifications—after all, opinions vary on everything. But realize audiences generally find it harder to see any political leaning at all in a news source with a political orientation similar to their own, so this guide can be a starting point. We suggest looking up other evaluations, too, of outlets' political leanings and judge for yourself.

Newspapers

- Liberal: *The New York Times*, the *Washington Post*
- Conservative: *The Wall Street Journal*, *The Washington Examiner*, *Epoch Times*
- Middle of the road (MOR): *USA Today*

Magazines

- Liberal: *The Nation*, *The New Republic*, *The Progressive*
- Conservative: *National Review*, *Newsmax*, *Human Events*
- Libertarian: *Reason*
- MOR: *Time*, *The Economist*

Broadcast News

- MOR: *WGN Newsnation* (satellite TV station)
- MOR but lean liberal: NPR's *Morning Edition* and *All Things Considered*, PBS' *News Hour*
- MOR but lean conservative: FNC's *Fox News Sunday* and *Special Report* weekdays
- Liberal: CNN's Don Lemon and MSNBC's Rachel Maddow
- Conservative: *Blaze TV* and Glenn Beck's radio show; FNC's Sean Hannity and Tucker Carlson
- Libertarian: Judge Andrew Napolitano, Kennedy (the one-word name she goes by) and Larry Elder, often guests on Fox News Channel.

International Views

- BBC news (carried on some public radio stations and PBS stations, and on satellite radio and satellite and cable TV)
- CBC News (carried on satellite and cable TV)
- France 24 TV (available free in English by app and at www.france24.com/en/)
- For more controversial views, you might also check Al Jazeera TV, for Arabic world views, ChinaNewsTV, and RT TV for Russian views. All of these are available in English. Check whether your TV service carries them, or look for possible apps.

Media Watchdogs

- Liberal: Fairness and Accuracy in Reporting, Media Matters, Project Censored
- Conservative: Accuracy in Media, Media Research Center
- Neutral: Pew, Annenberg, Center for Media and Public Affairs (although the left labels the latter right-wing)

Websites

- Liberal: Huffington Post, Daily Kos, Moveon.org, Slate, Salon
- Conservative: Dailycaller.com, Thefederalist.com, Washingtonexaminer.com

Fact-Checking Sites

The idea of creating fact-checking sites is a good one, but, unfortunately, we've seen plenty of examples where "fact-checking" turns out to be little more than partisan journalists reinforcing their own pre-held views. Often, they don't even realize that's what they are doing. So, do your own fact-checking using the steps we've mentioned. It should be easy enough to check the fact-checkers by using that system, and it's worth the time to do so.

There are a number of fact-checking sites designed to help the public determine whether news is legitimate—at least as the fact checkers see it. These include:

- PolitiFact (politifact.com), owned by the Poynter Institute, which also owns the International Fact-Checking Network that sets standards for fact-checkers. PolitiFact won the Pulitzer Prize for its work but has also been accused of leaning left (see, for one, www.allsides.com/news-source/politifact). And the International

Fact-Checking Network itself has been accused of leaning left because of funding from Google, George Soros and Bill Gates, and its being relied on by Facebook for labeling information as false, which can lead to demonetization of sites and bans of users.

- FactCheck.org, run by the Annenberg Public Policy Center at the University of Pennsylvania.
- Snopes.com and FactCheck.org seem particularly less biased than a number of other fact-check sites, although all have critics, as well.
- www.truthorfiction.com—a non-partisan website that focuses on the stories most often shared on social media.
- Lead Stories, which debunks rumors and hoaxes in hopes of keeping them from going viral.
- AP Fact Check, a service of the Associated Press.
- AFP Fact Check, a service of Agence France-Presse.
- Reuters Fact Check, a service of UK-based Reuters.
- Facebook's fact checking of users' posts—as well as its and Twitter's ban of a number of posts from conservatives—has come under much criticism from Republican politicians, conservative news outlets and others on the right for a left-wing bias. This has even prompted calls by Republicans in Congress to take away their Section 230 protections for acting as a publisher rather than a platform or even to break the companies up for antitrust. Democratic politicians tend to call for Facebook to fact check and ban more than it does
- Some newspapers, magazines and websites have created their own fact-checking systems. The more reputable the news organization's reputation, generally the more reliable it is. But take nothing for granted, and consult more than one (especially with different political leanings), and do your own fact checking, as well.

How to Fact Check

- Never just assume that something you find on an internet or social media site is accurate. Check, check and recheck. False conspiracy theories are prevalent on the web, especially social-media sites. One, for example, claimed that a Washington pizzeria was a front for a child sex ring run by Hillary Clinton and others. (For an overview of this conspiracy theory, see https://en.wikipedia.org/wiki/Pizzagate_conspiracy_theory)
- Beware of reports from researchers funded by a vested interest, such as an industry, lobbying group, political action group or media "watchdog" groups with a political agenda.

- Pay attention to the URL and domain. Abcnews.com is a reliable news source, but abcnews.com.co was a fake site that traded on name confusion and URL and design similar to the real site. Many people shared innocently its stories on social media thinking they were legitimate. Most sites have sections that describe the people or organization behind the site. Do an internet search to make sure those people or that organization check out as legitimate. For example, abcnews.com.co claimed (falsely) that it was owned by the Westboro Baptist Church.
- Isolate a specific claim in an article and look it up in a search engine like Google, Bing or another one (we like DuckDuckGo because it doesn't track you and doesn't seem to bias results as politically) to look up the topic by keywords. If it's unverifiable, it's suspect and likely false.
- Check to see that the story has direct quotes. Most good journalism contains lots of them, and the sources of those quotes can be checked for legitimacy at other sites. The absence of direct quotes is a tipoff that a story may be suspect.
- Check to see that the headline accurately reflects the story content. If it exaggerates, the story also may be false or misleading.
- If the story is accompanied by a photo, right click on the image and do an internet search for it. The source of the photo can be telling because those who produce fake news seldom take photos. They lift them from other sites. In this day and age, photos also are easily altered. Photos are also sometimes mislabeled and misused. For example, it turned out that widely disseminated pictures in 2019 of children in cages at the U.S.-Mexican border and labeled as something President Trump did, were actually of cages for children built in 2014 during President Barack Obama's administration, as many on the right pointed out. But for a fuller, more balanced account of the more complicated story than you likely got from either right-wing or left-wing media—although USA Today also fact checked this and reached similar conclusions—see www.snopes.com/fact-check/obama-build-cages-immigrants/. Snopes also found a widely disseminated photograph of a boy crying inside a cage during the Trump administration was mislabeled and was actually staged at a protest outside Dallas City Hall (www.snopes.com/fact-check/toddler-cage-photo/).
- Look at the fact-check sites we mentioned (such as factcheck.org, politifact.com, truthorfiction.com or snopes.com), as well as fact checks done by news organizations with good reputations, such

as *The New York Times*, the *Washington Post* and the Associated Press. But don't rely solely on them. Look for more than one fact check, because there are often competing claims and opinions, and even "fact-check" sites may have their own political agenda. Former CBS correspondent Sharyl Attkisson even has a name for biased fact checking: "fake fact checks."

- Avoid confirmation bias by making sure you don't just look for evidence supporting your side. And don't just assume that a second opinion is more correct than the first. But don't stop here!

- Do original research to determine whether the information is correct and whose information and arguments make more sense when you find contradictory ones. Note who says what, then make a judgment based on what is most probable and makes the most sense. Approach the topic with an open mind—look for the facts even (especially!) if they disagree with your own views, opinions or values. Check original sources wherever possible rather than someone else's summary of them. Look for trusted, impartial sources. Be transparent. List your sources, and explain your reasoning.

Google Search Hints

- **Use keywords to focus in on what you want.** For example, if you want to know whether the minimum wage actually helps or hurts the poor, don't just look for "minimum wage" but "minimum wage study" or "minimum wage poor."

- **Put key phrases in quotation marks.** The quotation marks force the search engine to give you only the results where that specific phrase appears. For example, type "media ecology" with quotes around it, so you won't get all articles that mention the media and the topic of ecology.

- **Use a tilde (~) to include any synonyms in the search.** If you put a tilde in front of a word (no space between), Google will search for that word and synonyms.

- **Use a minus sign (–) to exclude things you don't want.** If you put a minus sign in front of a word (no space between), Google will leave out those hits. For example, "tablet computers" –iPad will give you only articles about non-iPad tablets.

- **Use ellipses to specify a numeric range.** If you want to read about crockpots only in the $30–$50 price range, type in crockpots $30...$50 (no spaces).

- **Use site: to look only on a specific site.** If you want to look up media theorist Marshall McLuhan on www.nytimes.com, type "Marshall McLuhan" site:nytimes.com (no space after colon).
- **Use filetype: to look only for a specific file type.** If you want to look for a PowerPoint (ppt or pptx) file about journalism ethics, type "journalism ethics" filetype:pptx (no space after colon, pptx for new format ones).

Observations About Bias

- There can be valid reasons for statistical differences other than bias. See pages 252–253 on comparisons in science.
- When we see a bias in something, it may not mean prejudice but merely tendency. There's a difference between bias as prejudice and bias as tendency. For example, people can honestly say that they usually take a conservative or a liberal position but that they aren't close-minded to new evidence.
- Even people who are not racist or sexist in their beliefs sometimes unintentionally make statements that can be taken as racist or sexist in their effect, as when now President Joe Biden praised Barack Obama back when they were both running for president in 2008 as clean and articulate; see www.youtube.com/watch?v=vJSfBKQA_KQ.

Tips for Dealing with Press Bias

- Know the political leanings of TV and radio networks, newspapers, magazines, websites, think tanks and even fact-checkers. See pages 107–109.
- Don't get all your news from one source or one political outlook. Mix it up, and also throw in some foreign sources as a further check. Try some "affirmative action" for your news, not just picking sources that agree with you. Make a special effort to get the other side and to see multiple viewpoints.
- Review these tips and those in the book *unSpun* by Brooks Jackson and Kathleen Hall Jamieson for trying to decide among competing claims or even just checking out a critical piece of persuasive evidence.
- See what's there, not what you want to see. Trust evidence, not your own loyalties. Trust independent studies by neutral researchers more than your own limited "experience." Experience strikes many as the best evidence, but it's anecdotal, based on the limitations of our own background and is often colored and shaped by our own biases.
- Study common logical fallacies as presented in logic and debate texts or various sites on the internet.

- Don't trust something is true just because you've heard it said often. That was Hitler's "big lie" technique and is still used by unscrupulous politicians of all sides, advertising and PR.
- To sort out bias of any kind—race, sex, age, religion, politics, etc.— ask, "What if the shoe were on the other foot?" What, for example, would I think if it were said or done by a Democratic politician rather than a Republican? A man rather than a woman? A minority person rather than a white one? (Or vice versa, depending on the situation.)

Suggested Websites

Annenberg Public Policy Center's fact-check site: www.factcheck.org

For web searches: www.Duckduckgo.com

For searching magazine, newspaper, radio, TV and wire-service websites: HeadlineSpot.com

My Reference Desk: www.refdesk.com

Pulitzer Prize-winning political fact-check site sponsored by the *Tampa Bay Times*: www.politifact.com

A guide to fraudulent medicine claims: www.quackwatch.org

A great resource to verify the wording and source of famous quotations: www.quoteinvestigator.com

For checking out urban legends: snopes.com

The Center for Responsive Politics looks at political donations and lobbying: www.opensecrets.org

Washington Post's fact-checker: www.washingtonpost.com/news/fact-checker

Suggested Readings

Boller, Paul F. Jr., and John George. *They Never Said It: A Book of Fake Quotes, Misquotes, and Misleading Attributions*. Barnes & Noble, 1989.

Brunvand, Jan Harold. *Too Good to Be True: The Colossal Book of Urban Legends*. W.W. Norton, 2011.

Cohn, Victor. *News & Numbers: A Writer's Guide to Statistics*, 3rd edition. Wiley-Blackwell, 2011.

Huff, Darrell. *How to Lie with Statistics*. W.W. Norton, 2010.

Jackson, Brooks, and Kathleen Hall Jameson. *unSpun: Finding Facts in a World of [Disinformation]*. Random House, 2007.

Keyes, Ralph. *The Quote Verifier*. St. Martin's Griffin, 2007.

Kirchner, Paul. *Everything You Know Is Wrong*. General Publishing Group, 1995.

Morgan, Susan, Tom Reichert and Tyler R. Harrison. *From Numbers to Words: Reporting Statistical Results for the Social Sciences*. Routledge, 2016.

Paulos, John Allen. *A Mathematician Reads the Newspaper*. Basic Books, 2013.

5 MACRO EDITING FOR LEGALITY, ETHICS AND PROPRIETY

What to Publish? And Not?

Law, ethics and propriety involve principles that help editors decide what not to publish or how to present their stories in a way that poses fewer problems.

American media law is unique in that, theoretically, the First Amendment bans all government limitations on the press. But the Constitution provides for copyright laws the media are not free to violate, and freedom from government censorship doesn't exempt the media from lawsuits by private individuals for libel, invasion of privacy or negligence. Then, too, Congress and the courts have decided that electronic media don't deserve the freedom from regulation the print media have, so broadcast media are licensed, whereas print media are not. The situation with online media is less settled.

DOI: 10.4324/9781003011422-5

Americans arguably have in theory the freest media in the world, but the reality is not so simple. If the First Amendment's commandment that there shall be "no law . . . abridging the freedom . . . of the press" were taken by government to mean exactly what it says, journalism programs wouldn't need to require entire courses devoted to media law. Also, the law is constantly changing with new statutes and new court cases, and media law also varies from state to state. All of this adds to the complications.

Obeying ethical principles is more open to individual choice than obeying legal guidelines. But journalists, in addition to following their own moral compass, need to follow the ethics policies of their employers, which vary from place to place. Beyond their own ethics and those of their employers, journalists should also be familiar with policies that are standard industrywide. This will help them be better informed about what actions are normally acceptable and which aren't.

When we speak of making decisions about what to publish based on propriety and whether it's tasteful, we're trying to avoid giving unnecessary offense to our audience. Most American newspapers, for example, do not normally print cuss words beyond the relatively mild *hell* or *damn,* and do not normally publish pictures depicting nudity or anything gruesome. Broadcast media do likewise with video. This prudishness relative to increasingly looser pop-culture attitudes is not often the case in magazines and online media. And sometimes, journalists have to decide whether the news value trumps normal taste considerations, such as quoting what someone accused of a hate crime purportedly said to the victim.

The principles in this chapter should prove useful in avoiding lawsuits and sorting out other potential problems, as well. But principles provide rules of thumb, whereas life confronts us with individual circumstances that need to be taken into account—the particular subject matter, the way it's presented and other considerations such as the law of your local jurisdiction, and ethics and sensitivity standards of your particular media outlet and audience.

When you come upon a situation about which you're not sure, seek the help of the editor above you and, if necessary, your company's attorney. Consider this chapter the collective experience of some editors who have dealt with journalistic decisions on these issues. This is not legal advice, which must come from an attorney looking at your individual circumstances.

Freedom of the Press

The centerpiece of American media law is the First Amendment, ratified in 1791:

> Congress shall make no law respecting an establishment of religion, or prohibiting the free exercise thereof; or abridging the freedom of speech,

or of the press; or the right of the people peaceably to assemble, and to petition the government for a redress of grievances.

Most Americans have no clue what the First Amendment says or means. Time after time over the years, when Americans have been surveyed about it but not told they were being asked about the First Amendment, many haven't recognized it and have opposed it as too radical.

Many Americans even support the idea of government censoring opinions they themselves find offensive and support private actions creating a "cancel culture"—social ostracism of those who even in their youth violated today's activists' prescriptions that weren't even in place at the time.

College campuses led the way by imposing "Politically Correct" speech codes and requiring teachers issue "trigger warnings" and warnings against "microaggressions." *Trigger warnings* are alerts that some may take offense at what is to be presented, and *microaggressions* are statements based on stereotypes—usually based on race, sex or ethnicity—that are said typically with no conscious hateful intent but that can be offensive to others.

It could be argued, though, that our lawmakers and campus administrators haven't understood the First Amendment because we do have laws and policies abridging freedoms outlined in it. In 1966, U.S. Supreme Court Justice Hugo Black wrote that in his opinion, "no law" means just that: *no* law. He thought even libel and obscenity laws are unconstitutional, but that has never been the general opinion of the court.

Still, we're better off compared with many other countries. Many nations today license journalists or exercise other kinds of **censorship**. Even Canada and the United Kingdom could be said not to have as much press freedom as Americans do, despite Reporters Without Borders ranking them in 2019 18th best and 33rd best in the world, ahead of the U.S. at 48 (https://rsf.org/EN/RANKING).

In Canada, for example, judges can order the press not to cover a trial if they deem pretrial publicity could prevent a defendant's fair trial. In the U.S., judges instead must resort to measures short of that, such as sequestering the jury from the news, not depriving the entire public of it.

The Canadian Charter of Rights and Freedoms guarantees freedom of the press "only to such reasonable limits prescribed by law as can be demonstrably justified in a free and democratic society." The Canadian Human Rights Act makes it illegal to print or broadcast "any matter that is likely to expose a person or persons to hatred or contempt by reason of the fact that that person or those persons are identifiable on the basis of a prohibited ground of discrimination." It's also illegal in Canada to post such messages on the internet.

Meanwhile, in the UK, unlike in the U.S., the government may:

- Order the media not to publish something someone alleges, even without proof, is libelous. A defamatory statement is presumed to be false under British law until the defendant can prove it true. That's like being presumed guilty rather than innocent.

- Forbid publication of any information about a case being litigated, even information that has been brought up in open court.
- Prohibit publication of anything the government says involves national security, even though it's often merely something embarrassing to the government.

It usually surprises people to learn that unlike in Canada and Europe, hate speech is not illegal in the U.S., just hate crimes. Hate speech consists of name calling and criticism that demeans others by race, gender, sexual orientation, religion, disability, even intellect. It can result in a lawsuit, such as for slander or as evidence of discrimination or a "hostile workplace." But it is not a crime unless it rises to unlawful harassment, incitement or the inconsistently formulated idea of "fighting words" we'll say a bit more about later. Hate crimes are crimes motivated by such prejudice.

In other words, hate speech is mere words, whereas a hate crime involves the motivation for committing the action of a crime. The first is normally protected by the First Amendment as freedom of speech no matter how repugnant, whereas the second is a reason to enhance the punishment for a crime such as murder in the same way premeditation enhances the punishment for killing someone. For more on this, see UCLA law professor Eugene Volhk's piece at www.washingtonpost.com/news/volokh-conspiracy/wp/2015/05/07/no-theres-no-hate-speech-exception-to-the-first-amendment.

What Does "Freedom of the Press" Mean?

Freedom of the press means no government censorship. Alexander Hamilton asked what was meant by **"freedom of the press,"** and James Madison, the author of the Bill of Rights, responded that it meant freedom from despotic control by the federal government. The main idea was to avoid censorship by the government.

What *no censorship* means is *no prior restraint* by government. The government can't tell you beforehand what you must or must not publish. Sometimes students ask, "Could a newspaper print a story about . . .?" That's not an appropriate question because Americans are free to publish anything. No government censor looks over page proofs before a newspaper is printed or broadcast scripts and clips before radio or TV news is broadcast, saying what can or can't be included.

The media can severely criticize the government and its officials and have no fear that journalists will be jailed or the door to a publication or broadcast station will be padlocked.

What is legally permissible is that after something has been published or broadcast, a civil suit for libel or violation of privacy may be filed by someone mentioned in the story. In short, we don't have prior restraint by the government in the U.S., but journalists may have to face the consequences after the fact from lawsuits by individual citizens who feel their rights have been violated and who seek payment for damages.

Censorship, Pro and Con

Arguments for Censorship

- **We need to protect the young and the ignorant against "misinformation" (as defined, of course, by those in power).** The first great philosopher in Western civilization, Plato, around 2,300 years ago, said that in his ideal society the government would censor ideas that might mislead children or even adults. Later, during the Inquisition, the Catholic Church decided it was better to censor books with ideas not approved by the church than for people to be led astray and lose their souls. During the conservative McCarthy Era of the 1950s in America, people were blacklisted from working because of their left-wing politics if they were accused or suspected of ever having been a Communist. Today, many on the left accuse conservative news outlets and social-media posters of purveying "misinformation" and have proposed calling for regulations on privately owned social media to do more banning of certain people and information.

- **We should protect people from words or ideas that might offend them.** Some speech—such as racist hate speech, sexist language or pornographic depictions of women—doesn't help people get to the truth but rather distracts them from it by appealing to prejudice, not reason. This offensive language promotes contempt, not civil discussion. It shocks and intimidates, and it is a threat or a verbal assault.

But both of these ideas add up to this: "We know what's right, and you don't. Further discussion would only be harmful. Force is justified to make sure truth prevails. If someone says something with which I disagree or that offends me, they should be silenced."

Arguments Against Censorship

In 1644, John Milton, the English poet who wrote *Paradise Lost*, published an essay called "Areopagitica." He argued that licensing of the press, which Great Britain practiced at the time, was censorship, and he demanded that ideas be able to circulate freely. He said freedom of the press was the best way to get at the truth. His essay was one of the first great defenses of freedom of the press. The first two of the following defenses of a free press derive from him:

- **The censored idea might be true, and we'd be depriving ourselves of the truth.**
- **Even if it's false, being justified in our beliefs and being able to argue effectively for them require exposure to competing ideas.**
- **The truth is more likely to be discovered if there's a "free marketplace of ideas"—in other words, unconstrained debate.**
- **Freedom of the press makes possible an informed citizenry, which is necessary for wise self-rule.** Democracy demands an informed citizenry. As Thomas Jefferson wrote, "Our liberty depends on freedom of the press, and that cannot be limited without being lost."
- **A free press serves as a check on government power and can serve as a virtual fourth branch of government.**
- **Freedom of the press provides a safety valve for the public to let off steam without having to revolt.**
- **Free expression is a necessary right in order for human beings to realize their potential.** To achieve happiness, self-development and individuality, people must be free to gain information on which to base their beliefs and actions, and free to pass on their ideas to others.

People often ask whether censorship isn't legally justified by the "can't yell fire in a crowded theater" argument and also the "fighting words" argument—that some words are so offensive that they inflict injury by their very nature and as a result someone couldn't help but break the peace by fighting. "Fighting words" is the main excuse for many college bans on certain language. Why these arguments don't hold up is discussed in two excellent articles we recommend:

www.theatlantic.com/national/archive/2012/11/its-time-to-stop-using-the-fire-in-a-crowded-theater-quote/264449
www.thefire.org/misconceptions-about-the-fighting-words-exception

Although prior restraint is theoretically prohibited by the First Amendment, on rare occasions courts have allowed it. During the Vietnam War, one lower court temporarily restrained the press from printing the classified "Pentagon

Papers" when the government sought an injunction on national security grounds. The Supreme Court rejected the idea.

Government licensing of journalists is a form of prior restraint or censorship because countries often use licensing to prevent dissenting views from being published or aired by only granting licenses to those agreeing with those in power. For this reason, **the print media in the U.S. are not licensed. But when broadcast media were invented, Congress and the courts decided that those media should not receive the same full freedom as the print media.** Radio and television are licensed in the U.S. and face various regulations, including some regarding content.

If the approach to regulating broadcast content is allowed to continue and expands into the digital world of the internet, we are likely to lose our First Amendment freedoms. That's because people are spending more time with electronic media that are regulated by the government and less with purely print media that the First Amendment more fully protects.

Freedom of the press means freedom to exercise editorial judgment. Because censorship involves the government telling you what you must or must not publish, freedom of the press, then, traditionally means those who own the media have the freedom to choose what to publish.

Broadcast media, though, aren't allowed as full a degree of editorial discretion as print media and have had to face such content regulations as the now-repealed Fairness Doctrine, which we'll discuss later, as well as being

Figure 5.1 Editors should not assume they know what reporters meant in an unclear passage and rewrite it without consulting the reporter, especially in matters that could pose legal or ethical problems.

Photo by Christopher Parks.

required to satisfy the Federal Communications Commission (FCC) at licensing time that they have operated "in the public interest." Because the airwaves are considered publicly owned, broadcast stations are, to some extent, viewed as limited public utilities.

The opposite of censorship is the freedom to exercise editorial judgment—to accept or reject any story, advertisement, picture or letter. Free media would not have to publish, broadcast or post everything handed to them, the way a public utility must provide electricity to everyone in its area who requests it.

Over the years, many people have not understood the distinction between government censoring information and journalism outlets merely editing what goes into their publications, and so many have often incorrectly labeled both as "censorship." But in the years of the Trump administration, especially at the end, new questions were raised concerning problems posed by social media and other high-tech companies banning certain news, people and outlets favorable to Trump or conservative views in general.

These companies exert oligarchic control over much of the news audiences receive because more and more people get their news mainly from them, and even print and broadcast media reach much of their audience through them now. And app stores like Apple's and Google's, as well as large server suppliers, like Amazon, exercise further oligarchic control over what alternative services, like Parler, can even be carried on devices or on the internet at all.

So, are these big-tech companies, even though private businesses, exerting a kind of power equivalent to government censorship? Should the term "censorship" be applied to them, as well as government? And should this kind of private power be illegal? This gets us into the subject of U.S. Code Section 230 and whether it should be changed and in what direction.

Editorial Selection Under U.S Code Section 230

Before Section 230 of the U.S. Code was passed in 1996 (originally as part of the Communications Decency Act) online companies were advised not to edit what information they carried if they wanted to be protected against libel suits. This was established in three court cases, one against the then-popular online service CompuServe and two more against the even larger America Online. Courts let the companies off the hook legally because the two platforms were seen as common carriers merely passing on information unedited as a phone service does, not as a newspaper editing what it carried, which would make the services as open to lawsuits as newspapers are.

But then Section 230 came along, and part of it says this: "No provider or user of an interactive computer service shall be held liable on account of . . . any action voluntarily taken in good faith to restrict access to or availability of material that the provider or user considers to be obscene, lewd, lascivious, filthy, excessively violent, harassing, or otherwise objectionable, whether or not such material is constitutionally protected . . ." (You can read more at www.law.cornell.edu/uscode/text/47/230.) That language has been interpreted by many—although it has never been clear to us that's what it means or was intended to mean—that the older legal distinction between platform and publisher was now null and void and that internet companies are now legally protected even when they edit stories, attach fact-checks to them or ban them altogether. (For a detailed discussion about possible meanings of what Section 230 actually says, see www.journaloffreespeechlaw.org/candeubvolokh.pdf.)

But should such actions be more legally protected when taken by an internet company than by a print publisher? It seems questionable in that Congress had previously argued in the early 20th century at the introduction of broadcast that new media not explicitly named in the First Amendment weren't entitled to the same freedom of the "press." Not only that, but these internet companies now have so much more control over public discourse than any traditional media outlet ever did before.

The First Amendment was meant to guarantee a free press by preventing the government from censoring ideas, but what if the banning is done by corporations as opposed to government?

And what about actions such as the Biden administration admitted to in July 2021 of giving Facebook advice on what it thought should be banned or at least flagged to combat "misinformation" about Covid-19? (See www.msn.com/en-us/news/politics/biden-administration-s-admission-they-re-flagging-content-to-facebook-sparks-furor/ar-AAMcFjp.) Should government be able to use private corporations to ban what would be illegal for government to ban?

As we write this in 2021, some Republicans in Congress are calling for a return to the distinction between platforms and publishers, while some Democrats in Congress are calling for regulating internet companies *to require* them to exercise more labeling or banning of stories they deem "misinformation," even with Biden's White House Press Secretary Jen Psaki saying that if one social media outlet banned someone, all should. (See www.amren.com/news/2021/07/psaki-says-people-should-be-banned-on-all-social-media-if-they-are-banned-from-one-platform/.)

Freedom of the press means the media get to decide whether to publish or broadcast something—that's editorial judgment, not censorship—at least by the old definition. But as the news has come to be largely controlled by only about six major media corporations and even beyond that increasingly by a few high-tech companies rather than traditionally journalistic

ones, the definition of censorship may be broadened more and more beyond involving merely governmental action to include bans of information by private corporations.

More and more Americans are getting their news from online sources than from older media. Pew Research says 86% of Americans get their news from digital devices, compared with 68% from TV, 50% from radio and 32% from print. Of the online news audience, 68% get their online news from news sites or apps, 65% from searches, 53% social media and 22% podcasts (www.pewresearch.org/fact-tank/2021/01/12/more-than-eight-in-ten-americans-get-news-from-digital-devices/). This means that social media like Facebook and Twitter, and search engines, especially Google, control huge shares of the news people see.

Robert Epstein, former editor of *Psychology Today*, says high-tech companies such as these are "surveilling, censoring and manipulating"—collecting and selling your private information, banning stories that either don't accord with their own political views and secretly manipulating people to change their views by what the companies push you to see.

As examples, Epstein says 70% of videos people watch on Google-owned YouTube are suggested by the company. He also says his study of Google search-engine results found that Google is feeding people it considers conservatives more liberally biased content than liberals themselves are getting in nine out of ten searches. In other words, it looks as though Google is trying to change conservatives' political views by controlling what shows up in their searches rather than just citing the most popular results or those that fit the search criteria best. He says whistle-blowers also confirm this.

Epstein estimates this could change around 15 million votes in an election and that in 2020 Google was responsible for a minimum of 6 million votes by manipulating what people saw when they searched. Epstein says he's a liberal himself, so the results favor his own side but that he thinks it's dangerous for companies to have such power. (You can follow his research on internet matters at www.drrobertepstein.com/index.php/media-coverage.)

Social media banning of stories might have combined with lack of media coverage to change the outcome of the 2020 presidential election. A poll afterward by the Media Research Center (albeit a conservative media-watchdog group) reported that the mainstream media's not covering or actually banning eight key stories cost Trump re-election.

To quote MRC: "Looking at all eight of these issues together, our poll found that a total of 17% of [President Joseph] Biden's voters told us they would have changed their vote if they had been aware of one or more of these important stories. This would have moved every one of the swing states into Trump's column, some by a huge margin. The President would have trounced Biden in the electoral college, 311 to 227." (See list of stories, discussion and charts at www.newsbusters.org/blogs/nb/rich-noyes/2020/11/24/special-report-stealing-presidency-2020.)

Conservatives complain that social-media bans have been mainly against conservative voices, generally with the explanation or excuse that they are spreading "fake news" or even dangerous information. But at the same time, they say, the Iranian and Chinese governments, as well as the Taliban, have been allowed to post seemingly whatever they wanted, and few left-wing posts seem to be taken down. (For an examination of the controversy about political bias of social-media platforms, see www.bbc.com/news/technol ogy-54698186.)

In addition, unless you made a special effort to get the other side from what the mainly liberal mainstream media reported, you were unlikely to find out about the right's view that although Trump was often reported as spreading lies, much of the reporting itself throughout Trump's four years was arguably "fake news." Former CBS correspondent Sharyl Attkisson drew up a list of 154 such stories (see https://sharylattkisson. com/2021/04/50-media-mistakes-in-the-trump-era-the-definitive-list/).

What, if anything, government should do to regulate big-tech giants is an issue to keep an eye on. (See https://slate.com/technology/2021/03/ section-230-reform-legislative-tracker.html.)

It's unclear to us, though, whether losing platform protections against liability would change the situation much. It would only mean social media would lose protection against being sued but could proceed as they are at present, editing, banning and kicking off voices with whom they disagree, just like even the most partisan legacy media already do. On the other hand, federally requiring them to fact-check and ban more would mean they could also continue to proceed in a partisan manner with even more robustness. The biggest change would be if Congress decided to break them up under the antitrust laws for being too big and too powerful, as the government did with the old Bell Telephone System in 1982.

Freedom of the press is a right, not an entitlement. *Rights,* in the Bill of Rights, means protections from intervention in your life by the federal government. A right is not an *entitlement*—something the government gives you—as people often use the term today in phrases like *welfare rights* or *right to health care.* The *right* of freedom of the press is not something the government *gives* journalists but instead a *protection against* the government censoring the press. Freedom of the press also does not entitle you to force someone else to print your ideas or to provide you with a radio microphone or TV time.

Freedom of the press does not mean responsibilities of the press. You often hear people say, "With freedom come responsibilities." They go on then to say something like: "I believe in freedom of the press, but if the press doesn't start showing more social responsibly, the government might have to act."

But freedom of the press is not conditional on the media showing social responsibility by anyone's definition. The First Amendment doesn't say anything about responsibilities. This is the Bill of *Rights*—not the Bill of

Responsibilities. Besides, who's to define what is "socially responsible"? Does that phrase mean the same to Democrats as to Republicans? Wouldn't government-determined social responsibility lead to censorship of unpopular ideas or those the current party in power doesn't want aired? No government administration should be able to ban what it considers "fake news," which, as we've seen, often isn't fake at all.

Freedom of the press is not the same as the right to know. The First Amendment does not guarantee a **right to know**, which actually would be an entitlement, not a right. The phrase "right to know" is used when people think the government should have to give them information. The First Amendment doesn't say the government has to give the press any information—just that the government can't stop the press from printing any information.

The idea of a right to know in the U.S. was first proposed in the 1930s and 1940s. Its main legal apparatus is in state open-meetings and open-records laws passed since the 1950s, as well as in the federal Freedom of Information Act first passed in 1966. But "right to know" is neither a phrase in the First Amendment nor elsewhere in the Bill of Rights, nor a phrase in the Constitution. (By the way, the "right to privacy" is also not in the Bill of Rights or the Constitution. It was first proposed in a law review article in the 1890s.)

Freedom of the press doesn't give journalists special rights. The First Amendment doesn't give journalists any protection from prosecution if they break the law to get a story. If you trespass, misrepresent yourself as a police officer, or pay a bribe, you could go to jail. Nor are journalists protected from a lawsuit just because they quote someone else saying something slanderous. To the law, if you published it, you libeled the person, even though the words weren't your own.

The First Amendment does not grant journalists immunity from testifying at a trial. If you quote an anonymous source who accuses the mayor of being involved in criminal activity, you can be compelled in court to identify who told you that, even if you swore to your source you'd never reveal his or her name. If you refuse to answer, you can go to jail for contempt of court. If you do answer, your source can sue you for breach of contract.

Some states have tried to protect journalists by passing laws extending the same sort of professional–client relationship to them and their sources that lawyers, doctors and priests enjoy. These are called **shield laws**. But when someone's Sixth Amendment right to a fair trial conflicts with such a state statute, the Constitution wins out, and you still have to testify.

Are there really no restrictions on American media? In theory, yes, there are none. In reality, no, there are. Despite the absoluteness of the First Amendment's language, the media are restricted in various ways:

- Broadcast media have never been extended all the First Amendment rights of the print media. Electronic media are regulated by Congress, the FCC (broadcast) and, in some instances, by state and local governments (cable and telephones). The airwaves are considered public property, and broadcasters have to get permission from the government to keep their station on the air. License renewal is subject to approval of the FCC. In addition, various rules restrict "indecent" language, which topics can be discussed on the airwaves and even mandate that sometimes political ads must be broadcast with which station owners may not approve.

- Commercial speech is not fully protected by the First Amendment, either. The government regulates the content of advertisements. The Federal Trade Commission or the Food and Drug Administration can order a company to take corrective measures or pay stiff fines when false or misleading claims are made about products.

Even the print media are not totally free of restrictions. Publication cannot normally be stopped in advance—although that has happened, as in the Pentagon Papers case. And if you work at a school newspaper, the Supreme Court has ruled that the school can sometimes censor your paper. In addition:

- Publishers can be arrested and go to prison for printing obscenity, although the First Amendment makes no such exception when it says "no law" can be passed abridging freedom of the press.
- A publisher can face criminal charges over copyright infringement— for publishing someone's copyrighted material without getting permission.
- A media outlet can get in trouble for promoting information about a raffle that's technically illegal under state law.
- A publisher or a reporter can face civil suits for libeling someone, invading someone's privacy or treating someone negligently.

Legal Problems

Journalists don't need to be lawyers, but they should know enough about media law to know how to handle common situations and when it's necessary to call an attorney. Part of a print or web editor's job involves looking out for possible libel problems in stories, headlines, photos, graphics, captions and blurbs. If you can edit around the problem, do so, but also alert your supervisor to the problem and what you're doing. If you have doubts or questions, say so, and pass the problem on to your supervisor or the staff attorney.

The main legal problems editors must spot and fix involve libel and invasion of privacy. Not as common are issues of negligence, obscenity and copyright infringement.

Libel

Libel is one of the two kinds of **defamation**, meaning a statement that damages someone's reputation or livelihood by bringing that person into hatred, ridicule or contempt in the eyes of a substantial and respectable group.

Slander is when you say something that defames someone's reputation. Libel is when you publish or, in many states, broadcast something that defames someone's reputation. (California is one state that defines broadcast defamation as slander.) Making disparaging remarks to someone's face, with no one overhearing it, is neither slander nor libel—the comments may hurt someone's feelings but not damage their reputation.

Examples of defamation include accusing someone of a crime or of immorality; claiming someone is incompetent, dishonest or unethical; or accusing someone of association with a disreputable cause, such as fascism, communism, terrorism or the Ku Klux Klan. Nonetheless, politicians and media commentators make such accusations often, especially about people with political views with which they disagree. Less common ways of defaming someone include saying someone has what the public might consider a loathsome ailment, such as mental illness, venereal disease, or accusing a woman of being unchaste or a man of being impotent.

Don't confuse libel with liable. The second means "likely" and, in legal language, "responsible."

Don't think that libel means you must have told a lie about someone. A lie implies something knowingly false. Something unknowingly false may be libelous, too.

In addition, a statement may be untrue but not damage someone's reputation, and that's not libel. For example, it hasn't typically been a legal problem when newspapers incorrectly report that someone died. Or a statement may be true and damage someone's reputation, and that is technically **libel per se** but unactionable because it's true. California, though, includes as part of the definition that for something to be libelous, it must be false, and many definitions of libel include the idea that it must be untrue.

The idea that a statement always has to be false to be libelous comes about because essentially you're going to be legally in trouble in the U.S. for libeling someone only when you can't prove what you published or broadcast was true or otherwise protected. In other words, something may damage someone's reputation or business without being subject to legal action unless it is also false but even then may still be protected.

That a story damages someone's business or reputation doesn't necessarily mean you shouldn't publish it if it's true and newsworthy. For example, truthfully printing that someone was convicted of a crime may damage his or her reputation, but no one would argue that it shouldn't be published or that you would be in any danger legally if it were.

Some Common Libel Situations

Here are some common situations in which you should be on the lookout for libel:

Make sure accident, crime and court stories contain nothing that convicts a person before trial. All suspects are presumed innocent until they confess or are proven guilty by a jury. If a suspect you convicted in the media is later found not guilty, you could face a libel suit.

To be clear, merely accurately reporting evidence or statements presented in court is not what we mean by convicting a person—but editorializing that someone is guilty before a verdict of not guilty comes out would be. Even so, many times, especially on cable news shows, guests and hosts do just that and often get away with it. But there are also cases in which they've been sued and lost or settled out of court, as in the case of Nicholas Sandman, a Covington, Kentucky, high school student who was widely misrepresented in the media as confronting a Native American protester. Video later revealed the protester confronted Sandman, not the other way around. See www.nationalreview.com/news/cnn-settles-lawsuit-brought-by-covington-catholic-student-nicholas-sandmann/.

Make sure that any damaging statements in opinion pieces concern matters of opinion rather than matters of fact. Opinions are not true or false, but facts are.

Insist that news stories stick to observable, provable facts. Many libel problems could be avoided if editorializing value judgments were edited out of news stories.

Addresses of people who are the subject of damaging stories can be dangerous. Giving the wrong address could implicate the wrong person. But there's also a danger from *not* giving the address in the case of a suspect. If someone else in town has the same name, then—unless the age or correct address, or both, are given—the innocent person may complain because people who know the innocent individual thought the story was about him or her, but a correction usually suffices.

As for the victim, some news outlets use the block (for example, "the 2400 block of Main Street") rather than the exact address where the crime was committed. This can help protect the victim's privacy while still informing the public of the general area of the crime.

It's dangerous to make assumptions. For example, if someone has been laid off, that doesn't necessarily mean the person was fired. *Fired* suggests that someone erred and was kicked out. *Laid off* implies economic trouble, with no personal blame at all.

Headlines, captions and blurbs can pose special problems. People are more likely to read headlines, captions and blurbs than details in the story, yet the fact that an editor is writing them rather than the reporter means there's more opportunity to get things wrong.

Don't assume that if the details in the story are right, a damaging headline or caption or blurb isn't libelous. As editors, from a legal liability standpoint, it's important to consider the big type as standing alone. But when it comes to the story itself, the courts usually say that statements from it taken out of context are not libelous—the story must be considered as a whole.

Common Questions About Libel

How can it be libel when I'm just quoting someone else and not saying it myself? There's a common assumption that if something originated from an outside source, it's safe. That's wrong because the media are responsible for everything they publish, broadcast or post from whatever source—their reporters, wire services, syndicates and advertisers.

Don't think quoting a libelous statement by someone else protects journalists because "We're not the ones saying it— we're just reporting it." The news outlet is libeling the person by publishing the remark. This can be a problem not only in news stories but also in letters to the editor in newspapers and magazines, viewer feedback to broadcast stations, information given in press conferences and audience-feedback forums on web pages.

When news stories are written with accusations in direct quotes, try to get comments from the person being accused, giving him or her a chance to respond. Like printing a correction, this shows you're at least trying to be fair, although the person could still sue you. In fact, unless the person says "No comment" or refuses to speak, any comment can potentially be seen in court as tacit consent for running the story.

Can't I just protect myself with *alleged, allegedly, accused* or *suspected*? Not necessarily. Unfortunately, *The Associated Press Stylebook* is confusing on the matter.

The AP Stylebook acknowledges that *alleged* "must be used with great care" and that it should not be used "as a routine qualifier." It also says you should avoid the appearance of making the allegation. And if you follow AP's suggestion that you also see its rule for the related word *accused,* you are told not to write "accused slayer" because it implies someone is guilty without a trial.

So far, so good, but AP also suggests specifying the source when you use *alleged,* or substituting the words *apparent, ostensible* or *reputed.* Why these suggestions would be any better is not explained. Also, the examples AP has of using *alleged*—and *accused*—with attribution involve a district attorney bringing charges. That's legally fine, but in other instances merely using attribution with the words could still be problematic, and there's no explanation given.

So, what's the verdict on modifiers like *accused, alleged, allegedly, reputed* and *suspected*? Despite the fact that they are used often, a word like *alleged* before a word like *rapist* in a story may offer little or no legal protection, according to some books and attorneys consulted. But there's not total agreement, and the practice of using "alleged" and "allegedly" is common.

One argument against such words is that they—as well as phrases like *it's alleged that, investigators suspect, police charge* (police don't file charges, prosecutors do), *it's rumored that, sources claim* and *reports say that*—are prejudicial in that they suggest guilt to the reader without offering proof. In other words, they sound as though you're convicting someone.

Another argument against these modifiers is that they are no different from paraphrasing or quoting someone who is saying something slanderous—for example, that someone *allegedly is a thief.* But by publishing, broadcasting or posting a slander, you become responsible for libel unless you're repeating official charges issued in a warrant or in a courtroom, where you'd have **qualified privilege**, or protection in reporting the allegations in a way that was substantially complete and accurate. Such words, the argument goes, would not legally excuse printing a false, damaging statement if the statement were not privileged or the truth could have been found through reasonable reporting.

One attorney asked rhetorically who was doing the alleging in a phrase like "the alleged murderer." Then he answered: "You are." He added, though, that potentially the word *alleged* could help you with a jury because average people might interpret it to mean what those who misuse it think it means. Another attorney said she knew of no cases in which a journalist was sued and then lost over the word *alleged* in front of a word like *murderer.* Perhaps victims of the practice—that is, the "alleged" suspects—also are unaware that *alleged* may not be absolute protection.

For the reasons cited, though, **it's probably best to avoid *alleged*, *allegedly* and all similar modifiers. Constructions using *alleged* or *allegedly*, or *rumored* or *reports say*, should be rewritten to be more neutral and objective. Instead, ask: Has a charge been filed? What report says this?**

The **"a man" technique** often comes in handy: Change "John Smith allegedly raped the woman at gunpoint . . ." to "A man raped the woman at gunpoint. John Smith was later arrested and charged" (provided he was).

By the way, another mistaken use of *alleged* that's less dangerous but sillier is the misplacement of the word in front of something that is a nonlibelous fact: "Tuesday night, a convenience-store clerk was allegedly hit on the head with a hammer by an unknown assailant."

How can it be libel if I didn't name the person who's claiming damages? There is a common misunderstanding that if the person libeled isn't named, he or she can't sue. That's not true. If the person is described enough to be identifiable by someone in the know, then that can be the basis of a successful libel suit.

Also, if the harmful statement concerns a group, an individual member of that group can sue. If the group is small enough, such as a jury, a team or a council, each may have a case.

How can it be libel if the person's reputation is already so low it couldn't be damaged more? A man may be a notorious drunk, but that doesn't make him a thief.

How can it be libel when the story isn't about a person? Libel may involve a corporation, partnership or trust, or other business, as well as a nonprofit institution—not just individuals.

What Protects You from Libel Lawsuits?

Most of the time, the potential problems in a story are obvious enough that experienced editors handle them without calling an attorney. They'll reword the offending passages to convey the information without convicting a suspect or unnecessarily damaging someone's reputation or business. Experienced editors also are familiar with the legal defenses to libel suits if the story is important enough for the media outlet to run, despite the risk of even an unsuccessful lawsuit.

If a story is especially tricky though, it should be kicked up the line of authority and the attorney called if necessary. On some sensitive stories, a good attorney will dictate a legally precise wording that editors should not change. The headline, too, should be carefully phrased.

The best media attorneys understand that your purpose is to get out the news, and they will try to help you do just that in a way that protects you legally. The worst attorneys are the ones who always argue that the safest approach is not to publish or broadcast anything about which you have a legal question. But as Benjamin Franklin said, "If all printers were determined not to print anything till they were sure it would offend nobody, there would be very little printed."

A Social Media Case Over Libel

The 2019 case of Musk v. Unsworth involved a $190,000 lawsuit against Elon Musk, CEO of Tesla and SpaceX, over a tweet in which he called the plaintiff, Vernon Unsworth "pedo-guy." Unsworth was a famous British caver who helped save 12 boys on a soccer team and their coach from a flooded cave in Thailand in 2018.

This was one of the first cases of a private individual bringing a lawsuit to trial over a tweet. Musk's attorney had argued that the term "pedo-guy" was meant merely as an insult meaning "creepy old guy" and not an allegation of fact that Unsworth molested children. Musk's attorney also argued that Unsworth had failed to prove damages. The Los Angeles federal jury agreed with Musk's side.

Musk had tweeted the statement then later deleted it, then tweeted apologizing and calling for moving on from the matter. His attorney. Alex Spiro, invented a term for this: "JDart," meaning "a joking, deleted, apologized for, responsive tweet." Musk had clumsily made a statement online, thought better of it and then darted away from it, proving, he said, it was not serious.

BBC reporter Dave Lee, wrote online: "Expect the JDart 'standard' to be applied again and again, not just in libel trials, but in any arena where social media behaviour is under scrutiny—a parachute for anyone who, in the heat of the moment, says something idiotic online."

See also www.cnbc.com/2019/12/06/unsworth-vs-musk-pedo-guy-defamation-trial-verdict.html

www.bbc.com/news/world-us-canada-50695593

and www.wired.com/story/elon-musk-wins-defamation-suit-british-diver/.

The best defense to a libel suit is that the story is true and you can prove it. Legally in the U.S., the burden of proof is on the plaintiff—the person filing the libel lawsuit—to prove that the statements published by the media are false. But as an editor, make sure reporters can back up any damaging statements in their stories before publishing, broadcasting or posting them. For example, don't rely on the testimony of a doctor to back up a libelous claim if that would violate the doctor-patient privilege of confidentiality.

Courts will settle for substantial rather than absolute truth, meaning that the media must have the story right in at least the most important parts. That's not a license to libel—it's just an acknowledgment that honest mistakes can be made that shouldn't be punished if they don't go to the heart of the complaint.

A libel suit can also be defended by showing the story is a fair, substantially accurate and complete account of a judicial, legislative or executive proceeding of local, state or federal government. A quotation you might falsely think is protected is a police officer saying a person is "guilty" or that this arrest "solves a long string of crimes." A suspect is not guilty until convicted, and such remarks are potentially troublesome if printed, broadcast or posted.

But if the officer makes the remark in court, it is considered *privileged*—that is, not subject to actionable accusations of libel. Also, depending on the jurisdiction, if the officer makes the remark in the line of duty, such as during an official press conference or in a press release, the remark could likewise be privileged. Some states grant a privilege to publish fair and accurate stories based on police reports. But until you know the rulings in your jurisdiction, be hesitant to let such a statement be published or broadcast.

Quoting statements of attorneys unless made in a courtroom, press releases from government bureaus and statements by civic organizations are not considered privileged or exempt from actionable libel-suit claims. Nor in many states, surprisingly, are quotes from complaints, petitions or affidavits that have been filed.

Libel is not normally actionable when the damaging statement is clearly a joke, not to be taken as the truth. "It's only a joke" has traditionally been a libel defense, but after the Rev. Jerry Falwell's suit against *Hustler* magazine for emotional distress caused by a spoof of him, it appears that even jokes can pose legal problems. Falwell was awarded $200,000 in two courts before the U.S. Supreme Court reversed the ruling in 1986.

Libel is not normally actionable when the subject of the damaging statement is dead. The maxim is, "You can't libel the dead," meaning someone has to be alive to be libeled.

Traditionally, only the person libeled has cause for action—relatives have no recourse. The offended person must bring suit within the statutory period, ranging from one to six years, depending on the jurisdiction. If the plaintiff dies before—or even during—the trial, the survivors cannot continue the case.

But this is changing. Although the maxim about libel not applying to the dead is still true in most states, many—including California, Texas and New York—are now allowing ongoing suits to continue after the death of the plaintiff. We are also starting to see some lawsuits from trusts or foundations set up by the deceased that nibble away at this protection by claiming that false, damaging statements about their provider are damaging their ongoing legal entity.

Libel is not actionable when the story is "fair comment or criticism"—such as a book, movie, theater, concert or restaurant review—and none of the damaging statements is a matter of fact as opposed to a matter of opinion. But journalists are not protected, even in a review, for misstatements of facts. For example, a restaurant reviewer can safely say the fish tasted bad but could face a problem if he or she insinuates the menu misrepresents frozen fish as fresh, especially if the owner has the receipts to prove the fish was in fact fresh.

Nor could a journalist safely write in a column or editorial, "In my opinion, the mayor is a crook." This statement would not be legally protected. You'd have to have facts to back it up because it's not really a matter of opinion. You probably wouldn't guess this, though, from the many times politicians and news commentators make such statements. These often go unchallenged legally because to some extent such statements are somewhat protected when made about public officials or public figures because of the "actual malice" doctrine we'll discuss next.

A libel suit can be defended on the grounds that the statement was made without actual malice about a public official or public figure, or (in most states) without negligence if the person is a private individual.

In a landmark 1964 decision, the U.S. Supreme Court ruled in *New York Times Company v. Sullivan* that the constitutional provisions of the First and 14th amendments could be used as a defense against libel if the defamatory words were used to describe the public acts of public officials and were used without actual malice. Elected officials, political candidates and judges are generally held to be public officials or public figures.

The term *actual malice* is a bit misleading. Plaintiffs do not need to prove that the press had it in for them. **The Court has interpreted *actual malice* to mean a statement published in "reckless disregard" of the truth.** So, if a story comes to you near deadline and you have doubts, you shouldn't run with it anyway just to have a scoop, because that would be reckless disregard of the truth—the actual malice standard for a story about a public official or public figure.

In addition, not taking the usual professional caution, which is the standard in many states for a story about a private person, could open you up to a charge of negligence. And because the Supreme Court has said plaintiffs can probe journalists' "state of mind" when publishing a story to prove actual malice, you should never make a statement aloud about a story, such as "Sharon really nailed this S.O.B."

To be clear, the actual malice standard for public officials and public figures applies in all the states, but the standard for private individuals is different in various states. At least 20 states and the District of Columbia have decided that to collect damages, a private individual needs only to prove that the libelous statement was false and made negligently. A few have adopted the strict actual malice test for private citizens, but some states require that a private citizen show only that the press was at "fault," a lesser standard even than negligence.

Alaska, Colorado, Indiana and New Jersey require only that a journalist writing about a private citizen meet the same actual malice standard as when writing about public officials and public figures. New York requires that a private citizen prove "grossly irresponsible conduct" by the press to win a libel lawsuit. Generally speaking, though, as an editor, be more worried if the statement is about a private individual than a public official or public figure.

But the question is, how do you know whether someone is a public official or public figure as opposed to a private individual? Courts make that determination case by case.

Some people are obviously public officials in that they have prominent governmental decision-making jobs, such as presidents, senators, governors, mayors and city council members. Career government employees in the civil service, clerks and sanitation workers would probably not be public officials although they work for government. But it's unclear whether some government employees, such as teachers and police officers, are public officials.

As for what makes someone a public figure, the courts have said some people are **pervasive public figures** in all matters because they are so well-known or influential. A famous actor or musician would fit this category. Others may be public figures only in relation to certain controversial matters in which they have thrust themselves forward—voluntarily or not.

A libel suit can be defended in some jurisdictions on the grounds that the story was fair and included neutral reporting of both sides of a controversy. This is one of the newest defenses for libel and has not been universally accepted in all jurisdictions. Florida is one of the few states that has accepted it, for example, but California, Kentucky, Michigan, New York and Pennsylvania have all rejected it. In Illinois, it was accepted by one court and rejected by another. Where it does apply, a media outlet might be on more solid ground if it accords someone the right to reply and rebut an attack, and if the response remains pertinent to the charges without upping the ante on the attacker.

Should We Make a Correction?

Although making a correction admits the mistake, thus removing the strongest libel defense of truth, it's ethically the proper thing to do if, in fact, the media outlet was wrong. In many cases, a correction also will avert a lawsuit. In most states, statutes provide for retraction of libel, and the other states typically count corrections as evidence for lessening the damages.

In states with retraction laws, the plaintiff can collect only actual damages—not punitive damages—if the retraction is made on request and within a certain time limit. Sometimes, a newspaper, magazine, broadcast station or website will offer to run a correction in return for a release from further liability. This saves the time and cost of a trial and may eliminate the possibility of a major judgment against the media outlet.

Here's some advice on handling corrections:

- If you're not in charge and someone demands a retraction, apology or correction, pass the demand along to your supervisor. It's not your call. The angrier the person and the more potentially troublesome the problem, the more likely the paper's attorney needs to get involved.
- Before you pass the matter on, don't admit any error or wrongdoing to the person complaining, and don't speak to the complainant's lawyer.
- After investigating a complaint and finding it valid, a media outlet should quickly publish, broadcast or post a correction, and be sure to avoid republishing, rebroadcasting or reposting any libel in the explanation.

Negligence

When the media publish, broadcast or post something that could result in damage or injury to someone, they face a possible lawsuit for negligence. Negligence means a failure to show enough caution or care in a situation that results in damage or injury to another. As always, the media have no special exemption from laws that everyone has to obey.

Libel itself could be seen as a kind of negligence in that plaintiffs win a libel lawsuit only after being able to show that:

- The published or broadcast material damaged their reputation or business.
- The media did not take the same care that any reasonable journalist would normally under similar circumstances. This applies to private citizens in most states and the District of Columbia suing only for actual damages, not punitive ones.

But in nonlibelous situations, the media can be sued for negligence. In one Missouri case, a newspaper printed the name and address of a woman who had successfully fled from an attempted rape. Although the woman's name and address were public record at the police station where she had filed a report, after the paper printed them, the assailant knew her name and where she lived, and he began stalking her. She sued for negligence, and the paper settled out of court. A related example of a situation posing the possibility of a negligence lawsuit would be printing the name or address of a witness to a killing when the suspect is on the loose.

Invasion of Privacy

Surveys find that privacy is the right most cherished by U.S. citizens, so it's surprising that the right to privacy is found nowhere in the Constitution or Bill of Rights. In fact, as noted earlier, it was invented in 1890 in a law review article and has since been institutionalized in U.S. law by statute and various court rulings but not by constitutional amendment.

Invasion of privacy can include more than most people realize. To most, it probably means the publishing of embarrassing, private facts or perhaps the act of trespassing. Both of these constitute invasion of privacy under U.S. law, but so would depicting someone in a "false light," as well as using his or her name, voice or image in a commercial context without permission. Notify your supervisor if you spot any of the following four trouble signs:

A story or picture that reveals private facts about someone, especially embarrassing matters, could pose an invasion-of-privacy problem. This can be a difficult call. The legal questions are: Is the information really newsworthy? Would the information be offensive or objectionable to an average person? To avoid invasion of privacy, the answer to the first question should be "yes," and the answer to the second question should be "no."

Be especially concerned if the story or photo discloses information regarding the person's sex life, health or economic affairs. Even with public officials and public figures, it's safer to stick to reporting on their public life. Before revealing personal information, ask yourself, "Does the public really need to know this?"

The main legal defense against an invasion-of-privacy suit is that the information is newsworthy. You might think, "Of course, it's newsworthy, or we wouldn't be publishing or broadcasting it," but the jury will decide, second-guessing your news judgment by playing Monday-morning, armchair editors.

A second defense could be that although the information is embarrassing, it was already public. For example, the information could have come from the public record, or a photograph could have been taken in a public place where many people witnessed what was captured on film. But these two defenses, it should be noted, do not always work.

A reporter or photographer who enters someone's private property, without permission, to get a story or pictures could pose a trespassing or intrusion problem. In most states, an exception is typically made after a fire, disaster or crime, when police or fire officials let the press in, although it's sometimes been ruled that only the authorities themselves are privileged at such times against trespass charges, not the press.

Don't think journalists can automatically go anywhere and take pictures without permission. Schools, prisons and mental hospitals, for example, can require written permission. A shopping mall is private property, and mall authorities can ask the press to leave or require approval to take pictures. Even owners of a house or building that has burned down have a right to demand that you not take pictures on the property—and you must obey or be guilty of trespassing.

The best defense against an intrusion lawsuit is that you had permission to be there or to take pictures—usually from the owner but in some situations, in certain states, from law enforcement, fire or disaster authorities.

Also, note there may be state laws against using hidden cameras or privately recording someone's words without permission. This has sometimes been found to be a problem with undercover stories. In some states, you must have permission of the other person to record a phone interview. In other states, it's enough that only one of you wants to record the conversation. Ones in which both parties of a conversation must consent include California, Connecticut, Florida, Illinois, Maryland, Massachusetts, Montana, Nevada, New Hampshire, Pennsylvania and Washington.

A file photo of someone used to illustrate an unrelated story could bring a "false-light" invasion-of-privacy lawsuit. Depicting someone in print in a "false light" is similar in many ways to libel, and this is the only kind of invasion-of-privacy lawsuit against which truth is a valid defense. Using a picture of a woman standing on a street corner to illustrate a story about prostitution would be an example. If the woman in the photograph *is* a prostitute, you're off the hook. If she's a college student waiting for a bus, you're in trouble if she sues.

An advertisement using someone's image, name or voice without permission—considered appropriation—is legal grounds for a lawsuit. Celebrities have won lawsuits for this. More jurisdictions are even allowing surviving relatives to bring privacy actions against the exploitation of names, images or voices of deceased relatives. The best defense is to make sure permission was first obtained.

Anonymous Sources

Beware if you see an anonymous source quoted in a story, especially if allegations are being made that could result in criminal or civil actions. They can be a legal problem, and readers don't trust anonymous sources—they reduce a paper's credibility.

Most states, but not the federal government, have some form of **shield law**—a law protecting journalists from having to reveal the name of their source, similar to protections for attorneys and their clients, doctors and their patients, or priests and their penitents. But even with such a law, courts have sometimes forced journalists to reveal sources or go to jail. And at least one court case has also decided that if a journalist reneges on a promise of anonymity, the journalist may be liable in a breach-of-contract suit.

Instead of using anonymous sources, a reporter should try to get the source to go on the record. Failing that, the source should be asked to sign an agreement that the journalist will keep the source's name a secret short of going to jail.

As an editor, check on your media outlet's policy on the use of anonymous sources. If the use of an anonymous source violates your employer's policy, then point it out. If not, you might want to protect yourself by not trying to discover the source. If the reporter tells you, then you, too, risk being ordered to reveal the name in court or go to jail.

Obscenity

Chances are you won't have to worry about **obscenity** while working for a newspaper. But if you're working for a medium with less conservative standards, such as many magazines or websites, you should know that something is considered legally obscene if it:

- Appeals to the "prurient interest" of (or would arouse) the average person, applying contemporary community standards to the work as a whole.

- Depicts or describes sexual conduct in a patently offensive way.
- Lacks, as a whole, serious literary, artistic, political or scientific value.

Notice that all of these standards are problematic because they are vague and subjective.

Intellectual Property

Intellectual property rights are provided for by the Constitution, and the media are not free to violate them. To avoid problems, follow this advice:

Give credit where credit is due. If a wire service sends out a story based on the story of another media outlet, you should not delete the wire-service credit to the originator of the story. You may, if directed, compile stories from various sources into one comprehensive story, adding the sources from which the story was compiled.

Quote as little of the copyrighted work as possible. A rule of thumb is to avoid quoting 250-word-plus excerpts (some book publishers say 500 words) of books or articles without permission. But this is merely a rule of thumb, not a set number of words established by law. Instead, the law specifies that the work cannot be substantially appropriated without permission. That involves looking at what percentage of the work has been reproduced and what effect that might have on reducing the market value of the original for the copyright holder.

Don't lift photos, art or graphics, or audio or video clips, from other publications, including encyclopedias or websites, without permission or credit. AP warns against lifting "quotes, photos or video from social networking sites," even when you attribute them to the site where it was found. Instead, it says you should verify the information and make sure proper rights for reuse are obtained.

Merely linking to other pages from your web page doesn't usually pose a legal problem. Some websites, such as the Drudge Report (www.drudgereport.com) and WorldNetDaily (www.worldnetdaily.com), provide headlines and descriptions of stories that you click on to be taken to the web page of origin. A legal problem would arise, however, if the descriptions appropriated too much of the original story or if the linked pages appeared within a frame, making it appear they were part of the original content of your website.

Don't violate trademarks by using them lowercase as generic terms. Companies invest much money into making their brand names known. But if people generically use a brand name, the company can lose the right to its exclusive use, as happened with the former brand names *aspirin* and *nylon*.

So, if you let slip by a mention in a story of a brand-name product in lowercase as though it were a generic term—such as *kitty litter* for cat-box filler or *styrofoam* for foam plastic—your newspaper is likely to receive a letter from the company explaining you've misused its brand name and threatening a lawsuit if you do it again.

Avoiding Trademark Infringement

Here's a list of some of the most commonly misused trademark names and their generic alternatives.

Brand Name	Generic
Aqua-Lung	underwater breathing apparatus
AstroTurf	artificial grass
Band-Aid	adhesive bandage
Chap Stick	lip balm
Coke	cola
Crayola	crayons
Crock-Pot	electric earthenware cooker
Fudgsicle	fudge ice-cream bar
Google	internet search engine
Hi-Liter	highlighting marker
iPad	tablet computer
Jacuzzi	whirlpool bath
Jell-O	gelatin
Jockey shorts	underwear
Kitty Litter	cat-box filler
Kleenex	tissue
Kool-Aid	soft-drink mix
Krazy Glue	super adhesive
Little League Baseball	youth baseball
Magic Marker	felt-tip marking pen
Novocain	procaine hydrochloride
Oreo	cookie
Ping-Pong	table tennis
Popsicle	flavored ice on a stick
Post-it	self-stick note
Q-Tip	cotton swab
Realtor	real-estate agent
Rollerblade	in-line skate

Brand Name	Generic
Scotch tape	cellophane tape
Seeing Eye dog	guide dog
Sheetrock	gypsum wallboard
Styrofoam	foam plastic
Vaseline	petroleum jelly
Velcro	adhesive fastener
Viagra	erectile-dysfunction drug
Ziploc	zippered plastic bag

Censorship of School Newspapers

The courts have said student newspapers do not receive full First Amendment protection from censorship by school authorities. In 1988, for example, in the case of *Hazelwood School District v. Kuhlmeier*, the Supreme Court said a school board can decide what's appropriate to be printed in a school newspaper and upheld the decision of the school to delete two pages including an article on pregnancy and divorce.

Justice White wrote for the majority: "Exercising editorial control over the style and content of student speech in school-sponsored expressive activities" is the absolute right of school administrators, as long as their "actions are reasonably related to legitimate pedagogical concerns."

In various cases, the courts have said public school K–12 authorities may censor student publications that:

- Undermine school discipline.
- Violate rights of students.
- Fail to meet standards of academic propriety.
- Generate health and welfare concerns.
- Are obscene, indecent or vulgar.

The ability of colleges and universities to censor school newspapers is less clear. The Hazelwood decision applied to high schools but left open the matter of censorship of college newspapers. Could the same school discipline argument hold with college students, who are, after all, more mature?

Typical reasons administrators use to censor college and university publications include cutting out materials that:

- Portray the institution in an unfavorable light, such as stories and statistics about crime on campus that detract from the blissful image in the recruitment materials. Some colleges have even tried to hide from

the public statistics about crime on campus, refusing to release them, although this has been illegal under federal law since 1992.
- Might be confused with official school positions.
- Are not "politically correct" according to the college PC speech code (which, by the way, seems to get thrown out by courts whenever challenged, as in the case of *Doe v. Michigan* back in 1989).
- Are ads for potentially harmful products like tobacco or alcohol, or about controversial issues, such as denying the Holocaust or opposing reparations to African-Americans for slavery. Often, administrators claim that such ads might anger students—student activist groups have stolen entire runs of student newspapers 30 to 40 times some years to try to suppress views with which they disagree.

But for a while, it seemed as though the courts made a distinction between high school and college publications:

- A District Court ruled in 1967 that a student newspaper editor at Troy State College in Alabama could not be punished for failing to print an article the school's administration wanted printed.
- Another District Court ruled in 1983 that the University of Minnesota could not cut funding for the student newspaper when it was not a matter of reducing fees but to punish the newspaper for printing content that some thought was offensive.
- A U.S. Court of Appeals ruled in 2001 that Kentucky State University could not censor the yearbook because it was created as a public forum and was not made by students for a grade.

Then, however, in 2003, in the case of *Hosty v. Carter*, a U.S. Court of Appeals acting *en banc* (all the judges) overturned the decision of a three-judge panel of the same body and decided that the Hazelwood decision applies to colleges, as well. The Student Press Law Center was joined by other media-rights groups in trying to get the U.S. Supreme Court to overrule the decision, but the court declined to hear it.

Special Legal Issues Faced by Broadcast Media

The Federal Communications Commission (FCC) decides the locations where stations will be granted, assigns their frequencies and call letters, classifies them as to what kind of service they must render, regulates the kind of equipment they must use and issues licenses for the station operators (currently renewable every seven years). In addition, the FCC regulates decency of speech and political content.

Why are the rules so different for **broadcast media** than for print media? Why are they not as fully protected from regulation as the print media? Shouldn't the same First Amendment arguments against licensing the press or resorting to other forms of censorship also apply to broadcast and other electronic media, such as the internet? Here are two of the most common reasons given for regulation of broadcast, the original electronic media, along with opposing viewpoints:

First, those favoring the regulation of broadcast said radio and television are different from print because of the scarcity of the airwaves and the need to allocate frequencies so that stations don't interfere with each other.

But it can be argued that broadcast frequencies aren't scarce today and will become less so in the future. Newspapers are far scarcer now than radio or television stations. Most cities have at most one newspaper but many radio and television stations, not to mention cable stations and internet sources. And yet, broadcast is regulated, but print is not.

Also, new technologies are changing electronic media. Cable, satellite and internet delivery of radio and television are giving over-the-air broadcasting serious competition. And new compression technologies are making it possible to carry far more station signals in a smaller space, meaning new opportunities are opening up for more stations, even if new spectrum isn't discovered.

What about the idea that someone needs to license and assign frequencies so stations won't interfere with each other's signal? Congress assumed the only way to do this was for the government to own the airwaves and regulate content.

But why not use the same procedure as with land? The government said Western land belonged to whoever claimed it first. The government does not own all land and license it to you. Instead, the government registers deeds and adjudicates disputes. Ayn Rand wrote an article on this, "The Property Status of Airwaves," in *Capitalism: The Unknown Ideal,* and others, such as writers for the Cato Institute, have proposed similar ideas.

This led to the second main reason given for regulation: **Those favoring the regulation of broadcast said the airwaves should belong to the people.** Once Congress decided the government would hold ownership of the airwaves on behalf of *all* the people rather than let the people themselves own a deed on a frequency for a given locale like other property rights, the requirement followed that broadcast had to be operated for the "public interest, convenience and necessity" rather than the interest of the station owners. In other words, licensees had to be "socially responsible," as defined by whoever ran the government rather than by the stations themselves responding to their audience. This approach opened the gate to censorship—the government controlling speech.

Whichever side you take on the two reasons above most often given to support government regulation of the airwaves, the government has also regulated broadcast for less defensible purposes:

The government has limited eligibility to use the airwaves based on wealth. Historically, the best wavelengths were given to those with the most money and the best equipment. Those without as much money—educational, religious and labor-backed stations—got the worst frequencies and sometimes even had to timeshare them. The result? In 1927, there were 98 educational stations, but by 1937, just three years after the Communications Act was passed, there were only 43.

The government has used its licensing power to suppress political opponents. Both Democratic and Republican presidents have used their control over the FCC to harass political opponents. Richard Nixon ordered his people to look into making license renewals tough on the *Washington Post*'s broadcast holdings after that paper's Bob Woodward and Carl Bernstein started exposing him in its Watergate stories.

Likewise, President John Kennedy's assistant secretary of commerce, Bill Ruder, admitted:

> Our strategy was to use the Fairness Doctrine to challenge and harass right-wing broadcasters and hope that the challenges would be so costly to them that they would be inhibited and decide it was too expensive to continue.

Unfettering the Electronic Media

Our lawmakers and courts have never fully acknowledged that electronic media should be free for the same reasons as print. Justice Oliver Wendell Holmes said, for example, in the early 20th century: "The radio as it now operates among us is not free. Nor is it entitled to the protection of the First Amendment. It is not engaged in the task of enlarging human communication." To answer Justice Holmes, **here are some reasons electronic media should be as free as the print media and why journalists of all kinds should be concerned**:

- **Broadcast and online media have replaced print media as most of the public's main source of news. If these media aren't as fully protected as print, freedom of the press means less than the Founders intended by the First Amendment.** The First Amendment doesn't specifically mention radio, television, cable or satellite broadcasting, or the internet—they hadn't been invented, yet!—and Congress has regulated them as it legally can't print media.
- **Electronic media should be unfettered for the same reasons that we have the First Amendment for print.** We need a free marketplace of ideas, an informed public in a democracy, the right of self-expression and the right to consume what messages we want.

- **Regulation of broadcast creates a climate of opinion favorable to regulating all the media.** If broadcasters can be required to give equal time to opposing views, why can't newspapers or magazines or book publishers?
- **New technologies mean more voices and the democratization of the media, so why regulate the very technologies that are doing what press critics want? Where's the scarcity now?** Media critic A.J. Leibling used to say that, in the U.S., there's freedom of the press only for those who own one. But everyone can "own" one now posting something online.

Regulations That Have Applied Only to Broadcast

The famous Fairness Doctrine of 1949 is no longer legally mandated, although it's often confused with the still enforced Section 315 of the Communications Act of 1934.

The Fairness Doctrine was an FCC rule, not a statute. It applied not to candidates, as does Section 315, but to controversial issues of public interest. Each broadcaster was required to give "reasonable" opportunity for the presentation of conflicting viewpoints on controversial issues of public importance.

There were various later additions to the Fairness Doctrine provisions. The FCC ruled in 1963 that if a paid ad gave one side of an issue, the media had to give the other side free time if it couldn't afford to pay for an opposing ad. The FCC granted free time to anti-smoking messages under the Fairness Doctrine. A Court of Appeals went one step further, saying the cigarette ruling could not be limited to cigarettes. Friends of the Earth then argued that gasoline ads were only one side of the issue, and anti-pollution messages should be aired free. But the FCC refused, insisting that cigarettes were unique.

Also in the 1960s, the FCC ruled the Fairness Doctrine included an entitlement to reply to a personal attack and an entitlement to reply to an editorial.

The **Personal Attack Rule of 1967** said that when an attack was made on the honesty, character or integrity of a person or group during public discussion, that person or group must be given the opportunity to respond.

The **Political Editorializing Rule of 1967** said that when a licensee editorialized for or against a particular candidate—or even for or against an issue identified with a particular candidate, even if the candidate's name wasn't mentioned—the broadcaster had to notify rivals and afford them time to respond. For years, the broadcaster wasn't protected if someone given Fairness Doctrine time libeled someone else, but that was eventually changed.

With the Fairness Doctrine, the FCC was saying, in essence, that the public's entitlement to be informed took precedence over the right of the station to exercise editorial judgment. The government could override editorial discretion in the electronic media to force them to carry opposing views.

But in 2000, the U.S. Court of Appeals for the District of Columbia ordered the FCC to repeal the Personal Attack and Political Editorializing rules immediately. The court said that the rules "interfere with editorial judgment of professional journalists and entangle the government in day-to-day operations of the media."

As we said, the FCC established the Fairness Doctrine in 1949 to try to make sure there was a greater diversity of opinions presented in broadcasting. And in 1969, the FCC's power to require stations to air opposing views was upheld by the U.S. Supreme Court.

But the Fairness Doctrine didn't kick in until one side of a controversy was already aired, so stations would sometimes try to get around it by not airing controversy, especially after the Supreme Court ruled in 1976 that the licensee could determine what was a controversial issue of public importance. Broadcasting became more bland and less controversial for fear of having to provide free time to special-interest groups or face license challenges. Whatever the intention, the result was actually self-censorship and less presentation of public issues.

In August 1987, the FCC repealed the Fairness Doctrine. Congress tried to reinstate it by law, but it was vetoed by President Ronald Reagan. With the rule no longer in place, controversy returned to broadcast in the form of more news-talk radio formats and separate conservative and liberal talk and commentary shows, such as Rush Limbaugh on radio and Rachel Maddow on TV.

Although the Fairness Doctrine is gone, the FCC still regulates broadcast content in these ways:

All candidates in a primary or general election must be given an "equal opportunity"—not "equal time," as many people mistakenly think—to buy commercial time and be charged the lowest rate. Section 315 of the Communications Act of 1934 says that all candidates must have available to them an "equal opportunity" to air their views if one candidate for the same office has already done so on any given station. And you can't get around Section 315 by putting supporters on the air rather than the candidate, according to the Zapple rule. But news coverage is exempt from Section 315's equal opportunity provision under a 1959 amendment that says each candidate does not have to be equally covered because one may be making more news than another.

By the way, broadcasters cannot censor a political advertisement, but neither can they be held responsible in case of a legal action over the political ad. But broadcast stations generally don't have to accept ads they don't want to run. The Supreme Court ruled in the 1973 case of *CBS Inc. v. Democratic National Committee* that the "public interest" standard of the Communication Act does not require broadcasters to accept editorial advertising. Chief Justice Burger wrote: "For better or worse, editing is what editors are for, and editing is selection and choice of material. That editors—newspaper or broadcast—can and do abuse this power is beyond doubt, but that is not reason to deny the discretion Congress provided." One might wonder, then, why broadcast is regulated at all.

The FCC regulates indecency. The FCC traditionally outlawed what comedian George Carlin called "Seven Words You Can Never Say on Television" (*shit, piss, fuck, cunt, cocksucker, motherfucker* and *tits*) on his 1973 album *Class Clown*. In a 1978 case challenging the broadcast of an updated version of that comedy bit over the radio (that is, not the original one but the bit "Filthy Words" from his next album), the court ruled broadcasting it was not obscene but could be deemed unfit for broadcast by reason of indecency.

The FCC now defines *indecency* as "language or material that depicts or describes, in terms patently offensive as measured by contemporary community standards for the broadcast medium, sexual or excretory activities or organs." That standard, similarly to the standards for obscenity, is rather vague and subjective. Still, Congress passed a 24-hour ban of indecent broadcasts in 1988, but this was ruled unconstitutional in 1991. After a series of new partial bans by the FCC, eventually, in 1995, a panel of judges decided the FCC could ban indecency except between 10 p.m. and 6 a.m.

The Prime Time Access Rule of 1970 mandated non-network programming from 7:30 p.m. to 8 p.m. EST six days a week. The result of the rule was not more local programming but more syndicated programming, such as game shows and tabloid-television shows. The rule was repealed in 1995.

Every seven years at license-renewal time, each station owner must show that the station has operated in the public interest and be able to withstand any challengers from the community who might want to claim it has not. In 1943, the U.S. Supreme Court ruled in *NBC v. U.S.* that the Federal Communications Commission is not restricted merely to supervising traffic on the broadcast airwaves. The FCC must also make sure stations serve "public interest, convenience or necessity." This phrase was taken from a South Dakota public utilities regulation, and indeed the broadcast media are treated more like public utilities to be regulated than part of a system of free press left unlicensed and uncensored.

Satellite Broadcast Law

The FCC was going to exempt direct-broadcast satellite networks from ownership and political access requirements that other broadcasters must follow, but broadcasters sued. In *National Association of Broadcasters v. FCC* (1984), the court said satellite broadcasters must meet the same standards for these as over-the-air broadcasts. But **satellite TV and radio enjoy greater freedom when it comes to indecency.**

Special Legal Issues Faced by Online Media

Media law is constantly changing, and one of the latest major areas of development comes from the government's attempts to figure out what to do about the internet. This is where things stand so far:

It's safer to assume that laws applying to both print and broadcast—such as libel, privacy and intellectual property—also apply to the internet.

For example, the same standards for libel apply on the internet as in print, but jurisdictional issues make it harder to bring a lawsuit and win it, as we'll discuss later. Different states, for example, have different definitions of libel and different lengths for their statute of limitations.

One potential problem comes from a 2011 9th Circuit Court of Appeals case in which the court ruled the names of anonymous writers on a website can be subpoenaed in case of defamatory remarks.

Copyright laws in print also apply on the web. For example, the Digital Millennium Copyright Act of 1998 says that copyright law applies to material posted online, including emails and discussion forums. So, get permission before reprinting online material, including photos or graphics linked to another site but stripped out of the original context. But a brief description of an article with a link to the whole article on another site does not violate copyright unless the article was stripped out of context by being imported into a frame or page that makes it appear to be your own content.

Statements online that bully others pose legal problems online just as they would elsewhere. No federal law directly addresses bullying, but if it's based on race, sex, disability, national origin or religion, it can be addressed as discriminatory harassment. Titles IV and IX do not explicitly mention sexual orientation, but the law can be stretched to cover harassment based on nonconformity to sex-based stereotypes.

If you run a website, you should know, though, that in 2007, at least seven states passed laws against cyber bullying, and as of January 2016, altogether 24 states and the District of Columbia had. Even more—48 states and the District of Columbia—had passed cyber harassment laws. So these, along with libel, invasion of privacy and copyright violations, may be something to check for in posts.

In the area of privacy, online and mobile-media journalists may face additional problems over print and broadcast media:

- **It's not legally clear whether you forfeit privacy rights concerning things you post at sites like Facebook. For now, employers for one can and do use this information because you made it public.**
- **The Child Online Protection Act of 1998 said sites can't gather info on children under 18 without a parent's consent. Federal courts have ruled it unconstitutional. So they can.**

- **The USA Patriot Act of 2001 gave law enforcement power to intercept emails and web browsing.**

To what extent the internet will remain relatively free, like print, rather than more restrictive, like broadcast, remains open. Given the government's reluctance to apply full First Amendment protection to previous electronic media, it's probably more likely that the internet will see greater regulation in the future.

Attempts so far by the government to censor offensive content on the internet have largely failed, but there's still reason for concern. The FCC has claimed the Communications Act of 1934 gives it authority to regulate the internet, although it mainly hasn't tried.

The Telecommunications Act of 1996's Title V said government could regulate the internet for obscenity and also prohibited all discussion of abortion. The law prohibited sending indecent, patently offensive or obscene material to minors. But the Supreme Court said obscenity could be banned as in print but not things merely patently offensive because that was only one of three tests for obscenity. The law was overly broad, in other words. But possession of child porn on your computer, including cartoons or computer-generated images, can put you in prison.

Likewise, a federal appeals court struck down a federal judge's ban on an anti-abortion website, The Nuremberg Files, from publishing wanted posters of doctors who performed abortions. It had published the photo and address of a Buffalo, N.Y., abortion doctor who was then murdered. The reversal was because it hadn't been shown the murderer had found the information through the site.

But the Supreme Court ruled in *Reno v. ACLU* (1997) the internet should be treated legally more like print than broadcast, with full First Amendment rights, because it did not use a scarce spectrum like broadcast.

Posting your views opposing tax increases or some government spending can actually run afoul of state lobbying laws and even result in a prison term. John Stossel reported the following in 2014 about surprising possible legal dangers in posting political views online: In 14 states, it's potentially illegal to post on a website that you oppose a tax increase. Even without urging others to do likewise, and completely unconnected to a candidate or political party, your posting could be construed as lobbying under state law, and you could face imprisonment of up to four years in New York or 30 in Alabama. This would depend on its being a matter potentially before the state Legislature and crossing some dollar threshold defined by law. (By the way, it would be illegal, Stossel said, in 36 states to mail out a flier urging people to oppose some government spending unless you registered as a lobbyist.)

Keep an eye on possible changes in Section 230 of the U.S. Code, as we've said, over the power of internet companies, especially big near-monopoly ones controlling search engines,

popular social media sites, app stores and internet servers. (See pages 121–122.)

Lawsuits over web content can pose legal nightmares over jurisdictional issues. No one owns the internet, and although some individual countries regulate it within their borders, there is no international regulatory agency, except for ICANN, a California nonprofit corporation that sets technical standards and name allocations. Legal jurisdiction can involve the jurisdiction of the receiver, the sender and the server. There is no uniform international jurisdictional law.

The law is unsettled over how to treat online journalists. Citizen journalism with smartphones and blogs now means, in the words of one book title, "We're all journalists now." This poses a special problem for state shield laws for journalists as well as policies about granting journalists access to events both private and public, including presidential press conferences and Supreme Court hearings where space is limited.

This came up in a case in 2010 and two more in 2011. In 2010, the New Hampshire Supreme Court ruled a commercial website that presented information on mortgage lenders was covered by the journalist's privilege because "Freedom of the press is a fundamental personal right which is not confined to newspapers and periodicals."

But in 2011, the Supreme Court of New Jersey ruled that contributing to message boards did not make you a journalist covered by state shield law. And a U.S. District Court ruled in Oregon that year that a blogger was not a journalist because she was not affiliated with a traditional media outlet.

Ethical Issues Facing Journalists

The joke is that journalism ethics is an oxymoron, a contradiction in terms, like "military intelligence"—that in journalism, ethics don't matter, and that all that does matter is getting the story.

But most journalists don't think that way. People who go into journalism mainly care greatly about their fellow human beings. So, for most journalists, deciding whether to publish information shouldn't end with asking whether it's news and whether publishing it might pose legal problems. Sometimes, newsworthy, legally safe information won't get published because of ethical objections. **Ethics involves doing what's right even when it's legal to do what's wrong.**

Ethical Flashing Lights

You probably think of yourself as an ethical person and that a discussion of ethics is something you can skip over. **But many times, as a journalist you will find yourself facing a possible ethics problem and not even knowing it.**

The No. 1 reason journalism students give for going into the field is that they want to change the world. But consider this: **If you sign a petition, wear a candidate's button or have a bumper sticker on your car that supports a cause, you are probably violating your employer's ethics policy.** News outlets often ban such displays of political viewpoints even by journalists not covering politics. But, oddly, publishers may belong to groups like Rotary Club and be friends with the powerful people the paper cover. And increasingly, reporters and anchors at cable news outlets seem more like commentators, blatantly taking sides on political issues. The situation, then, can be confusing, especially for a young journalist starting out.

Here's another example of being in a possible ethics violation without knowing it. **Accepting anything from a source can be a conflict of interest.** For example, if you're a travel writer and accept a free trip to Cancún, you could find yourself out of work. It could also even be considered unethical to let a City Council member buy you a cup of coffee and a piece of pie while you conduct an interview at a cafe.

Even though you think you can't be bought, and that no strings are attached to the trip or the snack, your objectivity is compromised by the acceptance of favors, and your credibility, too. (But most news outlets wouldn't insist sports writers buy their own tickets to sporting events and not sit in the news boxes, and many would allow reviewers to receive free books, CDs or movie disks.)

To help you determine whether you may be facing an ethical problem, here are the kinds of ethical questions you might face as a journalist, along with a number of examples of each and even some typical answers. Think of this as a list of warning signs that what you are about to run deserves a second look—not that running such information would necessarily be ethically wrong in all cases.

Should you run information that is not objectively true or that may be deceptive?

- **Misinforming or failing to inform in a story if the deception might serve a public good.** What if the government asks you to run or not run certain information, perhaps to ease or prevent public fears or to deny a terrorist publicity? What if promoters of a good cause ask you not to report adverse reaction to a social program of theirs aimed at a desirable goal? (Most journalists would probably refuse.)

- **Leaving out information that might be relevant to a story if people involved ask you to.** What if the family of a person who died of AIDS or suicide asks you not to include that information in the obituary? What if the victim of a nonsexual assault asks you to leave his name out of the story because he's embarrassed he was beat up? (Most journalists would probably refuse.)

- **Stretching the facts or stressing only the most sensational angle to have a more interesting story.** (Most journalists would say this is wrong, but many nonetheless sometimes do it.)
- **Quoting out of context.** (Journalists would say this is wrong, but not everyone would likely agree on what the real context is.)
- **Selecting material to fit a preconceived story idea.** (Many journalists haven't thought about this one and do it more often than they would if they did think about it.)
- **Creating a pseudoevent, staging a photograph or writing a letter, ostensibly from a reader, to reveal certain information or to begin an advice column.** (This was more common in the past than now.)
- **Taking a side, other than in an editorial, a news analysis or, to a lesser extent, a sports story or a feature.** This extends not just to words in news stories but also in tweets and to broadcasters using a sarcastic tone of voice or gestures like eye rolls revealing clearly their own opinion about a quote or person, especially in a political context.

  But with the growing partisanship of many news outlets, the issue of whether to give the target audience what it wants or to try to be as objective as possible becomes a growing concern, not only for the ethics of individual journalists but also for the credibility of the news outlet and field of journalism as a whole.

  (Most journalists try to be objective or at least fair, but fewer seem successful at keeping out their biases. Journalists who go to work for partisan outlets at least think they're being objective or fair if the outlet's bias matches their own, but this can be a rationalization and illusion, and even as commentators they should try to mentally detach from their biases and comment fairly based on provable facts, not mere vitriol. As for social-media postings, journalists sometimes forget they are representatives of their news outlets as well as private citizens with opinions, so AP now advises in its "Social Media Guidelines" for its own employees that "if you or your department covers a subject . . . you have a special obligation to be even-handed in your tweets." It also advises them not to declare their views online on "contentious public issues in any public forum," even liking, following or friending on sites like Facebook any candidates, causes or movements "without a journalistic reason for doing so," according to *The AP Stylebook*.)
- **Blurring distinctions between ads and copy.** (Better publications, stations and websites avoid this.)
- **Not covering an important story or burying it inside as a small story.** (No one will tell you this is a good idea, but people disagree about the relative news value of stories.)

Should you obtain information in nonopen, nonlegal or questionable ways?

- **Use of anonymous sources.** (This can pose both legal and ethical problems but is commonly done.)
- **Use of off-the-record statements.** (This can pose not only an ethics problem, but also a legal one if a source sues you for breach of contract. But what would you do if someone told you, off the record, information that would be an important scoop? Some reporters might break their promise, for good or bad.)
- **Use of stolen or otherwise illegally obtained information.** If someone told you they'd broken into an office and found documents proving who killed a public figure, what would you say? (Printing stolen documents may or may not be illegal, as the 1971 Pentagon Papers case, more formally known as *New York Times Co. v. United States*, proved. That is, it's normally illegal, but the Supreme Court ultimately OK'd it in that case because of its importance. Is it ethical, though? Do the ends justify the means?)
- **Use of information obtained in trade for favorable treatment.** (Probably no one would tell you this is ethical, but it's sometimes done if the information is important enough and the favorable treatment is small enough.)
- **Use of sting operations, undercover investigations, eavesdropping, clandestine recording or photography, or other nonidentification of the reporter as such.** Is it ever OK to research a story without telling your sources you're a journalist and that what they say may be printed? Is it ethical to impersonate someone else to get a story? Is it ethical to go undercover as a patient to get a story about abortion counseling or conditions in a state mental hospital? (Sometimes, there may be no better way to get the information. But there is much debate about the ethics of such techniques, and such matters can seem ethical to you but still be illegal.)
- **The appearance of conflict of interest, even if it doesn't influence what is published**—such as holding stock investments in a company you or your paper covers; freelancing as a media consultant, PR adviser or speech writer; or taking honorariums to speak to corporations or lobbying groups your paper might cover. (Most media outlets would not allow this, but some well-known broadcast journalists have gotten away with things like this.)
- **Accepting special privileges or gifts not accorded the general public.** What freebies, if any, are acceptable while working as a journalist? Lunch bought by a source? Recordings or books that come in the mail for review? Tickets to concerts, games or speeches? Special

press seating at a game? Special preview showings not open to the public of movies or plays? Trips on chartered planes to cover sporting events? Transportation and accommodations for a travel story? (The policies on this are mixed. A common principle seems to be such freebies are acceptable only if they are not worth more than a certain small dollar amount—often about $20.)

- **Plagiarism**—Journalists often get facts from other stories, even without crediting them, but they usually won't take direct quotes. Lifted quotes should be kept to a minimum, and credit should be given to the original source unless it was another writer at the same publication.)

- **Involvement in politics or causes.** To what extent can you be a journalist—as opposed to a commentator—and be involved in politics? Should journalists mix their own personal political opinions into news stories or select information to support their opinions, even when they think (as people usually do) that they are right? Should journalists run for political office? What if it's for the school board? How about putting a political bumper sticker on your car or wearing a campaign button? What about becoming involved in the Rotary Club, the PTA or a neighborhood crime-watch group? Should a publisher have any more latitude than a reporter? Should a journalist publicly take sides on political or social issues such as abortion, the Black Lives Matter organization or protests against a pandemic shutdown? Would it make any difference if this were not an issue the reporter covers? Why do you suppose many newspapers take stands on issues like these on their editorial page but forbid their own reporters to speak or tweet out their private views if they are controversial? (Policies vary and are often inconsistent.)

Should you publish information that is harmful to individuals in stories?

- **Information that violates someone's privacy.** Is it ever ethical to invade someone's privacy to get the news? Is it ethical to go through someone's trash for information? To stake out a politician's house to see whether he or she is cheating on a spouse? To publicize crimes or sins of people related to someone famous? (Of course, this poses possibly severe legal consequences as well as ethical questions.)

- **Information that may conflict with someone's right to a fair trial.** (Although legal to print it, a media outlet should also consider the fairness of its coverage. After all, what if the suspect is not guilty and the coverage railroads him or her?)

- **Names and addresses.** What about victims of crimes other than sexual assaults? Are the common practices of routinely printing the ages and addresses of people in stories an invasion of privacy and possibly a threat to their safety? What about printing addresses in obituary notices? Burglars often use the obituaries in a newspaper as a shopping list. They know the survivors will be out of their houses attending the funeral, so they hit the best houses during the services. Should newspapers stop printing the addresses of the survivors of the deceased in an obituary, or doesn't it matter because the burglars could just look them up online?

(It's legal to print the names or addresses of victims of sexual crimes. The Supreme Court has said newspapers have the right to print the names of rape victims and details about the crime.

But addresses can be another matter. For example, printing in a newspaper or online the address of a victim of an attempted rape may constitute negligence if the assault had not been at the person's home and the assailant is still on the loose—he might use that information to find the victim again. Also, a news outlet might be legally and ethically safer giving the address and age of a person charged in a crime because if someone else in the area has the same name, the audience might mistakenly think he or she was the suspect.

Names and addresses are usually given in local newspapers except for victims of sex crimes and juvenile offenders. In obituaries, addresses aren't usually published for the deceased or survivors of the deceased. Broadcast outlets almost never give an address but may refer to a block or section of town. Online media's policy tends to vary along the lines of newspapers'.)

- **Names of juvenile offenders.** (Although the law may prevent authorities from releasing the names of juvenile offenders, it can't prevent a news outlet from publishing, broadcasting or posting those it knows. Not releasing such names, then, is an ethical rather than a legal consideration for the media. Most news outlets usually withhold these but may release them in the case of a particularly serious and famous crime.)

- **Expunged criminal records, information about previous convictions (especially misdemeanor crimes such as minor drug arrests), or information about mental-health problems.** (These are legally publishable if obtained, although all of them pose an ethics issue. Many news outlets typically won't publish, broadcast or post them—and in the case of someone's medical records, releasing such information could potentially spark an invasion-of-privacy lawsuit.)

- **Confessions.** (News outlets often won't publish, broadcast or post a confession until it is accepted as evidence in court, but if the case is important enough, one outlet is likely to release it, and the others will then typically follow suit once the information is out there.

It's legal to print that someone has confessed to a crime both before and after the confession is admitted into court. But many news outlets will tell you generally to avoid printing that someone confessed beforehand, even when police tell you this. Why? Confessions can be recanted or thrown out of court if they were derived under duress or before someone's Miranda rights were read to them. But it remains an ethical issue because it can influence a jury, perhaps denying someone a fair trial even if the confession is thrown out by the judge.)

Should you publish information that is potentially harmful to society?

- **How to commit a crime.** You learn that a con game is being played in your area to cheat elderly people out of their savings. Should you run a story explaining the con so readers can avoid it, or might that teach others how to run the con themselves? (Most outlets would run the story.)
- **Information that could hamper a criminal investigation.** (Most outlets probably won't publish such information if specifically asked not to. In big stories, the press does sometimes get in the way of police investigators as it pursues scoops.)
- **Information the government says must be kept secret for national security reasons.** You learn the president of the U.S. plans to invade a certain foreign country. Should you scoop your competition and announce this? (Most media outlets would not, but it has been done.)
- **Publicity crimes—when the press is held hostage.** This occurs when someone takes hostages until publicity is granted for a cause. (Taking such action should at least spark a debate in the newsroom before the decision is made.)
- **Ads of harmful products, such as tobacco and alcohol.** (Some publications exercise more restrictions than others on which products they will or will not accept for advertising.)

Should you accept restraints on the press?

- **From the government.** Should editorials champion a free press, then inconsistently promote the causes of "social responsibility" of the press, restraining sex and violence on TV, mandating more children's educational or quality programming, and banning or restraining certain kinds of advertisements? (Journalists often have mixed premises that prevent them from seeing how all of these positions place limits on the freedom of the press they cherish.)
- **From owners or managers.** If your publisher asks you to slant a story a certain way because it involves a friend or advertiser, should you abide by that wish? (Of course, the owner gets to make the rules, but you have to decide whether your job is more important than your ethics.)

- **From sources.** If someone gives you good information, then afterward asks that it not be run, should you abide by this request? Should you ever read a story back to a source to make sure it's accurate? If so, should you let the source reword a quotation to improve it or because he or she has now decided it would be better to say it in a less-pointed way? If a source says you've missed the point and taken an angle that suggests the wrong tone, what should you do? (Some papers see double-checking quotes with sources as responsible, but most see it as giving the source too much control over the story. The key if you do so is making clear that this is just an accuracy check, not a license for the source to rewrite the story as he or she would like.)

- **From yourself.** Should self-restraint over a story because you're shy or want to be a "nice guy" to sources be allowed to restrain you from getting to the truth? Are you willing to run negative news when appropriate, or will you avoid it because you're trying to be a town booster and want to focus on keeping up good relations with residents in order to survive economically? (You need to maintain independence to be objective, which may sometimes mean you have to put on your media hat and stand up for yourself as a journalist more than you might as a private individual.)

Deciding Ethics Issues

The Material Itself

- Is this newsworthy? Is this information relevant to the larger news story?
- Is this true, legal and ethical? Does this involve something that's ever right to run? Does the situation make this OK even though it may generally be wrong?
- Is this unbiased and fair? Does it sensationalize?
- Is this well-done?

Audience and Community

- Is this material appropriate for our audience? Is this something our audience needs to know, even though it may not want to?
- Should we decide whether the public should see this or have this information, or should we let people make up their own minds about its appropriateness?
- Would this information help our audience in any way, such as better understanding the world?

- Does this information point out a problem that needs to be solved?
- Would this information help prevent a similar situation from occurring again?
- Would this information hurt our audience by offending or prejudicing it? Does the information glamorize something destructive?

Sources and Those Concerned

- Is this fair to all concerned? What will be the consequences for everyone involved?
- Does the public's need to know this information count more than the harm we might be causing an individual?
- Would getting this information out violate anyone's trust?
- Does this information violate anyone's privacy? Is this public information?
- Would this information stigmatize innocent people?
- Are we exploiting anyone by running this?
- Are we treating this person as we treat everyone else in the same situation?
- Will this accomplish more good than harm? Is there a way to lessen any harm?

Yourself and Your Outlet

- What is my intent in running this? Is it honorable? Will I later feel proud or ashamed of myself for running this?
- How would I feel if someone ran this about me?
- Are we being consistent in our outlet's policies?
- Will publishing, broadcasting or posting this information damage our credibility?
- Will not publishing, broadcasting or posting this information look like we are hiding something or protecting somebody?
- Will this have repercussions on fellow journalists or the public's right to know?
- Can we afford the backlash in terms of lost subscribers, lost revenue, lost credibility and expensive lawsuits?
- If you work for an outlet aimed at a partisan market, or if you yourself are partisan regardless of your outlet, have you nonetheless told "the whole truth and nothing but the truth," as they say in court, sticking to the facts even while presenting opinion? (See pages 105–106.)

Finding Ethical Answers

Once you've identified a potential problem, where do you go for help in deciding whether it would be ethical?

- Consider your own religious and philosophical convictions about right and wrong.
- Consider the written or unwritten policy of your newspaper, magazine, station or online outlet on such matters. If there's not a written policy, consult with your editor.
- Consider the written policies of other media outlets or professional organizations. The Society of Professional Journalists publishes a code of journalistic ethics, available at www.spj.org/ethicscode.asp, as do a number of newspapers and other news organizations. Others are available in various books and on professional websites.

Propriety

When we speak of propriety in journalism, we mean selecting and presenting material that is appropriate for a specific audience. Media outlets with fairly selective, niche audiences—such as most magazines, newsletters and websites—may be liberal in the language and illustrations they use. Those with more general audiences—such as newspapers, broadcast outlets and some large websites—are typically more conservative in their standards.

A key question to ask is: Would this give unnecessary offense to our audience? Run the material if your audience would be receptive and if the material is newsworthy. Here are some examples for newspapers, which along with broadcast outlets, tend to be the most conservative in this area:

- **Nudity.** Usually, nude photographs are not published in a newspaper. But such photos might be if the nudity occurred in public or involved a legitimate news story, or if the nudity is covered enough in the photo to become less objectionable.
- **Obscene gestures, obscenity and profanity.** These, also, usually are not published in a newspaper without offsetting circumstances. An obscene gesture by a public official, candidate or religious leader might be published. Swear words might be published, provided they are mild, such as *damn* or *hell*. Offensive language might be published if part of a particularly powerful quote. Broadcast news outlets tend to be more conservative on such matters than the entertainment shows on the same channel or network.

- **Gore, tragedy and grief.** Newspapers usually reject these photos, despite the public's opinion that newspapers run them to increase sales. Actually, when such photos are run, people call to cancel their subscription in protest. Even television newscasters, for whom the slogan "if it bleeds, it leads" is well-known, face public outcry over broadcasting gruesome images or ones that intrude into private grief and suffering.

Sometimes, though, the news event captured is important enough or the message strong enough or the aesthetic quality great enough that the image is published anyway. But be prepared: Even photos that have won a Pulitzer Prize or other journalism awards have received large public outcries when originally published or broadcast. An example is Eddie Adams' famous Pulitzer Prize-winning photo of a Viet Cong prisoner being executed.

Being Sensitive

Included in propriety, and strongly related to both taste and objectivity, is the idea that journalists must show sensitivity to stereotyping or unfairly labeling people because of their race, ethnic or religious background, age, sex, sexual preference or handicap, or politics. More journalists by far are liberal rather than conservative, but whatever their politics, for most journalists, any bias along these lines is unconscious and unintentional, which makes it harder for an editor to spot. Journalists should strive to remove bias from their writing—not to push a politically correct agenda but because bias of any kind flies in the face of objective journalism.

We suggest these guidelines:

- **Avoid any obviously offensive language.** Examples: words like *bitch, cripple, geezer, gook, Holy Roller, wetback* and many others, including the infamous "N word." Sure, people have vastly different opinions about what is offensive, so it's impossible no matter how sensitive you are not to offend somebody at some time or other. But words like these are obviously offensive to many if not most, and why offend people needlessly, if it can be avoided?
- **Avoid merely gratuitous references to the categories of race, ethnicity, religion, age, sex, sexual preference and handicaps.** Examples: Why say, "Police are looking for a suspect who is a black male in his early 20s"? Such a description fits so many men as to be useless. Why comment on a woman's looks, dress or marital status when they have nothing to do with the story and when these would not be mentioned in a similar article about a man?

Awareness has been raised about these issues, and we see less of them these days, but they're still occasionally there. Some questions are less easy to answer: Is the practice many newspapers follow of routinely printing someone's age an ageist policy? Is it an invasion of privacy?

- **Avoid passages that may be prejudicial in effect even when not intended as such.** Both the *intent* and the *effect* of a statement deserve to be examined. After all, the severity of punishment for a crime is determined in part by trying to judge the intent of a perpetrator—a lighter sentence for unintended manslaughter than for a coldly plotted murder. Likewise, effect matters, too. We've all been a victim at one time or another of someone's ill-chosen words that stung deeply regardless of the innocent intent of the person speaking.

A difficult area in this regard involves the recent creation of lists of **microaggressions** to avoid, especially on college campuses. The term could be seen as a way of imposing the older idea of "political correctness" under another name. But many of these lists of microaggressions, or unintentionally offensive slights, generally having to do with stereotypes, especially racial ones, are dominated by things that should be considered obviously offensive and to be avoided regardless of political persuasion, such as "You're really pretty for a dark-skinned girl" or calling an Asian woman a "China doll" (see www.buzzfeed.com/hnigatu/racial-microaggressions-you-hear-on-a-daily-basis?utm_term=.gbBMqYNrK#.bjDO2gRqG).

In fact, items like those are no different from the kind of unintentional insults in stories we've warned for years against making. Examples: "He has such a good sense of humor, you forget he's handicapped." "She's a mother—and she's a doctor." "Tiger Woods is articulate" (as if you wouldn't expect that from a man who's an athlete or a minority, or both).

But others are more debatable, such as when Democratic presidential candidate Hillary Clinton said in 2016 "all lives matter" and was criticized. Another Democratic candidate, Martin O'Malley, also said "all lives matter" in a speech he made, was booed and later apologized. The statements were considered by many as racial affronts diminishing the slogan and the protest group "Black Lives Matter." O'Malley, as well as Clinton and fellow candidate Bernie Sanders learned from the rebukes, and at an early Democratic debate, when they were asked whether black lives matter or all lives matter, all three candidates answered, "Black lives matter."

But that sounded to many others as though they were implying "Only black lives matter, not all lives," which could be seen as a racist microaggression itself. There were widespread, heated arguments about the matter in social media, with each side accusing the other of bad intentions.

Likewise, President Obama's 2012 remark that "if you've got a business, you didn't build that—somebody else made that happen," was cheered by his admirers as reminding people that government provides infrastructure that aids the economy. But it was taken as an offensive remark by many small-business owners who felt their own investments, risk taking and hard work were being minimized—a microaggression against them in other words—and many heated words went back and forth on social media.

The point is it's a good idea for everyone, regardless of race, gender, sexual orientation, political persuasion and so on to be aware of possible ways words could be taken in effect, regardless of intention, and to avoid unintentional disses whenever possible.

Words and phrases offensive in origin but perhaps not recognized as such by a speaker may be offensive to the people involved, even if no offense was intended by the user. Examples: *to Jew someone down* (to drive a hard bargain), *basket case* (originally meant a paraplegic), *gyp* (from gypsy). Is there a difference between words like *gyp*, of which gypsies—although they prefer *Romany*—have made an issue, and *basket case*, which has not been made an issue by the disabled?

On a related note, the use of Native-American names for teams may be offensive to the people involved, even though racism may not be intended. But it shouldn't be too difficult to see that Native-American culture is demeaned by the spectacle of drunken sports fans in headdress and war paint—like old-time Hollywood's portrayal of "Indians"—beating tom-toms, swinging hatchets and shouting slogans such as "Scalp 'em, Braves!" Would similar stereotypes be tolerated today of African-Americans? Journalists can't change the names of the teams, but they should refuse to use cliché phrases like "the Chiefs are on the warpath."

Edit out assumptions that people who share a skin color, ethnic background, sex, disability, religion, sexual orientation or political affiliation are all alike, whether in negative or positive characteristics. Examples: "Women are bad drivers and are more emotional than men." "Vietnam veterans are powder kegs ready to explode." "African-Americans are poor." "Jews are smart and make great doctors." "Asians are model minorities, good at math and successful in life." "Elderly people are infirm, forgetful, stubborn, conservative, frumpy and stooped."

Edit out assumptions that certain jobs are male or female jobs. Examples: Calling a man a *male nurse* or *male secretary* assumes that nursing and secretarial work are female occupations. Calling a woman a *lady lawyer* or *woman doctor* assumes that law and medicine are male occupations.

A reporter began her story this way: "Mothers aren't the only ones who can tell us how to eat properly. A computer can, too." And so can a father. This reporter reinforced the stereotype that it is the mother's role to look out for the needs of children. The editor could have changed the lead to: "Parents aren't the only ones."

Don't describe a woman's appearance, clothing, marital status, motherhood or grandmotherhood in situations where you

would not say similar things about a man. Examples: "The first lady entered wearing a red dress and large gold earrings and received an ovation. Then the president arrived a minute later to thunderous applause." "The pretty mother of three was hospitalized following the accident." "Local Grandmother Wins Bowling Tourney."

Edit out assumptions that you can tell by physical characteristics alone, things such as someone's sexual orientation, religion, ethnicity or even race. Example: "According to the complaint filed at the Minocqua Police Department, [the secretary] reported that the threat came from a male Indian's voice." Just how does a male Indian (Native American?) sound? Besides, couldn't someone be faking a dialect to mislead authorities? Sometimes, such descriptions tell us more about the prejudices of the sources than about the person described, as when someone is described as "looking Jewish" or "sounding gay." Someone who looks white may be a light-skinned African-American, and someone who looks African-American may actually be from India, Pakistan, Haiti or Africa.

Make an effort to include women and minorities in stories that have nothing to do with their being women or minorities. Examples: Interview women and minorities, too, for business stories, for stories about community events and for lifestyle features, not just for stories about women or minority issues. But don't turn these into "He's black, but he owns a yacht" stories.

Generally speaking, use designations preferred by the group being covered.

- *African-American* has gained wide support, but *Black* is still OK. *Negro* is passé, *colored people* is offensive, but *people of color* is acceptable for nonwhites as a group.
- *Disabled* versus *handicapped* versus *special people* versus *otherly abled* versus *physically challenged*: Generally, use *disabled*, but follow group preference. But editors tend to resist terms like *special people*, which seem to imply you're special only if you're disabled.
- *Gay* is preferred in place of *homosexual* (for a male), but either is OK.
- Native Americans prefer their tribal name or *Native American* as a generic term. Avoid *Indian*. *American Indian* is gaining in acceptance.
- *Fundamentalist* versus *Pentecostal* versus *charismatic* versus *Holy Roller*: *Fundamentalist* is the broadest term. Only *Holy Roller* is offensive.

Exceptions: Be reluctant to accept loaded terms as standard designations—such as *sanitary engineer* in place of *garbage collector*. At some point, however, euphemisms and loaded terms may become so standard that they lose their emotional charge. When they seem preferred, widespread and neutral, it's time to adopt them—as has happened with *senior citizen* and with *pro-life* and *pro-choice*.

Taste in Broadcast

Broadcast news editors should be aware of all members of their audience—the young, the aged and the sensitive. Despite the broadcast TV cliché "If it bleeds, it leads," accident stories can usually be reported without bloody pictures or sordid details. Audience members often report that they are turned off by all the negativity of much of the news, especially on local television.

The anchor should know the content of any commercials sandwiched in news stories. For example, if a news story concerns a car crash in which several are killed, the item should not be placed ahead of a commercial for an automobile dealer.

Airlines generally insist that their commercials be canceled for 24 hours if the newscast contains a story of an airliner crash, a policy that is likewise applied to many metropolitan newspapers. But the sponsor should not control or censor the news. The story of a bank scandal should never be omitted from a news program sponsored by a bank. Nor should a sponsor ever expect sponsorship to earn news stories publicizing the business.

Some stations insist on getting the coroner's approval before releasing names of accident victims. If the release is not available, the tag would be, *"Police are withholding the name of the victim until relatives have been notified."* In stories containing condition reports on people in hospitals, the report should not carry over the same condition from one newscast to another without checking with the hospital to find out whether there has been a change.

Suggested Websites

American Society of Newspaper Editors, statement of principles: http://asne.org/content.asp?pl=24&sl=171&contentid=171

Ethical Journalism Network: https://ethicaljournalismnetwork.org/who-we-are/5-principles-of-journalism

First Amendment Center: www.firstamendmentcenter.org

Foundation for Individual Rights in Education: www.thefire.org

Markkula Center for Applied Ethics, "Journalism and Media Ethics Cases": www.scu.edu/ethics/focus-areas/journalism-and-media-ethics/resources/cases/

Media Law Resource Center: www.medialaw.org

Radio Television Digital News Association Code of Ethics: www.rtdna.org/content/rtdna_code_of_ethics#sthash.WnWzlyYe.dpuf

Reporters Committee for Freedom of the Press, "The First Amendment Handbook": www.rcfp.org/first-amendment-handbook

Society of Professional Journalists, ethics page: www.spj.org/ethicscode.
asp
Student Media Law Center: www.splc.org
Willsey, Marie, "10 Most Important U.S. Supreme Court Cases for Journalists":
https://money.howstuffworks.com/10-supreme-court-cases-journalists.
htm

Suggested Readings

Brooks, Brian S., James L. Pinson and Jean Gaddy Wilson. *Working With Words: A Handbook for Media Writers and Editors*, 10th edition. Bedford/St. Martin's, 2020.

Carter, T. Barton, Juliet Lushbough Dee and Harvey L. Zuckman. *Mass Communications Law in a Nutshell*, 8th edition. West, 2020.

Miller, Casey, and Kate Swift. *The Handbook of Nonsexist Writing*, 2nd edition. iUniverse, 2001.

Patterson, Philip, and Lee Wilkins. *Media Ethics: Issues and Cases*, 9th edition. McGraw-Hill, 2018.

Pember, Don R., and Clay Calvert. *Mass Media Law*, 20th edition. McGraw-Hill. 2017.

The Associated Press Stylebook. Latest edition. New York: The Associated Press.

6   MICRO EDITING FOR GRAMMAR AND USAGE

Know Grammar and Proper Usage

At first glance, micro editing may not seem as important or as fun as macro editing. Instead of dealing with the big, important problems of a story, micro editing focuses on checking for correct grammar and usage, making the mechanics conform to local and wire-service stylebooks, fixing spelling errors and typos, and tightening the wording.

Although many might consider micro editing to be an obsession with picky, little details, if the details aren't correct, they distract from what is important—the information the writer is trying to get across. The writer and editor both should try to make sure the mechanics are correct so that instead of becoming a distraction, the mechanics are invisible to the reader or viewer.

DOI: 10.4324/9781003011422-6

This is the hardest of the copy-editing skills to learn for most people because it involves mastering so many rules. Micro editing requires technical knowledge as well as skill and art. To be a master of micro editing, you must become a master of the language. Studying it makes you a better editor or reporter.

In this chapter, we'll look at the basic grammar and usage a journalist should know to communicate clearly. In Chapter 7, we'll look at common problems with style, spelling and tightening.

Grammar

Grammatical and usage errors can ruin otherwise clear writing or distort the meaning of a sentence, as well as damage credibility.

These tips are the minimum a good journalist should know, and after you master these, pick up some more detailed grammar guides—such as Margaret Shertzer's *The Elements of Grammar,* written for a general audience, or *Working With Words* by Brian S. Brooks, James L. Pinson and Jean Gaddy Wilson, a professional guide to grammar and usage written specifically for journalists.

Sentence Problems

Avoid fragments. To be a **sentence**, a group of related words must have a subject and verb, and express a complete thought. If it doesn't, it's a **fragment** and should be rewritten as a complete sentence.

> *Wrong:* The War on Poverty. An idealistic attempt to help people but largely a failure at reducing overall poverty rates.
> *Right:* The War on Poverty was an idealistic attempt to help people but largely a failure at reducing overall poverty rates.

Avoid fused sentences. When two sentences have been jammed together with no punctuation between them and without capitalizing the first word of the second sentence, it's called a **fused sentence**. To fix it, choose one of the following:

- End the first sentence with a period, and capitalize the first word of the second.
- Put a semicolon after the first sentence, and leave the first word of the second sentence lowercase. This is a grammatically correct choice but avoided in journalism because it makes the sentence look too intimidating for average readers.
- Put a comma and conjunction (*but, and*) after the first sentence, and leave the first word of the second sentence lowercase.
- In some cases, put a dash after the first sentence and leave the second one lowercase. This is used for a dramatic pause. In other cases, put

a colon after the first sentence, and capitalize the first word of the second sentence. This is used when the first sentence clearly points to the second.

Wrong: The Cleveland Guardians needed to do something they hadn't done all season they needed to beat the Detroit Tigers.
Right: The Cleveland Guardians needed to do something they hadn't done all season. They needed to beat the Detroit Tigers.
Right: The Cleveland Guardians needed to do something they hadn't done all season: They needed to beat the Detroit Tigers.

Avoid comma-splice sentences. A **comma splice** is like a fused sentence, but a comma has been used to separate the two independent clauses.

Wrong: The Cleveland Guardians needed to do something they hadn't done all season, they needed to beat the Detroit Tigers.

A comma by itself is not enough to separate two full sentences. The remedies are the same as for a fused sentence.

Avoid run-on sentences. A **run-on sentence** is not just any long sentence but one that rambles on forever, not knowing when to quit. As a result, too many ideas get jumbled together in an unclear way. The fix is to separate the ideas into separate sentences. Some books also refer to fused sentences and comma splices as *run-ons*.

Too long: Strict, new federal guidelines meant to improve homeland security by restricting access to explosives are also being applied now to fireworks displays, making it more difficult to hold Fourth of July celebrations in communities across the country, according to local officials and pyrotechnics-industry spokespeople who say their business was already heavily regulated and safe.
Better: Strict, new federal guidelines meant to improve homeland security by restricting access to explosives are also being applied now to fireworks displays. This is making it more difficult to hold Fourth of July celebrations in communities across the country, according to local officials. And pyrotechnics-industry spokespeople say their business was already heavily regulated and safe.

Be on the lookout for reader stoppers. Readers get stuck on passages that are fuzzy in meaning, often because the word order makes the sentence unclear. If you're not sure what a sentence means, ask the reporter to clarify it.

An insufficient water supply problem for firefighting at Fitch Senior School will be discussed next Thursday.
    (*Try this*: "The problem of insufficient water supply for firefighting at Fitch . . .")

Joseph H. Hughes Jr. of Los Angeles wrote to many of his late son's, Coast Guard Ensign Joseph H. Hughes III, friends.
(*Better:* "wrote to many friends of his late son . . .")

Gangs of white rowdies roamed the area last night, attacking cars bearing blacks with baseball bats, bricks and stones.
(*Who had the bats?*)

Three counties, Meigs, Pike and Vinton, get more than 85% from the state. Morgan gets 90.3%.
(*How many counties?*)

Many of the 800 executives and clerical people will be transferred, and some probably will be eliminated.
(*Some will probably be killed?*)

Victims in the other cars were not hurt.
(*Then how were they victims?*)

Parents protesting the closing of Briensburg School on Monday tried to . . .
(*A misplaced time element leads to awkward construction. Was the school closed on Monday? Did they protest on Monday? Or did they "try to" on Monday?*)

Avoid suggesting false connections by combining unrelated ideas in a sentence.

A guard at the Allied Kid Co., he died at 7:10 a.m., about five minutes after one of the youths implicated in the attack was taken into custody.
(*This implies that guards, or at least guards at that company, die at 7:10 a.m.*)

Planned by Jones, Blake and Droza, Detroit architects, the new school has 18 classrooms in addition to such standard facilities as cafeteria and library.
(*This implies it's natural to expect a school planned by that particular firm to have 18 classrooms and the other features.*)

Completed three years ago, the plant is 301 feet by 339 feet and is a one-story structure containing . . .
(*A plant of exactly that size could have been completed 50 years ago or yesterday.*)

Born in Iowa, he worked on two newspapers in Illinois before coming to St. Louis.
(*Being born in Iowa has nothing to do with working on two newspapers in Illinois.*)

Avoid mixed metaphors.

Legislative Hall was swarming with lobbyists as the second session of the 151st General Assembly got underway Monday.

With lawmakers treading water while awaiting the governor's budget message on Wednesday, lobbyists had a field day.

(*In two paragraphs, the story pictured Legislative Hall as a beehive, a swimming pool and an athletic field.*)

Breaking domestic ties with gold made the nation's gold stock a barometer of international fever for gold.

(*Do you shove a barometer under your tongue? Try thermometer.*)

Nouns and Pronouns

Pronoun-Antecedent Agreement

Every pronoun should clearly refer to a previous noun. The previous **noun** a **pronoun** refers to is called its **antecedent**. A pronoun without a clear antecedent makes for a **vague pronoun reference**, which needs to be fixed—perhaps by restating the noun.

Vague: When Beth and Dana were young, she was always the one who was more adventurous. (Which one?)
Clear: When Beth and Dana were young, Beth was always the one who was more adventurous.

Vague: The Smiths have two children. Both are 54. (The Smiths or their children?)
Clear: The Smiths, both 54, have two children.

A pronoun and its antecedent should be the same number. If the antecedent is singular, the pronoun should be singular, also. If the antecedent is plural, the pronoun should be plural, too.

Wrong: The committee will make their decision next week.
Right: The committee will make its decision next week. [*Committee* is singular.]

But AP now accepts the plural pronouns *them, they* and *their* as singular in meaning when referring to a person who could be either male or female.

Pronoun Case

Know the difference among subjective pronouns, objective pronouns and possessive pronouns.

- These pronouns are used as the **subject of a clause**: *I, you* (singular), *he, she, it, one, we, you* (plural), *they.* They are also used when the pronoun serves as a **predicate nominative**—a noun or pronoun following a **linking verb**, which is a verb that equates the subject with something else. The predicate-nominative use of subjective pronouns has largely disappeared from spoken English, however, so some, especially broadcasters or others preparing audio or audio-visual reports, may choose to be more conversational and use objective pronouns in such instances.

Marilyn and I are close friends.
(*I* is part of the compound subject.)

It is I.
(*I* is a predicate nominative here following the linking verb is: It equals I. But again, those not reporting for print, or even print journalists preferring to be more conversational, may choose *me*.)

- These pronouns are used as an **object** of a phrase or clause: *me, you* (singular), *him, her, it, one, us, you* (plural), *them*. They are also used as the **subject of an infinitive**—a noun or pronoun in front of a verb in its *to* form, such as *to go*.

The lawyer questioned her. (*Her* is the direct object.)
Many of us coal miners have black lung disease. (*Us* is the object of a preposition.)
The Cardinals wanted him to be traded. (*Him* is the subject of the infinitive.)

- These pronouns are **possessive**: *my, mine, your, yours, his, her, hers, its, one's, our, ours, your, yours, their, theirs, whose.*

My husband will mow the grass. (Possessive in front of word it describes, *husband*)
The book Joe has is mine. (Possessive after word it describes, *book*)

Gerunds (a form of a verb, usually ending in *ing* and used as a noun) require the possessive case form of the word before them. **Present participles** (also a form of a verb, usually ending in *ing* but used as an adjective, a type of modifier), do not. The difference is a matter of what modifies what.

It was the first instance of a city's losing its funds.
His dropping the course was ridiculous, the professor said.

(Both of these sentences use the possessive before the gerund ending in *ing* because the gerund is a noun, not an adjective, so the possessive forms *city's* and *his* act as the modifiers.)
An example of a present participle not taking a possessive in front of it could be:

I do not like the man standing on the corner.

(The possessive is not used for *man* if *standing on the corner* is a modifier describing *man*, at least if you meant to say you don't like that man. But if you meant you don't like anyone to stand on the corner, it would be *man's* because that possessive, adjective, form would stress not liking standing there as opposed to the person doing it.)

As with the subjective-pronoun use after a linking verb, using a possessive in front of a gerund but not in front of a participle is a rule often broken in conversation. But we still suggest following this rule because, unlike the other one, it can sometimes clarify the writer's meaning—at least to the few who may know the rule!

That Versus Who, That Versus Which, Who Versus Whom

Know the different uses of relative pronouns. A **relative pronoun** is used to connect a subordinate clause to the main clause of a sentence. These words are relative pronouns, and they are often confused with each other: *that, who, whoever, whose, whom, whomever, which.*

- When you find a relative pronoun in a sentence, first determine whether the sentence needs a word from the *that* family or the *who* family. Ask yourself whether the word refers to a person or to an animal with a pet name. If it refers to either of these, then you need a word from the *who* family. If it refers instead to a thing or an animal without a pet name, then you need a word from the *that* family.

  The book that she read . . .
      (The book is not a person, nor an animal with a pet name and so takes *that*.)

  Spot, the dog who loved him . . .
      (Spot is an animal with a pet name and so takes *who*.)

- If you need a word from the *that* family, choose between *that* and *which*. Ask yourself whether the word introduces something **parenthetical**—something not essential to the meaning of the sentence, like something you might put in parentheses. If it does, you need the word *which*, and you need to put a comma in front of *which* and another at the end of the parenthetical item unless that item ends the sentence. If the word doesn't introduce something parenthetical, you need the word *that* with no comma in front of it or after the clause it introduces.

  The deer that got away was a 10-pointer. (*That got away* is not parenthetical—it points to the exact deer we're talking about.)
  The deer, which was a 10-pointer, got away. (*Which was a 10-pointer* is parenthetical in this sentence. The main thought is that the deer got away—and by the way, it was a 10-pointer.)

- If you need a word from the *who* family, choose between *who* and *whom*—or *whoever* and *whomever*. To do that, use this trick:

  1 Start reading the sentence only after the choice between *who* and *whom*.
  2 Finish the sentence using either *he* or *him*, wherever either would fit. If neither works, it's probably because there is a *to* before or after the choice. Move the *to*, or cut it out, then try again.
  3 If *he* works, the answer is *who* or *whoever*. If *him* works, the answer is *whom* or *whomever*. It helps to remember the *m* in *him* goes with the *m* in *whom* or *whomever*.

  Hand the fliers back to who brought them. (*He* brought them, so the word is *who*.)
  To whom should he hand them? (Should he hand them to *him?* Yes, so the word is *whom*.)
  After his decision to cancel the trip, he sent a letter to all of the officials whom he had invited to attend. (He had invited *them*, so the word is *whom*.)

Possessives and Plurals

One of the most common mistakes in written English involves putting an apostrophe where it doesn't belong. Many people don't know how to write plurals and possessives.

Almost the only time an apostrophe is used to make a simple, non-possessive plural is when it's the plural of a single letter like A's. Here are some examples of common kinds of mistakes people make:

Wrong: Carbon arrow's are his favorite for archery practice.
Right: Carbon arrows are his favorite for archery practice.

Wrong: the decade of the 90's
Right: the decade of the '90s

(*The '90s* isn't possessive here, so there's no apostrophe before the *s*. There is an apostrophe before the *9* because it takes the place, as in a contraction, of the missing *19* in 1990s. Also, note that apostrophes always point left, never right.)

To make the plural of a noun ending in almost anything but s, add s. (There are exceptions, like the plural of ox is oxen.) If the noun ends in s already, make the plural by adding es. If a common noun ends in y, make the plural by changing the y to i and adding es. (Exceptions include boys and toys.) If a proper noun ends in y, just add s without changing the y to i.

gases	(ended in *s*, so *es* was added
jellies	(common noun ended in *y*, so the *y* was changed to *i* before adding *es*
the O'Reillys	(proper noun ended in *y*, so just add *s*

To make the possessive of a noun not ending in s, add 's. To make the possessive of a noun ending in s, add just an apostrophe if the noun is a name, is plural or if the next word starts with an s. Otherwise, add 's.

Bill's car	Bill didn't end in *s*, so 's was added
Jesus' home	singular possessive name, already ended in *s*, so just an apostrophe was added
the troops' weapons	plural possessive, already ended in *s*, so just an apostrophe was added
the hostess' seat	singular possessive but next word starts with *s*, so just an apostrophe added
the bus's windows	"bus" ends in *s*, but it's not a name, is singular rather than plural, and the next word doesn't start with an *s*. So an apostrophe *s* is added.

Here are a few examples of plurals and possessives using people's surnames:

	Singular	*Plural*
regular	Smith	Smiths
possessive	Smith's	Smiths'
regular	Jones	Joneses
possessive	Jones'	Joneses'
regular	Kelly	Kellys
possessive	Kelly's	Kellys'

The only possessive pronouns that end in 's are those ending in one or body.

theirs	yours
anyone's	everybody's

Verbs

Verbs express action or a state of being.

Parallel Construction

Keep verbs and other items in a series in a parallel, or similar, form.

> *Wrong:* We love to hunt, fishing and snowboards.
> *Right:* We love hunting, fishing and snowboarding.
>
> *Wrong:* First, read the instructions, then you should practice on your own.
> *Right:* First, read the instructions, then practice on your own.

Tenses

Don't confuse the word *of* with the word *have* or its contraction *'ve*.

> *Wrong:* could of, might of, must of, shall of, should of, will of, would of
> *Right:* could have or could've, might have or might've, must have or must've, shall have or shall've, should have or should've, will have or will've, would have or would've

Know the correct principal parts of the commonly misused irregular verbs. The **principal parts of a verb** are the present tense, the past tense and the past participle. (A fourth would be the present participle, or *ing* form.) The three principal parts are the basis for forming the six basic verb tenses in English. For most English verbs, you merely add *ed* to the end of the present tense to make both the past tense and past participle. (If the present tense ends in a single consonant and the last syllable is stressed, double the consonant before adding *ed*.)

For example, take the verb *correct*. If we use the *you* form to illustrate, an example of the present tense would be *you correct* and the corresponding past tense would be *you corrected*. The past participle form would also be *corrected: you have corrected*. From these three principal parts, all six of the following verb tenses can be formed:

past perfect:	you had corrected
past:	you corrected
present perfect:	you have corrected
present:	you correct
future perfect:	you will have corrected
future:	you will correct

Although the three principal parts of most English verbs will let us form the verb tenses this way, some verbs in English are **irregular verbs**—they don't form the past or past participle with *ed*. Look over "Principal Parts of Common Irregular Verbs" on pp. 179–180, and memorize any principal parts that you know you use incorrectly in conversation.

Use the correct verb tense to describe best the time when something took place. Here are some tips:

- Stick to one basic verb tense in a story as much as possible. Don't make a tense change for no apparent reason. For example, don't switch back and forth between *said* and *says* in the same story. Hard-news stories are usually written in past tense. Features are generally written in present tense. Of course, if a story requires writing at some point about something that happened earlier or later than something else, then it's appropriate to switch the verb tense.

- You know the order *past, present, future*. That's half of the six tenses right there. Next, remember that there's a tense that describes something further in the past than each one. Older than the *past* is the *past perfect*. Between the past and the *present* is the *present perfect*. And between the present and the *future*, there's the *future perfect*. If that seems confusing—as in how can something be further in the past than the past?—think of it this way: If you're writing about something that happened in the past and you want to mention something that happened even earlier, use the past perfect. Follow a similar rule for the other perfect tenses:

  Past: The City Council approved the anti-smoking ordinance in August.
  Even earlier: The City Council had considered the matter for three months when it approved the anti-smoking ordinance in August.
  Present: The City Council considers proposals at each meeting.
  But earlier: The City Council has considered proposals at each meeting.
  Future: The City Council will hold a retreat in the fall.
  And before then: The City Council will have held a retreat in the fall before it will start (or starts) its new term.

- Many editors insist on a rule that when you paraphrase after the attribution *said*, you must change the tense of the original remark. A statement that was originally in present tense will then be paraphrased in past tense (*correct* becomes *corrected*), past tense becomes past perfect (*corrected* becomes *had corrected*), and *will* in the future tense or future perfect becomes *would* (*will correct* becomes *would correct*, *will have corrected* becomes *would have corrected*).

  We generally follow this rule but don't insist on this if we think it could create confusion in the context, such as possibly in a sentence like "She said she loved him"—does she still? By the way, editors who do insist on this rule generally label it the sequence of tenses rule. But actually, that's a bit confusing because all of these things we've been talking about concerning the use of the right tense when there's more than one involve using the correct tense for the sequence of time covered.

original in present tense:	"I'm pleased."
paraphrased in past tense:	She said she was pleased.
original in past tense:	"I corrected the proofs."
paraphrased in past-perfect tense:	She said she had corrected the proofs.

Passive Voice

Use verbs in the active voice, generally, rather than in the passive voice. In the **active voice**, the subject does something:

The president fired the secretary of state.

But in the **passive voice**, the subject is not the one acting; rather, the subject is being passively acted upon:

The secretary of state was fired by the president.

The passive voice is wordier and less direct. Sometimes, it's even less clear, as when the actual doer is left out entirely:

The secretary of state was fired.

For these reasons, it's generally better to avoid passive voice.

Use passive voice only when you want to stress the receiver of the action rather than the doer. This is especially applicable in a crime or accident story:

The victim was assaulted and robbed as she left the convenience store.

Conditional and Subjunctive Moods

Learn to use the conditional mood. Use *could* or *would* instead of *can* or *will* when something is not now true but could or would be true under a certain condition. This is called the **conditional mood**. (Technically, the rule has also included that *shall* becomes *should* and *may* becomes *might* in the conditional, but in contemporary English, *should* is usually reserved to mean *ought to*, and *might* for the past tense of *may*.)

Wrong: The bill will cut taxes.
Right: The bill would cut taxes. (It would if passed into law.)

Learn to use the subjunctive mood. With verbs that convey a demand, desire, doubt, hope, prayer or wish, use the **subjunctive mood** form of a verb to express a condition contrary to fact.

Wrong: I wish I was rich.
Right: I wish I were rich. (But I'm not.)

Wrong: If she was here, something would be done.
Right: If she were here, something would be done. (But she's not here.)

Wrong: If dissent is treason, then we've lost our freedom.
Right: If dissent be treason, then we've lost our freedom. (The writer is suggesting dissent is not treason.)

Wrong: They demand that he leaves.
Right: They demand that he leave. (A demand requires the subjunctive.)

Note that the past tense of the subjunctive for the verb *to be* is always *were*, but the present tense of the subjunctive for *to be* is always *be*. For all other verbs, the subjunctive is used only in present tense and is always the infinitive minus the *to*. That means for most verbs, the only different subjunctive form from the normal present tense is the third-person singular, which typically just drops the *s*.

Subject-Verb Agreement

A singular subject needs a singular verb. A plural subject needs a plural verb.

Wrong: The monotony of the concrete walls painted in dull green and blue are broken only . . .
Right: The monotony of the concrete walls painted in dull green and blue is broken only . . . (*Monotony . . . is . . .*)

Wrong: A two-thirds vote of both houses of Congress and ratification by three-quarters of the states is necessary.
Right: A two-thirds vote of both houses of Congress and ratification by three-quarters of the states are necessary. (*A vote . . . and ratification . . . are necessary.*)

The verb must agree in number with the subject. Normally, ignore any other noun or pronoun when deciding verb number. It's common for a sentence to have a plural object of a preposition between the subject and verb or a plural predicate nominative after a linking verb. But remember, the verb agrees with the subject—not necessarily anything else.

(But common apparent exceptions, as we'll soon explain, is with fractions and percentages.)

Wrong: An American Bar Association team, in addition to a citizens' panel, have recommended this.

Right: An American Bar Association team, in addition to a citizens' panel, has recommended this. (*Team* is the subject, so the verb must be *has*. Parenthetical material should be ignored in choosing whether a verb should be singular or plural.)

Wrong: The majority of the senators favors the measure.

Right: The majority of the senators favor the measure. (*Majority* is often singular by itself, depending on whether it's preceded by "a" or "the," but like fractions and percentages, when followed by *of* should be plural if that is the sense.)

Wrong: The panel are Ann, Steve and Craig.

Right: The panel is Ann, Steve and Craig. (Make the verb agree with the subject, *panel*, which is singular. The phrase *Ann, Steve and Craig* is the predicate nominative.)

Principal Parts of Common Irregular Verbs

In this list, the present tense is shown first, then the past tense and finally the past participle. A fourth principal part would consist of the present participle, or ing form, of each verb.

awake, awoke, awakened
bear, bore, borne
bid (offer), bid, bid
bid (command), bade, bidden
break, broke, broken
bring, brought, brought
broadcast, broadcast, broadcast
burst, burst, burst
cling, clung, clung
come, came, come
dive, dived, dived (not dove)
do, did, done
drink, drank, drunk
drive, drove, driven
drown, drowned, drowned
eat, ate, eaten
fall, fell, fallen
flow, flowed, flowed
fly (to soar), flew, flown

fly (hit a baseball high), flied, flied
forbid, forbade, forbidden
get, got, got or gotten
go, went, gone
hang (suspend), hung, hung
hang (execute), hanged, hanged
have, had, had
hide, hid, hidden
kneel, knelt or kneeled, knelt or kneeled
lay (set down), laid, laid
lead, led, led
lie (recline), lay, lain
pay, paid, paid
plead, pleaded or pled, pleaded or pled
prove, proved, proved (proven is only an adjective)
raise, raised, raised
ring, rang, rung
rise, rose, risen
see, saw, seen
set (place or put down; also, hens, cement and the sun set), set, set
shake, shook, shaken
shine, shone, shone
show, showed, showed or shown
shrink, shrank, shrunk
sit (seat oneself), sat, sat
slay, slew, slain
spring, sprang, sprung
steal, stole, stolen
swear, swore, sworn
swim, swam, swum
swing, swung, swung
tear, tore, torn
wake, woke, waked
weave, wove, woven
wring, wrung, wrung

A conjunction in the subject influences the number of the verb. A **conjunction** is a word that connects other words, phrases, clauses or sentences.

- If the subject contains the word *and* connecting two or more items, the verb should be plural, unless the *and* is part of the name of a single item.

  Fran and Carol are here.

The potatoes and gravy tastes great! (*Potatoes and gravy* is considered one dish.)

- If the subject contains the word *or*, the verb should be singular unless one of the items it connects is plural. In that case, the verb agrees in number with the nearest of the items.

    A degree in journalism or English is necessary for the job.
    One or two guides are available.

- If the subject contains the words *along with, as well as, in addition to, including, such as, together with* or any other parenthetical words or phrases set off by commas or dashes, the number of the subject is not affected.

    Joseph, as well as Melissa, is a Republican.

Know the confusing singular words that are subject–verb stumbling blocks.

Collective nouns like *committee, council, jury* and *team* normally take a singular verb in America. The exception is when the focus is on the committee members (plural) rather than the committee as a unit (singular). Use the plural form of the verb when the members that make up the collective noun are *not* acting in agreement.

> *Wrong:* The committee have decided on an agenda.
> *Right:* The committee has decided on an agenda. (The singular verb *has* is used because *the committee* is acting as a single unit.)

> *Wrong:* The committee disagrees with each other.
> *Right:* The committee disagree with each other. (The plural verb *disagree* is used because *the committee* is *not* acting as a single unit.)

- These **uncountable nouns** (nouns with no separate singular and plural forms) are singular even though they end in *s: apparatus, athletics, civics, economics, kudos, linguistics, measles, mumps, news, shambles, summons, whereabouts.*
- These **indefinite pronouns** are normally singular, even though some of them may sound plural: *another, anybody, anyone, anything, each one, everybody, everyone, everything, little, much, nobody, no one, nothing, other, somebody, someone, something.*
- The word *none* normally means *no one* or *not one* or *no amount of,* so it usually takes a singular verb.

> *Wrong:* None were going.
> *Right:* None was going. (No one was going, or not one was going.)
> *Right:* None of it was left. (No amount of it was left.)

Occasionally, *none* means *no two* and will take a plural verb. (This is AP's older distinction, which is clearer than the latest AP explanation of making *none* plural when it means *none of them.* That's because one of its own examples of *none* as singular could be read also as *none of them*: "None of the seats was in the right place.")

> *Wrong:* None on the committee agrees.
> *Right:* None on the committee agree. (*No two* on the committee *agree,* assuming we're talking about agreeing with each other.)

- *Either* and *neither* are singular by themselves, but in the expressions *either . . . or* and *neither . . . nor,* the verb should agree in number with the closer noun or pronoun.

> *Wrong:* Neither were right.
> *Right:* Neither was right. (By itself, *neither* is singular.)

> *Wrong:* There are two things that either the Sloanes or Hollenbach have.
> *Right:* There are two things that either the Sloanes or Hollenbach has. (Hollenbach is closer to the verb *has* and is singular, so the verb should be singular, as well. Reverse the order of the two, and the verb should change.)

- The words *majority, number* and *total* are singular when preceded by the word *the.* But they become plural if preceded by the word *a.*

> The majority is in favor.
> A majority are in favor.

- Fractions and percentages are singular when referring to the amount of one thing but plural when referring to a number of things. A helpful guide is that what the fraction or percentage refers to is often stated immediately after as the object of a preposition, so make the verb agree with the object of that preposition.

> Half of the work is done.
> (Work, the object of the preposition *of,* is singular, so *is* is singular.)

> Half of the students were there.
> (Students, the object of the preposition *of,* is plural, so the verb *were* is plural.)

Learn these confusing plural words that are subject–verb stumbling blocks.

- These uncountable nouns are plural: *assets, barracks, earnings, goods, odds, pants, pliers, proceeds, remains, riches, scissors, shears, tactics, thanks, tongs, wages.*
- These indefinite pronouns are plural: *both, couple, few, many, others, several.*

Use your own judgment with these confusing words, which can be either singular or plural.

- These uncountable nouns are sometimes singular, sometimes plural: *ethics, headquarters, mechanics, politics, savings, series, species, statistics.*
- These indefinite pronouns are sometimes singular, sometimes plural: *all, any, more, most, plenty, some, such.*

Modifiers

Modifiers are words that describe other words. Adjectives, adverbs and interjections are modifiers.

Adjectives Versus Adverbs

Don't use an adjective in a sentence when an adverb is required. Many people mistakenly use an adjective in place of an adverb when they're describing the manner in which something is done.

- **Adjectives** modify a noun, pronoun or gerund.
- **Adverbs** modify a verb, adjective or another adverb.

Look at what's being modified, then pick the appropriate kind of modifier.

Wrong: The car ran smooth.
Right: The car ran smoothly. (The modifier tells *how* the car ran. It modifies the verb, not the car itself, so an adverb is needed.)

Once you can tell whether the adverb or the adjective form is required, how do you tell the two apart?

- Most adverbs end in *ly.* Exceptions include *well, very, quite, rather.*
- A few other words that are not adverbs end in *ly*: *friendly, lonely, manly, surly, ugly* (adjectives); *family* (noun).

Forms and Placement of Modifiers

Use the proper form of a modifier.

- The **positive form** for a simple modifier with no comparison.

    Adjectives: tall; controversial
    Adverb: quickly

- The **comparative form** when two things are compared.

  Adjectives: taller; less controversial, more controversial
  Adverbs: less quickly, more quickly

- The **superlative form** when three or more things are compared.

  Adjectives: tallest; least controversial, most controversial
  Adverbs: least quickly, most quickly

Notice that shorter adjectives form the comparative by adding *er* to the end of the positive and form the superlative by adding *est* to the end of the positive. Longer adjectives, as well as adverbs, tend to form the comparative by adding *less* or *more* in front of the positive and form the superlative by adding *least* or *most* in front of the positive.

Never combine an *er* form with *less* or *more*, or an *est* form with *least* or *most*:

Wrong: more quicker
Right: quicker

Some words have irregular comparative and superlative forms:

good, better, best
well, better, best
little, less, least
much, more, most

Some modifiers are considered absolute and have only one form. For example, something is either *unique* (one of a kind) or not—it can't be more one of a kind than something else, so don't say it's *more unique*. Other examples include *perfect, perpendicular* and *pregnant*.

Place modifiers next to what they describe. If you don't follow this rule, you may end up with the error called a **misplaced modifier**. The most common misplaced modifier is the **dangling participle**.

Wrong: If convicted of the assault-and-battery charge, the judge will impose the sentence. (*If convicted . . .* applies to the defendant, not the judge, so this is a misplaced modifier.)
Right: The judge will impose the sentence if the defendant is convicted of the assault-and-battery charge.

Wrong: Besides being cut on the left cheek and bloodied in the nose, Zeck's wallet was stolen with $825. (Zeck was *cut and bloodied . . .*, not his wallet, so this is a misplaced modifier.)
Right: Zeck's left cheek was cut, his nose was bloodied, and his wallet with $825 was stolen.

Wrong: Trying to arrest the man, the suspect fled from police. (*Trying to arrest the man* is a misplaced modifying phrase because it's next to *the suspect*, but the suspect was not trying to make the arrest.)

Right: The suspect fled from police as they tried to arrest him.

The last wrong example above is also an example of a dangling participle because "trying to arrest the man" is a modifying phrase built on the *ing* form of a verb—a **participle**, in other words—but it dangles because it's not next to what it modifies.

Coordinate Versus Compound Modifiers

Coordinate modifiers are equal adjectives that take a comma between them. The test is whether you could reverse them and put *and* between them. Exceptions: Don't use a comma if one or both of them refers to age, color, ethnicity, material, nationality, number or race. (Credit goes to Dan Ranly of the Missouri School of Journalism for developing this rule, which provides a clear standard anyone can apply to what had previously been a more arbitrary and less consistent decision.)

the tall, skinny boy	*tall* and *skinny* can be reversed with *and* between them, so use a comma.
the red brick building	*red* is a color and *brick* a material, so don't use a comma.

Compound modifiers are an adverb (or another word acting as an adverb) modifying an adjective, with the two together modifying a noun or pronoun. Punctuate with a hyphen between the adverb and adjective. Exceptions: Don't use a comma after the words *very* or *most* or after an *ly* adverb.

pressure-cooker situation	*pressure* modifies *cooker*, and together they modify *situation*. So use a hyphen.
heavily guarded entrance	*heavily* is an *ly* adverb, so don't use a hyphen.
family-oriented event	*family* is a noun, not an *ly* adverb. It modifies *oriented*, and together they modify *event*, so use a hyphen.

Interjections

An **interjection** is a word that expresses emotion and often takes an exclamation mark—one only!—either immediately after or at the end of the sentence it introduces, or both.

Ouch! That hurts.
Ouch, that hurts!
Ouch! That hurts!

When the interjection represents only a mild emotion, an exclamation mark is not used.

Gee, I don't know.

Connecting Words

Prepositions

A **preposition** is a connecting word that shows a relationship between its object and some other word in the sentence. Most prepositions show a spatial relationship, so if you think of a bird and some trees, you can think of a number of prepositions: The bird can fly *to* the trees, *from* the trees, *under* the trees, *over* the trees, *through* the trees and *around* the trees. All of the words before *the trees* are prepositions. In addition to spatial relationships, some prepositions show time relationships, such as *before* and *after,* and some show agency, such as *by* and *for.*

Don't end a clause or sentence with a preposition when you can avoid it.

Wrong: National security is something he said he cares deeply about.
Right: National security is something about which he said he cares deeply.

The object of the preposition should be in objective case if it's a pronoun. This doesn't change with a plural object of the preposition.

Wrong: Give it to I.
Wrong: Give it to myself.
Right: Give it to me. (*Me* is the object of the preposition *to.*)

Wrong: Give it to Sheila and I.
Wrong: Give it to Sheila and myself.
Right: Give it to Sheila and me. (*Sheila and me* is the plural object of the preposition *to.*)

In a headline, a prepositional phrase should not be split over two lines. But don't split apart on different lines a verb from a preposition that's part of the verb.

wrong:	Floods recede in	/	rural Missouri
right:	Floods recede	/	in rural Missouri
wrong:	Husband: Let's work	/	out our marriage problems
right:	Husband: Let's work out	/	our marriage problems

A preposition is part of the verb when it changes the meaning of the verb, as in the second example cited. *Work out* means something different from merely *work*.

Separate proper nouns. Instead of letting them run together, separate proper nouns with a preposition, or otherwise move them apart in the sentence.

> *Wrong:* He married Filipa Franks June 10, 2016.
> *Right:* He married Filipa Franks on June 10, 2016.
> *Right:* He was married June 10, 2016, to Filipa Franks.

Repeat a preposition or another word in a parallel construction if it will avoid confusion, or reverse the order of the items.

> *Wrong:* The prime minister said she would push for lower interest rates and tax cuts. (Does she want the tax cuts lower, as well? Make the wording clearer.)
> *Right:* The prime minister said she would push for lower interest rates and for tax cuts.
> *Right:* The prime minister said she would push for lower interest rates and lower tax cuts.
> *Right:* The prime minister said she would push for tax cuts and lower interest rates.

Conjunctions and Conjunctive Adverbs

Understanding conjunctions and conjunctive adverbs will help you make clearer transitions between ideas and help you correctly punctuate sentences.

It's OK to start a sentence with a conjunction like *and* or *but*. It's a common myth that you can't start a sentence with *and* or *but*, but there's no such grammar rule. You may start a sentence with any kind of conjunction, but it seems particularly odd to think you can't start one with a coordinating conjunction, like *and* or *but*, because by definition a **coordinating conjunction** is one that begins an **independent clause**—a clause that can stand alone as a complete sentence.

The comma goes in front of a coordinating conjunction, not behind it.

> *Wrong:* The FBI arrived at the scene and, agents began gathering evidence.
> *Right:* The FBI arrived at the scene, and agents began gathering evidence.

Put a comma between a **dependent clause** (one that can't stand alone as a sentence) and an independent clause, in general, only when the dependent clause comes first.

Wrong: They went home early, because the power went out.
Right: They went home early because the power went out.

Wrong: Because the power went out they went home early.
Right: Because the power went out, they went home early.

An exception would be when the lack of a comma could cause confusion. Then you might add a comma or rewrite for clarity:

Confusing: He didn't support her because she was a Republican. (Did he not support her for the reason that she was a Republican, or did he support her but not because she was a Republican?)
Clear: He didn't support her, because she was a Republican. (Meaning, because she was a Republican, he didn't support her.)
Clear: It wasn't because she was a Republican that he supported her.

If you're unsure whether a clause is independent or dependent, ask yourself whether it could stand alone as a complete sentence. The word that begins the clause can also help you decide. These are common coordinating conjunctions that begin an independent clause:

and	but
for	nor
or	yet

A **subordinating conjunction,** like any of the following, tells you what follows is a dependent clause—one that could not stand alone as a complete sentence:

although	as
because	if
since	until
whether	while

Learn how to use conjunctive adverbs. A **conjunctive adverb**—an adverb joining two clauses—in the middle of a sentence needs a semicolon in front of it and a comma behind it. Better still, in journalism, make the conjunctive adverb the first word of a second sentence with a comma behind it.

Wrong: The Gainesville City Council approved the plan, meanwhile the county had second thoughts.

Right: The Gainesville City Council approved the plan; meanwhile, the county had second thoughts.

Best for journalism: The Gainesville City Council approved the plan. Meanwhile, the county had second thoughts.

Some of the most common conjunctive adverbs include:

also	instead
as a result	in the first place
at the same time	likewise
besides	more important
consequently	moreover
first, second, third, etc.	nevertheless
for example	on the contrary
for this reason	otherwise
furthermore	so
however	still
in addition	then
indeed	therefore

The same word may sometimes be used as either a regular adverb or a conjunctive adverb.

He said that shouldn't have stopped him; however, it did.

(*However* is used as a conjunctive adverb, with a semicolon before it and a comma after it. This construction is generally not used in journalism, in order to avoid the use of a semicolon.)

He didn't, however, agree.

(*However* is used as a regular adverb, requiring only commas around it to set it off as parenthetical.)

Know which words go together as correlative conjunctions.
Some coordinating conjunctions are used in pairs. These are called **correlative conjunctions**.

as . . . as	neither . . . nor
not so . . . as	not only . . . but also
either . . . or	if . . . then

The most common mistake involving these is to forget to use *but also* after *not only.*

Usage

Correct usage is mainly a matter of vocabulary. But we're not talking about mastering big words that people seldom use in conversation. We're talking mainly about recognizing everyday words we use—and sometimes misuse—in conversations and knowing how to use them correctly.

Correct usage contributes to clearer communication. When some people use *prioritize*, for example, they mean to make something a priority rather than its actual meaning, to rank items in a list. You cannot prioritize an item, only a list.

Other times, though, correct usage and grammar seem to act more like signals to your audience that you're educated enough not to succumb to colloquialisms and slang. Before you put that down as superficial, realize that correct usage helps establish the credibility of a publication or station.

The problem is that language is always changing: Today's usage or grammar error may become tomorrow's preferred way, and today's preferred usage may come to sound stilted to your audience. But until a change becomes widely recognized—not only by the general public but also by writers, editors, teachers, stylebooks and usage manuals—it's usually safer to revise the wording.

The two main usage problems are confused words and misused idioms.

Confused Words

Some writers are not precise in their choice of words. By habit, they write *comprise* when they mean *compose, affect* when they want *effect.* Or they use *include*, then list all the elements. Each time a word is misused, it loses some of its value as a precise tool. Writers should learn some of the most common misuses of words, and editors should be able to spot ones like these:

> His testimony about the night preceding the crime was collaborated, in part, by his mother. (Corroborated)
> The two officers are charged with dispersing corporate funds. (The word is *disburse*—to pay out, to expend. *Disperse* means to scatter in various directions, to distribute widely.)
> A story indicating that a man might not be qualified for his job says: "Miller refutes all that," and then he says why he is capable. (*Denies* would have been much better because *refutes* means he proved the charges wrong.)
> He has been an "intricate part of the general community." (The writer meant *integral,* meaning essential, not *intricate,* meaning detailed.)

Mrs. Reece, a spritely woman . . . (She may be a *sprite*—an elf or pixie—but what the writer probably meant was *sprightly*—full of life.)

Other terms often misused:

- **A lot** two words; better yet, change to *much* or *many*.
- **Adopted, passed** Resolutions are *adopted* or *approved;* bills are *passed*. In legislative jargon, *passed* also can mean *passed by for the day* or *for that meeting*.
- **Affect, effect** For a noun meaning result, use *effect*. As a verb, *affect* means influence, and *effect* means cause.
- **Aggravate, annoy, irritate** The first means *to make worse*. The second and third mean *to incite, provoke* or *bother*, but the third also means *to make the skin itch*.
- **Although, though, while** *Although* is best used at the start of a clause, and *though* is best used in the middle. *While* may be used to show contrast, also, but should only be used when it means "at the same time."
- **Amateur, novice** An *amateur* is a nonprofessional. A *novice* is a beginner.
- **Among, between** *Among* is used for three or more. *Between* is used for two.
- **Amount, number** *Amount* indicates the general quantity. *Number* indicates an enumerable quantity.
- **Amused, bemused, confused** No one confuses *amused* and *confused*, but many people think *bemused* means slightly amused. Instead, it means confused. It's better to avoid the confusion by not using *bemused*.
- **Avenge, revenge** Use *avenge* for another, *revenge* for self.
- **Because of, due to, since** These can mean basically the same thing, but *due to* must always follow a *to be* verb, and *since* is best used when the stress is on something happening after something else rather than in the sense of cause.
- **Canvas, canvass** The first is a cloth. The second means *to solicit*.
- **Celebrant, celebrator** A *celebrant* presides over a religious rite. A *celebrator* celebrates.
- **Centers on, centers around** Something can be centered *in*, centered *at* or centered *on*, but it cannot be centered *around*. If you want to use *around*, try "revolves around."
- **Compared to, compared with** Use the first to stress similarities. Use the second to stress differences, or similarities *and* differences.
- **Complement, compliment** The first means to complete something by adding what's missing. The second refers to a flattering statement.
- **Compose, comprise, constitute** The whole *is composed of* the parts; the whole *comprises* the parts; the parts *constitute* the whole.

- **Continuous, continual** If it rains steadily every day for a week, it rains *continuously*. If it rains only part of every day for a week, it rains *continually* or *intermittently*.
- **Enormity, enormousness** The first means evil. The second means hugeness. A common error is to speak of the *enormity* of a task or issue that is not particularly evil, as in "The *enormity* of her new responsibilities overwhelmed her."
- **Etc.** The abbreviation for the Latin *et cetera* is *etc.*, not *ect.*
- **Farther, further** *Farther* is used for literal distance. *Further* is used to mean deeper.
- **Fewer, less** *Fewer* is used with plural nouns. *Less* is used for singular nouns. *Less* is also used with plural amounts of money or weight. A trick is to remember that *fewer* is used for things about which you could ask, "How many?" while *less* is used for things about which you could ask, "How much?"
- **Flaunt, flout** The first means *to make a showy display*. The second means *to mock or treat with contempt*. "The students *flouted* the authority of the school board."
- **Flier, flyer** *The AP Stylebook* prefers the first for either aviators or handbills, reserving the second only for proper names, as in the names of some buses, trains, bicycles or wagons.
- **Flounder, founder** Horses *flounder*—struggle, thrash about—in the mud. Ships *founder* or sink. And horses can *founder* when they become disabled from overeating.
- **Gender, sex** Originally, *gender* referred to whether a noun or pronoun was feminine, masculine or neuter. In recent decades, it has more commonly been used to refer to sex-based roles in society—a sociological distinction. The word *sex*, not *gender*, is the better word to refer to biological differences but is becoming less commonly used when not referring to the sex act itself.
- **Grisly, gristly, grizzly** "Karmel begins her work in a valley of shadows that deepens and darkens as she heaps one grizzly happening upon the next." One *grizzly* heaped upon the next produces only two angry or aroused bears. The word the writer wants is *grisly*, meaning *gruesome*. Tough meat can be described as *gristly* for having lots of *gristle*.
- **Half-mast, half-staff** The first term refers to a flag lowered on a ship or at a naval base. The second refers to any other flag that's lowered.
- **Hardy, hearty** A story of four visiting police officers from Africa said they expressed appreciation for their *hardy* welcome. If that's what they said, they meant *hearty*. *Hardy* means *bold* or *rugged*, and *hearty* means *jovial* or *nourishing*.
- **If, whether** *If* is used for conditions (if A, then B). *Whether* is used for choices ("I don't know whether I'll go"). Notice *whether* does

not require *or not* following it. Many people use *if* when *whether* is needed. To get the distinction right, see whether you could put *whether* in the sentence. If yes, *whether* is the right word. If no, then leave it as *if.*

- **Impassable, impossible** The first is *that which cannot be passed.* The second is *that which can't suffer or be made to show signs of emotion.*
- **Imply, infer** The speaker or writer does the *implying,* and the listener or reader does the *inferring.*
- **Its, it's** *Its* is possessive. *It's* means *it is* or *it has.*
- **Lay, lie** The first means to set or put something down. Its principal parts are *lay, laid, (have) laid,* and *(is) laying.* The second means to rest or recline. Its principal parts are *lie, lay, (have) lain,* and *(is) lying.* A common mistake is to use the first verb in place of the second.
- **Mantel, mantle** The first is a shelf. The second is a cloak.
- **More than, over** *The AP Stylebook* no longer insists that *over* should be used only in a spatial sense, and *more than* should be used for anything else, as in "The proposal costs *more than* (not *over*) $3 million."
- **Oral, verbal** All language is *verbal*—of words. But only *oral* language is spoken.
- **People, persons** A *person* is a human being. *People* is the plural.
- **Prejudice, prejudiced** The first means bigotry. The second means bigoted. Many speakers and writers make the error of leaving off the final *d* in the second.
- **Pretense, pretext** Both refer to putting on a false front, but the first refers to the false show itself. The second refers to a false motive behind it. Someone's flattery may be a *pretense* that he likes someone when he doesn't. But if someone acts under a false *pretext,* he gives a reason other than the real one.
- **Principal, principle** The first means main and by extension the supervisor of a school, who in England, was the main teacher. "The principal is your pal," is a mnemonic many have used to remember this spelling. The second means a rule or law.
- **Raise, rise** The first means to lift something up. Its principal parts are *raise, raised, (have) raised,* and *(is) raising.* The second means to get up. Its principal parts are *rise, rose, (have) risen,* and *(is) rising.*
- **Set, sit** To *set* means to put or lay something down. Its principal parts are *set, set, (have) set,* and *(is) setting.* To *sit* means to put one's bottom down, as in a chair. Its principal parts are *sit, sat, (have) sat,* and *(is) sitting.*
- **Stationary, stationery** The first means not moving. The second means writing paper.
- **Supposed to** Note the *d.*
- **Sustenance, subsistence** *Sustenance* is food. *Subsistence* is survival or means of support.

- **Their, there, they're** *Their* is possessive. *There* is used in the phrase *there are* or as the direction *over there*. *They're* means *they are*.
- **To, too, two** *To* is the preposition ("to the trees"). *Too* is an adverb meaning *also* or *excessive* ("That's too much, too"). *Two* is the number.
- **Used to** Note the *d*.
- **Your, you're** *Your* is possessive. *You're* means *you are*.

Misused Idioms

Careless use of idioms (accepted phrases in a language) occurs often in the news. Usually, the fault lies in the prepositions or conjunctions. In the following examples, the bracketed word is the preferred usage.

The economist accused him with [of] failing to make a decision. (You charge somebody *with* blundering, but you accuse him *of* it.)

He said the guns are against the law except under [in] certain specified situations. (But *under* conditions or circumstances.)

Dressen is no different than [from] other experts. (*Different* may only be followed by *than* when introducing a clause: "The patient is no different than he was the day before.")

Five men were pelted by [with] stones.

The reason for the new name is because [that] the college's mission has been changed.

He said he would not call on [for] assistance from police except as a last resort. (*Call on* the police, but *call* the police *for* assistance.)

These men and women could [couldn't] care less about Obama's legislative magic.

That begs [raises] the question of how to do it. (*To beg the question* refers to the logical fallacy of arguing in a circle.)

Suggested Websites

American Copy Editors Association: https://aceseditors.org/

American Heritage Dictionary, good for usage advice, too: https://ahdictionary.com

Associated Press Stylebook, but requires paid subscription: http://apstylebook.com

EditTeach, a great website for learning and teaching copy editing: www.editteach.org

English Grammar.org: www.englishgrammar.org

Grammar Girl (Mignon Fogarty): www.quickanddirtytips.com/education/grammar

The Slot: A Spot for Copy Editors (Bill Walsh): www.theslot.com

Suggested Readings

Bremner, John B. *Words on Words: A Dictionary for Writers and Others Who Care About Words*. Columbia University Press, 1980.

Brooks, Brian S., James L. Pinson and Jean Gaddy Wilson. *Working With Words: A Handbook for Media Writers and Editors*, 10th edition. Bedford/St. Martin's, 2020.

Burchfield, R.W., Ed. *Fowler's Dictionary of Modern English Usage*. Oxford University Press, 2015.

The Associated Press Stylebook. Latest edition. New York: The Associated Press.

7 MICRO EDITING FOR STYLE, SPELLING AND TIGHTENING

Remember, every time you make a typo, the errorists win.

The Basics of Editing

In this chapter, we continue our look at micro editing, or making sure the mechanics of writing are correct, by looking at three more areas. Correct style means writing something that matches the way your local or wire-service stylebook says is correct. Correct spelling means following those same stylebook preferences, and if a word isn't found there, then matching it to the spelling in the dictionary that's preferred where you work—generally in journalism, *Webster's New World College Dictionary.* Tightening means making sure the writing says everything that needs to be said but in no unnecessary words or words that are less conversational.

Style

By far, the main stylebook American journalists need to study and learn is the one published by the Associated Press, *The Associated Press Stylebook.* New editions come out regularly, and AP updates

DOI: 10.4324/9781003011422-7

it often at its subscription website, www.apstylebook.com. *The New York Times* stylebook is also readily available in print and e-book form. Less common are the stylebooks published by United Press International, Reuters, *Los Angeles Times*, the *Washington Post*, *U.S. News and World Report* and *Wired*, but these can be good to have and consult for issues not covered by AP.

Most newspapers also have local stylebooks, which sometimes differ from AP style. If you know the main rules of *The AP Stylebook*, it's easy to adapt to a local style. Just look for two things: where the local stylebook disagrees with AP and any entries that supplement AP. Often, the main differences are not disagreements but rather the addition of entries such as place names that have a strictly local value.

If you're familiar with *The AP Stylebook*—which journalism students are typically taught—you'll find when you look in any of the others that the rules usually differ from AP's in relatively few major ways. A number of news outlets, in fact, save money by publishing or putting online only the equivalent of a pamphlet of local additions and exceptions to use alongside *The AP Stylebook*.

To learn AP style, begin with the following list of rules any journalist should know. This will cover the most common rules—about 90% or more of those you regularly use—and the grouping here will make learning far easier than the alphabetical listing in *The AP Stylebook*.

When you have these rules mastered, read through *The AP Stylebook* at least once to get a feel for what's there. Sure, it's like reading a dictionary,

Figure 7.1 *The AP Stylebook* is the style bible for most newspapers and their websites. There are exceptions used by radio and TV stations.

Photo by Christopher Parks.

but how will you know what to look up if you don't have a passing familiarity with what's in it and where? You could just browse through it in spare moments, but we suggest you read a few entries a day until you get through it all.

Journalists with a special interest in sports or business should also study carefully the chapters on those topics following the main section of the stylebook. In fact, it's a good idea to note typical style issues that arise commonly in all the different types of stories you edit. We'll look at some of those in Chapter 8.

Here's a summary of some of the most often-used style rules typically followed by journalists. Most of this agrees with AP, but in some instances, we've gone outside its advice and suggested what we think is common practice or an improvement.

Abbreviations and Symbols

- Days of the week are never abbreviated.
- Months are abbreviated only when followed by a date during the month: Feb. 2 or Feb. 2, 2021, but not February 2021. The months with five letters or less are not abbreviated: *March, April, May, June, July.*
- AP used to abbreviate the name of a state after a city but now mainly does not. The new rules are more complicated. AP continues to use the older state abbreviations (the ones with periods, not the postal ones) in datelines except for the following eight states that are never abbreviated: *Alaska, Hawaii, Maine, Utah, Texas, Ohio, Iowa* and *Idaho.* But it now spells out the name of a state anywhere in the body of the story—whether it follows a city or stands alone—with the exceptions of using postal abbreviations for a state (*CA* for California) before a ZIP code in an address, or the older abbreviation after party affiliation (*Calif.* for California).
- See "Addresses" on page 206 for which names of thoroughfares are abbreviated and when.
- Most initials of three letters or more do not take periods. Exceptions: *c.o.d., U.S.S.R,* both of which refer to things you seldom see any more.
- Use a dollar sign ($) with any actual dollar amount, but always write out the word *cents* rather than using the cents symbol.
- AP now lets you use the percentage sign % instead of writing out the word after a numeral.
- An ampersand (&) is always written as *and* unless it's part of a company's actual name.
- AP now accepts the abbreviations *TV, U.S.* and *U.N.* in all text references, but some editors still prefer the old rule of using the abbreviations only as adjectives and writing out what they stand for as nouns.

In headlines, AP drops the periods from the abbreviations: *US* and *UN* but includes them when in the story.

Capitalization

- Common nouns are lowercase: *dog, apple.*
- Proper nouns are uppercase: *Leo, Barnes and Noble.*
- Names of months and days of the week are capitalized, but seasons are not: *Wednesday, January, spring.*
- Actual names of races are capitalized, but colors are not: *Caucasian, white.* An exception is *Black,* a common way to refer to African-Americans.
- Capitalize names of departments in government, but for departments anywhere else, capitalize only the parts that would be proper nouns by themselves: *State Department, Department of Defense, Fire Department, English department, history department, returns department.*
- For names of varieties of plants and animals or of particular foods, capitalize only the proper noun: *German shepherd, MacIntosh apple* (the fruit—the computer has a lowercase *i* and the brand Apple would be capitalized), *red delicious apple, Boston cream pie.*
- Political party names are capitalized, but not the names of philosophies unless based on a proper noun: *Democratic Party, socialist philosophy, Marxism.*
- Capitalize regions, but lowercase mere directions: *the South, Southern accent, driving south.* Exception: Do not capitalize a region in front of a proper noun, unless that forms the actual name or a place well-known around the country: *southern Colorado, southern U.S., South Carolina, Southern California.* Local stylebooks, however, often make an exception and capitalize a local region before a state name when it's known well to readers—such as *Southeast Michigan* in the Detroit area.
- Many product names that people think are generic terms (common nouns) are actually trade names (proper nouns) and should be capitalized: *Band-Aid, Frisbee, iPod, Jell-O, Kitty Litter, Kleenex, Scotch tape, Styrofoam, Vaseline* and *Velcro.* For more examples, see "Avoiding Trademark Infringement" on page 140.
- Oddly, AP lowercases pronouns for God or Jesus, but capitalizes *Mass* and *Communion.* It capitalizes *pope* only in front of the pope's name.

Numbers

- Generally speaking, the numbers zero through nine are written out, and the numbers 10 and above are written as numerals.
- Exceptions to the general rule about numbers: Use numerals, even if less than 10, with addresses, ages, clothes sizes, dates, dimensions,

money, percentages, recipe amounts, speeds, temperatures, times, weights and years. Most numbers in sports references are numerals, as well as the expressions *No. 1, No. 2,* etc.

- Despite the two previous rules, the only numeral that isn't written out at the beginning of a sentence is a year: *2020 was a bad year financially for many people after the pandemic shutdown.*
- Always write out the words *million, billion* and *trillion: 1 million, 13 billion.*
- Fractions are written out with a hyphen if the amount is less than one but written as numerals if greater (a mixed number): *one-third, $1\frac{1}{3}$.*
- Add the suffixes *nd, rd, st* and *th* to numerals for designations of courts, military terms and political divisions (such as precincts, districts and wards). Also, use them for amendments or street names in which the number has two or more digits: *First Amendment, 10th Amendment.*

Punctuation

Commas

- Use between independent clauses joined by a conjunction:

  Donald Trump was renominated for president in 2020 by the Republican Party, *and* Joe Biden was nominated by the Democratic Party. (*And* is a conjunction joining two clauses that each could stand alone as a whole sentence, so there's a comma before the *and*.)

- Use after a dependent clause followed by an independent one but not vice versa.
- Use to introduce a quote of one sentence.
- Use instead of parentheses around parenthetical items.
- Use between coordinate modifiers—when you can reverse them and put *and* between them. Example: *The tall, thin man . . .* Exceptions: See "Coordinate versus Compound Modifiers" on page 185.
- Use after an introductory word, phrase or clause. AP suggests a comma only after introductory phrases and clauses and says you may leave out the comma if a phrase is a short one. But for consistency, we suggest always putting one after an introductory element.

Introductory word:	No, we disagree.
Introductory phrase:	In the fall, it turned chilly.
Introductory clause:	Because he voted for the war, he came under attack.

- Differences between English usage and journalism usage:
  1. Don't put a comma before the word *and* in a series unless it would be confusing not to do so.
  2. Don't put a comma before *Jr.* or *Sr.* for names of people, or before *Inc.* or *Ltd.* in names of businesses
  3. Put a comma both before and after a state, after a city or a year, and after a date.

Semicolons

- Use a semicolon (;) to join independent clauses—those that could stand alone as complete sentences—when there is no conjunction between the two. A semicolon should never be used to join a dependent clause to an independent one. But journalists don't even often use semicolons to join independent clauses except in a headline. Instead, they typically would either make the clauses separate sentences or join them with a comma and a conjunction.
- Use a semicolon between items in a series when at least one of the items contains a comma. (And include a semicolon before the *and*.)
- Do not capitalize after a semicolon.

Colons

- A colon (:) is used to introduce a list or to join two closely related independent clauses when the first is meant to introduce and point to the second.
- A colon is also used instead of a comma to introduce a quote of two sentences or more.
- Capitalize after a colon only if what follows is a complete sentence.

Dashes

- Don't overuse them.
- Use a dash instead of a comma for a dramatic pause in a sentence.
- Use dashes in place of commas around parenthetical items already containing commas.
- You may use dashes as bullets to set off items in a list.

Hyphens

- Put a hyphen between compound modifiers—that is, when you have two modifiers in a row, the first modifies the second and the two of them together modify something else: the well-liked teacher. The main exceptions are that you should not hyphenate after the words *very* or *most*, or after an adverb ending in *ly*, and when the compound word follows the word it modifies:

lightly roasted nuts (no hyphen after ly adverb)
    She's a part-time worker, but she works part time.

- Hyphens are also used in some compound words and after some prefixes. Consult your official stylebooks and dictionary—generally your local one, AP and *Webster's New World*.
- AP now leaves the hyphen out of words with a *pre* or *re* prefix before a stem starting with an *e*: *preelection, reelected*.

Quotations

Attribution

It's important that the reader always be clear who's saying what.
    Every paraphrase needs to be attributed, but every quote does not as long as it's clear who said it.

Wrong: Privacy is our most cherished right. (Without attribution this paraphrase sounds as though the writer is editorializing.)
Right: Gonzalez said that privacy is our most cherished right.
Right: Gonzalez said it's important to protect citizens' privacy. "It's our most cherished right."

Whenever more than one person is quoted in a story, attribution is required—and it should be placed in front of the quotation whenever the speaker being quoted changes. This is important so the reader doesn't think it's the same person speaking. When there's only one speaker, it's not necessary to put an attribution with every sentence quoted as long as it's clear the same person is speaking.

"This type of evaluation isn't based on a score," he said. "It is based on ideas and areas that should be addressed." (Notice it's clear the same person is saying the second sentence even without another *he said*, which would only seem redundant.)

The first time a quotation is used, the speaker's qualifications are also usually cited, as well as the person's full name. On second reference, the person's last name only is cited. If the person has a title that was used on first reference—such as *the Rev., Dr.* or *Gov.*—that title is dropped on all following references. Sometimes, the title—written out and without capital letters—can be used in place of the name on some of the secondary references: *The governor said . . .*

In a detailed recounting of what someone said, rather than repeat *says* or *said* so often, introduce a longer account with a sentence like, "He gave the following account to police:"

A Memphis man was arrested early Monday morning after a high-speed chase through South Memphis that resulted in serious injury to a pedestrian.

Police arrested Jerome Caldwell, 22, of 303 S. Third St., and prosecutors charged him with resisting arrest, aggravated assault and burglary.

Police gave this account of the events:

Officers Jill Southerland and Carlos Rodriguez responded to a silent alarm at Southside Hardware, 2028 E. Miller St., about 4:30 a.m. They entered the building and surprised a burglar, who fled through a rear door.

The man jumped into a car and led the officers on a three-mile chase through South Memphis, which ended when another squad car was summoned to help block the intersection at Hernando and Main streets. The car came to a stop there but not until it had struck Antonio D'Amato, 29, who was crossing Main Street when the car and police arrived.

Here are some additional tips regarding attributions:

- **Reporters should stick to one tense in attributions—either *said* or *says* throughout but not both.** Don't mix the two because then you'll have unnecessary shifts in verb tense from past to present. Instead, use *said* for hard-news stories, and use *says* for feature stories.
- **The order should usually be *source said*, not *said source* in any medium, but especially broadcast.** The *source-said* order is more conversational because usually the subject precedes the verb in English. You may want to use the *said-source* order, however, if the *source* and the *said* are separated by a long description, such as a title.
- **Journalists prefer *said* and *says* to other attributions because of their brevity and neutrality.** For example, *stated* is longer. *Claimed* and *according to* can imply doubt. (Some editors prefer *according to* when a document is being quoted. *According to* is also correct when you mean "in accordance with rules" and then should refer to the content, not the speaker.) *Admitted* implies guilt. *Conceded* implies someone agreed reluctantly. *Refuted* means successfully answered. *Added* means the statement was an afterthought. And nobody ever *beamed, grinned, laughed, smiled* or *winced* in words.
- **Avoid attributions that imply mind reading such as saying that someone *believes, doubts, feels, hopes* or *thinks* something.** How does the reporter know? Only if he or she is a mind reader or the person *said* it.

Here are a few special problems with *said* and *says*:

- If *said* or *says* is followed by a time element, follow the time element with the word *that*.
- If a person is paraphrased as saying two clauses in one sentence, don't separate the clauses with a comma.
- If a person is paraphrased after the word *said,* the clause following it should whenever possible be in an earlier tense—further in the past— to maintain the proper sequence of tenses.

He said he was going. (Was, not is.)

How to Capitalize and Punctuate Quotations

- **Capitalize the first word of a quotation only when it is a complete sentence that is directly quoted.**
- **When the attribution precedes the paraphrased or quoted statement**:

  1. Quotations of more than one sentence are introduced with a colon.
  2. Quotations of one sentence are introduced with a comma.
  3. Partial quotes are not introduced with commas or colons.

- **When the attribution follows the paraphrased or quoted statement**:

  1. Put a comma before the attribution and after the paraphrase or quote when it's a full sentence or less long.
  2. If the quotation is more than a sentence long, move the attribution either after the first sentence or before both of them, punctuating according to the above rules.

- **A comma or a period will always go inside the final quote mark. An exclamation mark or a question mark will go inside or outside, depending on whether it's part of the actual quote.** *The AP Stylebook* says the latter is true for colons and semicolons, as well. But in practice, they always seem to go outside the quote.
- **Don't go from a partial quotation to a complete one within the same paragraph.** Don't write:

Jones said he was "happy to be alive. I can't believe it happened."

Instead, put a quotation mark after the period following *alive*, then begin a new paragraph with a quotation mark in front of *I*.

- **How to handle quotations of more than one paragraph**:

  1 Don't put quotation marks at the end of the paragraph if the quote in that paragraph is a full sentence and the quotation continues in the next paragraph.
  2 If the quotation in the paragraph is a partial one that continues into the next paragraph, it *does* have quotation marks at the end.

- **The use of quote marks should mean the reporter is using the exact words the speaker or writer used.** Reporters shouldn't rewrite another person's words and leave them in quotations. They should quote them exactly, paraphrase them (no quotations but attribution still used) or use partial quotes (paraphrase of some words with quotation marks around direct quotes).
- **Although AP permits ellipses (. . .), journalists don't usually use them to indicate words being left out of a quotation as a student would in a term paper. That doesn't mean journalists rewrite the quote and deceptively leave it in quotation marks.** Rather, journalists will instead use paraphrases (putting the quotation in the reporter's own words but taking off the quotation marks) or partial quotes (quotations of a few words or phrases only while paraphrasing the rest).

Miscellaneous

Time-Day-Place

- **Journalists write about events in time-day-place order because it is usually the most efficient way.** For example, don't say an event will take place "at City Hall on Friday at 3 p.m." Instead write that it will take place "3 p.m. Friday at City Hall" (saving two words).
- **Do not include both a day and a date.** Use only the day for events within a week forward or backward. Use only the date for events beyond a week forward or backward.
- **Do not write *yesterday* or *tomorrow*, but you may write *today* or *tonight*, *this morning*, *this afternoon* or *this evening* if you mean the day of publication.**
  Be careful, however, not to write *today* to refer to something you're writing today but that won't be printed until the next day.
- **If you write a month without a date, don't abbreviate the month.** If you write a month with a date, abbreviate it unless it's one of those with five letters or fewer (March, April, May, June, July): August; Aug. 9; Aug. 9, 2020; August 2020 (year but no date, so not abbreviated).

Addresses

- **Words like *street, avenue, boulevard, drive* and *lane* are always written out when a specific address is not given.** If an address is given, then the words *street, avenue* and *boulevard* are the only three such words abbreviated (*St., Ave., Blvd.*): *Ninth Street; 1039 Ninth St.; 1826 Circle Lane.*
- **If the street name has a direction in it, abbreviate the direction only with a specific street address**: *West Hickory Avenue, 103 W. Hickory Ave.; Southeast Avalon Drive, 2608 S.E. Avalon Drive.*
- **When an address follows a person's name, either separate them with the word *of* and no commas, or use commas around the address without the word *of***:
  Hank Jones of 678 S. Elm was arrested; Hank Jones, 678 S. Elm, was arrested. Some outlets also put commas in front of *of* and after the address in a sentence like the first example, but we consider that unnecessary.
- **When an address follows a person's name and age, separate them with both a comma after the age and the word *of* in front the address.** Do not put a comma after the address in this instance because the comma is there to separate the age, not the address: *Hank Jones, 36, of 678 S. Elm was arrested.*

Titles

- **A person's official title is always capitalized if it appears in front of the name, lowercase afterward or without the name**: *President Joe Biden; Joe Biden, president of the U.S.; the president.*
- **Mere job descriptions (such as astronaut, announcer, teacher) are not capitalized either before or after a name.** (If you are not sure whether a title is a formal, official title or merely a job description, put the title after the name and lowercase it.) AP always lowercases the titles *coach* and *professor*.
- **Use the abbreviations *Dr., Gov., Lt. Gov., Rep., Sen.* and the *Rev.* (note that the word *the* is part of the title) only in front of a name and on first reference.**
  In later references, just use the person's last name. The titles *president* and *professor* are never abbreviated.
- **Courtesy titles (*Mr., Mrs., Miss, Ms.*) are usually not used.** Instead, a person is referred to on first reference by first and last name, then on subsequent references by last name only. Exceptions include direct quotations or when a woman requests it. Newspapers also commonly use courtesy titles for the deceased in obituaries, and a few do in editorials.

- **In stories where it's necessary to distinguish between two people with the same last name, use the first and last name in all references.** Some newspapers will use only first names on second reference in cases where two people have the same surname, but they'd typically do this only in features.

Datelines

A **dateline** is the designation before the start of a story of the city from which the story was filed. It appears only in front of a nonlocal story. The name of the city in a dateline is written in capital letters, the name of the state or country in upper and lowercase: AUSTIN, Texas.

Some cities (such as Washington) are so well-known that they are not followed by a state or country. A list of cities in the U.S. and abroad that stand alone can be found in *The AP Stylebook* under the dateline entry. In addition, your editor may designate other cities within your state or readership area as dateline cities that stand alone in your publication.

Notice, especially, that *Washington* and *New York* always refer to the cities by those names, not the states, unless otherwise indicated. In other words, you would not normally write *Washington, D.C.,* or *New York City* but simply *Washington* or *New York.*

- If a city is a *dateline city*—that is, one that stands alone without a state or country in a dateline—it would also stand alone within the body of a story.
- The dateline is typically followed by parentheses in which is written the name of the wire service providing the story, then by a dash. The story would then follow, beginning on the same line:

WASHINGTON (AP)—The Senate voted 52–48 on Thursday . . .

Spelling

Average readers may never know when an editor misses a stylebook mistake so long as the article isn't inconsistent with itself. But spelling mistakes, like ones with grammar and usage, are ones that readers do catch, and when they do, the credibility of the publication goes down in their minds. They think, "If I can't trust this website to spell it right, why should I trust it to get the facts right?"

Remembering to click on the spell-checker or looking up the words your wordprocessor automatically highlights is a good start, but dictionaries vary, and no word-processing program follows the procedure journalists use.

Journalists have a specific and unique way of determining the way a word is spelled. This can result in some words being

spelled differently from how you may be accustomed. For example: *adviser, back porch, doughnut.* Follow these steps:

- Look it up in your local stylebook if it lists spellings that override AP's suggestions. Otherwise, start with *The AP Stylebook.* If the word is in there, spell it that way.
- If the word is not in your local stylebook or AP—and only then—look it up in *Webster's New World College Dictionary.* Don't look in a different dictionary. Don't look in the small paperback version of this one. If the word wasn't in your local stylebook or AP and it *is* in here, spell it that way.
- If the word isn't in either AP or *Webster's New World*—and only if it wasn't in either—AP used to suggest you look it up in the latest *Webster's Third New International* (unabridged). If the word wasn't in the previous two but it was in here, this was the way to spell it. AP has since dropped *Webster's Third New International* from its spelling procedure.
- If the word isn't in any of these, consider a different word. If the word isn't in any of the these, and it is a compound about which you wonder whether it should be one word, two words or hyphenated, then make it two words as a noun or verb, or hyphenate it as a compound adjective in front of a noun.

Here are some questions you might ask when checking spelling:

1. Have you checked for typos?
2. Have you looked up all compound words to see whether they should be written as one word, two words or hyphenated? There's really no overall consistency as to how AP or the dictionary might decide to spell them. You'd think by now, for example, that *baby sitter* would be one word, but AP spells it as two, with *baby-sit, baby-sitting* and *baby-sat* as two.

Spelling Words to Know

You should commit to memory some or all of these often-misspelled words. The following ones, for example, occur so often, it will save you time in the long run to know them. Also, they're likely to come up on internship and job tests.

acceptable	acknowledgment	advertise
accessory	Acoustics	adviser*
accommodate	adherence	aficionado
accumulate	admissible	afterward*

aggressor
all right
alleged
allotted, allotment
already
appall
Arctic
assistant
attendance
ax*
backward*
bankruptcy
battalion
beginning
bellwether
benefited
berserk
blond (adj., noun for male)
blonde (adj., noun for female)
boyfriend
burqa
buses (vehicles)
busses (kisses)
Canada geese
caress
Caribbean
cave-in
cemetery
chaperon
chauffeur
collectible
consensus
consistent
consul

council
counsel
deductible
demagogue
descendant
diarrhea
dietitian
disastrous
dissension
divisive
do's and don'ts
doughnut
drowned
drunkenness
embarrass
emphysema
employee*
espresso
exhilarating
existence
February
firefighter
fluorescent
forward*
fourth
fraudulent
fulfill
goodbye*
grammar
greyhound
guerrilla
harass
hemorrhage
heroes

hitchhiker
homicide
hypocrisy
ifs and buts
impostor
inadmissible
incredible
indestructible
indispensable
innocuous
innuendo
inoculate
irreligious
irresistible
irreverent
jeopardy
judgment*
kidnapped*
kindergarten
knowledgeable
lambaste
largess
leisure
liaison
license
likable
liquefy
marijuana
marriage
marshal
massacre
medieval
memento
misspell

naïve	preferred	surprise
nerve-racking	privilege	Tariff
nickel	procedure	theater*
ninth	prostate	thoroughly
nuisance	publicly	till
occasion	quandary	tomatoes
occurred	questionnaire	tornadoes
OK'd	queue	toward*
opossum	rarefy	traveled*
overrule	reconnaissance	tumultuous
paid	relevant	ukulele
papier-mâché	restaurateur	vacuum
parallel	rhythm	veterinarian
paraphernalia	rock 'n' roll	vice versa
pastime	sacrilegious	vilify
pavilion	Scotch)	villain
penicillin	seize	volcanoes
permissible	separate	voyageur
Philippines	siege	Wednesday
picnicking	sizable	weird
playwright	skiing	whiskey* (whisky for
pneumonia	skillful	wield
poinsettia	strait-laced	wondrous
politicking	strong-arm	X-ray (noun, verb and adj.)
pompom	subpoena	yield
potatoes	summonses	
preceding	supersede	

*Preferred spelling.

Tightening

A few words may say a lot, and a lot of words may say little.

The average newspaper reader reads the paper for only 22 to 24 minutes a day. The average broadcast story lasts 30 seconds or less. The average web reader doesn't want to waste time scrolling through a story that's longer than it needs to be. So, don't waste your audience's time with unnecessary words.

Get to the point as quickly as possible, conveying as much news as you can within the time the reader, viewer or listener spends with you.

For years, various readability formulas have been available to measure the difficulty of writing. Microsoft Word even has this function built in, although by default it's turned off. To turn it on in Microsoft Office 365, for example, go to File/Options/Proofing, then check under "When correcting spelling and grammar in Word" that "Check grammar with spelling" is selected. Finally, select "Show readability statistics." The reading level of the document will now be displayed after you check the spelling and grammar. If you use a different version of Word or a different word processor, consult the help function or search on the internet for how to check readability. This is a useful but often neglected tool for writers and editors.

Researchers have developed a number of readability measurements, some of which calculate the grade level of a writing sample. **The average American reads at an eighth- to ninth-grade level.** Readability measurements, including grade-level calculations, are based on some variation of three simple ideas:

1. Short sentences generally are easier to read than long ones.
2. Short words are easier to understand than long ones.
3. Familiar, conversational words are easier to understand than others.

If passages from a story or the whole story average more than 20 words to the sentence and the number of longer words in a sample of 100 words exceeds 10%, a majority of readers will find the passages difficult to understand. The number of unfamiliar words in passages also affects readability. A passage is more readable if it sticks as much as possible to the 3,000 most common words known by 80% of fourth-graders and that are the first words taught to learners of English as a second language.

Of course, anything that would be harder for a reader to understand would be even worse if written for broadcast, where the listener doesn't always have the luxury of looking again at what was not understood the first time.

So, here's our advice for making your writing for any medium easier to be understand and not to test your audience's patience:

Cut any words that wouldn't change the meaning of the sentence if they were gone. In the following sentences, the underlined words can be deleted:

She shopped <u>very</u> late each afternoon at the store <u>at the corner</u> of 10th and Elm <u>streets</u>.

The mayor read <u>from</u> a <u>prepared</u> statement.

She was on the operating table from 8 p.m. Monday night until 5 a.m. Tuesday <u>morning</u>.

He said the USDA is <u>currently</u> spending . . .

Justice said Double Spring had been <u>in the process of</u> phasing out its operation . . .

Hayley has some 30 <u>different</u> fish tanks in his home.

Tate slipped away to a secret retreat Tuesday for his first meeting with his daughter<u> he had never met</u>.

Cut unnecessary facts. News presents the pertinent facts. Every story should answer all the questions the reader or viewer expects answered. If a big story returns after having been out of the news, it should contain a short background or reminder. Readers don't carry clips to check background.

But if a fact isn't vital in telling the news, it should be cut. Don't ramble and let extraneous facts make it harder for your audience to follow the point.

Substitute fewer words for more if they mean the same thing.

prior to—before
applying its stamp of approval—approving
The field is 50 feet in length—The field is 50 feet long
The vase was blue in color—The vase was blue
He wrote a formal letter of resignation—He resigned

Use words that are more common. Usually, they're also the shorter ones. But sometimes, it's better to use a longer word, or two or three smaller words, rather than one less-common one.

Less common	More common
aggregate	total
attempt	try
component	part
conceptualize	think of
contusion	bruise
currently	now
discover	find
enable	let, allow to
enormous	big
frequently	often
implement	start, do
numerous	many
obtain	get

Less common	More common
remainder	rest
subsequently	later
transport	carry
utilize	use

Wordy Phrases to Avoid

Most experienced editors could add to this list. The preferred form is in parentheses.

a great number of times (often)
a large number of (many)
a period of several weeks (several weeks)
a small number of (few)
a sufficient number of (enough)
absolute guarantee (guarantee)
accidentally stumbled (stumbled)
advance planning (planning)
advance reservations (reservations)
all of a sudden (suddenly)
as a general rule (usually)
assessed a fine (fined)
at a later date (later)
at the conclusion of (after)
at the corner of 16th and Elm (at 16th and Elm)
at the hour of noon (at noon)
at the present time (now)
at 12 noon (at noon)
bald-headed (bald)
called attention to the fact (pointed out, reminded)
climb up (climb)
commute back and forth (commute)
completely decapitated (decapitated)
consensus of opinion (consensus)
cost the sum of $5 (cost $5)
despite the fact that (although)
disclosed for the first time (disclosed)
draw to a close (end)
due to the fact that (because)

during the winter months (in the winter)
end result (result)
entered a bid of (bid)
exact replica (replica)
few in number (few)
filled to capacity (filled)
first priority (priority)
first prototype (prototype)
for a period of 10 days (for 10 days)
foreign imports (imports)
free gift (gift)
free pass (pass)
funeral services (services—if in the context of an obit)
future plans (plans)
general public (public)
grand total (total)
heat up (heat)
hostile antagonist (antagonist)
in addition to (and, besides, also)
in back of (behind)
in case of (if, concerning)
in order to balance (to balance)
in the absence of (without)
in the event that (if)
in the immediate vicinity of (near)
in the near future (soon)
in the not-too-distant future (eventually)
introduced a new (introduced)
is going to (will)
is in the process of making application (is applying)
kept an eye on (watched)
large-sized man (large man)
lift up (lift)
made good his escape (escaped)
major portion of (most of)
married her husband (married)
merged together (merged)
midway between (between)
Muslim imam (imam)
new construction (construction)
new innovation (innovation)
off of (off)

old cliché (cliché)
on account of (because)
on two different occasions (twice)
once in a great while (seldom, rarely)
partially damaged (damaged)
partially destroyed (damaged)
past history (history)
period of time (period)
placed its seal of approval on (approved)
possibly might (might)
postponed until later (postponed)
prior to (before)
qualified expert (expert)
receded back (receded)
recur again (recur)
reduce down (reduce)
refer back (refer)
remand back (remand)
revise downward (lower)
rise up (rise)
rose to the defense of (defended)
short space of time (short time)
since the time when (since)
sprang a surprise (surprised)
started off with (started with)
strangled to death (strangled)
summer season (summer)
tendered his resignation (resigned)
total operating costs (operating costs)
true facts (facts)
underground subway (subway)
voiced objections (objected)
whether or not (whether)
widow of the late (widow)
with the exception of (except)

Cut clichés, or insist on a more original restatement. A good writer uses a fresh and appropriate figure of speech to enhance the story. Oscar Wilde said never to write anything you've heard before. The editor should distinguish between the fresh and the stale. This isn't always easy because some words and phrases are used repeatedly in the news.

Don't cut descriptions from feature stories if they help set the scene or add color.

On stage, she is surrounded by musicians in green suits and cowboy boots. Stuck there in the middle, Tammy looks like one smooth pearl in a bucket of green peas.

(Such descriptive language might be cut from a hard-news story but should be left in a feature to help set the scene and tone.)

Clichés to Avoid

110%
acid test
at the end of the day
average (reader, voter, etc.)
banquet (never a dinner)
belt tightening
best thing since sliced bread
bitter (dispute)
blistering (accusation)
bombshell (announcement, etc.) boost
bone-chilling temperatures
brutal (murder, slaying)
But one thing's certain.
call an audible
cardinal sin
caught the eye of (cautious, guarded) optimism
children (kids) of all ages
cold shoulder
crack (troops, etc.)
cutback
daring (holdup, etc.)
deficit-ridden
devastating (flood, fire)
devout (Catholic, etc.)
double down
dumped
epic (a web cliché)
eye (to see)
eyeball to eyeball
feel-good movie
fire broke out, swept
fire of undetermined origin

foot the bill
freak accident
gap (generation, credibility, etc.)
-gate (added to name to indicate a scandal)
gut (a program)
hammer out
hardcore, hard-nosed
hike (for *raise*)
historical document
hobbled by injury
in terms of
in the wake of
initial (for *first*)
. . . isn't just for . . . anymore
keeled over
led to safety
luxurious (apartment, love nest, etc.)
made off with
miraculous (cure, escape, etc.)
momentous occasion
name of the game
oil-rich nation
on the fly
Only time will tell.
one weird trick (a web cliché)
opt for
overwhelming majority
passing motorist
plush (hotel, apartment, etc.)
phones ringing off the hook
power (lunch, user)
relocate (for *move*)
reportedly, reputedly
roundly attacked
seasoned (observers, etc.)
senseless murder
shot in the arm
shovel-ready
skin in the game
slash (a program)
slowly but surely
staged a riot (or protest)
standing ovation
star-studded

stinging rebuke
sweeping changes
swing into high gear
take it one day at a time
task force
tax-and-spend (Democrats, liberals)
tense (or uneasy) calm
terminate (for *end*)
the same policies that got us into this mess
Think about it.
thorough (or all-out) investigation
timely hit
top-level meeting
touch base
turn thumbs down
uneasy truce
vast expanse
verbalize
violence (erupted, flared)
violent explosion
voters marched to the polls
wait-and-see attitude
whirlwind (tour, junket)
(80) years young
You be the judge.

Suggested Websites

American Copy Editors Association: https://aceseditors.org
Associated Press: www.apstylebook.com/
EditTeach, a great website for learning and teaching copy editing: www.editteach.org
Grammar Girl (Mignon Fogarty): www.quickanddirtytips.com/education/grammar
The Slot: A Spot for Copy Editors (Bill Walsh): www.theslot.com

Suggested Readings

Agnes, Michael, Ed. *Webster's New World College Dictionary*, 5th edition. Houghton Mifflin Harcourt, 2018.
The Associated Press Stylebook. Latest edition. New York: The Associated Press.
Bremner, John B. *Words on Words*. Columbia University Press, 1980.
Brooks, Brian S., James L. Pinson and Jean Gaddy Wilson. *Working With Words: A Handbook for Media Writers and Editors*, 10th edition. Bedford/St. Martin's, 2020.

Ross-Larson, Bruce. *Edit Yourself: A Manual for Everyone Who Works with Words,* 2nd edition. W.W. Norton, 1996

Siegal, Allan M., and William G. Connolly. *The New York Times Manual of Style and Usage,* 5th edition. Three Rivers Press, 2015.

Strunk, William, Jr., and Richard De A'Amorelli, Eds. *The Elements of Style: Classic Edition (2018): With Editor's Notes, New Chapters & Study Guide.* Macmillan, 2018.

8 HOLISTIC EDITING
Integrating the Macro and the Micro

Tying It All Together

In Chapters 4 through 7, we discussed macro versus micro approaches to editing. Earlier, in Chapter 3, we discussed our Three R's approach to editing and mentioned also Don Ranly's Seven C's Plus One formulation. All of these represent different ways to think about the editing process and to keep the basics in mind. You can use any or all of them that seem useful to you.

In this chapter, we introduce one more approach: what we call **holistic editing**, a particularly practical technique in helping you edit stories speedily yet thoroughly. The idea is simple. The news each day is full of the same kinds of stories—accidents, crimes, meetings, sports, weather and so on. After you've edited enough of each kind, you gradually learn what needs to be in each kind of story, even sometimes the typical order in which they're presented, as well as the most common problems, big and small.

DOI: 10.4324/9781003011422-8

When experienced editors read stories, they can edit more quickly because they know what to look for in stories of that type. As a beginning editor or writer, you can use this chapter as a checklist of the problems a seasoned editor looks for in various kinds of stories. Simply identify the type of story you're working on, then turn here for advice.

Of course, while editing or writing any kind of story, be on the lookout not only for what's typical in stories of that type but also for other kinds of problems, large and small, that might appear. For example, all fields of journalism stress short paragraphs; short sentences; short, common words; use of a common stylebook, usually AP; and some standard of objectivity, although that can mean different things in different contexts, such as hard-news versus features or even different media.

Speaking of that, hard-news stories share certain common formulas that differ from features and opinion pieces. So, we've arranged the story genres here under those three broad categories: hard news v. features and opinion.

Likewise, writing for a specific medium like newspapers has elements that differ from other media. So, refer to Chapter 3 for tips on how broadcast and web stories differ from print ones. Incorporate knowledge of these various formulas—what all journalism has in common, how hard news differs from features and how writing is different to fit the requirements of different media—into your editing and writing, as well as the story genres.

How you do that is up to you. You might, for example, read a story several times with a different focus each time—macro, micro, then headline writing. Or you might first read a story to get an overall sense of whether it's a hard-news story or a feature, then edit it according to which genre of story it is, then review it to look for anything you might have missed and to write the headline.

Remember, a story might be a combination of genres at once. You might edit, for example, a story from a police press release about the arrest of a man wanted for a crime reported previously in the paper. For that, you might want to review the advice for press-release stories, follows and crime stories (all discussed in this chapter).

It should also be pointed out that journalists tend to use two approaches in classifying stories: Sometimes they classify them by content, such as a crime story, and sometimes by approach, such as a chronological account, a first-person story, and so on. We've included these along with the genres, so that's another reason an individual story might fall into more than one type.

This holistic approach, then, involves recognition at once of all the various patterns a particular story fits and how it might differ from what's typical. The variances you spot will usually be errors to correct, but it's important to be on the lookout for creative variations that introduce intelligent, fresh approaches. Don't try to fit every story into a straitjacket of preconceptions. Being able to recognize the difference between a mistake and useful innovation takes experience and an open, alert mind—demonstrating that good editing requires lots of knowledge, but it's also ultimately an art, not a science.

Hard-News Story Genres

Here we list some tips for genres of stories that are typically written as hard news, but it's also possible some individual stories in these genres might be written with a feature approach, especially in the lead. It would also, of course, be possible to write some kind of opinion piece about a story of a genre listed here.

Accident and Disaster Stories

Car crashes, boating accidents, drownings, fires, tornadoes, floods—all fall under the category of accident and disaster stories.

Accident-story leads are often in **passive voice**, with the victim having been killed or injured or property having been damaged, rather than in **active voice**, with someone doing these things to the person or property.

In accident stories, the *who* is probably the victim or even the damaged or destroyed property, as in the case of a schoolbus. The what is that someone died or was injured, or that property was destroyed or damaged. If more than one of these happened, deaths are more important than injuries, injuries are more important than destroyed property, and destroyed property is more important than damaged property—unless the injuries were slight and the destruction or damage widespread or costly.

If the person in the lead is a delayed-ID—with the person described but not named there because he or she isn't in the news often enough to be recognized by your audience—then that person's name typically starts the second paragraph. The first full-sentence quote often appears in the second paragraph, as well, or sometimes in the third paragraph. The first quote in the story should be the most dramatic or the best summary of the significance, drama or tragedy of the accident.

From there on, the story's details will be presented from most to least important, while seesawing back and forth between the reporter's presentation of details and quotes from those involved.

Accident stories should answer these questions:

- **Who was involved?** What are the names, ages (especially children) and addresses? Are there any relatives or friends who might be able to add details to those gathered from authorities, participants and witnesses?
- **What happened?** What was the nature of the accident? What was the extent of injuries (condition of victims) and damages (monetary

or other description)? These should be answered by the investigating officer; participants, if possible; and witnesses, if available.

- **When did it happen?**
- **Where did it happen?**
- **How and why did it happen, as the officer on the scene, participants and witnesses understand it?**

Warning: Be sure the description of what happened doesn't assume or imply anyone's guilt. There has not yet been a trial, so don't convict anyone in the media for responsibility beforehand. Best bet: Tell what charges were filed or tickets given. For example, rather than saying, "While driving drunk, Jones crossed the median and hit an oncoming car," report that he was arrested for driving while intoxicated and striking a vehicle in the other lane.

In *train and plane crash stories,* you should include the train or flight number, the place of departure, the destination and the times of departure and expected arrival. Airplanes may collide on the ground or *in the air* (not *midair*). Let investigators *search* the wreckage, not *comb* or *sift* it.

Most *earthquake stories* describe the *magnitude* of the tremor. One measurement is the Richter scale, which shows relative magnitude. It starts with magnitude 1 and progresses in units, with each unit 10 times stronger than the previous one. Thus, magnitude 3 is 10 times stronger than magnitude 2, which in turn is 10 times stronger than magnitude 1. On this scale, the strongest earthquakes recorded were a 9.5 in Chile in 1960 and a 9.2 in Alaska in 1964. (The deadliest was in 1556 in the Shaanxi province of China and killed an estimated 830,000 people.) *Intensity* generally refers to the duration or to the damage caused by the shock.

In *fire stories,* the truth is that in nine of 10 cases when people are *led to safety,* they're not. Except for an occasional child or infirm adult, they simply have the common sense to leave the building without waiting for a firefighter to "lead them to safety." Eliminate terms such as *three-alarm fire* and *second-degree burns* unless they are explained.

In *fire and flood stories,* the residents of the area are rarely *taken from their homes or asked to leave.* Instead, they *vacate their homes,* or they're *told to evacuate,* or they *are evacuated.*

Accident-Story Usage

- **Accident, collision, crash**—An accident implies no one is legally responsible. Two objects can *collide* only when both are in motion and going—usually but not always—in opposite directions. It is not a *collision,* but a *crash,* when one car is standing still. If a car *collided* with a power pole, it must have been in the bed of a moving truck.
- **Damage, damages**—"The full tragedy of Hurricane Betsy unfolded today as the death toll rose past 50, and damages soared into many

millions." *Damage* was the correct word here. You collect *damages* in court. "An estimated $40,000 worth of damage was done January 29th." *Damage* isn't worth anything. Quite the contrary.

- **Damaged, destroyed**—*Damaged* refers to partial destruction, *destroyed* to complete. It is wrong, then, to say something was "partially destroyed" and redundant to say it was "completely destroyed."

Accident-Story Clichés to Avoid

- fiery holocaust
- flames (licked, leaped, swept)
- raging brush fire
- rampaging rivers
- searing heat
- tinder-dry forest
- (traffic, triple) fatals (police station jargon)
- tragedy, tragic
- tragic accident
- weary (firefighters, rescue workers)

Accident-Story Tightening

The preferred form is shown in parentheses:

- autopsy to determine the cause of death (autopsy)
- blazing inferno, flaming inferno (inferno)
- came to a stop (stopped)
- completely destroyed, partially destroyed (destroyed, damaged)
- vehicle (car, truck)
- went up in flames (burned)

Business and Finance Stories

Business news is increasingly consumer news. Back in the penny press era, it was discovered that business news could be made interesting to a wider audience by including more "news you can use." After all, news has the most impact when it has the power to affect people personally—in the pocketbook, in the way they live or in their emotions. But business features don't have to end with how-to articles. **Focus pieces**, analysis pieces, **personality profiles** and other feature stories play a big role on business pages, as well.

Some common recurring types of business stories include *personal finance stories* (on topics like jobs, credit, college, cars, mortgages, leases, investment, insurance) and *local business features*, which look at new businesses, earnings of big local employers, big shake-ups in management, heroes (personality profiles) and villains (investigations).

Stories about growth indicators look at recurring measurements such as:

- **Gross Domestic Product**—The quarterly total output of goods and services; newer than the Gross National Product, which included citizens abroad.
- **Consumer Price Index**—A monthly basket of about 400 items.
- **Unemployment rate**—Reported monthly.
- **Housing starts**—Responds quickly to interest rates; reported monthly.
- **Index of Industrial Production**—Monthly index of factories and cars, mines, electricity and gas.

Business news, like any other kind, is most interesting when focused on people rather than things. If a business story seems dull, check whether it's focused on a person, or merely on an abstract business topic. If the latter, let your supervisor know your concern and ask whether it might be sent back for refocusing on a person involved with the issue.

Pay attention to numbers in a business story. Sometimes, business stories get bogged down with lots of figures that are not clearly explained. Insist that figures be explained so readers can more easily relate to them and understand their significance. Also, don't let too many numbers be crammed into a lead. Pick the number that is most important to the reader, then move the others down. People are interested in how the news affects them, not in the figures per se (see Chapter 4).

All who edit business stories should have at least an elementary knowledge of business terms. If you can't distinguish between a *balance sheet* and a *profit-and-loss statement*, between *earnings* and *gross operating income*, and between a *net profit* and *net cash income*, you have some homework to do. It may be helpful to take classes in economics and accounting to learn economic concepts and be able to analyze a budget. At minimum, you should learn how to calculate percentages, read Henry Hazlitt's classic little book *Economics in One Easy Lesson*, and know a little about the federal agencies that regulate business.

Numbers in Finance Stories

Interest Rates

- Appear in stories about loans.
- To calculate *simple interest* for a set time, such as one month or one year: Multiply the loan amount (the *principal*) by the rate expressed in decimal form. (To do the calculation, a rate of 5% would be expressed as .05.)

- To calculate *compound interest* over a period of time, such as months or years:

   1. Express the interest rate in decimal form, but put a 1 in front of it. (A 5% interest rate would be written as 1.05.)
   2. Multiply this number times itself for each year of the loan past the first. (For a five-year loan, that would be 1.05 to the fourth power, or about 1.22.)
   3. Multiply the result times the principal to find the total amount paid by the end of the loan. You can find a calculator online that will do this for you in many places, including www.money chimp.com/features/debt_payment_calculator.htm.

Mortgages

- The *rate* is the interest rate paid on the loan. A *fixed-rate mortgage* stays the same rate during the life of the loan. An *adjustable-rate mortgage* goes up or down during the loan in relation to the *prime interest rate* set by the Federal Reserve Bank.
- *Points* are a percentage of the principal paid up front in order to get a lower interest rate on the loan.

Inflation

- Dollars not adjusted for inflation are called *nominal dollars* or *current dollars.*
- Dollars adjusted for inflation are called *constant dollars* or *real dollars.*
- To convert nominal to constant dollars, use the calculator at www. usinflationcalculator.com. For example, if you wonder what a $20,000 salary for a worker in 1980 would be equivalent to in 2019 dollars, input $20,000 in the dollar box, 1980 in the year box, and choose 2019 in the remaining box, then click on calculate. The answer: $62,271.36.

Sales Tax

- To calculate the amount that sales tax will add to a purchase, multiply the purchase price of an item by the sales tax rate expressed as a two-place decimal.
- Example: A $500 computer bought in a state with a 6% sales tax would carry $500 x .06 = $30 in sales taxes, for a total cost of $530.

Property Tax

- Assessed value is what the government appraiser says the property is worth. (The assessed value, though, may be only a percentage of the actual value. In Michigan, it's about half.)
- *Millage rate* is the tax rate per $1,000 value. Search on the web for the millage rate in your community.
- To calculate property taxes: Divide the property's assessed value by 1,000—in other words, move the decimal three places to the left. Then multiply the result by the millage rate.
- Example: A home assessed at $250,000 at a millage rate of 60.04 mills per $1,000 would require a total property tax of $15,010.

Business and Finance Story Usage

- **Ampersand**—Use an ampersand (&) in a company's name if that is how the company writes it—otherwise, write *and*. *Company, incorporated* and *limited* are abbreviated at the end of a name, not in the middle. But if a name ends with both *company* and *incorporated*, both are abbreviated.
- **Business names**—The way the company writes its name is not necessarily how it's written in AP style. For example, AP abbreviates *Company* at the end of a name and before *Inc.* or *Ltd.* Also, AP puts no comma between *Co.* and *Inc.* or *Ltd.* But AP does honor the company's use of an ampersand (&) in its name.
- **Dividends**—Dividends reports should use the designation given by the company—*regular, special, extra, increases, interim, quarterly*—or say what was paid previously if there is no specified designation. The story should say whether there is a special or extra dividend paid with the regular dividend and include the amount of previously added payments. When the usual dividend is not paid or is reduced, some companies issue an explanatory statement, the gist of which should be included in the story.
- **Dow Jones average**—The Dow Jones average is one of several indexes used to gauge the stock market. It bases its index on 30 stocks. Changes in it are changes in the index number, not a percentage change.
- **Firm**—*Firm* should not be used interchangeably with *company*. A *firm* is a partnership or unincorporated group. By the way, include the location of the home office.
- **Grant, subsidy**—A *grant* is money given to public companies. A *subsidy* is help for a private enterprise.

- **Lloyd's of London**—Contrary to what most people think, Lloyd's does not itself sell insurance. Instead, it's a market of insurance companies, one of which may sell you insurance.
- **Same-store sales**—In quarterly and annual reports, businesses often refer to "same-store sales" as a means of making valid year-to-year comparisons in sales.
- **Savings and loans**—These should not be called *banks*. They may be referred to as *companies, institutions* or *associations*.

Business and Finance Story Clichés to Avoid

- biggest, best, first, groundbreaking, revolutionary (these terms are too often used without checking that they are accurate)
- new and improved

Business and Finance Story Tightening

The preferred form is shown in parentheses:

- depreciate in value (depreciate)
- merchandise (goods)
- merchandize (sell)

Chronological Stories

Lead stories with the latest news, not the earliest chronologically. There are exceptions, however, in the body of a story:

Use the chronological approach when reporting a detailed event or the subject of an interview relates a complicated series of events. For example, an account of a gunman's siege may lend itself to this treatment. So might the reconstruction of a pilot's frantic final moments before an airplane crash or a step-by-step account of how the Legislature altered a bill to appease lobbyists.

Start with a lead summarizing the story, then transition to the chronological account, concluding, perhaps, with a dramatic ending or continuing in inverted-pyramid style.

Crime and Court Stories

The most important point to remember: Make sure the reporting does not incriminate anyone not yet convicted in court. Journalists are legally protected in reporting libelous statements made in court proceedings provided the coverage is fair and accurate. Similar statements made outside the courtroom, though, do not receive the same protection.

The Fifth Amendment guarantees the right against self-incrimination. The report should not suggest that the use of this protection is a cover-up for guilt. Phrases such as *hiding behind the Fifth* should be eliminated.

To say *the grand jury failed to indict Jones* implies it shirked its duty.

Consider the ethics of reporting names and addresses of victims. Names of victims in rape cases or attempted rape cases generally should not be used. Nor should the story give any clue to their addresses in a way by which they can be identified, especially if the perpetrator has not been apprehended.

Avoid legalese. For example, "In a petition for a writ of mandamus, the new bank's incorporators asked the court to . . ." should be changed to "The new bank's incorporators asked the court to . . ."

Referring on second reference to the *appellee* or the *appellant* is confusing. The best way is to repeat the names.

Lawyers are fond of word doubling: *last will and testament, null and void, on or about, written instrument, and/or.* "The maximum sentence is a $20,000 fine and/or 15 years' imprisonment." The maximum would be the fine and 15 years.

Make sure the headline accurately reflects the story. An accurate story with an inaccurate headline can still pose a legal problem, especially because many readers will read only the headline and not the story.

Court-Story Usage

- **Arraignment, preliminary hearing**—An *arraignment* is a formal proceeding at which a defendant steps forward to give the court a plea of guilty or not guilty. It should not be used interchangeably with *preliminary hearing,* which is held in a magistrate's court and is a device to show probable cause that a crime has been committed and that there is a likely suspect.
- **Bail, bond, parole, probation**—*Bail* is the security given for the release of a prisoner. *Bond* is cash or property given as a security for an appearance, as in court, or for some performance. *Parole* is a conditional release of a prisoner with an indeterminate or unexpired sentence. *Probation* allows a person convicted of some offense to go free, under suspension of sentence during good behavior and generally under the supervision of a probation officer. By the way, a farmer's hay is *baled;* water is *bailed* out of a boat; a prisoner is released *on bail.*
- **Decisions, judgments, opinions, rulings, verdicts**—A *verdict* is the finding of a jury. A judge renders *decisions, judgments, rulings* and *opinions,* but seldom verdicts, unless the right to a jury trial is waived. Although verdicts are returned by juries in both criminal and civil actions, a guilty verdict is found only in criminal actions. Attorneys general or similar officials give *opinions,* not *rulings.*

- **Divorce**—Divorces are *granted* or *obtained*, not *awarded* like a medal.
- **Fines, sentences**—Fines and sentences are not *given*—they are not gifts. Rather, the defendant was *fined* or *sentenced*.
- **Insanity**—Someone is found *not guilty by reason of insanity*, not *innocent by reason of insanity*.
- **Judge, jurist, justice**—Members of the Supreme Court are *justices*, not *judges* or *supreme judges*. The title of the U.S. Supreme Court's chief justice is "Chief Justice of the United States." A *jurist* is an expert in the law, not any judge or jury member.
- **Mistrial**—Judges *declare*, but do not *order*, mistrials.
- **Pleas**—Someone can plead *guilty, not guilty* or *nolo contendere* (not admitting guilt but not contesting the charge). There is no such thing as a *plea of innocence*. And the preferred past tense in a number of stylebooks and dictionaries is *pleaded*, not *pled*, but AP now accepts *pled*, also.
- **Sentences**—A jail sentence does not mean, necessarily, that a person has been jailed. The individual may be free on bail, free pending an appeal or on probation during a suspended imposition of sentence. Note also that if a person has been sentenced to five years but the sentence is *suspended*, he or she is given a *suspended five-year sentence*, not a *five-year suspended sentence*.
- **Statements**—Statements are either *written* or *oral*, not *verbal* (which just means in words).

Court-Story Tightening

The preferred form is shown in parentheses:

- apprehended (arrested)
- court litigation (lawsuit)
- file a lawsuit against (sue, file suit against)
- statutory grounds for divorce (grounds for divorce)
- sworn affidavits (affidavits)
- taken into custody (arrested)

Legal Terms Requiring Explanation

Knowing these terms will help make you a more knowledgeable journalist when it comes to court stories.

- **Accessories before the fact**—Those charged with helping another who committed the felony
- **Arraigned**—Brought to court to answer to a criminal charge

- **Bequest**—Gift
- **Continuance**—Adjournment of the case
- **Corpus delicti**—The evidence necessary to establish that a crime has been committed; not restricted to the body of a murder victim—it can apply as well to the charred remains of a burned house
- **Debenture**—Obligation
- **Demurrer**—A pleading admitting the facts in a complaint or answer but contending they are legally insufficient
- **Domicile**—Home
- **Felony, misdemeanor**—A *felony* is a crime graver in nature and usually punishable by imprisonment or death; a *misdemeanor* is a lesser charge and can carry a sentence of up to one year
- **In camera**—In the judge's chambers
- **Indicted**—Accused or charged by a grand jury
- **An information**—An accusation or a charge filed by a prosecutor
- **Plaintiff**—Person filing the lawsuit
- **Plat**—Map
- **Released on personal recognizance**—Released on word of honor to do a particular act, such as to not leave the district and to show up in court on a certain date
- **Remanded**—Sent the case back to a lower court for review
- **Res judicata**—Matter already decided
- **Stay order**—Stop the action or suspend the legal proceeding
- **Writ**—A judge's or a court's order
- **Writ of habeas corpus**—An order to bring the prisoner to court so the court may determine whether the prisoner has been denied rights
- **Writ of mandamus**—A court order telling a public official to do something

Crime Stories

As with accident and court stories, the worst thing you can do in a crime story is to imply someone is guilty who hasn't been convicted. Even if a police officer tells you someone is "guilty as sin" or that "this arrest solves 32 burglaries," such statements would convict the suspect if run. Here's an example of a lead that convicts:

> Two Marines are being held without bond after terrorizing a family, stealing a car and trading shots with officers.

As written, that lead convicted the men who had not yet stood trial. The writer, instead, should have reported what charges were filed against the Marines.

Listing the wrong name in a crime story can be a route to libel action. Thorough verification of names, addresses and relationships is a must.

Avoid *alleged* and *allegedly* as modifiers of the suspect or his or her possible deeds ("the *alleged* rapist," "the suspect *allegedly* raped"). Instead, use a construction such as, "The victim said a man climbed through her bathroom window and raped her. Police later arrested William Jones." See pages 129–130.

Don't identify someone as a *suspected criminal*. Also, don't say someone is a *reputed organized crime figure* unless you're quoting privileged reports, such as transcripts from hearings before Congress. The term *would-be rapist* asserts someone is guilty of attempted rape.

Crime stories usually have a delayed-ID lead because most perpetrators and victims aren't well-known to your audience. Of the two, the lead is most likely to focus on the victim, partly because a suspect may not have been identified, yet, and partly because the audience probably cares more about the victim. Also, focusing on the victim will result in passive voice, which is preferable in this instance because it will be less likely to convict the suspect before a trial than would an active-voice lead with the suspect's name. Examples:

> An Ann Arbor youth was severely beaten by a group of teenagers after a rock concert Monday night and robbed of $17. (Passive voice)
> An Ypsilanti woman was held at gunpoint for four hours Monday by her ex-husband before police were able to talk the man into releasing her. (Passive voice to focus on victim; although this says the ex-husband did it, it's the truth and would not result in a libel suit)
> A man in a ski mask abducted a Southfield woman from a shopping-mall parking lot Monday and forced her to drive to a secluded location where he raped her. (Active voice but no name of suspect that would convict him by saying he did it)

Other advice for editing crime stories:

- **Avoid printing confessions until they have been admitted into court as evidence.** This is more a matter of ethics than law and is subject to your outlet's policy.
- **Avoid printing names or addresses of juvenile offenders or victims as well as victims of rape, sexual assault or sexual abuse.** Again, this is more a matter of ethics than law.
- **Generally, avoid gruesome photos of victims.**
- **Avoid saying a victim was "unharmed" if he or she was involved in a psychologically harrowing situation such as a kidnapping or an attempted rape.**

Legal Term Problems

If you edit a story involving legal matters and you don't understand it, this in itself could pose a legal problem for you. The misuse of legal jargon can carry a high risk. Likewise, the following terms could get you in trouble if you think you know what they mean but don't really.

- **Arrested for**—*The AP Stylebook* says change *arrested for* to *arrested on a charge of* if a charge has been filed, or *arrested on suspicion of* if not.

  We think there are problems with that advice. First, although AP says not to write or say *arrested for* because it connotes guilt, that is the usual legal wording.

  Second, it's inaccurate to use automatically the wording *arrested on a charge of* if there hadn't been a warrant first. Many people are not arrested on a warrant and may never be charged, just questioned and released because the prosecuting attorney or judge didn't think the evidence was enough to charge. Contrary to common belief, U.S. police can't charge someone. Prosecutors or grand juries do that. Or the suspects may be charged after being arrested if there's enough evidence, which means they were not arrested on a charge but that the charge came later. It comes down to which came first. If the warrant, then the suspect was *arrested on a charge of.* If the arrest, then he was *arrested and charged.*

  The best thing is to find out whether the suspect has been charged and if so, whether he or she was charged first then arrested or the other way around. If no charges have been filed, you should follow your media outlet's policy whether the name should even be released, and if your outlet has no problem with that because it's true that he was arrested, then say the suspect was arrested in connection with the crime but that as of press time, no charges had been filed.

  Finally, AP's suggestion of the phrase *arrested on suspicion* is also problematic despite the fact you often hear that on TV police dramas. Sure, you can say that someone arrested or charged is a suspect if the police tell you he is—no problem there. But *arrested on suspicion* is a bit different, at least in the U.S.

  Yes, police and attorneys often use the wording, and you'd probably never face a lawsuit if you used it in a story. But technically, in America, suspicion alone is not sufficient for arresting someone—there should be some actual evidence—not just an officer's suspicion, such as because he was a Black teen in the vicinity of a crime. The standard for arrest is evidence, for charging is "probable cause" and for convicting is "beyond a reasonable doubt."

And while we're discussing charges, never predict in print that someone will be charged. That could pose a libel problem if the person isn't, in fact, charged.

- **Burglary, larceny, robbery, theft**—A *robber* steals by force, or threat of force against someone. If someone breaks into a house when no one is there and steals something, it isn't a *robbery* but a *theft*—more specifically, a *burglary*. If a person pulls a weapon on the homeowner and makes off with the family silverware, that person is a robber. By the way, money is not robbed. A bank is *robbed*; the money is *stolen*. "A man in uniform swindled $1,759 from a woman." No, the person is swindled, not the money.

    A *thief* steals without resorting to force. *Theft* suggests stealth. A *burglar* makes an unauthorized entry into a building. *Theft* and *larceny* both mean taking what belongs to another. *Larceny* is the more specific term and can be proved only when the thief has the stolen property. Pickpockets and shoplifters are *thieves*.

- **Drugs, narcotics**—All narcotics are drugs, but many drugs are not narcotics.

- **Homicide, murder**—Avoid calling a homicide a *murder* until someone has been convicted. But you may call the trial a *murder trial*, if the defendant has been charged with murder. A *murder* is a homicide involving malice and premeditation. A homicide without malice or premeditation is *manslaughter*. It is proper, however, to say someone is "charged with murder" if that is the official charge and that it is a "murder trial". That does not mean, though, that you can call the crime a murder. It becomes a murder if the person charged with murder is convicted.

- **Looting**—It is incorrect to write: "Thieves broke into 26 automobiles parked near the plant and looted some small items." Money or other property is not looted. That from which it is taken is looted.

- **Sheriff's deputies**—Not *deputy sheriffs*.

Crime-Story Clichés to Avoid

- daring daylight robbery
- hail of bullets
- police were summoned

- senseless murder
- thorough investigation
- tragic crime

Crime-Story Tightening

The preferred form is shown in parentheses:

- armed gunman (gunman)
- fatal killing (killing)
- self-confessed (confessed)
- was in possession of (had)

Education Stories

Examples of education stories are coverage of meetings of the local Board of Education or, for colleges and universities, the Board of Curators or Board of Regents; personality profiles of teachers, students or administrators; issues facing education, such as cheating, plagiarism, taxes to support education, cost of college, student debt; and so on.

Education-Story Clichés to Avoid

- facilitate
- teachable moment

Education-Story Tightening

The preferred form is shown in parentheses:

- educator, educationist (teacher)
- facilitator (teacher, leader)
- resource center (library)

Follows

A **follow**, or **follow-up**, is an update to a previous story. Both terms apply mainly these days to **developing stories** (ones that continue to develop with new information over a series of days, weeks or months) and **updates** (stories that revisit someone or something in the news in the past that hasn't been covered in some time).

In this age of round-the-clock news coverage on 24-hour news networks and the internet, most stories in any medium are follows in that they report in more detail information reported earlier, either by that outlet or another.

Make sure a follow stresses new information that advances the story. A cardinal sin is beginning with the old news rather than the new. This mistake is made for one of two reasons: Either the reporter has not kept up with the news and doesn't know the old information has already been reported, or the reporter is a newbie who makes the mistake of thinking that the old news is more important because it's more general than the newer news. But what's really important is what's new.

A follow may contain:

- Information not available earlier.
- Information obtained through reporter enterprise.
- Fresh details, such as color or background.
- Analysis about the news of the first story.
- Reaction from those affected by the original story.
- Local reactions to a state, national or international story.

Somewhere in the story, there should be a tie-back paragraph leading to a brief explanation of previous developments for readers who missed the original news or need to be reminded. Often, the **tie-back paragraph** will follow the lead, then the story will return to its main focus on new information, ending with more details recapping the original story.

Gun Stories

Journalists often use mistaken terms for guns, which lowers their credibility among those with a background in them. And readers who are not gun owners themselves often misunderstand and misuse the terms. So, when the issue of gun control comes up, there's a lot of confusion. Here are what common words and phrases used about guns actually mean and how they should be used.

Assault rifle, assault weapon—Both are carbine military-style and police-style weapons, shorter than a rifle. A true assault rifle is a military weapon with a selector switch to choose between automatic and semi-automatic fire. An assault weapon is the civilian version, incapable of firing fully automatically, just semi-automatically. The problem with both terms is they need to be explained because a reader or listener not familiar with guns will tend to think the word "assault" means they are designed only for mass killing of people. In addition, "assault weapon" will probably sound more dangerous to them than "assault rifle," even though an "assault weapon" is not fully automatic but an assault rifle is.

Automatic weapon, semi-automatic weapon—A fully automatic weapon will fire as long as the trigger is held down, whereas a semi-automatic weapon will fire only one shot per trigger pull. Any rifle that holds more than one bullet, such as a hunting rifle, and any pistol that holds more than one shot is a semi-automatic. The use of the term "semi-automatic" should also be explained because someone not familiar with gun terms will likely confuse it with "automatic" and not realize that average pistols and hunting rifles are semi-automatics.

Bullet, cartridge, shell—A bullet is a projectile fired by pistol, rifle, machine gun or submachine gun. A cartridge is a bullet with its metal casing. A shell is the casing for a projectile or ammunition for a shotgun or cannon.

Bump stock—This is a now outlawed device that uses the recoil of a semi-automatic weapon to reload faster and fire more like an automatic.

Clip, magazine—Both hold and feed ammunition for a firearm. The modern device is called a magazine and may be attached or fixed. A clip is the term for detachable storage devices used in obsolete military rifles.

Machine gun, submachine gun—Both are fully automatic weapons, but a machine gun is generally large enough to be on a mount, while a submachine gun is lighter and fires handgun ammunition.

Pistol, revolver—Both are handguns. Pistols can either fire a single shot or be semi-automatic, that is firing one shot per trigger pull. Revolvers have a cylinder that rotates, moving the next bullet in line with the barrel after a shot is fired.

Health and Medical Stories

Translate technical terms into plain English. See the Health and Medical-Story Tightening list below.

Avoid trade names of drugs. Use the generic term unless the story is about a particular manufacturer's drug: Lipitor (brand name)—atorvastatin (generic)

Health and Medical-Story Usage

- **Anesthesiologist**—A doctor who administers anesthesia is an *anesthesiologist*, not an *anesthetist*.
- **Babies**—Babies are *born*, not *delivered*. Mothers deliver. Use *Caesarian section*, not *C section*. Remember that weights of babies are always written as numerals even if in single digits, and ages of babies are always written as numerals, even if single digits or days or weeks or months rather than years.
- **Condition**—Don't write that someone is in *serious condition* if the person wasn't even taken to the hospital. Avoid *guarded condition* or *resting comfortably*.
- **Diagnoses**—The illness, not the patient, is *diagnosed*.
- **Epidemic, pandemic**—An epidemic is when a contagious disease is spreading rapidly among a population. A pandemic is when an epidemic spreads to a large region or becomes worldwide.

- **Healthful, healthy**—The first refers to something that promotes good health. The second refers to a person, plant or animal that has good health. A common mistake is to speak of "eating *healthy*" when what is meant is a person eats a *healthful* diet.
- **Heart condition**—To write someone has a *heart condition* means nothing. Everyone does. It's only news when the condition is abnormal.
- **Injuries**—An injury is *sustained* only if it is capable of causing death. If it wasn't sustained, it was *suffered*—injuries are not *received*.
- **Jaundice**—Jaundice is a symptom, not a disease.
- **Ophthalmologist, optometrist**—An *ophthalmologist* is a doctor who diagnoses eye disease. An *optometrist* tests for and prescribes glasses.
- **Slings**—A person wears a sling *on* his or her arm. That person doesn't wear his or her arm *in* a sling.
- **Temperature**—It means nothing to say someone *has a temperature* because everyone does. What's important is if it's abnormal.

Is it racist to call a disease by its place of origin?

Many media commentators objected to President Trump using the terms "Wuhan Flu" or "China Flu" as racist and said the term potentially posed a threat to Asians. But an internet search shows some of the same news outlets had earlier used the terms themselves. Still, is it racist to do so?

For context, often in the past, viruses have been labeled according to their perceived place of origin with no objections: German measles, Spanish flu (which actually first showed up in Kansas), MERS (Middle Eastern Respiratory Syndrome), Lyme disease (after Lyme, Connecticut), Ebola (after the Ebola River in Africa), etc. This has prompted defenders of the president to say the objection is just a political one against him. That still doesn't answer the question, though, about whether the name convention should change. Whatever you may think personally, we'd advise following any advice in the *AP Stylebook* or your local style rules about the name of a specific disease.

Health and Medical-Story Tightening

The preferred form is shown in parentheses:

- abrasion (scrape)
- contusion (bruise)
- fracture (break, crack)
- hemorrhaging (bleeding)

- laceration (cut)
- physician (doctor)

Health and Medical-Story Clichés

- new normal
- these difficult times
- We're all in this together

See also Science Stories.

Labor Disputes

Stories of labor controversies should give the reasons for the dispute, the length of time the strike has been in progress and the claims by both the union and the company. We've seen stories in which even major news outlets have run data and claims of one side without a mention of the other side's position.

Editors should be on guard against loaded terms. Avoid the tendency in labor stories always to refer to management proposals as *offers* and to labor proposals as *demands*. *Proposals* is more neutral for both.

Strikebreaker and *scab*, which are loaded terms, should be changed if used to describe men or women who individually accept positions vacated by strikers. The expression *honored the picket line* often appears in the news, even though a more accurate expression is *refused* (or *declined*) *to cross a picket line*.

Make sure you understand any math involved in the various claims or proposals. If a worker gets a 10-cent-an-hour increase effective immediately, an additional 10 cents a year the next and another 10 cents the third year, that worker does not receive a 30-cent-an-hour increase. The increase at the time of settlement is still 10 cents an hour, with additional 10-cent increases to follow the next two years.

Labor Disputes Terms to Understand

- **Arbitrator, conciliator, fact finder, mediator**—A *fact finder* listens to both sides' positions and tries to determine what the facts are when they are disputed. A *conciliator* or *mediator* in a labor dispute recommends terms of a settlement. The decision of an *arbitrator* usually is binding.
- **Closed shop, union shop**—In a *closed shop*, the employer may hire only those who are members of the union. In a *union shop*, the employer may select employees, but the workers are required to join the union within a specified time after starting work.

- **Labor leader, union leader**—*Union leader* is usually preferred to *labor leader.*
- **On strike, struck**—Don't say, "The company has been on strike for the past 25 days." No. The employees are *on strike.* The company has been *struck.*

Meeting Stories

- When only one main thing is decided at a meeting, use a **single-element-what lead**. To focus on the one most important thing decided of several that were discussed, use the **most-important-element-what lead**. The two look alike.

    The City Council voted 5–1 Monday to approve unit-plan zoning for a 60-acre tract north of Interstate 70 on U.S. 63 North.

- If a group decides at a meeting on several things that all have something in common, use a **summary-what lead** that summarizes them by focusing on what they have in common.

    The City Council took advantage Monday of a light agenda to approve a variety of zoning matters.

- Often, more than one thing is decided at a meeting, and each is important enough to mention in the lead. This is a **multiple-element-what lead**. It tells with parallel verbs two or more actions that were decided. Even though all the elements mentioned are important enough to be in the lead, you should still try to make sure that they're listed in the order of most to least important.

    The City Council on Monday rejected a bid by beverage-container-ordinance opponents to put a repeal measure on the ballot for spring election and restored $1.2 million in funding to the Orlando Arts Council.

- **If the group reached a decision about something, the story usually stresses the action taken, the vote, the reasons for it and against it, and the expected consequences of the action. If the group discussed an issue but failed to reach a decision, the story usually stresses the most significant issue raised, any consensus reached and reasons given on different sides of the arguments.**

Or the reporter may take a feature approach that stresses, for example, one person's colorfully expressed views. The body of the story might include the following:

- Background of the issue.
- Arguments for and against it.

- Name and identification of those on each side.
- Time and location of the meeting.
- Additional matters discussed.
- Makeup of the audience, the number attending, audience reaction.
- Agenda for the next meeting.

Meeting News About Government

City Council and *County Commission* are capitalized with or without the city or county; *council* and *commission,* however, are lowercase. In most states, the *Legislature,* without the state's name, is capitalized, but AP says *legislature* should be lowercase in states like Missouri that have a body with a different formal name like General Assembly.

Government Story Usage

Amendments, ordinances, resolutions, rules. AP says: "Amendments, ordinances, resolutions and rules are *adopted* or *approved.* Bills are *passed.* Laws are *enacted.*"

Bills, laws, legislation. A *bill* is proposed legislation. If it's passed, it becomes a law. *Legislation* is the law enacted by a legislative body. Do not write or say, as is often heard, "The president will send legislation to Congress." He may propose legislation, but it only becomes legislation if Congress passes it.

Obituaries

Obituaries typically appear mainly in smaller newspapers for average citizens, while larger papers may run only prominent people or some others with particularly interesting stories.

The **formula obit** is the most common type of obituary. It starts as a notice from the funeral home, often the result of filling out a form provided by the newspaper. The obituary is then written following a typical order that is varied primarily for the timing of the services and the individual circumstances of the person's life.

Each newspaper has its own obituary formula that will vary somewhat. Usually, you'll just have to figure out the formula from comparing previously run obits.

The standard formula obit usually leads with the person's name and date of death. A variation is to lead with the services if they are timelier than the date of death. The **feature obit**, though, usually leads with some distinguishing characteristic or achievement of the deceased.

Both the standard and feature obit should be distinguished from the paid funeral notice. Although it may look like an obituary, it's paid for and run as an ad. Because it's an ad, the family or friends can say pretty much what they want and not be edited the way the other two types would be.

Editors should check obits to make sure they conform to the local standard obit formula and local policy matters. Here are some typical policies concerning matters in obits. Of course, your newspaper's policy will likely vary in some ways, but this will give you an idea of the sort of issues involved.

Addresses. Burglars often burgle the homes of relatives of the deceased when the address is printed in an obituary. That's because they can safely guess the relatives will be out of the house at the time of the funeral. As a result, many newspapers will not print street addresses of the deceased or of survivors. All individuals' addresses, in town or out, are reported in obits simply by town.

Some addresses, however, are helpful in an obit: the place where visitation and services will be held (often the funeral home but many times a place of worship), as well as the cemetery. Notice, by the way, the spelling of *cemetery*—there are no *a*'s in it. Another common misspelling in obits is *cremation* (not *creamation,* as though the person was going to be made into a dairy product). Addresses for visitation, services and burial let interested people know where to go to pay their respects.

Cause of Death. All deaths are *sudden,* even ones preceded by long suffering; *unexpected* is the word you want. People die of injuries *suffered* or *sustained,* not *received.* People do not die of *an apparent heart attack*—it's not visible.

Also, people die *of* not *from* a disease; of *heart illness,* not *heart failure;* after a *long illness,* not an *extended illness;* and *following* or *after* an operation, not *as a result of* it unless malpractice has been proved.

Sometimes, relatives do not want the newspaper to list the cause of death if it is suicide or AIDS or some other cause embarrassing to them. Relatives may withhold it; they may tell you but ask you not to print it; they may actually ask you to lie about it. Newspapers will not want to investigate every unlisted cause of death, but no newspaper should ever knowingly lie.

Courtesy Titles. Use courtesy titles—for the deceased only—on second and subsequent references: *Mrs. Jones, Miss Jones, Ms. Jones* (ask family for woman's preference), *Dr. Jones, Mr. Jones.*

Dates. Because obits are clipped and saved for years, some newspapers use the date rather than the day for describing the time of death, visitation, services and burial. For dates of birth, wedding and death, use month-date-year order. For dates of visitation, services and burial, use time-month-date order.

Always check that the birth date subtracted from the death date agrees with the age listed. Remember, too, you cannot simply subtract the years and stop—you have to make sure the person's birthday has occurred this year, otherwise subtract one more. Example: A person born Aug. 3, 1938, who died May 18, 2020, was 81, not 82.

Flowers. If the family requests that flowers not be sent, ask whether they prefer that donations be sent to a favorite charity. If yes, get the name and address, and print that in the obituary—in addition to or in place of sentences like "The family requests no flowers," according to local policy. Some newspapers never used to print phrases like *in lieu of flowers* out of deference to the florist industry, but such a policy is now commonly rejected.

Negative Information. Sometimes, in the description of a person's life, journalists have to decide whether to include unsavory things about the deceased. Should a minor crime committed a quarter century ago be included in the obituary? Probably not. But good editors should not hesitate to include negative information if they deem it important.

Semantics. Never write euphemisms such as someone *passed away, succumbed, met her Maker* or *is resting in the arms of sweet Jesus.* The deceased is referred to as Mr. Jones, not *the dearly departed.*

Do not write that a spouse *preceded him in death.* Instead, write, *She died in 2014* or *She died earlier.* Do not make matters worse by writing *She died before him,* which sounds as though she died before his very eyes.

Survivors. A man is survived by his *wife,* not his *widow.* A woman is survived by her *husband,* not her *widower.*

Do not write that survivors are *of the home* when they live at the same address as the deceased. Instead, give the town for the address as for everyone else.

When listing groupings of survivors (usually only the spouse, parents, siblings, children, grandchildren and great-grandchildren), use a comma after the name of the grouping, commas within the items and a semicolon between them: "Survivors include two brothers, John Hill of Ann Arbor and Ben Hill of Ypsilanti; three sisters, Macy Weinhurst of Buffalo, New York, Sarah Peters of Port Huron and Jane Sommers of Detroit; and five grandchildren." Note the semicolon before the final *and* in the series.

Obituary Usage

- **Body**—Not *corpse* or *remains*
- **Burial**—Not *interment*
- **Casket**—Not *coffin*
- **Mortician**—Not *undertaker*
- **Services**—Not *obsequies* or *funeral services.* It is permissible to say a minister either *conducts* or *officiates* at services. If the deceased is Catholic, a funeral Mass is *celebrated,* not *said* or *held.*

Political Stories

Political stories include profiles of candidates, analyses of issues, stories about polls on issues or candidates, columns, stories about speeches and meetings and votes.

The single biggest problem with political stories is making sure there's no bias in them. Opinion pieces are a different matter, of course, than hard-news stories about politics because readers expect those to take a side. A good rule of thumb is whatever your own political beliefs, make a special effort to make sure the other side is represented fairly, even in an opinion piece.

Remember to cover the issues, not just the horse race. Too often, the media run horse-race stories—those concentrating on who's leading in the polls or has gathered more money—far more than issue stories. Readers need to see more stories explaining the issues better.

Beware of trusting seemingly outrageous quoted excerpts of politicians or commentators. Both parties hire media monitors to comb through opposition speeches and media commentary to gin up emotions against political opponents, often by taking quotes out of context, and sometimes even by altering the original quote by editing out words that change the meaning. Unfortunately, partisan media outlets often distort quotes themselves.

If an outrageous quote is distributed by a partisan group on social media in hopes it will go viral, don't trust in its accuracy and repeat it. It's usually easy to find transcripts or even video or audio recordings of the larger context to judge for yourself whether you think someone really said what partisans are saying that person said. The more outrageous the quote sounds, the more important it is to fact check it yourself, asking yourself questions like: Is the quote actually altered? Is the quote accurate but misleadingly taken out of context? Does the context and tone of voice suggest that the speaker said it sarcastically or jokingly?

Political-Story Clichés to Avoid

- arch conservative, arch liberal (the use of *arch* is more of a value judgment than the more simply informative *conservative* or *liberal*)
- closed-door hearing, closed-door meeting (drop the *door*)
- dark horse
- (Trump, Obama, Bush, Clinton . . .) derangement syndrome

Conservative Clichés

- bleeding-heart liberal
- dope-smoking liberal
- fake news
- family values
- Judeo-Christian values
- kneejerk liberal
- lamestream media

- loony left
- lunatic left
- ponytail liberal
- snowflakes
- tax-and-spend liberal
- What could go wrong?

Liberal Clichés

- assault weapons (for semi-automatics)
- bitter clingers
- climate denier
- commonsense gun control
- conspiracy theory
- cultural appropriation
- despicables
- far right
- flyover country
- for the children
- homophobe
- Islamaphobe
- It takes a village.
- mean-spirited (Republicans, conservatives)
- pay their fair share
- privileged
- social justice
- top 1%
- trigger warning
- undisputed fact
- Walmart shoppers
- we need to start a conversation about
- white male privilege
- woke
- worse than Hitler

Broadcast Media and Political Stories

Politicians have been taught by their media advisers for years to respond to broadcast journalists with prewritten speeches that get in their talking points and run out the clock on the interview rather than directly answering questions. Letting them ramble on irritates the audience, but so does interrupting the politician, especially if done argumentatively or in a way that seems impolite.

Poll Stories

Don't paraphrase a poll question in a story but rather report the actual wording. Never paraphrase a survey question in a story because good pollsters spend a lot of time wording them specifically to avoid misunderstanding by those surveyed. A big reason different polls on the same subject come up with widely different results sometimes is the wording of the questions.

Check that the headline and the story accurately reflect the questions. For example, CNN was called out by several outlets for misrepresenting a Gallup Poll's results. CNN reported that 68% polled said, in the words of CNN, that a COVID-19 vaccine was "needed before returning to normal life," The problem was that wasn't what the poll asked. The exact wording of the question was, "How important are each of the following factors to you when thinking about your willingness to return to your normal activities?" Sixty-eight percent said a vaccine would be a "very important factor," but that doesn't mean that percentage thought it was necessarily mandatory for things to return to normal as CNN's headline at its website seemed to suggest.

It was an easy mistake to make, especially because even reading it here, you probably had to stop and think about it. And to CNN's credit, the story did much further down contain the actual question, and it also responded to such criticism by changing its headline over the story adding a clarification.

Be sure the story reports both the margin of error and the number of people surveyed. Ideally, the "margin of error" should be 3%, although sometimes 5% is reported. This validity of a poll is based on the number of people surveyed as compared to the population about which the survey generalizes.

People are often suspicious of polls because of what they see as a low number of people interviewed. But actually, pollsters consult a standard chart for how many people they need to poll to be mathematically accurate within a 3% margin of error for the size of the population about which they want to generalize.

Make sure the story identifies who conducted or sponsored the survey as well as the exact wording of the questions. These measures will help weed out bias that might invalidate the survey. "Push polls" by activists to gather headlines for their own agenda will intentionally bias the wording of questions to nudge those surveyed to answer a certain way: For example, "Do you support the governor's unconstitutional quarantine orders?"

The story should tell when the survey was conducted and how—for example, over the phone, in person or on the internet.

Twitter is not a scientific poll of opinions and shouldn't be confused with one. A Twitter storm doesn't mean that's an accurate index of public opinion. Businesses and politicians make that mistake often.

On-the-street interviews are not scientifically accurate and can give biased impressions of public opinion. Although broadcast outlets and some newspapers often use them, they're often done on one street corner or in one shopping area, and the people there may not be representative of people in the entire city. Also, the people who agree to an interview are not necessarily representative of even the people there. Such interviews, like tweets, can be useful for a few quotes for stories, but the fact that most people who stopped to speak took one side can give a false impression of public opinion.

Republicans often argue that polls are biased because typically more Democrats are polled on political matters than Republicans. But actually, to be representative of the public, the percentages of Democrats, Republicans and independents polled should ideally be their same percentages in the population, and more people identify as Democrats than Republicans.

Public-Policy Stories

These are stories that examine issues of public policy themselves, as opposed to merely the politics involved. They may be mere factual explanations of the issues and what has been proposed to deal with them, or they may be news analysis and opinion pieces. Here are some tips about potential problems to watch out for:

Present fairly both the pros and cons of proposals, the advantages and disadvantages, as well as the costs of not doing something and the costs of doing it.

For example, many people, both journalists at mainstream media outlets and individuals on social media, focused only on the cost in lives of not shutting down the economy to fight the COVID-19 pandemic. Some politicians said the economy should be closed down until a vaccine was developed and added words like "even if it takes a year or 18 months." The mayor of Los Angeles even suggested that city wouldn't be fully reopened until a cure was found, even though no viruses so far have ever been cured—just prevented with vaccinations or treated with drugs to mitigate their effects.

They also often said those who supported ending the shutdown sooner than that, even in a gradual, monitored way, were heartless people who didn't care about people's lives. One typical comment by a Facebook user, as an example, asked: "Who would you be willing to sacrifice in *your* family?"

The problem with that approach, especially if it's the sole focus of a supposedly objective news article, is that it looks at only the cost of lives lost from COVID-19 infections themselves and not the cost of lives lost from shutting down the economy for a long period of time. What about the lives of Great Depression numbers of people who lost their jobs or their businesses because of the shutdown? Former *Wall Street Journal* editorial board member Stephen

Moore said that for each 1% increase in unemployment, deaths increase by about 1,000 people.

Why? Because as people lose their livelihood, there are increases in depression and suicide, child and spouse abuse, alcoholism and drug addiction, loss of ability to afford food and shelter, and so on. What about their lives? And what about the lives of those who were not able to go out for medical tests or treatments not related to COVID-19? How many lives might be lost to delayed procedures?

In other words, to focus only on the likely number of deaths from not shutting down, policy makers and those who were willing to let it go on for many months or even years were not taking full account of the other results of the policy that likewise carried a real cost in lives.

A clichéd saying of those who focus exclusively on the cost of not doing something while neglecting the cost of doing it, is "If it saves just one life, it would be worth it." The fallacy of that emotional appeal can be seen if you look at the number of people killed, maimed or injured in car accidents. Should we ban all driving because it would save many lives? How realistic would that be? Maybe we should never travel at all because lives are also lost on planes, trains and boats. Should we also ban all swimming because sometimes people drown?

See also the tips on poll stories and science stories.

Public-Policy Story Usage

- **Mean, median**—*Mean* is the average. If the high is 80 and the low is 50, the mean is 65. *Median* means that half are above a certain point and half are below.

Religion Stories

Make sure the terminology is correct for the particular religion.

Religion is an all-inclusive word referring to the three Abrahamic religions that trace their history back to Abraham—Judaism, Christianity and Islam—as well as others, such as Eastern religions (like Hinduism, Buddhism and Taoism), as well as a number of older and newer religions (paganism, Druidry, witchcraft and Wicca, shamanism, New Thought, and so on).

A growing number of people classify themselves as "spiritual but not religious." These people tend to mean by spirituality, not necessarily a belief in spirits, but rather that they see *spirituality* as your own personal relation to God, the universe, nature, other people and yourself, rather than *religion*, which they view as accepting someone's else's dogma on faith. They also tend to especially disfavor "organized religion," which most of them have left. Some of them have turned to one or more of the second or third group above but often as "solitary practitioners" who select their own individual path, beliefs and practices from one or more forms of spirituality.

Not all denominations use *Church* in the organization's title. It is the First Baptist Church but the American Baptist Convention. It is the *Episcopal* Church, not the *Episcopalian* Church. Its members are Episcopalians, but the adjective is *Episcopal*: Episcopal clergymen.

Mass is *celebrated*. The rosary is *recited* or *said*. The editor can avoid confusion by making the statement read something like this: "The Mass (or rosary) will be at 7 p.m." The Benediction of the Blessed Sacrament is neither *held* nor *given;* services close with it.

The order of the Ten Commandments varies depending on the version of the Bible used. Confusion can be spared if the commandment number is omitted.

The usual style in identifying ministers is *the Rev.*, followed by the individual's full name on first reference and only the surname on second reference. The title *Reverend* should not be used alone as a noun, nor should plural forms be used, such as "the Revs. John Jones and Richard Smith." Churches of Christ do not use the term *reverend* in reference to ministers. They are called *brothers*.

Priests who are rectors, heads of religious houses or presidents of institutions and provinces of religious orders take *the Very Rev.* and are addressed as *Father*. Priests who have doctorates in divinity or philosophy are identified as *the Rev. Dr.* and are addressed either as *Dr.* or *Father.*

The words *Catholic* and *parochial* are not synonymous. There are parochial schools that are not Catholic. The writer should not assume that a person is a Roman Catholic simply because he is a priest or a bishop. Other religions also have priests and bishops. Use *nun* when appropriate for women in religious orders. The title *sister* is confusing except with the person's name (Sister Mary Edward).

Mormons are more formally known as the Church of Jesus Christ of Latter-day Saints. Although AP says "Mormon" is acceptable in all references to the church and its members, the church prefers the full name on first reference and prefers people not use the terms "Mormon church" or "LDS church" at all, but rather a term like "the church" on subsequent references.

Mormons consider themselves Christians, but other churches tend to reject classifying them as such because their beliefs differ in a number of ways from most Christian denominations. (The same goes for the New Thought churches discussed later.)

A number of smaller groups have split off from the Mormon church, the ones in the media most often being Mormon fundamentalist groups that practice polygamy. The Mormon church rejected polygamy in 1890 after practicing it openly the previous 38 years. Be careful in news reports to make the distinction between the Mormon church and these breakaway groups.

Also, make a distinction between the Mormon church and the largest other group that splintered in the 1800s after the death of Mormon founder Joseph Smith Jr. Rather than follow Brigham Young, the Community of Christ (formerly known as the Reorganized Church of Jesus Christ of Latter Day Saints, a name it also still owns) rejected polygamy and some other Mormon teachings. It's more liberal than the other groups and resembles increasingly more of a mainstream Christian church in its beliefs although still honoring Smith, and some of his work.

Islam is the world's second-largest religion. Its followers are called *Muslims*. The adjective is *Islamic*. *Islamist* refers to Muslims who favor ordering society according to Islamic laws. The correct spelling is now *Quran*, not *Koran*. *Muslim imam* is redundant—just say *imam*. But titles for Muslim clergy vary from group to group but include, *ayatollah, hojatoleslam, imam, mullah* and *sheik*.

Jewish congregations should be identified in news stories as *Orthodox, Conservative* or *Reform*. Most Orthodox congregations use *synagogue*. Reform groups use *temple*, and Conservative congregations use one word or the other, but *synagogue* is preferred. The term *church* only applies to Christian bodies.

Israelis are nationals of the state of Israel, and *Jews* are those who profess Judaism.

Rabbis take *Rabbi* for a title. *Jewish rabbi* is redundant—just use *rabbi*.

Hinduism, the world's third-largest religion after Christianity and Islam, has no formal clergy, but it does have *monks*.

Buddhism is the world's fourth-largest religion. Many Christians think Buddhists worship Buddha as God, as Christians think of Jesus. But Buddhists instead revere Buddha as a man who became *enlightened*—woke up to the truth about life—not as a god. In fact, Buddhists don't necessarily believe in God at all. Buddhist clergy may be called *priests*, and Buddhism also has *monks*.

Don't misuse the anthropological term "cult" as a propaganda term. Don't use it as many Christian authors do to imply that a religion like that of the Christian Scientists, Jehovah's Witnesses or Mormons is inherently dangerous because their doctrines differ from "traditional" Christianity. Especially, don't use the term to imply that such groups practice brainwashing or devil worship. *Sect* is also a derogatory term.

Don't confuse neopagan religious people like Wiccans and Druids with devil worshippers. *Pagan* was the term that first the Romans then later Christians used for the pre-Christian indigenous religions. The word means country dwellers—in other words hicks who didn't accept the religion of Rome or later Christianity but preferred their own religion. Pagans didn't even believe in the devil—that's a later Christian belief. The original pagan beliefs were largely lost, and neopagan groups have tried to revive and reinvent them. They practice a nature-based religion that generally sees the divine in everything and all beings, and personified as split between a god and a goddess, male and female polarities, with the female often more important. Also, Wiccans consider themselves witches, but not all witches are Wiccans. Wicca is the most popular variety of witchcraft today, although solitary practitioners with their own beliefs increasingly outnumber those formally initiated by a Wiccan coven.

Don't confuse New Thought and New Age. New Thought grew in the middle to late 1800s out of Christianity but stressed using the mind to heal, as Christian Science does, or to heal and prosper, as Unity School of Christianity and Centers for Spiritual Living (formerly Church of Religious Science) do. Those three churches could be called the major New Thought denominations, although Christian Scientists separate themselves from the other two and vice versa.

Don't misuse the terms atheist and agnostic. An atheist is not necessarily someone, who as Christians tend to think, believes there is no God. Atheists more often define the term as simply not believing in a God—no belief one way or the other is involved. An agnostic is similar to the latter definition of atheist and means someone who's on the fence, such as thinking there's not enough evidence one way or the other to decide.

Science Stories

Science stories may be written as hard-news stories, but they are often turned into features by focusing on a researcher or someone dealing with science research, by following a wire story with reactions from local experts or people involved, by analyzing a new development and explaining what it means, or in some cases by taking a how-to approach. Some tips on problems to keep an eye out for:

There are more kinds of causation than one, and it can make a big difference. Science distinguishes among at least three kinds of causes:

Necessary cause—You must have A to get B.
Sufficient cause—A alone can result in B, but C alone can also result in B.
Contributory cause—A alone may not cause B, but A combined with C can, or at least act as a catalyst.

Don't confuse causation with mere correlations. Correlations can be useful *in* formulating hypotheses to test but are not in themselves proof of **causation**. A **correlation** is simply two variables that seem to rise and fall together when charted—they can be intriguing indications of a possible cause, but jumping to the conclusion that one causes the other is illogical.

A correlation means that when A is found, B is too, at least to some degree; A may cause B, or B may cause A, or the correlation may be accidental, with C actually being responsible. So, when A and B correlate, does A cause B, or does B cause A, or neither?

An example: A study found watching violent TV shows as children correlated with children who became violent adults. But did watching the TV shows turn normal people violent, or were more violent people more likely to watch violent TV shows?

But actually, the problem is worse. Correlations between variations that rise and fall are often completely unrelated. How about this: Did you know that everyone who eats meat will eventually die? It's true. But everyone eventually dies, vegetarians and vegans, as well.

To see more examples that correlations don't prove causation, take a look at this website: www.tylervigen.com/spurious-correlations. It shows actual charts of hilariously amazing correlations between totally unrelated true data, such as the number of people who die of drowning after falling out of a fishing boat correlates with marriage rates in Kentucky, and the age of Miss America correlates with the number of murders from steam, hot vapors and hot objects.

Don't confuse causation with simple comparisons. By "comparisons" here we mean when people look at numbers for two groups and because the numbers differ, they assume a particular reason explains it without further investigation into other variables.

For example, don't assume that it's proof positive of discrimination if a demographic's percentage in a group doesn't match its percentage in the larger population. It certainly may be taken as evidence worth examining further, but there might ultimately be a nondiscriminatory explanation. This can be seen by the fact that the percentage of white players in the NBA is less than their percentage in the population, but no one seems to think seriously it's because white players are discriminated against. Nor do people seem to think the NHL discriminates against black players because their percentage is lower in the league than in the population. One possible explanation for both might be cultural differences in preferences by athletes for what sport they'd like to play.

This also is a problem with many of the comparisons of pay differences between men and women, in which it's shown women earn less on average than men. Although these often are presented as "women earn less for the same job," check the way the figures were actually calculated. The less the number is based simply on adding up all women's salaries then dividing by the number of women working, then doing the same for men and comparing them, the less the pay difference is between the groups.

That is, when the calculations take into account other variables like actual job-to-same-job comparisons (because women and men often take some jobs more than the other sex does), that some jobs taken more often by men often entail more risk, and so on, the difference gets smaller. Of course, men and women should be paid the same for the same job, once education and experience levels are taken into account. But the figures cited often don't take into account these other variables and assume discrimination as the only possible reason. A website we like that advocates for equal pay for women (www.payscale.com/data/gender-pay-gap) but takes these other variables into account, says that as of 2020, if you didn't account for other variables, women were earning 81 cents on the dollar compared to men, but that when you did, they earned 98 cents on the dollar.

Don't overhype scare stories—try to put the stories in some context. The nature of news is to focus on the latest developments—including out-of-the-ordinary things that scare the public. These stories attract viewers, listeners and readers, but this can have the effect of distorting the public's understanding of policy decisions, and in turn affect policy makers, as well.

The harmful result is that policy, funding and research may be misplaced by focusing the public's attention on problems disproportionate to their actual comparative importance. So, AIDS gets the sixth most research funding of all causes of death, although it doesn't make the list of the top dozen killers (www.healthline.com/health/leading-causes-of-death). Cancer is the No. 2 killer but receives the most funding, but AIDS research receives more funding than the No. 1 killer heart disease, the ranking of which in dollars is ninth (www.fiercebiotech.com/research/top-15-nih-funded-disease-areas).

But even AIDS was replaced in the media spotlight in 2017 when Ebola emerged. Health journalist Tim Chen wrote in Forbes on April 6, 2017, in an article titled "The Ebola Effect: How Media Hype Distracts From Silent Epidemics": "Yet, globally more people died from HIV in a week than the entire period of the Ebola outbreak . . ." (www.forbes.com/sites/chentim/2017/04/06/the-ebola-effect-how-media-hype-distracts-from-silent-epidemics/#442968e855e9).

The point isn't that we shouldn't report on scary new developments like potential pandemics but rather a context should be provided so that they're not overhyped.

Avoid "the science is settled" fallacy. This is a phrase that shows up often in climate-change stories, but what we have to say is not a critique of climate-change theory itself. Rather, we're critiquing an invalid argument that might be misused in many other science stories, as well, such as those on COVID-19, that betrays a misunderstanding of the nature of science.

It's closer to the truth to say science is never settled—at least permanently—or that the science is temporarily settled. For example, Isaac Newton's principles of physics were widely accepted for several hundred years until Albert Einstein's theory of relativity overthrew them, only to be shortly challenged by a stream of quantum physics theories.

It's better to say "the majority opinion of experts is" whatever it is at present. It can be potentially a bit problematic to say "the consensus is" because that connotes to many that everyone agrees. But it is technically correct when referring to the vast majority of opinion because it actually means most or all think a certain way.

Seldom does everyone agree on something, but the closer there is to total agreement, as opposed to a bare majority, the more acceptable the term is. So, if 97% of scientists believe in the manmade global-warming theory (a figure widely cited but that's also been disputed), then that can accurately be described as the consensus view. But you would probably not write of a 5–4 Supreme Court decision as a "consensus."

To know why science is settled only temporarily, even if that consensus lasts for hundreds or more years, it's important for journalists and the public to understand that science is a self-correcting method of studying the world that by its nature results in constant upheaval of old ideas.

Science advances the most the more phenomena are observed that don't fit the accepted **theory**, **model** (a representation of something, whether it's a model train or a model of the atom) or **paradigm** (a set of concepts that define an area of science at a particular time). These outlying phenomena, called **"anomalies"** prompt scientists to look for explanations of why the theory "leaks," which ultimately results in tweaking the theory to make it more accurately inclusive or even result in a larger alternative theory to replace it.

What all this means is that science is always advancing. Its nature is to not be settled.

Don't use propaganda terms like "climate denier" or "science denier." These terms are not objective but a kind of name calling meant to equate people with different views from the person using them with Holocaust deniers. No one denies there's a climate or that the climate has changed many times or is probably changing now. Rather, they should more accurately be called "skeptics of manmade global warming theory."

Likewise, the term "science denier" is name calling often thrown around by people who themselves may not support the current scientific consensus on a number of things like vaccinations, nuclear power, fracking, genetically modified food, gluten, and so on.

Avoid the vague phrases "scientists say," "experts say," "studies say," "emerging science says," and so on. Be more specific.

Science Story Usage

- **Ecology, environment**—*Ecology* can mean the interrelationship of organisms and their environment but more properly it refers to the science that studies that. *Environment* means surroundings.

Speech Stories

Speech stories are based on the answer to the question: *Who said what to whom, when* and *where? Some speech stories also describe how it was said, why it was said and to what reaction.*

An important point to note about both speech and meeting stories is that the reporter should not try to include everything that was said. If the better story were the one closest to having everything, then we might as well fire the reporters and just run uncut transcripts of speeches.

Instead, a reporter's job is to select what is most important. The reporter shouldn't bother with unimportant points. Usually, speech stories cover no more than the three or four most important points. Also, the reporter shouldn't overquote but use only the quotations that best make the points—not every one that was relevant.

The speech-story lead usually follows the order of who said what, although if what was said is more important than who said it, this order may be reversed.

> Researchers at Springfield University are charging that the U.S. Food and Drug Administration is dragging its heels on approval of a new treatment for COVID-19.

or

> The U.S. Food and Drug Administration is dragging its heels on approval of a new treatment for COVID-19, researchers at Springfield University are charging.

Time, day and place may follow in the lead but often appear in later paragraphs instead, especially if they would make the lead unwieldy.

The *what* in a speech story is the most important point made in the speech, which the journalist must decide was most newsworthy. It's not necessarily what the speaker thought was the main point or spent the most time on.

The most important point, and each subsequent point presented in a speech story, should be written as a thesis statement, not a mere statement of a topic. A *topic* can be like a vague title that hints at the subject but doesn't say exactly what the speaker said or what position was taken. A *thesis*, however, takes a specific stand.

To say, for example, that someone "spoke about cancer" is to state a topic, not a thesis. A thesis might be that someone "said new studies have found that secondary smoke is not nearly so big a cancer threat as earlier studies had indicated."

A hint for making sure a speech-story lead states a thesis rather than a topic is to see that it avoids the following attributions: *commented on, discussed, spoke about* or *spoke on, talked on* or *talked about.* It's grammatically impossible to use these with a thesis statement. On the other hand, if the lead uses *said* (for a hard-news story) or *says* (for a feature), it's almost impossible *not* to follow the attribution with a proper thesis.

After the lead paragraph summarizes the most important news of the speech, the speech story typically uses a quote in the next paragraph or two to back up the thesis. It should come no later than the fourth paragraph.

Much later than that and the reader probably wonders where the quotes are or stops reading. A full-sentence quote earlier, in the first paragraph, doesn't usually summarize the story as well as a statement of the thesis and looks like a beginner's work.

The second paragraph, in addition to containing a quote amplifying the thesis from the lead, as well as the name of the speaker (if this was a delayed-ID lead), often includes the name of the organization sponsoring the speech and sometimes when and where it was given.

After the lead, the story should proceed using the seesaw technique. The story seesaws back and forth between paraphrasing key points and direct quotations that are one, two or three sentences long.

The order of the story typically follows an inverted-pyramid style. The most newsworthy point in the lead is followed by supporting points and points of lesser importance as the story proceeds.

The body of the story might also include some facts about the speech if they weren't already given in the lead: the purpose, time and place of the speech. It might describe the nature and size of the audience, including any prominent people in attendance, and describe the audience's reaction—such as a standing ovation or the number of hecklers.

The story might include background information about the speaker and material gathered from a question-and-answer period or from an interview with the speaker.

Occasionally, in the case of misstatements of fact made by the speaker— as opposed to a mere difference of opinion—the reporter might include corrections.

Don't say, "The president said in prepared remarks . . ." because presidential speeches—indeed most speeches—are typically prepared.

Review the guidelines in Chapter 7 about selecting quotations.

Speech-Story Usage

- **Dais, podium, lectern**—A speaker stands on a *dais* or *podium* but behind a *lectern*.

War Stories

Find out what the policy is at your newspaper, magazine, station or website about whether war reports must be neutral and whether it's permissible to wear flag-style clothing or accessories, such as a flag lapel pin, when interviewing sources or on air.

Military titles use numerals when a number is involved: *1st Sgt. Bill Taylor*. Also, it's redundant to say someone was promoted to the rank of major. She was simply *promoted to major*.

War-Story Clichés to Avoid

- massive attack
- pitched battle
- powder keg (used as a metaphor)

Weather Stories

Every so often, a story will refer to the *eye of a hurricane* as turbulent when instead it's the dead-calm center.

Blizzards are hard to define because wind and temperatures may vary. The safe way is to avoid calling a snowstorm a *blizzard* unless the National Weather Service describes it as such. Generally, a blizzard occurs when there are winds of 35 mph or more that whip falling snow or snow already on the ground and when temperatures are 20 degrees above zero Fahrenheit or lower. A *severe blizzard* has winds that are 45 mph or more, temperatures 10 degrees above zero or lower and great density of snow either falling or whipped from the ground.

The National Weather Service insists that *ice storms* are not sleet. *Sleet* is frozen raindrops. The service uses the terms *ice storm, freezing rain* and *freezing drizzle* to warn the public when a coating of ice is expected on the ground.

The following tips will help editors use the correct terms:

- Temperatures can become *higher* or *lower,* not *cooler* or *warmer.*
- A *cyclone* or *tornado* is a storm or system of winds rotating about a moving center of low atmospheric pressure. It is often accompanied by heavy rain and winds.
- A *hurricane* has winds above 74 mph.
- A *typhoon* is a violent cyclonic storm or hurricane occurring in the China Sea and adjacent regions, chiefly from July to October.
- The word *chinook* should not be used unless so designated by the National Weather Service.

Weather Story Clichés to Avoid

- adverse weather conditions
- biting (bitter) cold
- blanket of snow
- a bolt of lightning (lightning)
- current temperature
- fog rolled (crept or crawled) in fog-shrouded city
- golf-ball-sized hail
- hail-splattered
- hurricane howled

- mercury dropped (dipped, zoomed, plummeted)
- rain failed to dampen
- storm-tossed
- winds aloft

Feature Stories

See also Chapter 4 for advice on editing feature (soft-news) stories in general and how that differs from editing hard-news stories

Advance Pieces

Advance pieces announce an upcoming event but go beyond a simple calendar-style listing by providing a fuller story.

These stories often, but not always, originate from a press release. When a press release arrives at a newspaper or other media outlet, editors judge whether it will be covered at all by asking themselves whether it gives some genuine news that readers would want to know or whether it is just a request for a free ad disguised as a press release.

A press release should never be run as a publicity puff but rather be rewritten and expanded into a news feature. Make sure all self-serving, self-promoting, nonobjective language gets removed and that the focus is on what the readers might find interesting, not merely what the sponsor wants to say.

Advances are often written as an interview with a performer or group before a concert or other event, a personality profile of a key person involved or as a historical piece about the person, group or event. In such a case, the news-peg event may be teased in the story, but often it's best to take the time-day-place and cost details out and put them into a box.

Don't save calendar items just for post-mortems. If you're ever called on to open the mail and sort through the press releases for likely stories, don't simply set aside an announcement of an interesting event for a story *after* the event occurs. By letting your audience know in advance of an event they might want to attend rather than simply documenting it afterward, you serve your audience better. Also, the one event can now be the subject of two stories, one before and one after, giving the paper or other news outlet more news and making the sponsor happier, as well.

Press-Release Stories

Don't let any press release be published without a reporter checking it out and rewriting it. Why? Press releases are often written not by professional PR people but by people with no journalistic training. The result is some press releases come in written more like ads than news—full of self-serving propagandistic language. Often, there's no sense of what in the release is the real news that would interest your audience—sometimes, important information such as the time of an event is even left out. And, of course, releases written by amateurs will probably not be in AP style, much less your own publication's local style, and may even contain misspellings, poor grammar and awkward, vague or wordy writing.

People send press releases to news outlets to get free publicity. You're not obligated to give it to them. Read the release, and determine whether it's really news. Ask yourself: Does it contain information your audience would want to know or should know? If not, don't run it.

Be on the lookout for any nonobjective language the reporter might have missed. Cut everything that is self-serving rather than informative—anything that editorializes or sounds opinionated or like an advertisement.

Improve the wording, if necessary, to make it clearer and simpler while leaving in all the real information. Look for anything that's unclear or missing or could mean more than one thing. Were any of your questions unanswered? If so, then if you're an editor, ask the reporter to make a call to find the answers, or get on the phone to the source yourself, depending on your outlet's policy.

Consider whether the press release could be made more effective by restructuring it. Does this have the best lead for your audience? Does it stress something that affects people? If not, does it stress something that would interest your readers? At the very least, people should be the focus rather than things.

Be especially careful editing for AP and local style, as well as spelling. As we said, press releases from nonprofessional PR people seldom come written in AP style, and you usually find capitalized words like *association, board, center, club* and *institute* on second reference, such as "The Center will begin a weekly newsletter next month." Lowercase such words when standing alone on second reference.

Calendar Items

Usually, these items run in the community calendar part of a newspaper or magazine—smaller than briefs, with a time and date rather than a headline. They can also be a good source of feature stories.

Many press releases are mailed at the last minute and don't arrive in time to get the information into the calendar before the event. Conversely, if the press release has a later **release date**—a time before which the people who sent it don't want it run—honor the release date, and don't run the story earlier than that time.

Remember the time-day-place formula (and don't use both day and date unless that is your paper's policy with calendar items). Time examples: 7 a.m. to 5 p.m.; 3 p.m. to 5 p.m.

Know your news outlet's policy about whether profit-making events are given free publicity. For example, some newspapers may put a listing in the calendar for a band playing at a bar. Others demand this be promoted only through paid ads.

Look out for profit-making enterprises trying to appear as nonprofit to avoid taking out an ad—for example, a mutual-funds investment company promoting a "free lecture on how to achieve financial independence," when the lecture is really just a vehicle for selling shares in a mutual fund.

Here are some other tips to keep in mind when writing or editing calendar items:

- The plural of *person* is *people,* not *persons.*
- Don't write "For additional information, *contact* Jan Smith at 555–1212." Instead, write: "For more information, *call* Jan Smith at 555–1212" (or ". . . stop by the Ithaca Art League at . . .").
- Rather than say *No admission,* say *The event is free.*
- Normally, change *The event is free and open to the public* to *The event is free.* If it weren't open to the public, why would we be running this calendar item? But you may want to include the phrase about being open to the public if you think your audience might otherwise think the event is for members only.
- Change "A *free-will offering* will be taken" to "An *offering* will be taken" or "*Donations* will be collected." If it isn't *free-will,* it's not a *donation* but a *cost* or *admission charge.*

Biannual, biennial—The first means *twice a year.* The second means *every two years.* The copy editor could help the reader by substituting "every six months" for *biannual* and "every other year" for *biennial.*

Personnel: Appointments, Promotions, Training, Retirement

Find out your paper's policy on these. Community newspapers often run these items as briefs, often without headlines, on the business page or in the feature section, often on Sunday, under some standing heading like "Local Celebrities" or "About Town." Most larger outlets ignore them, and even for those that do run them, they're seldom worth a larger story.

Remove self-serving plugs for the employer, as well as quotations by or about the employee, leaving just the news of who got promoted to what at which company.

Does this item let burglars know someone will be out of town during a certain time to attend a training program or take a long retirement trip? If so, reword.

Personal: Weddings, Engagements, Anniversaries, Reunions

Larger newspapers tend to ignore these items except for prominent people.

Look at previous examples from your newspaper for the format. For example, for names in the headlines or captions, does your newspaper print the woman's name first or the man's name first? Are courtesy titles used? Find out, too, whether your paper limits anniversaries to significant numbers like 25th, 50th, etc.

Avoid pretentious words and phrases. Examples include *holy matrimony, bonds of matrimony* and *exchanged nuptial vows.* (Even *exchanged wedding vows* could be tightened to *married.*)

Avoid non sequiturs such as "Given in marriage by her parents, the bride wore . . ."

Couple is a collective noun, so it's singular when referring to the pair as a unit, but plural when referring to individuals acting separately.

Cause-Promoting and Image-Building Releases

Is it a "good" cause? Is it a "legitimate" cause? Newspapers will generally run announcements about a wide variety of causes on various political and religious spectrums, weeding out only those of a commercial, fringe or hate-group nature.

Often, these are noncontroversial press releases promoting something like a community blood drive, a fundraiser for United Way or an American Cancer Society smoke-free day. These are usually worth at least a brief, sometimes even an 8- to 10-inch story.

Ask yourself whether image-building releases are only self-serving or also public-serving. Generally, these may come from an individual or an organization but generally from politicians trying to keep their name before the public or candidates seeking office. Ask yourself whether it's just an attempt at free advertising, or does it contain some legitimate news? Sift out the self-serving quotes and self-congratulations, leaving in only the real news, if any. And consider whether the other candidate or other side in a controversy should be called for comment.

Color Pieces

The purpose of a **color piece** is to make the readers feel as though they are there—to give them a word picture of the sights, sounds, smells, and even touch and taste, if possible, of an event or locale. Color pieces are often assigned as sidebars or follows to hard-news stories.

Use a nut graf near the top of the story to give readers a main point on which to focus.

Don't overuse modifiers. Although a color piece involves more description than is typical in news stories, that's not a license to overuse modifiers. Modifiers are usually unnecessary when a more specific noun or verb is available, or when the reader may have a sense that details are coming fast and thick with no apparent theme or reason

Entertainment and Celebrity Stories

Entertainment stories can be reviews of movies, plays, books, music, art shows or restaurants; personality profiles of celebrities; advance stories on entertainment events, such as movie or theater openings, new TV shows or new music; focus pieces on issues, controversies and trends in the arts; entertainment columns; and so on.

One of the main characteristics that makes something newsworthy is the prominence of the person involved. Prominence has to do with how famous, powerful or rich someone is.

Celebrities are newsworthy. Sure, their doings may not be the most important things going on in the world on a given day, but they are talked about by your audience. The trick is to not become too tabloid-ish, though, because too much focus on such news can damage your credibility.

A number of legal points discussed in Chapter 5 should be kept in mind when editing stories about celebrities:

Celebrities have less protection than an average person when it comes to suing the media for libel. Celebrities must prove that the article was published, broadcast or posted with "actual malice," meaning "reckless disregard of the truth," not just that it was wrong and negligent. This doesn't mean, however, that journalists should intentionally lower their standards when reporting on celebrities.

The public fascination celebrities engender doesn't mean they don't deserve private lives. The main defense the media have against an invasion-of-privacy lawsuit is newsworthiness, but celebrity status doesn't mean the media should seek and reveal all embarrassing private information about prominent people for public titillation. Nor does it entitle the press to stalk or trespass to get stories.

Celebrities have a right to endorse or not endorse products and causes of their own choosing without advertisers appropriating their name, voice or image without permission. Appropriation of these for commercial purposes can result in an invasion of privacy lawsuit.

Entertainment and Celebrity News Usage

- **Concert, recital**—Two or more performers give a *concert*. One performer gives a *recital*.
- **Debut, host, premiere**—*The AP Stylebook* used to say none of these words should be used as a noun. The movie *will debut* or *have its premiere*. The star *will be host* of the event. These rules have been dropped from the latest editions, but some editors may still insist on them as good usage.

Entertainment and Celebrity Story Clichés to Avoid

- controversial
- feel-good movie
- lovely and talented
- star-studded
- whirlwind (courtship, romance)

Also, see the entries for the specific kind of story it is, such as a review, advance piece, focus piece or column.

Fact-Check Stories

Many news outlets and internet sites offer fact checks on claims that seem to be important in the news. We're putting them here under Feature Stories and Opinion Pieces because although their purpose is to determine the facts of something for an audience, the media outlet is involved in offering its opinion about the fact and taking a position like an editorial.

It's important that fact checks be rigorously honest and not based on looking only for evidence that backs a previously held viewpoint by the fact checker.

Fact checks should hold all sides to the same standards, not change standards to favor one side.

Don't quote statements out of context. For example, don't fact check jokes or satire and present the quoted material as though it were seriously stated.

Don't label a statement false or partly false that was true as stated. Often, fact-check sites make the mistake of labeling something false, partially false or mainly false for not also saying something else, even when the fact-checked statement was not misleading without the additional information.

Don't make what we call "the second-opinion fallacy." A number of "fact checks" make the mistake, intentional or not, of asking one other source for a second opinion, and when that source disagrees, labeling the original claim false.

But if you ask one doctor to diagnose an ailment then go to another for a second opinion, you'll often find that even medical doctors are like experts on anything: They don't necessarily agree. And it's a fallacy to assume that the opinion offered second is automatically better than the one offered first.

What's needed is a more rigorous standard, such as consulting more sources to see what the most common wisdom of authorities on the matter is. Even then, realize that someone with a new idea is always in the minority at first and that the conventional wisdom often turns out to be wrong.

Social Media Tip

The second-opinion fallacy shows up often in social media posts. Someone will post an article on a matter, then someone else will angrily post another article that takes a different view from the first. This is fine if it's part of a peaceful discussion of views and among openminded people mutually capable of changing their minds. But too often participants just end up arguing with each other and one or both calling the other names when they frustratedly run out of possibly persuasive proof.

Don't assume that half of a sites's fact checks on policy matters should favor one side, half the others. That presupposes that each side is equally right or wrong, which may not be the case. What would be more objective would be to look honestly at the evidence on each issue independently rather than ignoring the evidence and trying to balance the number of fact checks decided for each side.

Feature Obituaries

Feature obits are written as feature stories about the deceased rather than in the typical formula-obit fashion.

Obituaries have always been one of the most often read parts of a newspaper that run them (especially community newspapers as opposed to big-city ones, which may only run obits of prominent people, such as leaders and celebrities), but the obit beat has traditionally been given to **cub reporters**. Perhaps that's because obituaries were usually among the most formulaic of newspaper writing, and seasoned reporters were called to the task only when the deceased was prominent enough to warrant a feature obit, which often ran on one of the news pages rather than with the regular obits.

Now, however, journalists are at last beginning to recognize the importance of obits. If obit reporters have enough time before deadline, they should consider making a few calls to the deceased's friends and family and writing a feature obit.

The feature obit is usually organized around a theme—a distinguishing characteristic or achievement of the deceased that serves as a summing up of that person's life. Here's an example of a lead from a feature obit that demonstrates this:

> Ben Jeffers had a city in his basement.
>
> Mr. Jeffers himself built all the houses, factories, schools, churches, even the farm buildings in the surrounding countryside. He also built the roads and laid the train track connecting them all. It was a 27-year project for the model railroader, who died May 25, 2019.
>
> "Ben loved playing with his trains and building a little world around them," said Fran Jeffers, his wife. "He told me once that one of his first memories of life was traveling with his father on a train to Chicago."

One of the biggest problems with feature obits is that writers sometimes try to build the feature around a trite theme rather than finding something unique or more interesting. Here are two examples:

> Stephanie Benson dreamed of one day dancing on Broadway. But the 21-year-old University of Nebraska theater major will never get her chance. She was killed in a car wreck Aug. 18, 2019.

> His family and friends remember Hank Petrovik as a man who never had an unkind word for anyone.

Although the structure of a feature obit is different from that of the typical formula obit, it obeys the same style rules.

First-Person Stories

First-person accounts—where the reporter speaks as I—should be used sparingly because the focus should normally be on the news, not on the reporter. But first-person stories are perfectly acceptable when the reporter is an eyewitness to an event. A personal column is often written in first person, as is a story such as one based on a day the journalist spent riding along with an ambulance driver or a police officer (participatory journalism).

Follow-up Stories

When a big news event breaks, a feature story will often be assigned to provide color and human interest as a sidebar to the main story, or to provide a new angle that can keep a story in the public eye and move it along in the absence of fresh developments.

As with any follow, the news that should be stressed in a follow-up feature is what's new, not merely a repeat of what's already been made public. A color or human-interest piece may not have any new developments to report, but what's new are the details or the inside angle reported here first. So, for example, a feature follow to a plane crash providing a firsthand account by an observer or passenger should begin with what's new to this story—calling attention to the inside scoop—not simply repeating that a plane crashed the day before.

Make sure there's a nut graf near the top that lets readers know what's going on and ties this piece to the news peg.

Commemorative features appear at the first anniversary of an event and perhaps every fifth anniversary thereafter, reminding people of important events on this date in history. Reporters typically interview survivors who experienced the event firsthand and try to capture its color and significance for people today.

Food Features

Often, these stories are written as a personality profile of a cook or a feature story about a particular kind of food—ice cream, barbecue or Chinese food, for example—to which some relevant recipes are added at the end.

Unless your local paper's style is to uppercase all the main words in the recipe title as though it were a book title, remember that the wire-service rule for names of foods is that only words that would be proper names by themselves are capitalized:

> *Wrong:* Boston Cream Pie
> *Right:* Boston cream pie

Recipes use numerals and fractions exclusively—don't follow the usual rules for writing them out.

Recipe writers shouldn't forget the rule about putting a comma before an independent clause. A sentence like "Mix thoroughly and bake for 30 minutes" should take a comma before the "and." After all, we have two independent clauses with *you* as the understood subject of each. How do we know this isn't a compound predicate? You are supposed to bake for 30 minutes, but you don't mix for 30 minutes, as well.

History Pieces

Local-history stories can be immensely popular features both for longtime residents and newcomers. The basic structure is often like that of the personality profile or sometimes that of a chronological narrative topped with a teaser to interest readers in the story that follows.

The more the piece is written like a short story, the more questions you should ask the reporter about the details (such as

the weather) and the quotes (especially dialogue) to make sure these parts are not simply made up for the sake of the story.

How-To Articles or Service Journalism

Not all **service-journalism** pieces are in the how-to format. Others, for example, include calendar listings, lists of the 10-best type, and focus pieces on lifestyle issues. But the how-to is the most common service-journalism piece, and the two terms are sometimes used synonymously. Car care, food, home improvement, interior design, gardening and photography are some subjects often written about in the how-to format.

The reporter should not pretend to be an expert if he or she isn't. How-to features take either the **writer-as-expert approach** or the **outside-expert approach**. Unless the feature writer is an expert on the subject, the latter approach should be taken, with an interview of at least one expert to quote in the piece. A common mistake of beginning feature writers is to try to write a how-to piece like a term paper—consulting published sources and then writing as though an expert.

Make sure the directions are clear and easy to follow. If they're not, get clarification from the reporter before assuming you know what was intended. Explain any technical jargon in everyday language.

Suggestions that will make the how-to work better for the readers are to include possibly a list of materials needed for a project, cost of materials, safety-precaution notes and a sidebar about how to troubleshoot.

Human-Interest Stories

The term **human-interest story** is often used as a synonym for *feature*, but here it refers more specifically to a story focusing on an unusual or emotionally involving event. Such stories often appear on page 1 in a newspaper, despite the lack of a news peg, because they are interesting, humorous or odd and are likely to cause people to talk about them.

Beware of human-interest stories lacking specific source names that could verify the story. Folklorist Jan Harold Brunvand has documented a number of urban legends that have been reported as news by the media. Beware, too, of common hoax stories. (See Chapter 4.)

Opinion pieces can take the form of analysis, editorials, op-eds or reviews.

Movies, books, music, drama, art and restaurant reviews are the main kinds of reviews.

Negative reviews are protected from libel judgments provided they state opinions about things that are matters of opinion and facts about things that are matters of fact. Reviewers create legal problems if they make false statements about matters of fact—as opposed to matters of opinion—that can harm a person's reputation or business. They can also create problems of objectivity and even legality by offering opinions about matters where they should stick to facts (see Chapter 5).

As opinionated pieces, allow reviews more latitude when it comes to standards of objectivity. That is, reviews are more opinion than fact, aren't neutral, aren't impersonal in style and don't have to be fair in the sense of giving both sides. But they should be fair in the sense of being honest and open-minded rather than prejudiced beforehand.

Personality Profiles

A personality profile is used when the focus is on a person rather than an event or thing.

Although personality profiles are generally about a living person the reporter has interviewed, the feature obit, in which the reporter interviews friends and family of the deceased and perhaps researches the paper trail, is also a kind of personality profile.

The personality profile is also often used as a top for cook-of-the-week features and for odd-hobby and odd-occupation stories that focus on one person engaged in the activity. But with rare exceptions, we are past the days when the point of a story can acceptably be about a person engaged in a hobby or occupation that's odd only because of a person's race or sex.

Remember that personality profiles are selective and themed—they shouldn't just be a collection of assorted facts about someone. Instead, they should focus on particular telling details that reveal the personality in striking ways.

Beginning writers often overquote in personality profiles. You'll know this is the case if the writer is a cub reporter (an intern or a new hire) and you see many long quotations that remind you of a student trying to fill space in a term paper. The solution is to cut out the unnecessary, but alert the person doing the page layout that the size won't end up near what it measured at originally.

Question-and-Answer Interviews

The Q-and-A interview should be used in place of a more conventional personality feature only when the words of the person interviewed are so important or unique that readers would rather read the person's words quoted in full than a more selective, arranged and descriptive account.

Raffles

That warm story about neighbors holding a raffle to help raise money for a little girl's surgery could cost your publication. Why? **All lotteries not run by or licensed by the state are illegal and illegal to promote.** The law defines a **lottery** as any contest involving the three elements of prize, consideration (paying to enter) and chance.

Seasonal Features

Some features are assigned every year like calendar work. July seems to be the time, for example, when food editors assign stories about homemade ice cream, and sometime during the summer, there will likely be a spread on barbecuing and another on picnics.

In October, look for a feature on Halloween safety and another on the latest fashions in costumes.

In November, look for a food page on Thanksgiving-dinner ideas, and the day after Thanksgiving, look for a story about the biggest shopping day of the year.

In December, look for a story on what the items in "The Twelve Days of Christmas" would cost at today's prices and another on the latest toy fads.

You get the idea. As you might guess, many feature editors keep a **futures file** of seasonal story ideas. You might prepare yourself for advancement by beginning your own futures file as you find repeatable ideas in various newspapers or even on TV, radio and web reports.

Seasonal stories may be assigned each year, but that doesn't mean they have to be trite. Whenever possible, insist on new angles in seasonal stories. Every Yuletide, for example, there are countless stories beginning "Christmas came early" for a certain family. Don't let writers get away with such stale approaches. If you're assigned such a feature to edit, take it to your supervisor, and suggest that it be sent back for a new lead.

Opinion Pieces: Analysis, Columns, Fact Checks and Reviews

Analysis articles explain and interpret news events, offering the perspective of an expert in the field or at least of a reporter or commentator who has closely followed the events.

Alert your supervisor if you are ever mistakenly assigned an analysis piece to brief. A **brief**—a small two- or three-inch story in a print publication—appears in a **digest**, which is a collection of small stories under a heading like "News in Brief." A newspaper slot person tends to assign digest items on the basis of the wire-service budget rather than after reading the whole story, so it happens fairly often that you'll be mistakenly given an analysis piece that the slot thought was a news story that could be cut. Likewise, don't try to brief an analysis piece in other media. Briefs should generally only be made from news stories, not opinion ones, which require more explanation.

Don't remove the byline in a print, web or mobile story from an analysis piece unless it has a byline logo with it, like those

you see with regular contributing commentators. When paginating or proofing a news page with an analysis piece on it—as opposed to an editorial or opinion page—make sure the story has an *Analysis* or similar logo with it if your publication uses one.

The headline on an analysis or opinion piece should reflect the opinion taken in the story, so it does not have to be objective.

A focus piece is used primarily for writing an analysis of an issue, but it's adaptable to other kinds of features, as well. The writer E.B. White once advised: "Don't write about Man. Write about a man." That's basically what the focus piece does. It's also sometimes called *The Wall Street Journal* approach.

A story about a particular person dealing with a particular problem serves as a frame around a discussion in the middle of the broader issue. After starting with this person, the article has a **nut graf** in which readers find out why they're reading this—the larger controversy, issue or problem of which this person's experience is an example. The nut graf is actually a transition to the discussion and analysis that makes up the bulk of the story, then the ending is often a return to the person with whom the story started.

Make sure there is a nut graf in a focus piece, and make sure it comes right after the feature lead. If the nut graf is missing or too far down in the story, readers get confused and put off.

A common variation of the focus piece is the multiple-interview story that starts with a single person, moves to a nut graf, then quotes from various sources to develop points in the body of the text. The ending may return to the person who was in the lead, or it may end, instead, with a strong quote from one of the other sources.

In any story with more than one source, make sure that it's always clear which person is being quoted and that all second references to names (last name only) are preceded by a first reference with full name and title.

Sports Stories

Sports stories are often player interviews and profiles, advances on upcoming games and tournaments, analysis and commentary about games, focus stories on issues in sports, and personal columns on anything sports or recreation related.

Sports journalists too often assume their audience is as knowledgeable as they themselves are and don't define technical terms. Often, they are. But why limit sports coverage to those in the know? If sports journalists would take a little time to define technical terms, perhaps more casual readers would find the stories useful, as well.

Put statistics in perspective so that their relevance is clear to the readers. Comparisons are always a useful way to promote understanding.

Local people love to see their kids' names in print in high school sports stories. Remember, too, that these players _are_ just kids and be less critical of their mistakes than if they were professionals.

Review the special section on sports style in _The AP Stylebook_. Most helpful hint: Almost every number is a numeral.

Look out for flamboyant overuse of modifiers and sports-writing clichés—use genuine color instead, such as great quotes. Examples of clichés are listed below. Also, make sure reporters press beyond the clichés athletes use when they're talking:

> I just try to take it one day at a time, and always give 110%.

Insist on better, fresher quotations.

Closely related to watching out for overuse of sports clichés is insisting that reporters resist the temptation to use synonyms extravagantly. For example, use the verbs _wins_, _beats_ and _defeats_, not _annihilates_, _atomizes_, _batters_, _belts_, _bests_, _blanks_, _blasts_, _boots home_, _clips_, _clobbers_, _cops_, _crushes_, _downs_, _drops_, _dumps_, _edges_, _ekes out_, _gallops over_, _gangs up on_, _gets past_, _gouges_, _H-bombs_, _halts_, _humiliates_, _impales_, _laces_, _lashes_, _lassoes_, _licks_, _murders_, _outscraps_, _outslugs_, _orbits_, _overcomes_, _paces_, _pastes_, _pins_, _racks up_, _rallies_, _rolls over_, _romps over_, _routs_, _scores_, _sets back_, _shades_, _shaves_, _sinks_, _slows_, _snares_, _spanks_, _squeaks by_, _squeezes by_, _stampedes_, _stomps_, _stops_, _subdues_, _surges_, _sweeps_, _topples_, _tops_, _triggers_, _trips_, _trounces_, _tumbles_, _turns back_, _vanquishes_, _wallops_, _whips_, _whomps_ or _wrecks_.

Reporters should let the ball be _hit_, not always _banged_, _bashed_, _belted_, _blooped_, _bombed_, _boomed_, _bumped_, _chopped_, _clouted_, _clunked_, _conked_, _cracked_, _dribbled_, _drilled_, _driven_, _dropped_, _hacked_, _knifed_, _lashed_, _lined_, _plastered_, _plunked_, _poked_, _pooped_, _pummeled_, _pumped_, _punched_, _pushed_, _rapped_, _ripped_, _rocked_, _slapped_, _sliced_, _slugged_, _smashed_, _spanked_, _spilled_, _stubbed_, _swatted_, _tagged_, _tapped_, _tipped_, _topped_, _trickled_, _whipped_, _whistled_, _whomped_ or _whooped_.

Reporters should let a ball be _thrown_ and only occasionally _tossed_, _twirled_, _fired_ and _hurled_. They should let a ball be _kicked_ or _punted_ and never _toed_ or _booted_.

Reporters should resist the shopworn puns: Cardinal (Eagles, Orioles) _soar_ or _claw_; Lions (Tigers, Bears, Cubs) _roar_ or _claw_; Mustangs (Colts, Broncos) _buck_, _gallop_, _throw_ or _kick_.

Sportswriters, like feature writers, are allowed more lee-way as far as objectivity, but this shouldn't be abused. Sports editors tend to tolerate much more opinion in their writers' stories than elsewhere in the paper. Although often thought of as necessary for a lively sports page, the same argument could be made for other categories of news, as well. As for objectivity in sportscasters, we find that although they give their opinions more than other reporters, they usually are more objective in the sense of being fair and fact-based than many political reporters.

Sport-Stories Cliches to Avoid

- coveted trophy
- crunch time
- drought
- field of (battle, dreams)
- give 110%
- good speed
- hammered
- He'd [she'd] like to have that one back.
- hoopsters
- in your face
- last-ditch effort
- new record (record)
- paydirt
- the pride is back
- roared back
- roared from behind
- rocky road
- sea of mud
- seconds ticked off the clock
- a shooting contest
- slammed
- standing-room-only crowd
- sweet revenge
- There's no I in "team."
- turned the tables
- unblemished record
- What a difference a season makes.

Travel Pieces

Travel stories tell about interesting places to visit and often suggest tours, routes, accommodations and restaurants.

If the story is about a nearby locale and no sidebar or graphics are included, suggest that a map be made or a directions-box included, as well as, perhaps, a list of accommodations or tours, with prices, pulled from the story.

Don't let travel stories fall into the trap of long, boring descriptions. Remember, most readers find lengthy descriptive passages a turnoff because mere description focuses on things being rather than on people acting.

Because travel pieces contain more description than most other features, editors are more likely to find adjectives and adverbs overused in them. Remember Mark Twain's advice that modifiers should be used only sparingly.

Be on the lookout for travel-piece clichés such as a particular locale that is "a quaint blend of old and new." This description applies to almost everywhere. Likewise, rather than simply labeling a place "historic" or "scenic," describe what makes it historic or scenic, *showing* the readers rather than *telling* them.

Be aware that it's usually considered a conflict of interest to accept free travel arrangements.

Columns

Sports, entertainment, humor, editorial, food, garden, home improvement, religion, antiques and advice are some of the main kinds of columns.

Unlike hard-news stories where the writing should be impersonal, columns depend upon the writer being more personal in style and in information.

Columns are generally the most personal of feature stories, and nothing will infuriate a reporter so much as an editor needlessly rewriting a column.

Columns often contain elements of a review, so it's important for legal purposes to beware of false statements about matters of fact as opposed to mere negative opinion.

Columns are one of the places where the news media most often pass on famous misquotations or misinformation. So, look out for these because columns are more personal and involve more writing off the top of the head rather than reporting. (See Chapter 4.)

Suggested Websites

Bureau of Labor Statistics: www.bls.gov
MedlinePlus: https://medlineplus.gov/
National Association of Broadcasters: www.nab.org
National Weather Service: http://weather.gov/
Quackwatch: www.quackwatch.org Guide to fraudulent medicine claims
Radio Television Digital News Association: www.rtdna.org
Radio–Television News Directors Association and Foundation: www.rtnda.org
The Most Mispronounced Words in English: www.alphadictionary.com/articles/mispronounced_words.html

Suggested Readings

Angler, Martin W. *Science Journalism: An Introduction.* Routledge, 2017.
The Associated Press Stylebook. Latest edition. New York: The Associated Press. (There's a section called "Broadcast Guidelines" at the back.)
Block, Mervin. *Rewriting Network News: Wordwatching Tips from 345 TV and Radio Scripts.* Washington, DC: CQ Press, 2010.

Block, Mervin. *Writing Broadcast News Shorter, Sharper, Stronger: A Professional Handbook*. Washington, DC: CQ Press, 2010.

Brooks, Brian S., James L. Pinson and Jean Gaddy Wilson. *Working With Words*, 10th edition, 2020.

Cohn, Victor. *News & Numbers: A Writer's Guide to Statistics*, 3rd edition. Wiley-Blackwell, 2011.

Hazlitt, Henry. *Economics in One Lesson*. Three Rivers Press, 1988.

Gisondi, Joe. *Field Guide to Covering Sports*, 2nd edition. CQ Press, 2017.

Huff, Darrell. *How to Lie with Statistics*. W.W. Norton, 2010.

Missouri Group. *News Reporting and Writing*, 13th edition. Bedford/St. Martin's, 2020.

Morgan, Susan, Tom Reichert and Tyler R. Harrison. *From Numbers to Words: Reporting Statistical Results for the Social Sciences*. Routledge, 2016.

Paulos, John Allen. *A Mathematician Reads the Newspaper*. Basic Books, 2013.

Schultz, Bradley, Edward T. Arke and Ed Arke. *Sports Media: Reporting, Producing, and Planning*, 3rd edition. Routledge, 2015.

Standling, Suzette Martinez. *The Art of Opinion Writing: Insider Secrets from Top Op-Ed Columnists*. RRP International, 2013.

Tompkins, Al. *Aim for the Heart, Write for the Ear, Shoot for the Eye: A Guide for TV Producers and Reporters*. New York: Bonus Books, 2002.

9 EDIT YOURSELF

The Impact of Disappearing Editors

Earlier in this book, we mentioned that newspapers, in particular, have made large cuts in the number of editors in their newsrooms and in some cases have eliminated copy desks entirely. Just why corporate moguls seem to think editing is not important is a mystery. As we explained in Chapter 2, editors are extremely important in battling the decline of credibility, not to mention their roles in ensuring accuracy in every area from avoiding libel suits to double-checking facts to correcting spelling and grammar errors.

The goal of this book, however, is to prepare beginners in the field for what they will encounter when they take their first jobs. **Two trends in the industry are clear**:

- **Those headed for newspapers (and many magazines) will find that fewer editors are editing stories than ever before.**

DOI: 10.4324/9781003011422-9

- **Those headed for jobs with online sites will find that while the number of editors at websites is growing exponentially, the volume of information processed at such sites means that many stories may be handled by only one writer/editor.**

Indeed, working at an online site can often be quite similar to what wire-service reporters have done for decades, particularly on night shifts at the smallest bureaus. A reporter in Tulsa, Oklahoma, for example, may find herself covering the University of Tulsa football game, perhaps including taking photos and recording audio or even video clips, then writing the story, then editing the story herself, then filing it online and maybe even updating the story. Across the country, reductions in the number of editors are making the need for skills in self-editing increasingly important.

So, what is self-editing all about? In its simplest form, it's following best practices of reporters while writing the story, then following best practices of editors while editing the story. All writers need editors to produce the best journalism—even if your editor is only yourself. To do that, and do it correctly, it's useful to understand the perspectives and techniques used by both reporters and editors. Doing that is not easy for several reasons:

- Many reporters have never worked as editors and simply don't understand the reason an editor changed the lead, organization or wording of a story. Those reporters don't have the critical eye of an editor, and they don't think their story needs work.
- Some editors, on the other hand, try to rewrite stories as they would have written them rather than allow the reporter to have a voice. And some editors entered the business as copy editors and never worked as reporters.
- Many reporters have the notion they are great writers and that their golden prose needs no editing. Neither, they believe, should it be trimmed in length. We'd argue vociferously that this is an absurd position.
- Some editors have forgotten how much work goes into putting together a story and don't appreciate the reporter's difficulty in getting all the information needed and phrasing it so an audience can understand.
- And even if all those barriers are overcome, it's still much easier for an independent editor to find errors or inconsistencies in your story than it is for you. You, after all, know what you were trying to say. Another editor may not and would attempt to clarify it.

Those are just a few of the dozens of things that prevent reporters and editors from having a kindred perspective. That gap in understanding is unfortunate in an era in which writers often must also be editors. In this chapter, we'll suggest a few ways to bridge the gap between the reporter's perspective and that of the editor. We'll do that with the intention of melding those two perspectives into one in situations when the reporter must also serve as the editor.

The Reporter's Perspective

Reporters have a lot on their plate, and entire textbooks are written to help beginners learn how to report a story correctly. We won't attempt to re-invent the reporting textbook here, but let's take a look at some of the key techniques reporters use to gather information and write a story.

Let's assume that an editor has assigned you to write a story about the growing problem of homelessness in your community. Where do you start? The starting place for most stories, including this one, is to check your news-paper or magazine library to see what has already been written about the problem. If you find some earlier stories, they are likely to give you leads about who handles the homeless issue within city government, agencies in town that provide services to the homeless and perhaps data about the extent of the problem locally, statewide or nationally.

The newsroom library, or morgue, as it is often called, is the place we'd like to see reporters start on almost any subject. It will include previously pub-lished stories and photos, as well as possibly reporters' notes available only to staff and not the public. Generally, these days, the newsroom library is primarily online, and some of its archives can be searched also by the public. A search there would give you an initial list of local people who might have expertise on the subject. Add to that any others you can think of.

The Editor: Manager or Leader?

Editors aren't just editors; they also are managers, and the best ones are leaders. It's extremely important to understand the distinction between management and leadership. And make no mistake about it, they are different. **The distinctions are important for both editors and reporters, and even for reporters who are their own editors.**

Management is getting things done through other people. Man-agers focus on maintaining standards. They watch for declines in produc-tivity and quality, and seek to move the organization back to the point of achieving standards. To some extent, it's fair to say that managers look backward and fix things that are broken.

Leadership results from people who are innovative, see the need to change, embrace change and implement change. Leaders look forward and plan for the future, all the while honoring and recognizing the organ-ization's historic strengths. Leaders definitely manage, but they also lead.

Managers, at the base level, must do five things—hire people, organize these people into a cohesive unit, communicate with these people, plan for the future through budgeting and other processes, and control the operation by maintaining at least minimum standards. Leaders do more. They inspire a collective vision for the organization. Leaders inspire. They show the way. They lead by example. They empower others. The leader, then, pulls from the bottom up, while the manager pushes from the top down.

One of the most important lessons to learn before you enter management is that people enjoy being led, but they merely tolerate being managed.

Managers push, but leaders pull. Managers drive people to perform. Too often, they treat employees like parts of a machine. They demand and insist, they cajole, and, if necessary, they punish to get results. The worst are sometimes even compared by their staff to "slave masters." Employees of those who manage may dread visiting with the boss. Those same employees generally enjoy visiting with a leader.

Leaders create an environment in which employees feel pulled to greatness—inspired, empowered to make changes and do great things. Leaders praise accomplishment. They show respect for the employee's opinions. They show interest in the employee's family. They are good at being human. Finally, leaders have one other significant characteristic: They don't profess to know it all. They often provide all or most of the vision, but they seek advice from those closest to the situation—those in the trenches performing daily journalism.

What happens if you are now the editor, as well, and not just a reporter? You may not have others to manage or lead, but the import thing is you will need to take the reins and become your own leader. You must demand the best performance of yourself.

Then, we'd suggest a search of other online databases for earlier stories about homelessness. While these likely won't provide as much useful information about local sources, they will give you a better perspective of the problem regionally or even nationally.

Find a few local people to talk about how they view homelessness. Are they put off by homeless people asking for handouts in the street? Do they think that homeless veterans should get help from the Veterans Administration? Have they ever considered what they would do if suddenly they found themselves homeless?

Finally, consider whether it's possible to write a good story on this subject without doing the obvious—talking with homeless people. It isn't. So, learn where homeless people congregate in your community. It might be near a soup kitchen or shelter, or it might be beneath a bridge. Go there to find subjects to interview.

The Foundation of Good Reporting

Why is searching for possible sources important? Because **the basis of any good news story is the *Discipline of Multiple Sources*.** Call it being thorough. You should never write a story based on talking to only one source—unless that source is the only one you can find while on deadline. And even if a person is the subject of a mere personality profile, it would be good to talk also to people who know him or her.

Having only one source can lead to an unbalanced story that conforms to the source's biases without providing contrasting viewpoints. One expert source may suggest building tiny houses for homeless individuals and providing financial assistance. Another expert may have a different suggestion, like updating and converting unused buildings for living spaces. Interviewing multiple sources helps to ensure that you are not missing any important perspectives on the issue.

Another key to good reporting is the related idea of the *Discipline of Verification.* The information you get must be validated for accuracy, and a reporter does that in many ways. First, the reporter asks the same question of several experts on the subject. If the same answer surfaces each time, it's likely to be accurate, or at least the conventional opinion. If, however, sources differ, it's important to do more reporting, perhaps even calling a national expert to help explain the nuances of different approaches to the problem.

A third key is the *Discipline of Accuracy.* This is also related to the concept of objectivity we've previously discussed (see pages 102–106, and all of Chapter 3). It's a passion for getting to the facts—to reporting what's the best you can discern at the time is actually true, not what you *want* to be true. In the age of abundant online data sources, a check of the internet can be one way to help ensure accuracy. Just make sure the sources you find online are good ones.

Together, the *Discipline of Multiple Sources*, the *Discipline of Verification* and the *Discipline of Accuracy* form the foundation on which all good news stories are built.

Macro and Micro Editing

As we've seen in earlier chapters, editors look at a story on both the macro and micro levels. **Remembering to attend to both macro and micro issues is an important part of an editor's job. It's also an important part of a reporter's job as he or she writes the story, and it's also an important aspect of self-editing.**

Macro editing (Chapters 4–5) **looks at the bigger picture—things like:**

- **Is this easy for readers to understand?**
- **Are there ambiguities?**
- **Is the story internally consistent?**
- **Are there any obvious questions left unanswered?**
- **Does this agree with previous stories on the subject? If not, why not?**

Micro editing (Chapters 6–7) **is the process of paying attention to detail—things like:**

- **Are all the facts correct?**
- **Is our publication's or website's style followed throughout?**
- **Are all the names and other words spelled correctly?**
- **Is the grammar correct?**

Now that copy editors no longer exist at many publications and websites, it falls to the writer to pay meticulous detail to all parts of the story, including spelling, grammar, adherence to style rules and the like. No longer can a reporter say, as many once did: "I don't care about style rules. I'm worried about accuracy, being thorough and making sure the story flows. The copy editor will fix the small stuff."

The Editor's Perspective

Reporters are human, and their attitude toward the subject of a story can easily affect the finished product. That's why it's important to think like an editor. Doing that requires detaching yourself from your emotions long enough to make an objective evaluation of the story.

For example, what about that story on homelessness your editor assigned you? Do you have the same drive to be thorough and execute it as well as one you came up with the idea for yourself? Perhaps you do, and, if so, you should be commended. But what if you're not comfortable around homeless people, and the subject is not one you're happy to deal with? It becomes a chore to write and report it, and the story is likely to suffer as a result.

Not only that, but also, if you're covering a story on a subject you like or dislike, your own views could add bias to the questions you ask, the angle taken and your wordings. That's why it's good to have an editor to offer a second set of eyes or ears to spot such things. But if you're your own editor, you need to learn to detach your own judgments and opinions from the story.

Reporters should do that anyway—and when your goalie is out of the net, a good field player needs to cover.

We could write several pages repeating the ways editors look critically at a story, but here are some reminders of the most important perspectives they may take:

- **Is the opening paragraph—the lede—crafted to draw the reader into the story? Is it quick to read and to the point?**
- **What's the point of this story? Is that clearly defined in what editors call a *nut graf*? A nut graf tells the reader what the story is and why it's important.**
- **Does the story flow well? Has the writer included transitions that encourage the reader to keep reading?**
- **Is the story well-organized, or does it skip aimlessly from point to point?**
- **Does the writer answer all questions the reader might ask? If not, is there a sentence or two explaining why those questions weren't answered?**
- **Has the writer used direct quotations throughout to break up the monotony of potentially boring text?**
- **Are points made in the story supported with attribution or sourcing? Are the most important ones reinforced by more than one source?**
- **Does the story include context to help explain its importance? For example, how does homelessness in our community compare to that in other similar-sized cities?**
- **Is the story accompanied by charts or graphs that help explain it in quantifiable ways?**
- **Is the story accompanied by photographs that reinforce important points?**
- **Is the story a good literary effort? Are grammar and spelling correct throughout?**
- **Is there any part of the story that makes it seem impossible to believe? If so, is the veracity of that part well-documented?**
- **Does the story pose any problems of legality, ethics or taste?**

Use this list as you approach self-editing. Step back from the story you wrote and view it as an objective editor or reader who knows little to nothing about the subject. That's not the easiest thing to do with a story you wrote, but **thinking like an editor could be the difference in publishing a mediocre story or a great one**.

The Self-Editing Process

In Chapter 3, we suggested this approach to editing a story:

- **Read the story.**
- **Edit it thoroughly.**
- **Reread the story and make any final corrections.**

But when the writer is also the editor, we need to expand the process to ensure a story is as close to perfect as we can possibly make it. Here's a suggested procedure for doing that:

- **Complete the background research by checking your library and online sites for possible story themes and sources.**
- **Look for statistical information.** How many are homeless locally? Statewide? Nationally? Statistics always make a story seem more thorough in the readers' eyes. And more accurate.
- **Make a list of subjects to interview.** You may well add to that list later as sources point you to others with expertise on the subject.
- **Interview your sources**, leaving the person you view as the most important source for last. That person, presumably, could help you resolve ambiguities and perhaps provide the best information.
- **Write the first draft of your story.** Any meticulous writer will produce several revisions and constantly make changes as he or she reads through the story. Reading through a story multiple times helps you find questions you may have left unanswered and helps you resolve inconsistencies or ambiguities.
- **Edit your draft as often as needed to make the story as clear and concise as possible.**
- **Then, switch gears. Assume the role of editor, and edit your story with the critical eye of an editor. Look at it as if you hadn't written it.** Complete a first read of the story while making few changes. Evaluate how easily readers will be able to understand it. Look for the big-picture items on this read.
- **Now, edit it thoroughly.** Work your way through the story with the skeptical eye of an editor, searching for both macro and micro problems. Is the lead the best it can be to catch the readers' attention? Is the flow of the story both logical and easy to follow? Are there still unanswered questions a reader might ask? Are there any internal inconsistencies in the story? Are any passages potentially libelous? Are the style, spelling and grammar correct? All those things, and more, would be done by an editor if you had one. Now if falls on you to do them.
- **Reread the story a final time, looking for punctuation, style, spelling and grammar errors in particular.**

In the end, it's important to understand this key point: **The more times you read the story, the more likely it is you will detect and fix all the problems.** Redundant editing is the key to creating good, understandable and accurate journalism. If it falls to you to accomplish all of those readings, so be it.

All this takes time. If one writes a story then edits and makes tweaks in seven or eight revisions, hours, not minutes, are involved. And when confronted with frequent deadlines at newspapers, it may not always be possible to read and edit a story multiple times. That's even more true at websites, where there's a deadline every minute, not every day. And that, in turn, may well be why we're seeing more errors in the media than ever before. So, there is an increasing demand for those who can get it right—and get it right the first time.

Understand that not all stories merit such meticulous attention. The process we outlined here ideally would be used to write and edit all stories, but shorter, simpler stories may not require that level of attention. We say that with the caveat that many of the errors we see online and in newspapers occur in the shortest of stories. All stories are important. Cast a critical eye on even the shortest ones.

Self-Editing versus Peer Editing

We've focused here on self-editing, which is, in fact, the worst-case scenario for media writers. Having a dedicated, independent editor or editors go through your story is still the best way to ensure production of a good, accurate news story. We know from experience that redundant editing (editing by two or more individuals) almost always produces a better finished product. That's why publications with the time to do so write, edit, rewrite, edit, edit and edit again. Even editors need editors!

Time magazine is a great example. It often is edited so heavily that the writer barely recognizes what he or she originally submitted. But *Time*'s goal in doing so is quite different from the editing process that occurs at newspapers. In daily journalism as opposed to weekly, tight deadlines mean that speed is more important than writing the tightest possible story, which is *Time*'s goal. For a weekly publication compiling multiple days of news into a limited amount of space, conciseness is important.

It's important to understand, then, that there are several levels of editing that range from highly desirable to least desirable. These are:

- Intensive redundant editing by multiple editors. (Similar to what occurs at *Time*.)
- Less intensive redundant editing as historically occurred at newspapers. (At least two editors, typically a metro editor and a copy editor, edit your copy).

- Editing by just one editor. (One metro editor, for example, with no copy editor.)
- Peer editing. (Reporters exchange stories and edit each other.)
- Self-editing. (You're on your own.)

We haven't discussed peer editing here, but it should be considered if time allows. An Indonesian research study of peer editing versus self-editing found that peer editing improved the quality of copy significantly more than self-editing alone.

In the end, it's clear that the more editing a story undergoes the more likely it is to be accurate, clear and concise. Those are the primary goals of any piece of journalism.

Suggested Websites

American Copy Editors Society: www.copydesk.org
The Poynter Institute: www.poynter.org
The top ten golden rules of self-editing: www.writermag.com

Suggested Readings

Davis, Steve and Emilie Davis. *Think Like an Editor: 50 Strategies for the Print and Digital World.* Boston: Walsworth, 2014.
Ross-Larson, Bruce. *Edit Yourself.* New York-London: W.W. Norton, 1996.
Saleh, Naveed. *The Writer's Guide to Self-Editing: Essential Tips for Online and Print Publication.* Jefferson, NC: McFarland, 2019.

10 WRITING HEADLINES, TITLES, CAPTIONS AND BLURBS

Getting People to Listen, Read or Watch

To persuade people to read newspapers and magazines, listen to radio, watch television and surf the web, you first must get their attention. Radio accomplishes this with sound, while television provides a compelling combination of sound and video. The print media, on the other hand, rely primarily on still photographs and large type to accomplish the same end. Then there is the web, which has all those assets and is well on its way to becoming America's news medium of choice.

In this chapter, we review the importance of what print and web journalists call *display type—headlines, titles and blurbs—*and the words, called *captions* or *cutlines,* that accompany still photographs. For the print or web journalist, these are critical means of drawing an audience.

DOI: 10.4324/9781003011422-10

Editors Are the Most Widely Read Writers

Newspapers and magazines developed **headline** writing, or **title** writing as magazine journalists call it, into an art form. The editor who writes compelling *heads* or *titles* is a valuable member of the staff. **While the editor's first task is to correct and refine copy, as explained in earlier chapters, a second task is to write a headline that:**

- **Attracts the reader's attention.**
- **Summarizes the story.**
- **Helps the reader index the contents of the page.**
- **Depicts the mood of the story.**
- **Helps set the tone of the newspaper, magazine or website.**
- **Provides adequate typographic relief.**

Although all these functions are important, none is more important than attracting the reader's attention.

The Sad Truth About Readership

We get a much clearer view of the job of a newspaper, magazine or website journalist when we grasp this simple truth: **The average reader does not read the average story**. That's a depressing thought at first—one most editors don't want to hear and don't want to believe. But, unfortunately, it's true. Take newspapers for example. The average reader reads the paper only about 20 minutes a day, according to the most recent studies.

TICKS
The best defense? A good, strong dose of prevention.

Mayor orders investigation of park police

5 Days of Testimony End
Jury Gets Zimmer Case

Police Expand Task Force
Missing Persons Bureau Placed Under Redding's Command

Figure 10.1 Headlines come in all sizes and typefaces. Sizes are measured in points, a printer's unit of measurement equal to 1/72 of an inch. Because there are 72 points in an inch, 24-point type would be about one-third inch in height. Typefaces are given distinctive names such as Bodoni and Helvetica.

But, of course, that 20 minutes is not all spent reading news. Not by a long shot. From that time, we should subtract the minutes spent looking at the classifieds and other advertising, as well as the TV listings, the horoscope, the comics and the bridge column. We should also subtract the time spent reading advice columns, like Dear Abby, and lifestyle and cooking ones. Some also would suggest subtracting the time spent reading sports scores and obituaries, but to many these are the most important news in the paper.

How much time is left to read the news? Not much. But do you read the whole paper word for word? Few people, even journalists, do so. Why should we expect the average reader to spend more time with a newspaper than we do? What almost all newspaper readers do, journalists included, is look at the pictures, graphics and big type—the headlines, titles and blurbs— and use them as both a quick news summary and an index to what we may want to read in depth. Readers of magazines and websites consume news much the same way. Now, here's the good news: If we accept this as a fact of life rather than get depressed about it, we're in better shape to make better papers, magazines and websites.

Another axiom of the industry is this: **The people most likely to read a story in its entirety are those most likely to find fault with it.**

Let's start with a word of encouragement for reporters, those most likely to find this news disturbing. After all, we've just told you that the prize-winning stories you labored to craft and are so proud of probably aren't read by many of your subscribers.

If you write a story about a new kidney machine at the local hospital, it doesn't matter whether Ernest Hemingway himself could have done a better job. The people most likely to read it, aside from your editor and maybe your family and friends, probably work at the hospital or have kidney problems. Those are the same people who likely know more about the subject than you do and who are most likely to find fault with your story.

That's encouraging? It can be. If you're in the doldrums about complaints over stories, let that motivate you to be more accurate. But mainly consider who's complaining before you let frustration burn you out.

Editors and publishers who pay more and more attention to studies showing low credibility ratings for newspapers should keep that reality in mind— not just as an excuse but also as a part of the problem that now can be more easily tackled because we've identified it. Magazine editors face the same problem. So do web editors. The fact is that regardless of the medium, readers will consume only a tiny part of the content you offer.

Assume the Reader Won't Read the Story

Let's turn our attention to page designers and headline writers for whom the implications are particularly strong for our initial observation—that the average reader doesn't read the average story. If the average reader is mainly reading just the big type, then a big part of a reader's impression of the usefulness of the publication or website—and how interesting it is—is determined by the editor who writes the headline or title.

That big type is likely to be all a reader will read of a story. As a result, it should be so clear that the news consumer will feel informed by reading the big type alone. Thus, we offer the single most powerful bit of advice for improving headlines: **When you write a headline or title, assume the reader won't read the story.**

The problem with many heads is that the editor has forgotten that he or she had the benefit of having read the story before encountering the headline. The reader does not. Too many headlines by beginners read like vague titles on term papers. That won't do.

The test is this: After you've written a headline, forget you know what the story is about long enough to read the headline and ask yourself whether you have a clear idea of the news from reading just the headline. If the answer is that you don't, then the headline should be rewritten, or the page designer should redesign the story's space to include a longer headline, a second deck, a blurb or some other display-type device.

Here's a tip for newspaper and magazine page designers and website screen designers: You can design pages that will better inform your readers if you recall the advice that readers are big-type readers. **Every bit of big type on a page is another chance to give them additional news they might not otherwise read.**

For example, why use an **underline** (a one-line caption) with a photo when a full **cutline** (a multiple-line caption) would allow the editor to pull some additional information from the story and highlight it? This is especially helpful when the photo is a portrait of someone prominent in the story and the only information the photographer gives you is the person's name. Allow room to put in a cutline with an interesting quotation that otherwise might remain unread in the body of the story.

And, of course, when you place any story on the page or on the web, ask yourself how complicated the story is and whether the headline specifications you're considering will allow enough space to summarize it adequately.

Although the size of type is important to attract attention, and the number of words the designer allows is critical to communication, **the most important part of the headline-writing process is crafting a head that says as much as possible**.

Good headlines and titles attract the reader's attention to stories that otherwise may be ignored. The day's best story may have little or no impact if the headline fails to sell it or attract attention. **Headlines sell stories in many ways, but often they do so by focusing on how the reader's life will be affected.** For example, if the City Council has approved a city budget of $30 million for the coming year, one approach is to headline the story:

Council approves $30 million budget

Another approach, which does a better job of selling the story, might be this:

City tax rate to remain unchanged

Headline Writing Is Fun

It's fun to write headlines and titles because writing them is a creative activity. Editors have the satisfaction of knowing that their headlines will be read. They would like to think that the head is intriguing enough to invite the reader to read the story. When they write heads that capsulize the story, they get smiles from their supervisors, and sometimes, some praise.

Somerset Maugham said you cannot write well unless you write much. Similarly, you can't write good heads until you have written many. After editors have been at that task for a while, they begin to think in headline phrases. When they read a story, they automatically reconstruct the headline the way they would have written it. A good headline inspires them to write good ones, too.

Sometimes they dash off a head in less time than it took them to edit the copy. Then they get stuck on a small story. They might write a dozen versions, read and reread the story and then try again. As a last resort, they may ask a colleague or supervisor for an angle. The longer they are on the desk, the more adept they become at shifting gears for headline ideas. They try not to admit that any head is impossible to write. If a synonym eludes them, they search the dictionary or a thesaurus until they find the right one. If they have a flair for rhyme, they apply it to a brightener:

Nudes in a pool play it cool as onlookers drool

Every story is a challenge. After the writer has refined the story, it almost becomes the editor's story. The enthusiasm of editors is reflected in the headlines of a newspaper, magazine or website. Good editors seek to put all the drama, the pathos or the humor of the story into the headline. The clever ones, or the "heady heads," as one columnist calls them, may show up later in office critiques or in trade journals:

Council makes short work of long agenda
Hen's whopper now a whooper

> **Stop the clock; daylight time is getting off**
> **Lake carriers clear decks for battle with railroads**
> **'Dolly' says 'Golly' after helloful year**
> **Tickets cricket, legislators told**
> **Quints have a happy, happy, happy, happy, happy birthday** (First birthday party for quintuplets)

The second approach answers the question the reader is most likely to ask about the council's action: How will it affect me?

Some headlines attract attention because of the magnitude of the event they address:

> **Earthquake in Algeria kills 20,000**

Others attract attention because the headline is clever or unusual:

> **Hunger pangs**
> **Thief finds sandwich goodies, wine provide appetizing loot**

Magazines, in particular, have mastered the art of clever title writing. They often do so with far fewer words than a newspaper headline writer might need. Of course, magazine editors have more time to do their jobs because magazines aren't published daily like newspapers. There is more time to edit carefully and more time to craft clever, eye-catching titles. Each story requires a different approach, and the headline or title writer who is able to find the correct one to attract the reader's attention is a valued member of the staff.

Most headlines that appear over news stories are designed to inform, not entertain, so the headline that simply summarizes the story as concisely and accurately as possible is the bread and butter of the news headline writer:

> **US, China agree to major grain deal**

Such headlines seldom win prizes for originality or prompt readers to write letters of praise. But a newspaper full of headlines that get right to the point is a newspaper that is easy to read. The reader knows what the story is about and can make an intelligent decision about whether to read more. The headlines summarize the news, much as brief radio newscasts do.

If the headlines on a page do a good job of summarizing the stories, the editors have created for their readers an index

to the page. This also helps readers determine what to read and what to bypass. In one sense, good headlines help readers determine what *not* to read. Although that may seem counterproductive to the objectives of the publication or website, it's realistic to recognize that readers will partake of only a small percentage of the offerings. Publications and websites help by providing a choice of fare, much as supermarket managers offer their customers various brands of green beans. That may not be an appealing comparison to those who view the news media as entities above that sort of thing, but it *is* realistic. To ignore that is a mistake.

The headline also sets the mood for the story. The straightforward news headline indicates that the story it accompanies is a serious one. Similarly, a headline above a how-to-do-it story should reflect the story's content:

It's easy to save by regularly changing your car's oil

Setting the mood is even more important when writing headlines for humorous stories. One newspaper hurt readership of a bright story during the 1970s streaking craze, when students on college campuses tried to outdo each other by getting as many students as possible to run across campus in the nude. That newspaper used a straight headline:

Judge lectures streaker

Figure 10.2 At smaller newspapers, copy editors or city editors may also design pages.

Photo by Philip Holman.

The story was a humorous account of the court appearance of a group of students who had run across a softball diamond in the nude. In the second edition, the headline writer did a much better job:

Streaker gets the pitch;
it's a whole nude ball game

In a way, that's a teaser head because it is intended to draw the reader into the story. Clearly, though, the mood was set for the reader to enjoy it.

Headlines probably reveal as much about the tone, or character, of a publication or website as anything it contains. If the top story on the front page is headlined **Cops seek lover in ax murder** and the second story carries the headline **Janice flips over new beau**, there can be little doubt about the nature of the publication or site. Serious tones, as well as sensational ones, can be set with headlines.

Shorter Stories Can Add Up to More

All the jokes about *USA Today*'s short-article, fast-food journalism aside, that newspaper could teach even *The New York Times* a thing or two about being informative. That's because *USA Today*, one of the largest in circulation among U.S. newspapers, is probably most in tune with how people actually read, not how journalists think they should.

In an ideal world, everyone would have the time to read in-depth articles about everything. But that's not the world in which readers live. **Readers skim the headlines because they don't have time to read more than the articles of particular interest to them.**

When we as journalists say *The New York Times* has long been one of the standards for journalistic excellence—and in many ways it is despite critics on the right—we are not looking at how readers actually read. A typical *Times* inside page may have only one or two stories on it because they're so long and in-depth. But what does the average reader read? The big type. How much information, then, did the reader really get from that page?

Compare a *Times* inside page with a typical inside page in *USA Today*, loaded with photos and graphics and numerous small stories. More stories means more items can be covered in the same amount of space with a larger array of big type. The average reader probably spends more time reading the average page of *USA Today* than the average page of *The New York Times*. That reader will, in turn, be more informed on a greater number of topics.

We're not suggesting that *The New York Times* change what it does. For one thing, the average *Times* reader is probably an atypical newspaper reader—one who buys *The Times* for the greater depth it offers compared with the alternatives. But most of us can better serve our readers—actually better inform them and keep them more interested—if we put together newspapers in a way that takes into account how most people actually read.

That same advice applies to our websites and even to magazines. **Long, unrelieved masses of gray text aren't very appealing to the average reader.**

Shorter Stories—and More of Them

If we take the ideas outlined above and apply them to our local paper, a magazine or a website, it clearly would make sense for us to run shorter stories and more of them. We're not ruling out occasional lengthy, in-depth pieces. Readers should get these, too, but they should probably be limited to one per open page or one to the front page of a website. It's unrealistic to think readers will read much more than that. Magazines may well get away with more long stories, and many do.

Despite our suggestion to include more and shorter stories, it sometimes seems that reporters think every planning and zoning committee meeting is worth 15 to 20 inches of space or more. When papers or magazines run a plethora of lengthy stories, others are held until they are less timely or are squeezed out of the publication or website altogether. Reporters' efforts are wasted, and the readers are less well-informed.

The Headline- or Title-Writing Process

Readers read the headline or title first, then the story. Editors work in reverse; they first read the story, then write the headline. This often leads to confusing heads because editors mistakenly assume that if readers will only read the story they will understand what the headline is trying to convey. **Except in rare cases deliberately designed to tease the reader, the headline or title must be instantly clear. In most cases, the reader will not read a story simply to find out what the headline means.**
Headline writing, then, involves two critical steps:

- **Selecting which details to use.**
- **Phrasing them properly within the space available.**

The editor exercises editorial judgment in completing the first step in the process. Which words must be included in the headline to convey to the reader the meaning of the story? In its simplest form, this involves answering the question: Who does what? Thus, most good headlines, like all good sentences, have a subject and predicate, and usually a direct object:

Tornado strikes Jonesboro

That done, the editor tries to make the headline fit. Synonyms may be necessary to shorten the phrase, and more concise verbs may help:

Tornado rips Jonesboro

That, in simplified form, is the essence of headline writing.

Understanding Headline Orders

Traditionally, specifications for headlines are written as three numbers separated by hyphens. Here are four examples: 1–24–3, 2–36–2, 4–48–1, 6–60–1. The first number in a headline order is the number of columns the headline will cover; the second is the **point size** of the headline (its height in points measured from the bottom of a descender like *g* to the top of an ascender like *h*); and the third is the number of lines in the headline. So, a 1–24–3 headline is one column wide, 24-point type, three lines long.

This is less important to understand today now that headlines are written right into InDesign pages, but many newspapers still refer to headline sizes this way. Think of it as a shorthand way of talking about headline sizes within the office.

A note on print measurements: In publishing and printing, we don't measure in inches or centimeters but in picas and points. There are 12 points in a pica and 6 picas (or 72 points) in an inch.

Traditionally, graphic elements and column widths are measured in picas and points, but the height of type is measured only in points. So, we'd say a headline is 36 points (half an inch tall) but a column is 12.2 (12 picas and 2 points) wide, and a photograph is 38.6 picas wide and 24.6 picas deep.

By the way, 38.6 (read as 38 point 6) means 38½ picas. Why? The point is not a decimal point but a dividing mark between picas and points. The photograph referred to is 38 picas and 6 points wide—or, since there are 12 points in one pica, 38½ picas. In many design programs, 38 picas 6 points would be written 38p6. (In so-called new math terms, we are in base 12, not base 10.)

It will save you time writing headlines if you first visualize their size so you'll have an idea about how much to write and where to break lines. It's easy to "see" the number of columns and lines, but visualizing the point size may be difficult at first. Just remember that 72 points equal an inch, so a 54-point headline would be three-fourths of an inch in height, 48 would be two-thirds of an inch, 36 half an inch, 24 one-third of an inch and 18 one-fourth of an inch. Other common point sizes can be visualized like this: 60 would be between three-fourths of an inch and an inch tall, 30 would be between one-third and one-half inch tall.

Headline Terminology

Editors have various terms for different kinds of headlines so that editors doing the design can tell copy editors editing the stories and writing the headlines exactly what they want. Here are the terms you should know:

Main head. If there's only one headline over a story, it's usually just called the *headline*. But if there is more than one, the headline that makes the primary point is the **main head**. The main head typically would have one to three lines or perhaps even more in a narrow column.

Deck or second deck. If the story has more than one headline, the **deck** adds additional details or a different angle beyond what's said in the main headline. A deck may be one to five lines long. Don't confuse a deck with merely a second line of the main head. Here are some differences:

- The second deck will be a sentence of its own and not simply a continuation of a sentence in the main head.
- The second deck will be in a lighter typeface than the main head and at some papers, magazines or websites, it will be italic.
- The second deck will be either half the point size of the main head or the next larger standard point size above half. (The standard head sizes are 14, 18, 24, 30, 36, 42, 48, 54, 60, 72, 90 and 96.) So, a second deck under a 48-point head would be either 24 or 30 points.

Example:

This is a main head
This is a deck beneath the main one

Hammer. A *hammer* is a label head, typically one or two words long, above a main head. It's used mainly with features. When a story has a hammer, the hammer is in bold type, and for once the main head is in lighter, smaller type. When you have a hammer, the main head is either half the point size of the hammer or is the next larger standard point size above half. The hammer itself should not be longer than half the width of the main head.

Example:

Hammer
Here's the main head beneath the hammer

Kicker. Like a hammer, a *kicker* is a label head (up to about five words in length) above a main head. But with a kicker, the main head is the bold one while the kicker is half the point size (or the next standard size above half) of the main head and in lighter type. At some papers, a kicker is italic or underlined, or some combination of lighter, italic and underlined. Kickers are much less common today than hammers because people tend to read type from biggest to smallest, so a kicker tends to be read after the main head—not what the designer wants—and leads people's eyes away from the story. Example:

This is a kicker up here
Here's the main head

Headline Mechanics

There are a few headline conventions with which all headline writers must be familiar. Here, by category, are a few must-know items about the mechanics of crafting a headline:

Punctuation

- Most editors write **downstyle** headlines and titles in which only the first word of the headline and other proper names are capitalized. **Upstyle** headlines, in which the first letter of most words are capitalized, still prevail at some newspapers, but they are increasingly rare.
- Don't put a period at the end of a headline unless your publication style calls for a period at the end of a **conversational deck** (a deck written in complete sentence form as opposed to the abbreviated sentence form found in most headlines and titles).
- If you have two sentences within one headline, separate them with a semicolon (and do not capitalize the first word of the second sentence unless it is a proper noun). A semicolon should not be used in a headline unless both what precedes and follows are complete sentences (less the articles, adjectives and adverbs) with subjects and predicates.
- Use single rather than double quotation marks in headlines and titles to avoid graphic clutter.
- In headlines and titles, a comma often is used in place of the word *and*.
- Attribution is best shown with the word *says*, but it is sometimes shown with a colon instead. If a colon is used, capitalize the first word that follows if it begins an independent clause. A third way to show attribution, a way that is the least desirable, is with a dash at the end of the thought, followed by the name of the person who said it. But beware of headlines that could be misread like this one:

Cause of virus found—Fauci

Grammar

- Except for hammers, kickers, **catchlines** (one or two words in head-line type accompanying a photograph) and a few magazine-style titles, headlines should be complete sentences but with the articles, adjectives and most adverbs missing. Magazines tend to use more short titles that are labels, and websites tend to use longer headlines that contain words for which readers might search.
- Write in present tense about events that have happened since the last day's newspaper or the last issue of the magazine. Present tense also works well—almost universally—on websites.
- Past tense, usually used for events in a more distant past, is rarely used. Example:

Battle of Hamburger Hill was 'no picnic,' witness recalls

- Future action is shown by changing *will* to *to*. Example:

City Council to discuss sewer bonds

- Write in active voice to avoid the space-wasting passive.
- Eliminate articles (*a, an, the*) and *to be* verbs.

Line Breaks

More and more newspapers are ignoring headline "splits," but it's better to learn to write heads without them in case you end up working for a newspaper that bans them. Split heads are easier to write. So, for our purposes:

- Multiple-line headlines should break at logical places—at pauses between natural breath units.
- If you have a literary background, think of multiple-line headlines as little poems, and put the line breaks only where they would come in a poem.
- Don't split modifiers from the word they modify.
- Don't split a prepositional phrase over two lines.
- Don't split the parts of an infinitive over two lines.
- Some leeway is permitted in one-column heads—but only as a last resort.
- Typically, this involves modifiers (prepositional phrases would still not usually be split).

Abbreviations

- Never abbreviate days of the week.
- Never abbreviate months unless followed by a date.

- In headlines, most newspapers allow abbreviations for states without a city name preceding.
- Never abbreviate months or states that AP does not.
- Typically, it is permissible to abbreviate these cities: Kansas City as K.C. or KC, Los Angeles as L.A. or LA and New York as N.Y. or NY based on the publication's style.
- Never abbreviate a person's name (Wm. Henderson, J. Jones).
- Do not eliminate *the* in front of *Rev.*
- In a headline, most newspapers and magazines will permit use of a numeral for a number less than 10.
- Use a percent sign (%) for the word *percent.*
- As in text, you may abbreviate any headline reference for *U.S., U.N., CIA* or a university commonly known to readers (*M.U., USC*, etc.). But oddly, AP drops the periods in headlines in *US* and *UN.*
- Some, but probably not most, newspapers will let you abbreviate *county* as *Co.* or department as *Dept.* if the rest of the name is present.

How to Write the Headline

The wire services often include a suggested headline at the top of major stories. Some editors use that headline to help them get started. If you do this, don't rely too heavily on it, or your headline will sound too much like those of other papers. But it does make a good starting point, a check that you've understood the story and a fallback if you're stuck.

Start by writing your ideal head for the story—what you'd like to say if space were no object. Then try to fit it into the space you have. Cut the head to its essentials if it's too long. If it's too short, add more information. To improve the fit, you can also simply pick synonyms that say the same thing in a shorter or longer space.

Many editors find it useful to jot down key words from the story that need to be in the headline. Then they build the head around these key words. Others simply ask: If I ran into a friend, what would be the first thing she would ask about this news? That should be the basis of the headline.

Headlines That Tell

Here are some tips on writing informative headlines:

- Remember that the headline and other big type may be all the reader will read, so get in the key words and be as specific as possible in presenting the news.
- After you've written a headline, forget for a moment what you've read in the story. Would you have a clear understanding of the news just

from reading the big type (headlines, titles, blurbs and captions)? If not, rewrite the head. Example:

No: **Jury hears how man was slain**
Yes: **Victim slain with his own gun**

- Make sure the headline is accurate—don't exaggerate or mislead. Reread the story to make sure.
- Try to match the tone of the story in the headline. A light story demands a light head. A tragic story should not have a head that is a pun.
- Don't editorialize. Attribute all controversial statements. Make sure the headline over a news story is neutral and fair.
- Get information from the top, but don't repeat the lead or give away a punch line or ending. If the best headline information is farther down in the story, consider moving that information up. Don't, however destroy a story with a suspenseful ending by moving that up or putting it in the headline.
- Be conversational and clear. Make the language vivid, and appeal to the reader.
- Avoid writing a headline in the negative (using *not*)—it's harder to grasp quickly.
- Don't try to get more than one idea in a deck, or things can get confusing.
- Don't overabbreviate. Use only abbreviations everyone knows: *CIA, FBI, UFO.* Examples of unacceptable abbreviations: *DOS* for Department of State, *FD* for Fire Department.
- Don't use obscure names or terms in the headline.
- Don't use common last names (Jones or Smith) in a headline. Use a name only if the person is well-known and easily identifiable. The exception, of course, is an obituary.
- Pay special attention to verbs. Write in active, not passive, voice. Try to get a verb in the top line, but don't start with a verb, or the headline may sound like a command. Likewise, avoid label heads (those without verbs) except in hammers, kickers and catchlines. If a label head is appropriate, beware of nouns that can also be read as verbs because they can introduce double meanings:

Dead cats protest

- Avoid "headlinese" whenever possible: *blasts, rips* (ridicules); *nixes* (rejects); *solons* (lawmakers, Legislature). Reserve, when possible, the old standby headline terms for deadline.
- Don't just pad a line to make it fit. Use the space to say something.
- Question heads seldom work. Avoid them unless the point of the story is to raise a question to which it doesn't present the answer.
- Don't repeat words in the big type—within a headline, or between heads or captions or blurbs.

- If your paper still uses **upstyle** or **all-cap heads** (few do anymore), be especially aware of how some names may be misread:

Right: **Chargers may lose Butts for rest of year**
Wrong: **CHARGERS MAY LOSE BUTTS FOR REST OF YEAR**

Headlines That Smell

To the advice above, let's add more tips based on examples of actual headline bloopers by professionals. *Columbia Journalism Review* publishes examples like the following at the back of each issue. We've gathered these mainly from *CJR, American Journalism Review* and the *National Lampoon's* True Facts issues.

Beware of Typos

Poll says that 53% believe media offen make mistakes
Defective show officially starts new TV season
Schools to call for pubic input
Nicaragua sets goal to wipe out literacy
13% of U.S. adults unable read or write English
Man booked for wreckless driving
56-year-old man shoots shoots daughter twice
Despite our best efforts, Black employment is still rising

Avoid Vague Headlines That Say Nothing or State the Obvious

City Council to meet
Tribal council to hold meeting in June
School board agrees to discuss education
New bar exam to include test of legal skills
Researchers call murder a threat to public health
Some students walk, others ride to school
Don't leave kids alone with molester
Carcinogens cause cancer, book says

Beware of Double Entendres

Marijuana issue sent to joint committee
City Council takes up masturbation
Breaking wind could cut costs
Textron Inc. makes offer to screw company stockholders
Narcolepsy may be more prevalent in women than thought
Man who moved to Florida leaves after death
High-crime areas said to be safer
Beating witness provides names
Unpaid subway fare led police to murder suspect

Culver police: Shooting victims unhelpful
Police begin campaign to run down jaywalkers
Man executed after long speech
More judicial fertilizer use advised
Condom Week starts with a cautious bang
Jerk injures neck, wins award
Blind workers eye better wages
Woman off to jail for sex with boys
Stiff opposition expected to casketless funeral plan
Dr. Tackett gives talk on moon
Aging expert joins university faculty
No dad's better than abusive one
Prostitutes appeal to pope
Wives kill most spouses in Chicago
Teacher strikes idle kids
USA to seek new location
Woman dies after 81 years of marriage
Clinic gives poor free legal help
Lebanon chief limits access to private parts
Potential witness to murder drunk
ISU revokes doctorate in plagiarism
Jude delays ruling on paddling principal
A record walker admits she skipped 1,000 miles
Jessica Hahn pooped after giving testimony

Beware of Misplaced Modifiers

Scotland Yard arrests three men carrying explosives and seven others
40,000 at Mass for Polish priest reported killed
Threatened by gun, employees testify

Write Accurate Headlines

The key to ensuring accuracy is close and careful reading of the story. Erroneous headlines result when the copy editor doesn't understand the story, infers something that is not in the story, fails to portray the full dimension of the story or fails to shift gears before moving from one story to the next. Some examples:

Minister buried in horse-drawn hearse
   (The hearse and horse participated in the funeral procession, but they were not buried with him.)
Cowboys nip Jayhawks 68–66 on buzzer shot
   (The lead said that Kansas [the Jayhawks] beat Oklahoma State [the Cowboys] by two points in a Big XII conference basketball game.)

Paducah's bonding law said hazy

(The details were hazy; the subject of the story was hazy about the details.)

3 in family face charges of fraud

(They were arrested in a fraud investigation, but the charge was perjury.)

Child's adopted mother fights on

(The child didn't select the mother; it was the other way around. Make it "adoptive.")

Do-nothing Congress irks U.S. energy chief

(The spokesman criticized Democrats, not Congress as a whole, and the "do-nothing" charge was limited to oil imports.)

Don't Rehash Old News

Some stories, like announcements, offer little or no news to invite fresh headlines. Yet, even if the second-day story offers nothing new, the headline cannot be a repetition of the first-day story lead.

Suppose on Monday the story says that Coach Stoops will speak at the high school awards dinner. If Stoops is prominent in your community, his name can be in the head: **Stoops to speak at awards dinner.** On Thursday comes a follow-up story, again saying that Coach Stoops will be the awards dinner speaker. If the headline writer repeats the Monday headline, readers will wonder if they are reading today's paper. The problem is to find a new element, even a minor one, like this: **Tickets available for awards dinner.** So, the dinner comes off on Friday, as scheduled. If the Saturday headline says **Stoops speaks at awards dinner**, readers learn nothing new. The action is what he said: **Stoops denounces 'crybaby' athletes**. Or, if the story lacks newsworthy quotes, another facet of the affair goes into the head: **30 athletes get awards**.

Watch for Libel

Because of the strong impression a headline may make on a reader, courts have ruled that a headline may be actionable even though the story under the head is free of libel. Here are a few examples:

Shuberts gouge $1,000 from Klein brothers
Doctor kills child
A missing hotel maid being pursued by an irate parent
John R. Brinkley—quack

A wrong name in a headline over a crime story is one way to involve the paper in a libel action. The headline writer, no less than the reporter, must understand that under the U.S. justice system a person is presumed innocent of any crime charged until found guilty by a jury. Heads that proclaim

Kidnapper caught, **Blackmailer exposed**, **Robber arrested** or **Spy caught** have the effect of convicting the suspects (even the innocent) before they have been tried.

If unnamed masked gunmen hold up a liquor store owner and escape with $1,000 in cash, the head may refer to them as "robbers" or "gunmen." Later, if two men are arrested in connection with the robbery as suspects or are actually charged with the crime, the head cannot refer to them as "robbers" but must use a qualifier: **Police question robbery suspects.** Even *in* may cause trouble. **Three women arrested in prostitution** should be changed to **Three women charged with prostitution.**

In their worst days, newspapers encouraged headline words that defiled: **Fanged fiend, Sex maniac, Mad-dog killer**. Even today, some newspapers permit both reporter and copy editor to use a label that will forever brand the victim. When a 17-year-old boy was convicted of rape and sentenced to 25 to 40 years in the state penitentiary, one newspaper immediately branded him "Denver's daylight rapist." Another paper glorified him as "The phantom rapist." Suppose an appeal reverses the conviction? What erases the stigma put on the youth by the newspaper?

Don't Overstate

Akin to the inaccurate headline is one that goes beyond the story, fails to give the qualifications contained in the story or confuses facts with speculations. Examples:

> **West Louisville students at UL to get more aid**
> (The lead said they may get it.)
> **Pakistan, U.S. discuss lifting of embargo on lethal weapons**
> (The story said, correctly, that the embargo may be eased. And aren't all weapons lethal?)
> **Arabs vote to support PLO claim to West Bank**
> (The story said that Arab foreign ministers voted to recommend such action to their heads of state. The head implies final action.)
> **Schools get 60% of local property tax**
> (The story said that although the local property tax contributes 60% of schools' funding, the amount is far less than 60% of the total local property tax.)

Don't Command the Reader

Headlines that begin with verbs can be read as commands to the reader and should be avoided. A New York City newspaper splashed a 144-point headline over the story of the shooting of a civil rights advocate. The head: **Slay NAACP leader!** Another head may have given the impression that a murder was being planned: **Slaying of girl in home considered.** In reality, police were trying to determine whether the murder took place in the girl's house or in a nearby field.

Here are some examples of heads that command:

Save eight from fire
Buy another school site
Arrest 50 pickets in rubber strike
Find 2 bodies, nab suspect
Assassinate U.S. envoy

Avoid Editorializing

The reporter has ample space to attribute, qualify and provide full description. The editor, however, has a limited amount of space in the headline to convey the meaning of the story. As a result, there is a tendency to eliminate necessary attribution or qualification and to use loaded terms such as *thugs, cops* and *deadbeats* to describe the participants. The result is an editorialized headline.

It's often difficult to put qualification in headlines because of space limitations. But if the lack of qualification distorts the head, trouble arises. Was the sergeant who led a Marine platoon into a creek, drowning six recruits, drunk? Most headlines said he was, but the story carried the qualification "under the influence of alcohol to an unknown degree."

Even though the headline reports in essence what the story says, one loaded term will distort the story. If Syria, for reasons it can justify, turns down a compromise plan offered by the U.S., the head creates a negative attitude among readers when it proclaims **Syria spurns US compromise.**

Avoid Sensationalizing

Another temptation of the headline writer is to spot a minor, sensational element in the story and use it in the head. A story had to do with the policy of banks in honoring outdated checks. It quoted a bank president as saying, "The bank will take the checks." In intervening paragraphs, several persons were quoted as having had no trouble cashing their checks. Then in the 11th paragraph was the statement: "A Claymont teacher, who refused to give her name, said she had tried to cash her check last night, and it had been refused." She was the only person mentioned in the story as having had any difficulty. Yet the headline writer grabbed this element and produced a head that did not reflect the story:

State paychecks dated 2018
Can't cash it, teacher says

Don't Miss the Point

The process of headline writing begins as soon as an editor starts reading the story. **If the lead can't suggest a headline, chances are the lead is weak. If a stronger element appears later in the story, it should be moved closer to the lead.**

Although the headline ideally emerges from the lead, and generally occupies the top line (with succeeding lines offering qualifications or other dimensions of the story), it often has to go beyond the lead to portray the full dimensions of the story. When that occurs, the qualifying paragraphs should be moved to a higher position in the story. Example: **U.S. company to design spying system for Israel.** The lead was qualified. Not until the 15th paragraph was the truth of the head supported. That paragraph should have been moved far up in the story.

The head usually avoids the exact words of the lead. Once is enough for most readers. Lead: "Despite record prices, Americans today are burning more gasoline than ever before, and that casts some doubt on the administration's policy of using higher prices to deter use." Headline: **Despite record gasoline prices, Americans are burning more fuel**. A paraphrase would avoid the repetition: **Drivers won't let record gas prices stop them from burning up fuel**. Since the story tended to be interpretive, the head could reflect the mood: **Hang the high price of gasoline, just fill 'er up and let 'er roar**. Most editors try to avoid duplicating the lead, but if doing so provides the clearest possible head, it is a mistake to obfuscate.

Don't Give Away the Punch Line

Some stories are constructed so that the punch line comes at the end, rather than at the beginning. Obviously, if the point of the story is revealed in the headline, the story loses its effectiveness. One story, for example, told of a man who went shopping with his little girl and yielded to her pressure to buy a life-sized doll despite the fact that it cost only $1 less than his weekly salary. That led to an argument with his wife about frivolous spending, and the man left home in a huff. The woman put the child to bed with her doll and went in search of her husband. She found him at a nearby bar, but when they returned home they saw firefighters battling a blaze at their apartment. Firefighters had to restrain the father from trying to rescue the girl. "You wouldn't be any use in there," a police officer told him. "Don't worry, they'll get her out."

A firefighter, himself a father, climbed a ladder to the bedroom window, and the crowd hushed as he disappeared into the smoke. A few minutes later, coughing and blinking, he climbed down, a blanket-wrapped bundle in his arms. The local newspaper headlined its story with the punch line that should have been saved for the finish:

Fireman rescues life-size doll as child dies in flames

Headlines That Sell

A good headline tells the story; a great headline tells it and sells it. Remember, though, that headlines that sell must also tell.

Selling is something you do in addition to telling, not in place of it. Here are some techniques to make a headline sell a story by explaining it in a way that is striking:

Alliteration

Alliteration is the repetition of sounds. It's often overused but can still be effective. Alliteration should sound natural or at least make sense.

Crowds cry encore to street-corner Caruso
(about a man who dresses in a tux and sings opera arias on the street for tips)

Rhymes

Rhymes can sometimes work.

Dollars for scholars
(hammer over scholarship story)
The urge to merge
(hammer on a story about business mergers)

Balance and Contrast

Examples of this technique are:

They bring new life to old towns
(about remodelers of historic buildings)
Hot pursuit of the common cold

Graphic Devices

Graphic devices occasionally work but can be cheesy, too.

Photocopying made easy Photocopying made easy
Missing l tt rs in sign puzzl curators at mus um
It's a boy, it's a boy, it's a girl, it's a girl: Quadruplets born to local couple

Puns

This is one of the most-often used headline tricks. In fact, it's used so much, most editors, if not readers, get tired of it. Not only that, but it's also often misused. Don't try to brighten a serious story with an inappropriate one. Still, puns can be effective when they are appropriate to the mood and content of the story.

> *No:* **Mother of all deadbeat dads gets six months in prison**
> *No:* **MacMassacre! 23 killed in Big Mac attack**
> (about a mass murder at a McDonald's)
> *Yes:* **Clockmaker puts heart into tickers**
> *Yes:* **Business picking up for pooper-scooper firm**

Put a Twist on the Familiar

This technique is similar to the pun but specifically involves taking a well-known saying, title or cliché, and playing off it. (We're indebted to journalism professor and magazine expert Don Ranly for many of these examples.)

> **Forgive us our press passes**
> (story about criticism of the press)
> **'Tis a Pity' it's a bore**
> (review of production of play *Tis a Pity She's a Whore*)
> **Where there's smoke, there's ire**
> (about no-smoking controversy)
> **Take this job and love it**
> **There's no business like shoe business**
> (feature about a shoe-repair shop)

Learn From Magazines, Tabloids and *USA Today*

Although these sometimes sensationalize, you can learn from some of them.

- Headlines with personal pronouns such as *you* or *we:*

> **We're eating out more**
> (survey story, *USA Today* style)

- Advice headlines:

> **How to sell your old baseball cards for a fortune**
> **Five ways to flatten your thighs**

- Analysis headlines:

> **Why the US is losing the drug war**

- Striking or superlative statements:

> **The iron woman of softball** (hammer)

Avoid 'Headlinese'

Avoid the words that get overused in headlines and that make them sound alike. Examples of "headlinese" to avoid include: *blasts, cops, eyes, gives nod* (approves), *grill* (question), *hike, OKs, probe, raps, row* (clash), *set, slated*. These are all overused.

Speak the Language of the Story

Think of words associated with the subject of the story, and use them in the headline to bring the reader into the spirit of the topic:

> **What a long, strange trip it's been: Summit marks LSD's anniversary**
> **After the pomp, tough circumstances**
> (about poor job prospects for grads)

Let the Story Speak for Itself

Sometimes you don't want to be cute, and the story is odd or interesting enough by itself. Stories about dinosaurs, space aliens, diets and medical breakthroughs fit this category. You just need to get the keyword in the headline and people will read it.

> **Are 33 orgasms a day normal at age 75?**
> (Sex-advice column)
> **Man acquitted in mayonnaise slaying case**

What to Do if You're Stuck

Every headline writer has a mental block at one time or another. Here are some tips for when that happens:

- If you can't get a line to fit, look for synonyms for each individual word in that line that might be longer or shorter as needed. If that doesn't work, only then should you try rewriting the whole headline with a different approach.
- Look at the suggested head from the wire service, if it's still atop the story. Maybe that will help you come up with a different idea.
- Ask another editor for help. If neither of you can think of something, ask your superior. If none of you can come up with something, ask that the size or number of lines be changed or that a blurb or second deck be added.
- If you're having trouble capturing a feature story's focus, the story itself may need more focus. But if it's too late to send it back, consider turning a quote from the story into the head. This is an especially helpful technique for a personality profile. But don't get in the habit of doing this all the time.

- This last idea is sneaky and should be used only as a last resort: If you're having trouble not repeating a great lead in the headline, consider stealing the great lead for the head, then rewriting the actual lead. But don't even think of doing this with a local story—only a wire one where the reporter won't be around to chew you out.

Title Heads in Magazines

As noted earlier, newspapers have headlines, and magazines have **titles**. Sometimes they are similar, and sometimes they are not.

Typically, a newspaper uses illustrations to focus the reader's attention on a page. It relies on the headline to lure readers into the story. But in a magazine, the whole page—title, pictures, placement—is designed to stop readers in their tracks. They may get part of the story from a big dramatic picture before they ever see the title. This combination of elements must make readers say to themselves, "I wonder what this is all about?"

The magazine editor is not confined to a few standardized typefaces for headings. Instead, the editor may select a face that will help depict the mood of the story. Nor is the editor required to put the heading over the story. It may be placed in the middle, at the bottom or on one side of the page.

The heading may occupy the whole page or only part of a page. It may be accented in a reverse plate or in some other manner. It may be overprinted on the illustration. More often, it will be below the illustration rather than above it. Almost invariably it is short, not more than one line. Often, it is a mere tag or teaser. A **subtitle**, then, gives the details:

Oil from the Heart Tree

An exotic plant from Old China produces a cash crop for the South.

I Can HEAR Again!

This was the moment of joy, the rediscovering of sound: whispers . . . rustle of a sheep . . . ticking of a clock.

The Pleasure of Milking a Cow

Coming to grips with the task at hand can be a rewarding experience, especially on cold mornings.

In magazines, only a few of the rigid rules that apply to newspaper headlines remain in force. Rules of grammar and style are observed, but almost anything else goes. Magazine title writing is freeform in both style and content.

Writing SEO Headlines for the Web

Almost all of the basic conventions of headline and title writing apply equally to the web. Typically, news sites follow the conventions of newspaper headline writing, and other sites employ a mixture of headline and title writing. But editors increasingly realize there are significant differences between writing heads for print and websites.

Primary among those differences is the need to craft a web headline so the story can easily be found by search engines such as Google and Yahoo! Editors call this an SEO (search-engine optimized) headline. Suzanne Levinson, former director of site operations for MiamiHerald.com and ElNuevoHerald.com, argues that **for several reasons SEO headlines must be different from those that appear in the newspaper or magazine:**

- Keywords often are missing in print heads, a fatal flaw in online heads. A print story about a football game, for example, may have a head without *Miami* or *Dolphins,* words that are essential if a search engine is to find it. Even when entire texts are indexed, without the requisite keywords the story will rank lower in the list of search results.
- There often is no context for the head. In other words, on the web there may not be a section label (national, international, sports, etc.) to help the reader figure out what the story is about. And even if some of those exist, search engines allow readers to drill straight to the story, sometimes without the surrounding context.
- Print headlines often are too long or too short for the web. As a result, they don't automatically work on the internet.
- Print headlines often are written awkwardly to fit space available in the print edition, which might not correspond to the space available online.
- Clever heads for which print editors are known often don't work on the web.
- Website scanners want information and don't want to be teased. Levinson argues that readers tend to search for topic and location. Example:

Schools in Miami

If those words aren't in the headline, there's a strong possibility the user will never find it. Why is this important? Websites must attract as many readers as possible to become financially viable. Web editors, then, must write headlines that index the news even better than printed publications. Levinson cites examples of headlines from the *Miami Herald* that were rewritten for the web:

Print: **Ripe for growth**
Online: **Wine superstore sign of industry's growth**
Print: **Divorce was out of the question, husband says**
Online: **Divorce was never an option, Terry Schiavo's husband says in new book**

So, **SEO headlines typically are longer (column restraints are largely nonexistent on the web) and contain more information,**

including key words that search engines will need to help readers find the story.

Levinson suggests that editing text for the web is different, too. As an example, she notes that *here,* when used in the *Miami Herald,* clearly refers to Miami. But with readers coming directly to a story on MiamiHerald.com from a search engine, the reader may not even be aware that he or she is reading an article from Miami. Similarly, *today* may work well in a printed publication for the date of publication; it doesn't work at all on the web, where the day of week or date is essential.

Teresa Schmedding, former news editor of the *Daily Herald* in suburban Chicago, agrees with Levinson that the web demands a different approach. Like Levinson, she warns against cute headlines that tease rather than inform. Says Schmedding, "Studies show that readers do not like headlines that force them to click on something by teasing, but they do like those that help them evaluate whether they want to read."

Like Levinson and Schmedding, executives nationwide are rethinking how they edit their websites. Increasingly, they realize that while the fundamentals of editing and headline writing for print remain, the web is a different medium that requires new approaches.

Blurbs and Captions

Most readers, as we learned earlier, don't completely read many stories they find in publications or on news sites. Instead, they look at the photos, graphics and big type. They use the headlines, captions and blurbs as an index to the news, deciding which stories to read. **It's important, then, that editors try to sneak as much information as possible into the big type. Readers should feel—and be—informed merely by perusing the paper, magazine or website in their normal way.**

So, tell the story as completely as possible in the main head, then use any additional devices available to you—second decks, blurbs or captions—to add as much other important news as possible. Editors should:

- View decks, blurbs and captions as opportunities to get across more information to people who won't be reading the story, as well as hooks to people who might be tempted to read more.
- Put the main idea in the biggest type, the next most important idea in the next biggest type, and so on. Usually, this means the following order: *main head, deck, blurb, caption.*
- Don't repeat information from one graphic element to another. That's just wasting the opportunity to get across more information.
- Make sure none of the information contradicts information in the other elements or in the story. Especially, make sure the spelling of names is consistent.

- Write in full sentences. Don't cut articles or *to be* verbs from blurbs or captions.
- You don't have to worry about where the lines break with blurbs or captions.
- Learn local style on matters like whether your paper uses single or double quote marks in blurbs and captions.

Blurbs

***Blurbs* go by different names at different papers—*pullouts, pull quotes* and so on—but the key thing to remember is that whatever they're called, they are information in big type that either provides a summary or a sample of the story.**

External blurbs are always summary blurbs. They generally come between the headline and the lead of the story, in which case they're sometimes called *read-out blurbs*, although they have many other names, as well. **Read-out blurbs** are similar in function to second decks, but they permit more flexibility and generally greater space to say more.

Sometimes, generally on feature stories, an external blurb may be above the headline, in which case it's called a **read-in blurb** because it reads into the headline.

Internal blurbs are always sample blurbs. They are placed somewhere within the story itself, usually with rules above and below them. Most often, they're used for pull quotes, the most interesting quote or quotes from the story. Sometimes, especially when none of the quotes are that colorful but the page designer has planned for the space, an internal blurb may simply be interesting information from the story rather than a quote.

Captions

Writing photo *captions* is an art. Here are some tips to remember:

- Don't waste the opportunity to get across more information. Fill up the space as much as possible and don't say obvious things like "Janet Hemmings looks on as . . ."
- Feel free to add information from the story to the cutline if you have extra space. It's also fine for the cutlines to have information not in the story.
- If there are multiple captions, put the main cutline information under the dominant photo, the one people will look at first.
- Write in present tense. It's helpful to avoid days or dates in cutlines. This will avoid the awkward mixing of present tense with past days.
- When more than one person is pictured, a caption usually names them *from left.*

There are several kinds of captions:

- **Nameline.** A **nameline** is a one-line caption under a **mugshot** and consists only of the person's name. A nameline under a full-column mugshot will have the person's first and last name. A nameline under a thumbnail (half-column mug) will have only the person's last name.
- **Nameline-Underline.** Some papers will put a one-line description under a nameline. That's called a nameline-underline. Example:

Joseph Biden
Mum on prison uprising

- **Underline.** An *underline* is a one-line caption. Except for when it's part of a nameline-underline, the underline should be a full sentence and have a period or question mark at the end. An underline should never be less than half the space width that was allowed for it, and ideally, it should fill the line.
- **Cutline.** A *cutline* is a multiline caption and is used to provide more information than a mere underline would allow. A cutline in one or two columns may be any number of lines long. In three columns or more, a cutline is usually divided into two or more wraps (such as two wide columns of type under a three-column photo), and each column should have an equal number of lines so the wraps are equally long.
- **Catchline.** A *catchline* is a label head (like a hammer) over the cutline of a **standalone photo** (a photo with no story other than the information in the cutline). It's typically one to three words.

Publications and websites that do a great job of crafting headlines, titles and other display type give their readers a big assist. Those that put little effort into this part of the craft do their readers a big disservice.

Suggested Websites

American Copy Editors Society: www.copydesk.org
Folio (the magazine of the magazine industry): www.foliomag.com

Suggested Readings

Brooks, Brian S., Beverly Horvit and Daryl Moen. *News Reporting and Writing*, 13th edition. New York: Bedford/St. Martin's, 2020.
Dunham, Steve. *The Editor's Companion: An Indispensable Guide to Editing Books, Magazines, Online Publications and More.* Blue Ash, Ohio: Writer's Digest Books, 2015.

11   USING PHOTOS, GRAPHICS AND TYPE

Only one news medium—radio—attempts to reach large audiences without strong graphic appeal. We live in a world in which visual stimulation is important in attracting and holding the attention of television viewers, newspaper and magazine readers, and web surfers. Indeed, in today's world it's almost unthinkable to ignore the power of design and the impact of video, photos and graphics.

Unfortunately, so many journalists are focused on written or spoken content that they fail to appreciate the power of visuals. Too often, older, word-oriented journalists view visual journalists as those who merely add ornamentation to the news rather than as content providers. But visuals are content, too, and an important part of content at that. Research from the Poynter Institute tells us:

- About 90% of readers enter pages through large photos, artwork or display type (such as headlines and promos).

DOI: 10.4324/9781003011422-11

- Running a visual element with text makes it three times more likely that at least some of the text will be read.
- Headlines are more likely to be read when a photo is nearby.
- The bigger the photo, the more likely readers are to read the caption.

While these findings relate most directly to newspapers and magazines, it's equally undeniable that visuals make television what it is and that visuals are extremely important in driving traffic through websites. ESPN's website (www.espn.com) has become one of the most popular in the country, thanks to strong content, good design and ample use of digital video and graphics.

Today, print, television and web journalists need to be aware of the power of visuals. The wordsmith on the magazine editing staff and the newspaper city hall reporter need to be just as attuned to visuals as the television **videographer** and the magazine designer. Although one journalist may spend all or part of her day working entirely with visuals, and another may spend all of his day working with words, both must recognize and respect the power of visual communication. Consider that:

- **Photographs and information graphics markedly increase both comprehension of text and interest in stories.**
- **Graphics, photographs and headlines get far more attention from readers than text does.**

The same is true in television and on the web. When television stories are merely read by anchors, and web stories are told only with text, news consumers show little interest. Add video, photos, graphics and display type, and the equation changes for the better.

Television, of course, lives and dies with video and graphics. The television videographer oversees all aspects of the video image, including lighting and the operation of the camera. The videographer in many ways is TV's ultimate editor because of the incredible power of sound and video in that medium. And in today's world, television reporters often shoot their own video as two-person television teams become increasingly rare. That effectively makes them not only reporters but also videographers.

Whatever the medium—except, of course, radio—the power of visuals is strong and undeniable. And even radio has websites, where the power of visuals is real. In this chapter, we address the fundamentals of using photos, graphics and type, devices available in all of the media capable of visual communication.

Editing for Graphic Appeal

Editors can do much to help increase graphic appeal. Here are some tips that apply equally well to newspapers, magazines and websites:

Be on the lookout for sidebars. If a story seems too long and moves in several directions, consider breaking it into a main story and separate

sidebars. Remember, the average newspaper reader reads only about 20 minutes a day—perusing the photos and reading mainly the headlines and other big type except on a few stories of interest. Breaking sidebars out of longer stories means the material looks shorter and more inviting. In addition, you spoon-feed the readers some extra information in the sidebar's headline.

Boring: A 30-inch story describes the events of an upcoming town-history festival, relates some of the history to be commemorated and profiles the organizer of the event.

Better: The three parts of the story should be made separate stories, packaged with appealing photos or artwork. The events should probably be listed in an accompanying box. Don't automatically make the history the centerpiece; the profile may be the better choice. People usually prefer to read about people rather than things or events.

Boring: A 75-inch investigative piece examines who lives in public housing, the history of public housing in the area, the complaints people in public housing have about life in the projects, the complaints neighbors have about having public housing nearby and responses from officials in charge.

Better: Organize this into separate stories that can run over several days as a series. Or run the stories as a package, probably on a Sunday, on a special page devoted to the issue. Promo it on the front page, or even consider starting the main story, probably a summary, on the front page and then jumping it to the special page. Another alternative: It could run in the Sunday magazine if you have a locally produced one. The less earth-shattering the revelations, the more likely this alternative would be considered.

People will be more attracted to stories with photos or graphics, so keep the visual possibilities of each story in mind when designing a page. If you're a copy editor, it may be helpful to your designer if you mention that a particular story has great quotes that could be used for blurbs or a list that could make a good chart. Is the story so complicated that the headline or title could use an extra deck? Adding that may result in better communication. Encourage reporters to think about visual possibilities for their stories. Remind them that stories almost always receive better play if accompanied by photos or graphics. Visual possibilities should be considered early in the writing and editing process, not as an afterthought.

Bullets permit you to list a lot of items in a minimum amount of space and with added contrast. Bullets are solid circles, dashes, check marks or black boxes used to set off items in a list. *USA Today* makes extensive use of bullets to keep its stories short.

If a story is long, subheads could help break it into shorter, logical parts. Use subheadings instead of transitional paragraphs between the parts. Magazines and websites use them often, but newspapers use them less often, except in the longest of stories.

Make sure the photographer knows the mood and theme of the story and takes pictures of the main people being

interviewed. Too often, newspapers will have a sad piece with a smiling photograph or a feature with a photograph of one person and a story about someone else. When you see that, you know the illustration was an after-thought, not part of a carefully crafted package.

Drawings, often called *line art*, are sometimes preferable to photos for series logos and for times when a camera may be intrusive. They also can explain complicated processes or things by strip-ping away the exterior and showing the inner workings of the object.

Double-check charts for accuracy of figures.

Using Photos

Good newspapers, magazines and websites treat graphical elements—photos, charts and illustrations—as the editorial equivalent of stories. The days are gone when an editor would say to a reporter, "That's a good story; now get me a photo to go with it." Today, photos are assigned with the same care, and preferably at the same time, as news and feature articles.

That development came about late in the last century as newspapers and magazines faced increasing competition for readers' attention. Editors found that their publications needed to be more attractive if they were to hold read-ership. The result was an era in which newspaper design became almost as important to many editors as content. In general, the size and quality of news-paper photographs increased, and charts, graphs and maps proliferated. All of these elements were increasingly likely to be printed in color.

None of that should be surprising. We live in a visual society in which color and design play important roles. Visual appeal is used to market everything from television to mobile phones, and printed publications are not exempt. This has necessitated a change in the way almost all of them look. The gray, vertical columns of the past have given way to modular design, color, more and larger pictures, and charts, graphs and maps, which editors call *infor-mation graphics*. To make these changes, newsrooms have been forced to change their internal structures, too.

Photo editors today are key members of the newsroom man-agement team, usually equal in rank to news, city or metropol-itan editors. Design desks have been added in many newsrooms to relieve the copy desk of the chore of designing as well as editing. Many metros have gone so far as to appoint assistant managing editors for graphics. And graphics departments, which produce charts, graphs and maps, have sprung from nowhere, even at relatively small dailies.

Not surprisingly, technological advances have helped. Computers with design and charting software allow editors and artists to create graphics that would have taken days to execute through traditional methods.

Now, the art of photography itself has changed as digital cameras have made silver-based photography and darkrooms obsolete. Both local and wire-service photos are processed with computers and digital-imaging software. No fancy technology, however, can make a bad picture good or help an editor determine whether a graphic accomplishes what it purports to do.

This chapter is designed not to make photographers or graphic artists of editors but to give editors an appreciation of the role of photos and graphics in the appeal of newspapers, magazines and websites. **Visual literacy** is critical for all editors. That's true even for those in radio if they also edit the station's online and mobile sites.

Rewriting can turn a poorly written news story into an acceptable one. Little can be done to change the subject matter of clichéd photos—tree plantings, ribbon cuttings, proclamation signings and the passing of checks, certificates or awards from one person to another, and "firing-squad photos" where people are "lined up and shot." Some newspapers, magazines and websites use photographs of these situations simply because of the tradition that "chicken-dinner" stuff must be photographed. It is a tradition that should be scrapped, and most good publications have already done so.

A photo editor (Figure 11.1) is almost as essential to today's newspaper as a city editor. Some executive—preferably one with a background in photography—should be responsible for assigning photographers to news and feature events. Someone in authority should insist that all photos, including those from news agencies, be edited and that captions be intelligently written.

Figure 11.1 Photos are now edited on computer workstations at most newspapers and magazines.

Photo by Philip Holman.

If it is a good picture, it should get a good play, just as a top story gets a big headline. If pictures are a vital part of the story, editors should be willing to cut back on words, if necessary, to provide space for photographs. Some events can be told better in words than in pictures. Conversely, other events are essentially graphic, and editors need little or no text to get the message across.

Photographer–Editor Relationships

An encouraging development in recent years has been the trend toward making photographers full partners in the editorial process. Historically, photographers were second-class citizens in the newspaper and magazine hierarchy. They did not enjoy the prestige of the reporter or the copy editor, and with rare exception their opinions were not solicited or were ignored.

Many editors now have reached what should have been an obvious conclusion—that photographers may have higher degrees of visual literacy than even the best wordsmiths. After all, that's a photographer's job. So, photographers should have a voice in how their pictures are displayed, and editors who have given them that voice invariably have been pleased with the results. The number of publications using pictures well is increasing each year, although leading photo editors agree that there is still room for improvement.

A key to improvement in the quality of pictures is allowing the photographer to become involved in the story from the outset. If possible, the photographer should accompany the reporter as information for the story is gathered. If that is impossible, allowing the photographer to read the story—or to take time to talk with the reporter about the thrust of it—will help ensure that a photograph complements the story. Publications throughout the country each day are filled with pictures that fail to convey a message because the reporter, photographer and editor failed to communicate with each other.

An important part of this communications process involves writing the photo order, the document given to the photographer when an assignment is made. A photographer for the *Columbia Missourian* once received an order for a picture of an elementary school principal. The order instructed the photographer to meet the principal in his office at 3:15 p.m. and to take a picture of him at his desk. It mentioned that the principal would be unavailable until that time. The story focused on how the principal went out of his way to help frightened first-graders find the right bus during the first few weeks of school. Because the reporter failed to mention that when he wrote the photo order, the photographer followed his instructions exactly. He arrived at 3:15 and took the picture. Only after returning to the office did he learn the thrust of the story and discover that the principal was unavailable 15 minutes earlier because he had been helping students find their buses. The best photo opportunity had been missed.

Photographers should also be told in advance, if necessary and when possible, whether particular shots need to be vertical or horizontal and the various sizes in which the photos might need to work. That's because photos are often used these days in different ways in different media by the same news outlet—in a print publication, online and for a mobile device app, for example.

Photo Editing Decisions

Most photographs, like most news stories, can be improved with editing. The photo editor, like the copy editor, must make decisions that affect the quality of the finished product. The photo editor must determine:

- Which photo or photos complement the written story or tell a story of their own.
- Whether cropping enhances the image.
- What size a photo must be to communicate effectively.
- Whether retouching is necessary.

Selection

Photo selection is critical because valuable space is wasted if the picture does nothing more than depict a scene that could be described more efficiently with words. The old adage that a picture is worth a thousand words is not necessarily true. If the picture adds nothing to the reader's understanding of a story, it should be rejected. Conversely, some pictures capture the emotion or flavor of a situation more vividly than words. In other situations, words and photographs provide perfect complements.

A talented photo editor, experienced in visual communication, can provide the guidance necessary for successful use of pictures. Smaller newspapers, magazines or websites without the luxury of full-time photo editors can turn to their photographers for advice, but often the news editor or copy editor must make such decisions. When that is necessary, an appreciation for the importance of visual communication is essential for good results. At websites, there are sometimes no photographers or photo editors, which means those who produce the site must possess visual literacy.

The best picture may not always be the best choice to run if it doesn't match the story. Some media outlets allow the photographer to make the decision as to the photos to run, and the pictures he or she submits to the desk are the only ones considered for publication. This procedure may ensure selection of the picture with the best technical quality, but that picture may not best complement the story. A better idea is to have a photo editor, working closely with the photographer, the reporter, the assigning editor and the page designer or copy editor make the selection.

Printouts or a computer review of the photographer's usable shots allow the photographer, reporter and editors to review all frames available so the best selection can be made.

Cropping

Certain elements within the picture could be stronger than the full picture. A prime job of a photo editor is to help the photographer take out some unnecessary details to strengthen the overall view. A photograph is a composition. The composition should help the reader immediately grasp the picture's message. If the picture is too cluttered, the viewer's eyes scan the picture looking for a place to rest. But if the picture contains a strong focal point, the viewer has at least a place to start.

The editor also searches for compositional patterns that could be strengthened by cropping. These are the same patterns used by artists and graphic designers in various media. Common patterns help give the picture harmonious and balanced composition: letter shapes—L, U, S, Z, T, O—and geometric patterns such as a star, a circle, a cross or a combination of these.

Another important overall compositional device is the **rule of thirds**. Imagine a photo divided into thirds both horizontally and vertically. The four points where these lines intersect are considered the best focal points, or centers of interest, for the photo.

Some photo editors try to find these interest points and patterns by moving the digital photo around in an art box with a mouse or by moving two L-shaped pieces of cardboard over the picture. This helps to guide in cropping. The editor looks for a focal point, or chief spot of interest. If other points of interest are present, the photo editor tries to retain them.

Because most news and feature photos contain people, the editor strives to help the photographer depict them as dramatically as possible. The editor must decide how many people to include in the picture, how much of each person to include and what background is essential.

Historically, publications opted for the tightest possible cropping to conserve valuable space. Severe cropping, however, may damage a photo to the point that not printing it would have been preferable. Those who win awards for photo editing appreciate the fact that background is essential to some photographs. As a result, they tend to crop tightly less often than editors with more traditional approaches to picture editing. In Figure 11.2, tight cropping allows the reader to see interesting detail. But in Figure 11.3, tight cropping eliminates the environment and damages the picture. Those who can distinguish between these approaches are valuable members of newspaper and magazine staffs. They possess visual literacy.

Figure 11.2 Footprint on the lunar soil. This is an example of how cropping (B) can bring out an interesting detail in a photograph (A). The close-up view was photographed with a lunar surface camera during the Apollo 11 lunar surface extravehicular activity.

Photos courtesy of National Aeronautics and Space Administration.

Sizing

The value of the picture, not the amount of space available, should determine the reproduction size of a photograph. Too often, editors try to reduce a photograph to fit a space and destroy the impact of the photo in the process. Common sense should dictate that a picture of 15 individuals will be ineffective if it appears as a two-column photo. More likely, such a photo will require three or even four columns of space.

Talented photo editors know that the greatest danger is making pictures too small. If the choice is between a two-column picture and a three-column picture, the wise photo editor opts for the larger size. Photos can be too large, but more often they are damaged by making them too small. Another alternative may be available. Modern production techniques make it easy for the editor to publish a half-column photo with text wrapping around it to fill the space.

Sizing of any photograph is an important decision, but sizing of pictures in multiphotograph packages is particularly important. In such packages, one photograph should be dominant. The use of multiple pictures allows the editor flexibility that may not exist in single-picture situations. If a picture editor selects a photo of a harried liquor store clerk who has just been robbed and a photo of the outside of the store where the robbery occurred, the editor has three choices:

- Devote equal space to the two pictures. This is the least desirable choice because neither picture would be dominant and, consequently, neither would have eye-catching impact.
- Make the outside shot dominant and the close-up of the clerk secondary. This would work, but the dominant photo, which serves merely as a locater, would have little impact. The impact of human emotion, evident in the clerk's face, would be diminished.
- Make the facial expression dominant with good sizing and make the outside shot as small as 1½ columns. The outside shot, standing alone, would look ridiculous if used in that size, but used in conjunction with another, larger photo, it would work well.

Dramatic size contrast is an effective device in multipicture packages (Figure 11.4). An editor trained in visual communication understands the usefulness of reversing normal sizing patterns for added impact.

Electronic Enhancement

Some photographs can be improved by electronic enhancement, once called retouching, the process of toning down or eliminating distractions within the frame. Minor imperfections in photos can be repaired with computer programs such as Adobe Photoshop. Care must be exercised, however, to ensure that electronic enhancement does not change the meaning and content of the photo. Changing a photo to alter its meaning is as unethical as changing a direct quotation to alter a speaker's meaning.

Figure 11.3 Tight cropping can occasionally destroy the impact of a photo (A). Tight cropping takes the farmer out of his environment by making it difficult to determine that a setting is a barn (B).

Columbia Missourian photos by Manny Crisostomo.

Pictures as Copy

When the picture has been processed, someone—reporter or photographer—supplies the information for the **caption**, the most common type of which is the **cutline**. The picture (Figure 11.4) and caption information then go to the appropriate department, where the editor decides whether to use the photo and, if so, how to display it.

Before submitting a picture to the production department, the editor supplies information to get the correct picture in the correct place with the correct caption. Today, most photos are sent from desk to desk within a newsroom electronically, although at some magazines actual photographic printouts are still used. A picture, like a story, generally carries an identifying word or words. If photos are handled as prints, a slip of paper clipped on the picture or taped to the back normally contains information such as:

- The identifying word or name of the picture.
- The size.

- Special handling instructions.
- The department, edition and page.
- The date the photo is to appear.
- The date and time the picture was sent to the production department.
- A notation of whether the photo stands alone or accompanies a story.

In computerized photo editing, this information is contained in metadata that accompany the file.

Sometimes the photo may be deliberately separated from the story. A teaser picture may be used on page 1 to entice readers to read the story

Figure 11.4 Many editors would run the overall flooding shot larger than the picture of the farmer laying sandbags in place (A). The pairing, however, has more impact if the close shot of the farmer is run larger than the scene-setting overall photo. By itself, the wider shot would have to run much larger.

Columbia Missourian photos by Lee Meyer and Mike Asher.

on another page. If a long story has two illustrations, one illustration often is used on the page where the story begins and the other on the jump page. For major events, such as the death of a president, pictures may be scattered on several pages. In this case, readers are directed to these pages with a guideline such as "More pictures on pages 5, 7 and 16," or "More pictures on website."

Changing Photo Technology

Most photographs today are taken digitally and electronically processed—lightened or darkened, sharpened, cropped and sized—using programs such as Adobe Photoshop. Then, newspapers and magazines flow photographs directly onto the page using computer programs such as Adobe InDesign. From there, entire pages, with all photos and graphics in place, are output to paper proofs, to film or even directly to the printing plate.

Scanning of photos is sometimes necessary because a few publications still prefer to use conventional photography to take pictures and because some are submitted in photographic print form by readers. Now that digital photography is widely accepted, darkrooms and chemical processing are, for the most part, a thing of the past. Digital processing saves time, which is of paramount importance for publications, particularly newspapers and websites.

Taste in Picture Editing

Picture selection can sometimes pose hard choices between news value and sensitivity. It was a tragic fire in the Boston metropolitan area. A woman and a child took refuge on an ironwork balcony. As firefighters tried to rescue them, the balcony collapsed, sending the woman to her death and the child to a miraculous survival. Photographers took sequence shots of the action (see Figures 11.5 and 11.6). Should a photo editor use the pictures?

Some readers would be incensed, accusing the papers of sensationalism, poor taste, invasion of privacy, insensitivity and a tasteless display of human tragedy to sell newspapers. Picture editors could reply that their duty is to present the news, whether of good things or bad, of the pleasant or the unpleasant. Defending the judgment to use the pictures on page 1, the editor of a Michigan newspaper said,

> The essential purpose of journalism is to help the reader understand what is happening in this world and thereby help him [or her] to appreciate those things he [or she] finds good and to try to correct those things he [or she] finds bad.

Figure 11.5 One of the controversial sequence shots of a fire tragedy at a Boston apartment. Scores of readers protested use of these widely distributed photos.

StanleyFormanPhotos.com; Pulitzer Prize 1976.

Figure 11.6 The second shot of the balcony collapsing in Boston. Most editors defended use of the tragic photos.

StanleyFormanPhotos.com; Pulitzer Prize 1976.

Of the flood of pictures depicting the war in Vietnam, surely among the most memorable were the Saigon chief of police executing a prisoner on the street, terrified children fleeing a napalm attack and the flaming suicide of a Buddhist monk. Such scenes were part of the war record and deserved to be shown. A photograph of an airplane striking one of the towers of the World Trade Center in 2001 in New York is similarly memorable.

Photos of fire deaths may tell more than the tragedy depicted in the burned and mangled bodies. Implicit could be the lessons of inadequate inspection, faulty construction, carelessness with matches, arson or antiquated firefighting equipment.

Picture editors have few criteria to guide them. Their news judgment and their own conscience tell them whether to order a picture for page 1 showing a man in Australia mauled to death by polar bears after he fell into a pool in the bears' enclosure at a zoo. Of the hundreds of pictures available that day, surely a better one could have been found for page 1.

Caption Guidelines

Picture texts are known by many names—**captions**, **cutlines**, **underlines** (or **overlines**), **namelines**, **nameline-underlines**, **ellipse lines** and **legends** are some. **Caption** originally suggested a heading over a picture, but most editors now use the term to refer to the lines under the picture. In that sense, the term is often used only in a generic sense, with the more specific type of caption specified by the designer for the editor to write. **Legend** may refer either to the text or to the heading. If **catchline**, or heading, is used, it usually is placed under, not over, the picture, but placement often depends on the publication's style.

The editor sells the reporter's story by means of a compelling headline. By the same token, the picture editor can help control the photographic image with a caption. The primary purpose of the caption is to get the reader to respond to the photo in the manner intended by the photographer and the picture editor.

Readers first concentrate on the focal point of the picture, then glance at the other parts. Then, presumably, most turn to the caption to confirm what they have seen in the picture. The caption provides the answers to questions of who, what, where, when, why and how, unless some of these are apparent in the picture.

The caption interprets and expands on what the picture says to the reader. It may point out the inconspicuous but significant. It may comment on the revealing or amusing parts of the picture if these are not self-evident. The caption helps explain ambiguities, comments on what is not made clear in the picture and mentions what the picture fails to show if that is necessary.

The ideal caption is direct, brief and sometimes bright. It is a concise statement, not a news story. It immediately gets to the point and avoids the "go back to the beginning" of the background situation.

If the photo accompanies a story, the caption shouldn't duplicate the details readers can find in the story, but it should contain enough information to satisfy those who will not read the story. Ideally, the picture and the caption will induce readers to read the story. Normally, the caption of a picture with a story is limited to two or three lines. Even when the picture relates to the story, the caption should not go beyond what the picture reveals. Nor should the facts in the caption differ from those in the story.

Captions stand out in the sea of words and strike the reader with peculiar force. Every word should be weighed, especially for impact, emotional tone, impartiality and adherence to rules of grammar.

No one should write or rewrite a caption without seeing the picture, and the page design, too, if it's part of a multipicture package. The cropped photo should be examined, not the original. The caption has to confine itself to the portion of the picture the reader will see. If the caption says a woman is waving a handkerchief, the handkerchief must be in the picture. In a design containing two or more photographs with a single caption, the editor should study the design to make sure that left or right or top or bottom directions are correct.

When dealing with the photo on a computer, as most publications and websites now do, simply copy the caption to a text field and edit as necessary. Time permitting, a proof sheet showing pictures and their captions should be given to the photo editor to make certain all the pieces have been put together properly and that the caption matches the content of the photo.

When Photos Lie

"Photos never lie" is one of the oldest media industry axioms. It's doubtful whether this was ever true, and it certainly isn't today. Computerized processing of photos makes it easier than ever to manipulate pictures in ways that are totally unethical.

National Geographic magazine moved a pyramid closer to the Sphinx to improve the composition of a photo, then listened to cries of outrage from photographers and others who objected to the practice. *TV Guide* put Oprah Winfrey's head on another person's body and suffered a similar fate.

One can't help but wonder, though, how many similar things have occurred without someone noticing. The fact is that tampering with the content of a photo is just as wrong as printing a manufactured quotation and attributing it to a senator, the mayor or a police officer at the scene of a crime. It is unethical, and at many publications it's now grounds for dismissal.

Quality publications limit computerized alteration of photographs to the equivalent of minor electronic enhancement. Editors and photographers are allowed to make a photo lighter or darker. They also are allowed to do electronic edge sharpening, the equivalent of improving the focus.

Most other forms of alteration are prohibited, although some publications allow the removal of distracting background elements. This might include removal of an electric wire dangling behind a subject in such a way as to appear the wire is emerging from the person's head. The best photographers eliminate such distractions the right way by making sure they aren't there in the original photo.

Writing the Caption

Here are some tips on caption writing:

- **Don't state the obvious.** The picture will tell whether a person is smiling. It may be necessary, however, to tell why he or she is smiling. An explanation need not go as far as the following: "Two women and a man stroll down the newly completed section of Rehoboth's boardwalk. They are, from left, Nancy Jackson, Dianne Johnson and Richard Bramble, all of West Chester." An editor remarked, "Even if some of the slower readers couldn't have figured out the sexes from the picture, the names are a dead giveaway."
- **Don't editorialize.** A writer doesn't know whether someone is happy, glum or troubled. The cutline that described a judge as "weary but ready" when he arrived at court must have made readers wonder how the writer knew the judge was weary.
- **Use specifics rather than generalities.** "A 10-pound book" is better than "a huge book."
- **Omit references to the photo.** Because the readers know you are referring to the photograph, omit phrases such as "is pictured," "is shown" and "the picture above shows."
- **Use "from left" rather than "from left to right."** The first means as much as the second and is shorter. Neither *left* nor *right* should be overworked. If one of two boys in a picture is wearing a white jersey, use that fact to identify him.
- **Avoid "looking on."** One of the worst things you can say about a person in a photo is that he or she is "looking on." If that is all the person is doing, the photo is superfluous.
- **Don't kid the readers.** They will know whether this is a "recent photo." Give the date the photo was taken if it's an old photo. Also, let readers know where the picture was taken—but not how. Most readers don't care about all the sleet and snow the photographer had to go through to get the picture.

- **Write captions in the present tense.** This enhances the immediacy of the pictures they accompany. The past tense is used if the sentence contains the date or if it gives additional facts not described in the action in the picture. The caption may use both present and past tenses, but the past time element should not be used in the same sentence with a present-tense verb describing the action.

- **Make sure the caption is accurate.** Double-check the spelling of names. The paper, not the photographer, gets the blame for inaccuracies. Caption errors often occur because someone, the photographer or the reporter accompanying the photographer, failed to give the photo desk enough, or accurate, information from which to construct a caption.

- **Double-check the photo with the caption identification.** The wrong person pictured as "the most-wanted fugitive" is a sure way to invite libel.

- **Be careful.** Writing a caption requires as much care and skill as writing a story or a headline. The reader should not have to puzzle out the meaning of the description. Notice these jarring examples:

  Fearing new outbreaks of violence, the results of Sunday's election have been withheld.
  Also killed in the accident was the father of five children driving the other vehicle.

- **Don't hit the reader over the head with the obvious.** If the photo shows a firefighter dousing hot timbers after a warehouse fire, it is ridiculous to add in the caption that "firefighters were called."

- **Avoid last-line widows or hangers.** The last line of the caption should be a full line, or nearly so. When the lines are doubled (two two-columns for a four-column picture), write an even number of lines. Short last lines are known as **widows** or **hangers**.

- **Captions should be humorous if warranted by the picture.** But biting humor and sarcasm have no place in captions.

- **The caption should describe the event as shown in the picture, not the event itself.** Viewers will be puzzled if the caption describes action they do not see. Sometimes, however, an explanation of what is not shown is justified. If the photo shows a football player leaping high to catch a pass for a touchdown, viewers might like to know who threw the pass.

- **Update the information.** Because there is a lapse between the time a picture of an event is taken and the time a viewer sees the picture published, care should be taken to update the information in the caption. If the first report was that three bodies were found in the wreckage, but subsequently two more bodies were found, the caption should contain the latest figure.

- **Be exact.** In local pictures, the addresses of the persons shown may be helpful. If youngsters appear in the photo, they should be identified by names, ages, names of parents and other relevant information.
- **Credit the photographer.** If the picture is exceptional, credit may be given to the photographer in the caption, perhaps with a brief description of how he or she achieved the creation. On picture pages containing text matter, the photographer's credit should be displayed as prominently as the writer's. Most newspapers and magazines now credit every photograph to the photographer who took it.
- **Pictures without captions.** Although photographs normally carry captions, mood or special-occasion pictures sometimes appear without them if the message is obvious from the picture itself. Not all who look at pictures will also read the captions. In fact, the decline is severe enough to suggest that many readers satisfy their curiosity merely by looking at the photo.
- **Know your style.** Some papers use one style for captions with a story and another style for captions without a story (called **standalone** or **no-story picture**). A picture with a story might call for one, two or three words in boldface caps to start the caption. In standalones, a small head or catchline might be placed over the caption.
- **Give the location.** If the dateline is cut from a caption, make sure that the location is mentioned later. Example:

GUARDING GOATS—Joe Fair, a 70-year-old pensioner, looks over his goats Rosebud and Tagalong, the subject of much furor in this northeastern Missouri community, boyhood home of Mark Twain.

The "northeastern Missouri community" was Hannibal, Missouri, but the caption did not say so.

- **Rewrite wire-service cutlines.** The same photos from news agencies and syndicates appear in smaller dailies as well as in metropolitan dailies. Some papers merely use the caption supplied with the pictures. Most, if not all, such captions should be rewritten to add to the story told in the picture and to indicate some originality on the paper's part.
- **Watch the mood.** The mood of the caption should match the mood of the picture. The caption for a feature photo may stress light writing. Restraint is observed for photographs showing tragedy or dealing with a serious subject.
- **After the caption has been set in type or readied for the web, the editor should compare the message with the picture.** The number of people in the picture should be checked against the number of names in the caption. Everyone appearing prominently in the photo should be identified. If a person is obscured in the crowd, that person need not be brought to the reader's attention.

Using Information Graphics

Photographs help the reader gain a visual appreciation of reality, while information graphics help the reader understand the intangible or the hidden. A map of part of the city is usually a better locater than an aerial photo of the same area. A chart often helps the reader track trends over time. An artist's cutaway can show the undersea levels of a sinking ship.

In recent years, **information graphics**, as these illustrations are known, have appeared with increasing regularity in newspapers and magazines, large and small, and on websites. Personal computers are ideal for creating such graphics quickly and inexpensively, and newspapers and magazines rushed to embrace them in the 1980s. Suddenly, publications that once had only photographers and artists added graphic designers to create charts, graphs and maps. Contests added categories for graphic design, and the Society of Newspaper Design was formed.

Many believe this transformation was sparked by the arrival of *USA Today* in 1982, and there is no doubt that it set new standards for the use of color and graphics. Colorful charts, graphs and maps play a key role in *USA Today*, which was designed for the busy reader. Charts, graphs and maps are a good way of communicating lots of information in a hurry, and *USA Today*'s editors were quick to embrace them.

USA Today is far from alone in adopting information graphics. *The New York Times* and other prestigious newspapers now publish full-page graphics on section fronts, *Time* magazine produces startling graphics, and syndicated services of graphics material proliferates. The Associated Press greatly increased the quality and quantity of the graphics it provides.

Like photographs, however, information graphics can be good or bad. Confusing charts, graphs and maps hinder readers rather than help them. Graphics that are too busy may confuse rather than enlighten.

Types of Information Graphics

Some information is conveyed best in words, some in pictures and some in information graphics. The editor who knows when to choose each of these devices helps to create an easy-to-read publication.

Illustrations help the reader understand complex things or concepts, including information that may be extremely difficult or impossible to describe in words. They take many forms, from the simple illustration to the complex diagram.

Maps, of course, help the reader locate things. Local maps help the reader locate places within the city. Maps of counties, states, regions or nations help readers locate sites with which they may not be familiar (see Figure 11.7). Good graphics departments maintain computerized base maps of various locales. When an event occurs, it is a simple matter to add specific locater information to the base map to create a helpful aid for the reader. Secondary windows within maps sometimes are used to pin down specific areas within geographic regions or to show the location of the specific region within a larger area.

Tables are used to display numerical information graphically (see Figure 11.8). They are useful when lots of numbers are involved, as in precinct-by-precinct election results.

Bar charts help the reader visualize quantities (see Figure 11.9), and **fever charts** show quantities over time (see Figure 11.10). **Pie charts** are used to show the division of the whole into components (see Figure 11.11). **Process drawings** help readers visualize detailed plans (see Figure 11.12).

Photos and graphics have strong eye appeal and therefore rank as important elements in creating visually attractive newspaper, magazine and web pages. Even television uses a fair amount of graphics, and wise selection of typefaces is important in all the media.

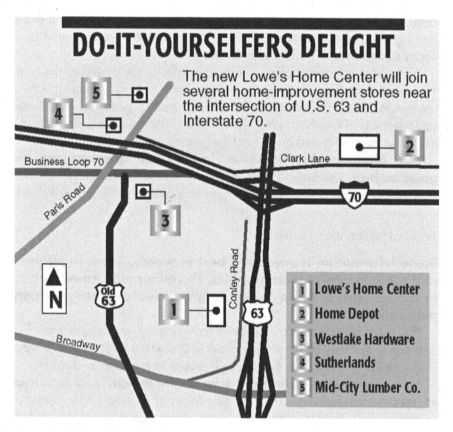

Figure 11.7 Maps help readers locate news events.

Courtesy of the *Columbia Missourian*.

TOP 10 U.S. OIL FIELDS

Texas dominates the list of top U.S. oil fields with four sites in the top 10, according to the U.S. Energy Information Administration. Texas has 27 fields in the top 100, more than any other state.

Rank	Field Name	Location	Production* (2013)	Year discovered
1	Eagleville	TX	238,050	2009
2	Spraberry Trend Area	TX	99,787	1949
3	Prudhoe Bay	AK	79,080	1967
4	Wattenberg	CO	47,259	1970
5	Briscoe Ranch	TX	62,046	1962
6	Kuparuk River	AK	29,487	1969
7	Mississippi Cnyn	Gulf of Mexico	15,833	1969
8	Wasson	TX	19,996	1937
9	Belridge South	CA	23,703	1911
10	Green Canyon	Gulf of Mexico	27,346	1998

*thousands of barrels of 42 U.S. gallons

Source(s): U.S. Energy Information Administration   Columbia Missourian

Figure 11.8 Tables are a form of information graphics used to make numerical information easier to understand.

Courtesy of the *Columbia Missourian*.

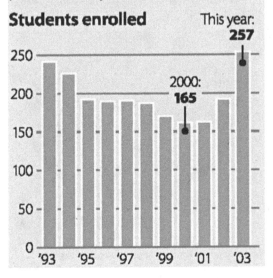

RECENT INCREASE

Enrollment in the Hotel and Restaurant Management program at MU increased 31 percent this year.

Students enrolled   This year: **257**

2000: **165**

Figure 11.9 Bar chart.

Courtesy of the *Columbia Missourian*.

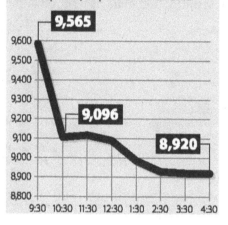

Figure 11.10 Fever chart. ·

Courtesy of the *Columbia Missourian*.

Figure 11.11 Pie chart.

Courtesy of the *Columbia Missourian*.

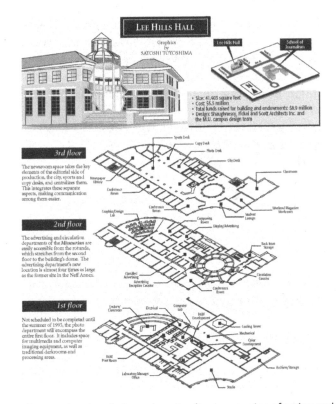

Figure 11.12 Process drawings help readers visualize progression of action or detailed plans.

Courtesy of the *Columbia Missourian*.

Using Type

Type is used in the print media as both body type and display type. **Body type** is the primary typeface used for the text of a publication's stories. **Display type** is that used for headlines, blurbs, pull quotes and similar items that use large type. Although some magazines (and a few newspapers) switch body type styles with regularity, most stick with one basic typeface chosen for its legibility. **Legibility** refers to the ease with which a reader navigates a story. If a typeface is easy to read, it is legible. If it's difficult to read, it's not legible. Here are examples of some typefaces considered to be legible:

> This typeface is called Palatino.
> This typeface is Baskerville.
> This typeface is Times.
> This typeface is Goudy.

It's obvious that some of those faces have a wider set width than others. Typefaces with wide sets require more space to print the same amount of copy (compare Palatino and Times in the example above). Newspapers often opt for more compact typefaces, such as Times, because they allow much more information to be printed in a given space than less compact faces such as Palatino. Magazines, often more concerned about overall appearance rather than space restrictions, frequently opt for the more attractive typefaces with wider sets.

Almost always, body typefaces are chosen for a combination of legibility and set width (see Figure 11.13). Here are other factors to consider, based on various legibility studies:

| Typefaces | Bookman | Helvetica | Tiffany | Times |

Figure 11.13

These letters were all set in 24-point type, yet each has a different basic design. The names of the typefaces appear below the letters.

- **Italic** (slanted) type is more difficult to read than **roman**, or upright, type.
- A line set in all capital letters is more difficult to read than a line set in caps and lowercase.
- Ornamental and cursive typefaces are more difficult to read than simple ones.
- **Serifs**, the small strokes at the ends of letters, aid legibility, particularly in body type. A serif is a relatively fine line at the bottom and top of letters such as *d, h, i, l, m, n, p, r, u, x* and *z*. Serifs also appear on capital letters of a serif typeface.
- Conversely, **sans serif** type is more difficult to read as body type.
- **Reverse** type, white letters on a dark background, is more difficult to read than black on white.

Generally, once a publication or website is designed, editors stick with the same body typeface all the time, with the possible exception of some feature pages the graphic editor might think deserve a special artistic touch. Although the body type is an important part of the overall design of a publication, it has far less impact than display type on luring readers. Therefore, we'll focus on the importance of display type—headlines, blurbs, pull quotes and similar devices that employ large type. First, however, let's review the basics of typography.

How Type is Measured

Most type measurements are carryovers from the old days of hot type and are identical to those used by traditional printers.

Although desktop computers allow measurement in inches, many people retain the printers' practice of measuring in picas and points. Following are the basic traditional measurements:

- **Points.** 72 points equal 1 inch (a point is 1/72 of an inch). The height of all type is measured in points. An editor can specify 12-point or 6-point type or any point size. Headline type may even be quite large, such as 120 points.
- **Picas.** 6 picas equal 1 inch (a pica is ⅙ of an inch). 12 points equal 1 pica. The width of a line of type is usually expressed in picas—for example, 14 picas wide.
- **Page measurements.** The trim size is usually measured in inches. For example, a page may measure 7 by 10 inches. (Width is usually expressed first and length second.) But the type area (the trim size minus the margins) is usually measured in picas. A page 7 by 10 inches with a half inch margin all the way around has a type area of 36 by 54 picas.

Differentiating Typefaces (Fonts)

An editor or designer specifies a particular typeface, or font, when preparing copy to be set. Specifications for any particular type may vary in several ways, including point size (see above), typeface (also called a **font**), weight and width (light or bold, condensed or expanded, for example) and style (roman or italic), as shown in Figure 11.14.

Differences in Typeface or Font

Just as members of the same human family tend to have similar facial characteristics, so do members of a type family. A type family includes all variations of a given type with common characteristics. Some type families have many variations, while others have few. Figure 11.15 shows one of the large families of typefaces. Any one of the styles within that family may be referred to as a **typeface** or **font**.

Five Ways Typefaces Differ and Sample Specifications					
How these could be specified:	(1) By point size	(2) By typeface	(3) By weight	(4) By width	(5) By style
Example 1	24 pt.	Bodoni	Lightface	Regular	Italic
Example 2	60 pt.	Century	Boldface	Condensed	Roma

Figure 11.14 Differences in typefaces.

All of those in Figure 11.15 are sans serif typefaces, which means they do not have fine closing strokes at the ends of the letters. The body type in most newspapers has serifs, as does most of the body type in this book. The three examples of large type in Figure 11.16 also have serifs. **Research shows that typefaces with serifs are easier to read in large blocks of type, so most publications prefer a face with serifs for text. Headlines may be either serif or sans serif.**

Type letters also differ in their use of thick and thin elements, which can be placed in slightly different positions on each letter. Figure 11.16 illustrates the differences among three typefaces. The type user, however, should not pay too much attention to slight variations of single letters but should concentrate on their appearance in mass form, as in a typical newspaper or magazine paragraph. A paragraph of about 50 words can show the overall look of a typeface.

Differences in Type Weight and Width

Type may be differentiated by the weight or width of the letter. Most typefaces are created in regular and boldface. Some

Futura Light

Futura Regular

Futura Bold

Futura Extrabold

Futura Regular Italic

Futura Bold Italic

Futura Light Condensed

Futura Regular Condensed

Futura Bold Condensed

Futura Extrabold Condensed

Futura Bold Outline

Figure 11.15 Some members of the Futura type family. Although each typeface is different, each also has family characteristics. When mixing different typefaces on the same page, use different members of the same type family.

Differences Among Typefaces

Shown below are three typefaces often used on desktop computers. Study the differences and read the comments.

Here is an example of 24 pt. Bookman

Here is an example   of 24 pt. Times

Here is an example   of 24 pt. Palatino

Comments

- The letters in one typeface are designed to be wider than others.
- Some letters in one face are taller than others.
- Compare the design of an "e" or "a" in each typeface. Note the differences.
- Each typeface has its own set of peculiar characteristics.
- Note the mass effect of each typeface below.

How Sample Typefaces Look in Paragraphs

10pt. Bookman

Typefaces have been designed to have unique characteristics. In selecting typefaces for a story, think of the connotation (or feeling) of the typeface and its relationship to the story. Is one typeface better than another? Some typefaces are warmer, more legible, more powerful or more delicate. Some are more feminine or masculine.

10pt. Times

Typefaces have been designed to have unique characteristics. In selecting typefaces for a story, think of the connotation (or feeling) of the typeface and its relationship to the story. Is one typeface better than another? Some typefaces are warmer, more legible, more powerful or more delicate. Some are more feminine or masculine.

10pt. Palatino

Typefaces have been designed to have unique characteristics. In selecting typefaces for a story, think of the connotation (or feeling) of the typeface and its relationship to the story. Is one typeface better than another? Some typefaces are warmer, more legible, more powerful or more delicate. Some are more feminine or masculine.

Figure 11.16 Some of the more important ways typefaces differ.

faces are also created in lightface medium, demibold, heavy and ultrabold as well. The terminology tends to be confusing. One type designer calls its medium-weight type **demibold**, whereas another calls a corresponding weight **medium**. The terms **heavy**, **bold** and **black** also may mean the same thing.

Figure 11.17 shows common examples of type weights. Most typefaces are manufactured in normal (or regular) widths (see Figure 11.18). Regular widths are used in most reading matter, but wide and narrow widths also are available. Type manufacturers have created extra-condensed, condensed, expanded and extended typefaces in addition to regular. These additional widths, however, are not manufactured in all type sizes or families.

Differences in Type Style

The most common classification of type style is into broad categories termed roman, italic and script. It is best to think of these classifications as style characteristics that help in differentiating and identifying typefaces. Each of them helps the editor find some unique quality in most typefaces.

Roman Type. Roman type (see Figure 11.19) has a vertical shape and serifs. It usually has combinations of thick and thin elements in each letter. The body copy is always set in a roman typeface with serifs. Some type experts consider all vertical letters to be roman, even those without serifs or with no

LITHOS EXTRA LIGHT

LITHOS LIGHT

LITHOS REGULAR

LITHOS BOLD

LITHOS BLACK

Figure 11.17 Various weights of typefaces within the Lithos family.

Figure 11.18 Variations in widths of type. Each variation is chosen for a specific purpose.

A B C D E F G H I J K L M N O P q r s t u v w x y z

Figure 11.19 A roman typeface (Bodoni) showing a vertical look with thick and thin elements.

ABCDEFGHIJKLMNOP qrstuvwxyz

Figure 11.20 Italic version of the Bodoni family.

variations in the width of letter elements. This form of classification, therefore, may be confusing to the beginner because the roman designation will have two purposes: one to distinguish it from sans serif and the other to distinguish it from italic.

Italic Type. Sometimes called cursive despite not being joined like handwriting, italic types are characterized by their slanted letter shapes (see Figure 11.20). Although italic typefaces were originally designed to print many letters in relatively little space, their use today is limited to citations or words that must be emphasized. They are also used in headlines and body types. Italic types are designed to accompany roman types to provide consistency in the family of design.

Electronic Distortion of Type

Computers and computer design programs such as Adobe InDesign have simplified typesetting and design. But the software is so powerful that it also permits distortions that can seriously damage the legibility of type.

For example, some software makes it possible to take a roman typeface and artificially create an italic version by slanting the type. But as any good typographer knows, that's an abomination. Good italic fonts have the italicized sweep built right into the design of each letter. Publications that care about typography have set limits on the ability of designers to distort type electronically. Such distortion should be used rarely and then only in small doses as in a headline (or title) for a magazine feature story.

How to Measure Type from a Printed Page

If you're analyzing a printed page, it's possible to measure the type but with less than complete accuracy. The height of type is measured from the top of the ascenders (the top stroke of a lowercase *d*, for example) to the bottom of the descenders (the bottom stroke of a lowercase *p* as an example).

Figure 11.21 The dashed lines define ascenders, descenders and x-height.

Figure 11.22 Measure the distance between the top ascender and the bottom descender to determine type size.

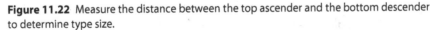

E E E E E E E

Figure 11.23 Why printed type is so difficult to measure. Each of the E's is 48 points high, but the shoulder (or descender) space of each varies.

Figure 11.21 shows imaginary lines by which letters are created. These lines are called the *base line*, on which all letters other than *g, j, p, q* and *y* rest; the cap line, to which most capital letters and tall letters rise; the lowercase line, where small letters align (called the **x-height** of letters); and the descender line. Each line helps in aligning letters.

For example, the ascender of the letter *h* rises above the lowercase line, but there is no descender below the base line. Thus, the shoulder underneath the letter must be included in the measurement. To accurately determine ascender space, simply look for a capital letter or one with a high ascender. If it is necessary to measure the point size of a line of capital letters, take the space normally used for descenders into consideration (see Figures 11.22 and 11.23).

Still, measuring type this way is far from accurate. Most typefaces have built-in leading to ensure white space between lines of type that is set solid. Further, on occasion printers enlarge or reduce pages during the printing process, so the end result might not be quite the same size as the original. So, at best, measuring type on a page is an estimate.

An Introduction to Leading

The space between lines of type is called **leading** (pronounced "ledding"). Leading should make lines of type easier to read because it gives readers more white space between lines, which helps them focus their eyes on the type.

Leading for body type usually has been determined when a newspaper, magazine or website creates its basic design. Therefore, computerized typesetting systems may be preset to control the amount of line spacing that the designer recommended. The computer automatically provides the leading desired. Occasionally, though, a publication may choose to increase the leading of a special story to make it pop out on a page (see Figure 11.24).

The Typography of Headlines

A primary purpose of a headline is to attract the reader's attention. Indeed, type is most noticeable in publications and on websites when it is used in headlines. As noted earlier, a headline often does this best when

LINE SPACING

The principle of making each line of type an easy eyeful can be aided by the generous (but not too generous) use of space between the lines. This provides a "right-of-way" for the eye along the top and bottom of each line. Types with short ascenders and descenders and large lowercase letters need more space between lines than faces with long ascenders and descenders and small lowercase letters. A fairly safe rule is to let the spacing between the lines approximately equal the space between words.

The above paragraph is set with generous spacing (3-point leads) between lines, while *this* paragraph is set with no leads and is consequently tougher reading for the consumer. The type is the same size but looks smaller. Educated instinct will in time tell you the difference between jamming and scattering type lines.

Figure 11.24 The top paragraph has been leaded three points. The bottom has been set solid, meaning that there is no leading between lines. Leaded lines are usually easier to read.

used in conjunction with photos or information graphics. Nevertheless, the bold display type used in headlines can be effective in attracting attention even when used alone.

Most headlines are set in a downstyle in which editors use the same rules of capitalization as in sentences:

Bush defends decision to invade Iraq

Older forms of headline writing are increasingly out of style:

TRUMP DEFENDS DECISION TO ABANDON KURDS

Trump Defends Decision to Abandon Kurds

The all-cap style is out of vogue, based largely on research that shows legibility is best, even in headlines, when normal rules of capitalization are followed. Occasionally, however, the news demands a splashy headline that conveys the added drama of the moment:

UNTHINKABLE TRAGEDY

Thousands die as airliners hit World Trade Center

Bigger type certainly attracts attention, but designers now know that any headline-size type can help draw readers into

a story. As a result, newspapers, magazines and even websites also use devices such as blurbs or pull quotes to draw readers into a story:

Eyewitness describes horror of trapped victims leaping to their deaths 100 stories below.
'I thought I had seen everything, but this was the pinnacle of hell.'

—James Culligan, New York firefighter

Suggested Websites

National Press Photographers Association: www.nppa.org
Pictures of the Year International: www.poyi.org
Society for News Design: www.snd.org

Suggested Readings

Franz, Laura. *Typographic Web Design: How to Think Like a Typographer in HTML and CSS*. Chichester, Sussex, England: John Wiley & Sons Ltd., 2012.
French, Nigel. *InDesign Type: Professional Typography with Adobe InDesign*. San Francisco: Adobe Press Books (Pearson), 2018.
Kobre, Ken. *Photojournalism: The Professionals' Approach*. New York: Focal Press (Taylor & Francis), 2017.
Lupton, Ellen. *Thinking With Type: A Critical Guide for Designers, Writers, Editors & Students*. New York: Princeton Architectural Press, 2010.
Lupton, Ellen. *Design Is Storytelling*. New York: Cooper Hewitt Smithsonian Design Museum, 2017.
Lupton, Ellen, and Jennifer Cole Phillips. *Graphic Design: The New Basics*. New York: Princeton Architectural Press, 2015.

GLOSSARY

active voice a verb is said to be in active voice when the subject is doing the action of the verb rather than being acted on by something else

adjective a word that modifies a noun or pronoun

adverb a word that modifies a verb, adjective or another adverb

all-cap head a headline in which all letters are capitalized

antecedent the noun that a pronoun names

art director one who oversees the design of the newspaper or magazine

assigning editor an editor who assigns a writer or reporter to a story

associate and assistant editors those who assign, write and edit articles for particular departments of a magazine

association publications magazines produced by associations of various kinds, such as trade- or hobby-related groups

audience fragmentation the erosion of audience size caused by the proliferation of television channels and other new media

bank see *deck*

banner a headline that spans the width of the page and is placed at the top

bar chart a chart that helps readers identify quantities

barker see *hammer*

bleed a design technique that pushes illustrations or background screens outside the margin to the trimmed edge of the paper

blog a journal or opinion website usually in reverse chronological order; short for web log

blurb display-sized type pulled from the text to attract the reader's attention; sometimes called a *pullout* or a *pull quote* (if a quotation)

browser a computer program used for navigating the web

budget a list of stories being readied for publication

caption the words that accompany and explain a photograph; sometimes called a *cutline* or other specific type of caption

catchline a headline-sized word or words placed over a caption and designed to help attract attention to a photo, usually a standalone

censorship when government forces the media to publish or broadcast, or not to publish or broadcast, certain information; the opposite of editorial discretion; increasingly, bans of stories, posters or outlets by high-tech companies with enormous power over what audiences get to see are also being referred to as censorship

chat room an online interactive discussion forum on the web

citizen journalism content provided by the public rather than by professional journalists

city editor the assigning editor in charge of assigning and editing all locally written stories other than sports and editorials and, depending on the newspaper, perhaps lifestyle-section stories

clause a group of related words containing a subject and a verb

collective noun a noun that is singular in form but that names a group, such as *media, committee* or *council*

color piece a story, often a sidebar or follow, that mainly tries to make the reader feel what it was like to be there

comma splice something punctuated to look like a sentence but that really consists of two sentences joined with only a comma between them

community-engagement editor one in charge of building relationships between a news organization and its viewers or readers

comparative form of a modifier the form of a modifier used when comparing two things; comparative adjectives, for example, end in *er* or have the word *more* or *less* in front of the positive form

compound modifiers two modifiers in a row, with the first modifying the second, and together the two modifying another word; compound modifiers usually have a hyphen between them

conditional mood a verb that expresses not what's true now but what could, might, should or would be true if a certain condition were met

conjunction a word that connects other words, phrases, clauses or sentences

conjunctive adverb an adverb like *although* that can join two clauses

contributing editor a regular freelancer that a magazine often employs who tends to be an expert in the field on which he or she writes

convergence the practice of sharing and cross-promoting content from a variety of media through newsroom collaborations and outside partnerships

conversational deck a blurb written in sentence style

coordinate modifiers two modifiers in a row that are equal (they can be reversed with *and* between them); coordinate modifiers should have a comma between them

coordinating conjunction a conjunction that introduces an independent clause, such as *and, or* and *but*

copy desk the place on a publication where final editing of a story takes place

copy-desk chief the person in charge of the copy desk at a newspaper or magazine; also called the news editor or the slot

copy editor an editor who does the final editing of a story and writes the headline

copy flow the steps through which a story moves from reporter to various editors on its way to production

correlative conjunctions words that must appear together when connecting words, phrases or clauses, such as "not only" with "but also"

correspondent a writer who writes from a distance for a publication; sometimes a staff member but often a freelancer

cover line a teaser headline on the cover of a magazine; also known as *cover blurb*

crossline a horizontal headline that covers multiple columns

cub reporter a beginning, or novice, reporter

cutline specific name for a multiple-line caption

dangling participle a participial phrase that has not been placed next to what it modifies, resulting in confusion

dateline the city—and sometimes the state or country—written before the first line of a story's lead (city in all capital letters but the state or country, if present, in upper and lowercase); in the past, datelines contained the date of the story, but with modern electronic transmission, the date is almost never included now

deck a section of a multiple-bank headline

defamation slander or libel that damages someone's reputation or business

delayed-ID lead a brief description of the *who* of a story in the first paragraph rather than the person's name (the name often appears at the beginning of the second paragraph); used when the *who* of a story is not famous or does not appear often in the news

dependent clause a clause that cannot stand alone as a complete sentence

developing story a story that is followed each day for a period of time

dingbat a decorative font mark

display type headline-sized type

downstyle a headline writing style that follows sentence-style rules for capitalization

drop cap a large capital letter at the start of a paragraph, whose top is lined up with the top of the smaller letter to its right

drop head a second headline between the main headline and the article; also known as *second deck* or *subtitle*

editor anyone who assigns, selects, edits or arranges stories, images or sounds

editor in chief an editor in the chain of command below the publisher but above the managing editor

editorial-page editor the editor in charge of writing editorials for the editorial page and selecting columns, cartoons, letters and op-ed pieces for the opinion section; he or she typically reports to the publisher rather than the managing editor

electronic media broadcast media (radio and television) and the internet

ethics morality, a code of behavior, principles of right and wrong, doing what's right even when what's wrong is legal

executive editor at a newspaper, an editor above the managing editor but below the publisher; at a magazine, often someone who balances the skills of the managing editor

e-zine a small, personal magazine published on the web

feature a story with a feature lead and a story structure with a dramatic beginning and end

feature lead a story introduction that tries to introduce the news dramatically rather than telling the news immediately in the first paragraph

feature obit an obituary written with a feature-story approach focusing on what the deceased's achievements were or what kind of person he or she was; also called a *life story*

fever chart a chart that shows quantities over time

flag a publication's nameplate (usually a newspaper term)

flow smooth movement in a story from point to point, making it easy for the audience to follow

focus group a representative group of readers or viewers used to evaluate or suggest changes in news content

focus piece a feature story taking *The Wall Street Journal* approach of focusing in the lead, and often the ending, on a person whose story exemplifies a particular issue

follow a follow-up story; a story that updates a previous story

formula obit an obituary written to a formula a newspaper uses for all obituaries except its feature ones

four-color process the method of printing photos or graphics of any colors from four basic inks: black, magenta, yellow and cyan

fragment a group of words that does not have both a subject and verb or present a complete thought

freedom of the press the idea that the media should be able to publish or broadcast without censorship

fused sentence a group of words punctuated to look like one sentence but which really consists of two joined sentences without punctuation between them

futures file a file a reporter or editor keeps of upcoming events and story ideas

gatekeeper an editor who controls the flow of information to the public

gerund a form of a verb, usually ending in *ing*, used in a sentence as a noun

graphics designer a person who does page design at a news outlet

graphics editor the editor in charge of designing graphics for stories and, at some papers, especially larger ones, in charge of laying out the paper

hammer a headline with a large word or two designed to attract quick attention

hanging indention a typesetting style in which the first line is flush left and all subsequent lines are indented

hard-news stories typically written with a summary lead and an inverted-pyramid structure

headline the display type designed to attract readers to a story

hoax a fraud perpetrated as a practical joke; after a while, as with many widely circulated emails, people circulate them thinking they are true

holistic editing recognizing the various journalism formulas that apply to a particular story and noticing when the story differs from them in non-intelligent ways, helping an editor spot at once various macro and micro problems in a story

hook anything in any medium that serves to grab attention and hook in the audience's mind

human-interest story a story that focuses on an emotionally involving or unusual situation; more broadly, used synonymously with *feature*

ICE desk interactive copy-editing desk, where websites are produced

idiom common expression in a language

illustration a graphic artist's effort to explain something

immediate-ID lead putting the name of the *who* of a story in the first paragraph; used when the *who* is famous or appears in the paper often

indefinite pronoun a pronoun that has no expressed antecedent (*all, any, each, everybody, few, nobody*), so it is sometimes difficult to tell whether it is singular or plural

independent clause a clause that can stand alone as a complete sentence

information graphics charts, maps, graphs and other illustrations used to convey relationships, statistics and trends

intensity density the idea that a work of any kind is usually considered better by its audience the more interesting elements it has in a given amount of space or time

interjection a word that expresses an emotional outburst

internal blurb a sample of the story, usually a pull quote, printed in large type inside a story

invasion of privacy publishing, broadcasting or posting personal information that is embarrassing, trespassing on someone's property, presenting someone in a false light or using someone's image or voice for commercial purposes without approval

inverted pyramid a news-writing style in which information is presented in order of most to least important

irregular verb a verb that doesn't follow the normal forms for verbs

keyword method a headline-writing technique in which the writer seeks to determine which words are most important to include

kicker a headline style in which a smaller subhead appears above the main headline

layering a technique for leading readers through a story on a website

lead the introduction to a story; often the first sentence or first paragraph of a story, but a long lead may sometimes run for several paragraphs; sometimes spelled as *lede*

leadership the process of inspiring employees

leading the amount of space between lines of type

leg a column of type under a story

legibility the ease with which a typeface can be read

libel a published (or in many states, broadcast) statement that defames; becomes a civil-court matter (not a criminal one) if the object sues and can show the statement to be false

line art a drawing or graphic with little or no shading made up primarily of solid strokes of a pen

linking verb a verb that draws an equation between the subject of the clause and a noun, pronoun or adjective following the verb

linkmeister a person designated to search for links to place on a website

links uniform resource locator (URL) ties to other pages within a website or outside to other websites

macro editing looking for big problems in stories, such as accuracy, objectivity, legality, ethics and propriety

main head the primary headline as opposed to a secondary deck

management the process of directing employees

managing editor the editor directly in charge of the newsroom as a whole; reports directly to either the publisher or an editor above him or her with a title such as "executive editor" or "editor in chief"

metropolitan (or metro) editor the assigning editor in charge of assigning and editing stories relating to the city in which the paper is published

micro editing looking for small things in stories, such as grammar, usage, spelling and style

misplaced modifier a modifier not placed next to the word it modifies, resulting in confusion as to what's being referred to

modifier a word that describes another one; adjectives, adverbs and interjections are modifiers; phrases and clauses can also act as modifiers or be modified

morgue a term used for a news outlet's library of stories, pictures, video or audio

most-important-element lead a lead that focuses on the most important news out of several things that happened related to the story

mugshot a photo of a person's head and neck, usually one-column or one-half-column wide

multimedia journalist a person capable of functioning in more than one medium, usually print, broadcast and online

multiple-element lead a lead that lists several things that happened related to the story

nameline a one-line caption under a mugshot

negligence failure to show enough caution or care in a situation that results in damage or injury to another

news director the person in charge of the news department at a broadcast outlet

news editor the copy-desk chief at a newspaper

newsletter a short, newsy publication with a frequent publication cycle and a high degree of specialization; usually distributed exclusively through subscription to a limited circulation

news peg a timely, newsworthy event on which to base a story

Nielsen Ratings the results of surveys used to determine levels of television viewership

noun a word that names a person, place, thing, idea or quality

nut graf a paragraph that summarizes the bottom line of a feature story, following the lead

object a noun, pronoun or other substantive that receives the action of a verb, verbal or preposition

objectivity traditionally, in journalism has meant being factual, neutral, fair and, in a hard-news story, impersonal in style; in Chapter 3 of this book, we argue for a redefinition of the term more along the lines of science and the law that stresses facts (even when judgments are expressed) and fairness and open-mindedness to new evidence that doesn't fit any preconceptions the journalist has (even if the journalist or outlet is a partisan one)

obscenity legally defined in the U.S. as something that appeals to the "prurient interest" of (would arouse) the average person, applying contemporary community standards to the work as a whole; that depicts or describes sexual conduct in a patently offensive way; and that lacks, as a whole, serious literary, artistic, political or scientific value

online editor an editor in charge of content for a news outlet's website

parenthetical in common grammatical terms, "nonrestrictive," or in AP style terms, "nonessential"; *parenthetical,* though, more clearly expresses the idea that something is an aside or an afterthought and could be put in parentheses, but since journalists don't normally use parentheses, they set off parenthetical items with commas instead

participle a form of a verb, usually ending in *ing,* that's used in a sentence as an adjective

passive voice a sentence is said to be in passive voice when the subject is not doing the action of the verb but is being acted on by something else

personality profile a story focusing on a person rather than an event

photo editor the editor in charge of choosing photos for a news outlet and recommending their cropping and sizing, as well as designing the photo-story packages

photojournalist a master of graphic aesthetics as well as a journalist who happens to work with a camera

play the location of a story within a publication; a story on page 1 is said to have received "good play"

podcasting the process of producing audio reports for a website

positive-form modifier modifiers have three forms, the positive being the one about which no comparison is made to anything else—for example, one person is *tall* (the "positive" form), but that person is *taller* than another (the "comparative" form) or the *tallest* of three or more (the "superlative" form)

possessive one of the three cases of nouns and pronouns, the one showing ownership

predicate nominative a noun or pronoun following a linking verb that renames the subject

preposition a connecting word that combined with its object acts as a modifier; in the sentence "He ran toward the trees," *toward* is a preposition, *trees* is its object, and the phrase *toward the trees* is a prepositional phrase that modifies "ran"

principal parts of verbs the main present-tense, past-tense and past-participle forms of a verb; some books add the "ing" form

process drawing an artist's drawing that helps readers visualize detailed plans

production editor an editor who follows the work of the assigning editor

pronoun a word that takes the place of a noun

proof a copy of a completed page, ready to print except for any last-minute changes you may be able to make

proofreading reading the proofs of a page after it's been formatted but before it goes to press, to check one last time for errors

proofreading symbols the symbols used in the proofreading stage after the stories have already been copy edited and laid out on the page; these are increasingly obsolete as proofreading is now done mostly on the computer

propriety the selection and presentation of material that is appropriate for a specific audience

public journalism journalism that seeks citizen participation in key issues involving a community; also called *citizen journalism*

publisher the owner or a person appointed by the owner to be the chief executive officer of a newspaper or magazine, ultimately the person locally in charge of both the news and business operations

pullout see *blurb*

pull quote a quotation from an article repeated in big type as an internal blurb to break up the page

pyramid a headline style in which lines get progressively wider, emulating the appearance of a pyramid

Q-and-A interview an interview written not as an article but in the form of a transcript of the questions and answers

ragged right type that is not justified (not lined up on the right side of the column as on the left)

readership studies measure of the relative popularity of features in a publication

read-in blurb a conversational headline element that reads directly into the main headline

read-out blurb a subhead that comes between the headline and the text; often conversational and sometimes called a *conversational blurb*

relative pronouns the pronouns *who, whom, whose, whoever, whomever, what, which* and *that* used to connect a subordinate clause to the main clause of a sentence

release date a date on a press release before which time the information should not be made public

retouching correcting imperfections in a photograph, usually done with a computer program like Photoshop

reverse white letters on a black background; also called *reverse type*

reverse kicker see *hammer*

reverse plate a headline with white type on a dark background

ribbon see *banner*

right to know the idea that the government must provide certain information to the public

rim editor a copy editor who edits stories and writes headlines and blurbs

run-on sentence a group of words punctuated to look like a sentence but that really consists of several sentences run together

sans serif type without the ending strokes called serifs

second-day story a follow story to one appearing earlier in your paper

second deck a second headline between the main headline and the article; also known as *subtitle* or *drop head*

section editor an editor who looks over a particular section of the magazine, such as letters to the editor, reviews of new products, etc.; also known at magazines as a *senior editor*

Section 230 of the 1996 Communications Decency Act; before it was passed, court cases had decided internet service providers were legally protected from liability if they acted as a mere carrier of information rather than as a publication that edits content; but Section 230 says, in part: "No provider or user of an interactive computer service shall be treated as the publisher or speaker of any information provided by another information content provider"; the controversy now is whether powerful tech giants like Facebook, Twitter and Google should be able to ban or suppress speech

SEO search engine optimized; usually used when referring to headlines on web stories

serifs the ending strokes that appear on the ends of letters in some typefaces

service journalism articles of practical use to a reader in more than a merely informative way; often used more narrowly as synonymous with *do-it-yourself article*

shield laws laws that shield a journalist's relationship with a source of information in states with laws providing such protection

slander spoken defamation that damages someone's reputation or business

slot person the copy-desk chief; the person in charge of the copy desk

soft lead an introduction typical of a feature story or the mixed-approach story in which the writer does not reveal the bottom line in the lead but instead introduces the story dramatically before turning to the bottom line several or more paragraphs later in the story

soft news another name for features

special-interest publications magazines devoted to a particular, specialized subject

spread head a multiple-column headline

staff writers at a newspaper or magazine, the salaried writers as opposed to freelance contributors

standalone a photo that stands by itself without an accompanying story

stet head a standing headline

stick-up initial a larger font capital letter at the start of a paragraph, whose base is lined up with the base of the smaller letter to its right

story count the number of articles per page, per issue, per writer, or so on

streamer see *banner*

stringer a writer paid by the column inch for contributing to a publication

style the rules of such things as abbreviation, capitalization, numbers and punctuation

subject of a clause the noun, pronoun or other word or words that the verb says is doing or being something

subject of an infinitive a noun or pronoun immediately preceding an infinitive; in the sentence "They mistook her to be Joan," *her* is the subject of the infinitive *to be*

subjunctive mood the form of a verb used when the speaker or writer of a sentence means to imply that something being expressed is contrary to fact or is a wish, doubt or prayer

subordinating conjunction a conjunction that introduces a dependent clause, such as *because* or *since*

subtitle a second headline between the main headline and the article; also known as *second deck* or *drop head*

summary lead a lead that summarizes several things that happened related to a story

superlative form of a modifier the form of an adjective or adverb when comparing three or more items; superlative adjectives, for example, end in *est* or have *least* or *most* in front of the positive form of the adjective

sweeps periods periods of time in which television audience ratings are conducted

table an information graphic composed of rows and columns of numbers

tabloid a half-size newspaper format

talk radio a radio format featuring discussion rather than entertainment

taste judgment in matters of aesthetics; sensitivity to how your audience is likely to regard something

tie-back paragraph a paragraph in a follow-up story that transitions from the latest news back to previous developments to update readers who might have missed them or forgotten

timeliness one of the main characteristics of news; to be news, something must have happened recently or have been recently revealed

title a term used for headlines, usually in magazines

trade publications specialized publications aimed at people in a particular field, such as farming, automaking or plumbing

uncountable nouns nouns with no different singular and plural forms

undated story a story with no place of origin at the start of the first paragraph; often used for roundups from multiple locations

underline a one-line caption

uniform resource locator the location of a site on the web; most often called a *URL*

update a follow story looking back weeks, months or years later at what happened since the original story was in the news

upstyle a headline style in which the first letter of all words except short conjunctions and prepositions is capitalized

urban legend a tale that is actually modern folklore, although it masquerades as a news story

usage the use of the correct word; mainly a matter of the meaning of commonly misused words

vague pronoun reference a pronoun whose antecedent is unclear

verb a word that expresses action or state of being

videographer one who operates a video camera

visual literacy understanding the importance of visually conveying information with photographs and information graphics

vodcasting the process of producing video reports for a news site

web editor an editor in charge of a website or who works on one

writer-as-expert approach a how-to story based on the knowledge of the writer

INDEX

Note: page numbers in italic type refer to Figures.

14th Amendment of the U.S. Constitution 133–134
24-hour news channels 6
247 Sports (247sports.com) 9
1984 (Orwell) 32

"a man" technique 130
abbreviations and symbols 198–199; broadcast media 72; headlines 297–298
ABC 7; reliability and political bias rating 21
Abcnews.com 110
abortion 149
accident and disaster stories: holistic editing 222–224; and libel 128
accuracy 5, 51, 93, 94; captions 331; Discipline of Accuracy 279; headlines 120, 301–302; imprecise/misleading words 99
Accuracy in Media 99, 108
ACES, the Society for Editing 47
Acosta, Jim 18
active voice: accident and disaster stories 222; of verbs 177
actual damages 135
actual malice, and libel 133–134
Adams, Eddie 160
Adams, John 27
Adams, Samuel, Journal of Correspondence 23
addresses 128, 154–155; obituaries 155, 242; style 206; of victims 229, 232
adjectives, and adverbs 183
Adobe InDesign 326, 343
Adobe Photoshop 323, 326
advance pieces 258

adverbs: and adjectives 183; conjunctive 188–189
adversarial journalism 18
advertising: appropriation of image, name or voice 138; distinction from copy 152; harmful products 156; regulation of 126; school publications 142; taste issues 164
"advertorial" copy 63
advocacy journalism 39
age 160, 161; broadcast media 75
Agence France-Press 55; AFP Fact Check 109; reliability and political bias rating 21
Ailes, Roger 28–29
airwaves, as public property 126, 143
Al-Jazeera 25, 108
All Things Considered (NPR) 107
all-cap headlines 345
alleged/allegedly, and libel 129
alliteration, in headlines 306
all-news radio 7
allsides.com 20
Altschull, Herbert J. 35
America Online 121
ampersands, in business names 227
Annenberg 108
Annenberg Public Policy Center, University of Pennsylvania 109
anonymous sources 138, 153
AP (Associated Press) 54–55, 57; AP Fact Check 109, 111; AP Graphics Bank 55; reliability and political bias rating 21; style 52, 52–53, 61, 76, 99
AP Stylebook 94, 99, 129, 139, 152, 196–198, 197, 208; legal terminology 233–234

apostrophes: possessives and plurals 173–174

"Areopagitica" (Milton) 27, 118–119

Aristotle 40, 41

arrogance, of journalists 26

Associated Press (AP) see AP (Associated Press)

association publications 59

assumptions, and libel 128

Atlanta Journal-Constitution 63

Attkisson, Sharyl 111, 124

attribution 202–204

audiences 9; audience fragmentation 7; audience-focused stories 48; difference btween online and traditional news audiences 62–64; engagement of 63–64; ethical issue 157–158

audio clips: intellectual copyright 139

average *versus* mean 101

Babylon Bee, The 97

Bagdikian, Ben 35

balance of opinion 13, 40–41; "Fairness Doctrine" 28

bar charts 334, *335*

Bartlett's Quotations 94

BBC 6, 108

Beck, Glenn 6, 107

Bell Telephone System 124

Bernstein, Carl 144

bias 11–12, 13, 35; biased sources 97–99; broadcast media 11, 13, 65; and credibility 18–21; observations about 112; political stories 244; public perceptions of 17; reliability and political bias ratings 21; tips for dealing with 112–113

Biden, Joe 105–106, 112, 122, 123

Bill of Rights 26, 117, 124–125

Bing 110

Black, Hugo 116

Black Lives Matter 154, 161

black type 341

Blaze TV 29, 107

blogs, as biased sources 98

Bloomberg: reliability and political bias rating 21

blurbs 311–312; accuracy 102; and libel 128–129

body type 337, 338

boldface type 340, 341

Boller, Paul F. Jr., *They Never Said It* 94

books 76

Boston.com 25

broadcast media: 24-hour news channels 6; acknowledgement of errors 14; bias 11, 13, 65; changing environment 6, 10–11; criticisms of 19; editing process 53, 66–68, *67*, *69*, 70–72, *73*, 74–75; legal issues 142–145; licensing and regulation of 120, 126, 142–145; local stations 7, 68; political leanings 107; political stories 245; redundant editing 76; satellite broadcast law 147; style 67–68, *69*, 70–72, *73*, 74–75; taste issues 164; see also radio; television

Brunvand, Jan Harold 94, 267

budget 55–56

bullets 316

bullying, online 148

Bush, George W. 98

business and finance stories 224–228

business names 227

bylines: opinion pieces 269–270

cable television 7; and bias 11; criticism of 19; partisanship and sensationalism 28–29

calendar items: holistic editing 259–260

Callender, James 23–24

Canada: freedom of the press 116

"cancel culture" 116

capitalization 199; quotations 204

captions 311–312, 312–313; accuracy 102; and libel 128–129; photographs 324–326, *325*, 328–332

Carlin, George 147

Carlson, Tucker 107

Carrington, Edward 27

catchlines 297, 313, 328

causation 251–253

cause promoting stories 261

CBC 6

CBC News 108

CBS 7, 98; criticisms of 19; reliability and political bias rating 21

CBS Inc. v. Democratic National Committee (1973) 146–147

celebrity stories 262–263

censorship 116, 117; arguments against 118–119; arguments for 118; by private corporations 122–123

Center for Media and Public Affairs 108

Chen, Tim 253
Chicago Manual of Style 76
Child Online Protection Act 1988 148
child pornography 149
ChinaNewsTV 108
chronological stories 228
citizen journalism 150
Civil War 27
clauses: dependent 187, 188;
   independent 187
clear stories 49–50
clichés 215–218; accident and disaster
   stories 224; business and finance
   stories 228; cliché leads 82, 88;
   conservative 244–245; crime stories
   234–235; education stories 235;
   entertainment and celebrity stories
   263; liberal 245; photographs 318;
   political stories 244–245; sports
   stories 271, 272; travel pieces 273;
   war stories 257; weather stories
   257–258
climate-change stories 253–254
Clinton, Hillary 109, 161
CNBC 6
CNN 6, 12, 19, 107; and objectivity
   29; reliability and political bias
   rating 21
CNN website: reliability and political
   bias rating 21
collective nouns 181–182
college campuses: speech codes 116,
   142, 161
college publications, censorship of
   141–142
college websites 66
Colonial Press Era (1492–1776) 23
colons 201
color pieces 261–262
Columbine Massacre, 1999 95
columns 273
commanding the reader, avoidance of
   in headlines 303–304
commas 200–201
comma-splice sentences 168
commercial speech 126
commercials *see* advertising
Communications Act 1934 *see* Federal
   Communications Act 1934
Communications Decency Act 121
companies 227
comparative form of modifiers 184
comparisons 252–253

compound modifiers 185; punctuation
   201–202
CompuServe 121
concise stories 50
conditional mood 177–178
confessions 155–156, 232
confirmation bias 111
conflict 9
conflict of interest 151, 153
confused words 190–194
conjunctions 180–181, 187–188;
   conjunctive adverbs 188–189;
   correlative 189–190
connecting words 186–190;
   conjunctions and conjunctive adverbs
   187–190; prepositions 186–187
conservatives: conservative clichés
   244–245; conservative talk radio 28;
   criticism of the media 18–19
consumers: and bias 20; changing
   patterns of consumption 4–7, 8,
   10–11; consumer news stories 224;
   Modern News Consumer study (Pew
   Research Center) 10–11
contractions: broadcast media 72
conversational decks 296
coordinate modifiers 185; punctuation
   200
coordinating conjunctions 187–188
copyright 114, 126, 139; and online
   media 148
corporate communications publications
   59, 76
corrections: and libel 134
correlation 251–252
correlative conjunctions 189–190
Cosmopolitan 59
court stories: holistic editing 228–231;
   and libel 128
courtesy titles 206; obituaries 242
COVID-19 pandemic 122, 246,
   247–248, 253
credibility 11–14, 16–42; arrogance
   and insensitivity 26; and bias
   18–21; demise of 30–32; and fake
   news 23–25; and mistakes 25;
   and negative news 22–23; online
   journalism 64–66; Party Press and
   Yellow Journalism 26–30; and
   sensationalism 21–22
crime stories: ethical issues 155–156;
   holistic editing 228–229, 231–235;
   and libel 128

criminal records 155
Cronkite, Walter 7
cropping, of photographs 321, *322*, *324*
cub reporters 264
cults 250
cutlines 288, 313, 328
CW, The 6
cyber bullying 148

Daily Kos 108
Dailycaller.com 108
Damon, William 38
dangling participles 184–185
dashes 72, 201
datelines 56–57, 207; *see also* time-day-place formula
dates: obituaries 242; *see also* time-day-place formula
day: leads 86
dead people, and libel 133
deadlines: magazines 60–61
death, cause of in obituaries 242
decimals: broadcast media 74; *see also* numbers
decks 295
defamation 116–117, 127, 133–134
delayed-ID leads 86, 89; accident and disaster stories 222; crime stories 232
demibold type 341
Democrats 19, 109; distrust in media 17, 18; fake news 23; online regulation 122; political use of broadcasting licensing powers 144; poll stories 247
demographics: news consumption 11; online audiences 63
DeMott, John 33, 34
dependent clauses 187, 188; punctuation 200
developing stories 235
Digital Millennium Copyright Act 1988 148
disability 160; terminology 163
disaster and accident stories 222–224
Discipline of Accuracy 279
Discipline of Multiple Sources 279
Discipline of Verification 279
Discovering the News (Schudson) 28
discriminatory harassment 148
display type 337

Disraeli, Benjamin 96
dividends 227
Doe v. Michigan (1989) 142
domain names 65–66, 110
dots 72
double entendres in headlines 300
Douglas, William O. 26–27
Dow Jones average 227
downstyle headlines 296, 345
drawings 317
Drudge Report 139
drugs: trade names 237
DuckDuckGo 110
Duranty, Walter 28

earthquake stories 223
Economist, The 107
editing: art of 43–44; evolution of 1–15; for graphic appeal 315–317; philosophy of 43–45; soft-news (feature) stories 90–91; *see also* editing process; editors; holistic editing; macro editing; micro editing; self-editing
editing process 43–78; basics of 48–51; broadcast media 53, 66–68, *67*, 69, 70–72, *73*, 74–75; magazines 59–61; mistakes introduced during 51–52, 100–102; newsletters and books 76; newspapers *52*, 52–59; overediting 44, 53; radio 53; stories 51–53, *52*; web editing 53, 61–66; wire copy 54–59; *see also* editing
editorial judgment 120, 121; U.S. Code Section 230 121–122
editorializing, avoidance of: captions 330; headlines 304
editors: as agenda-setters 5; changing role of 1–3, 4–5; credibility 13; employment opportunities 14–15, 59–60; functions of 44, 45, 45–47; as gatekeepers 4–5; as headline writers 286; impact of reduction in 276–277; key functions 8–9; management and leadership 277–278; perspective of 280–281; photographer-editor relationship 319–320; self-development 46–47; *see also* editing; self-editing
education stories 235
Elder, Larry 107

elections: candidates' "equal opportunity" for airtime 146
electronic enhancement of photographs 323, 326
Elements of Journalism, The (Kovach and Rosenstiel) 12, 35, 36, 105
ellipse lines 328
Emerson, Ralph Waldo 96
Empire News 25
entertainment stories 262–263
entitlement 124
Epoch Times 107
Epstein, Robert 123
errors *see* mistakes
ESPN 7
ethical issues 47, 51, 115, 150–159; decisions on 157–158; finding answers to 159; information sources 151–158
ethnicity 160, 162, 163
experience, and bias 112
external blurbs 312
e-zines 60

Facebook 14, 109, 122, 123; hoaxes 97
fact checking 93; and bias 20; fact-check stories 263–264; "fake" fact checks 111; Google Search Hints 111–112; methods of 109–111; websites 108–112; *see also* accuracy; facts
FactCheck.org 65, 109, 110
facts: adherence to 39; from biased sources 97–99; determination of 105; incorrect 96; *see also* accuracy; fact checking
"fair comment and criticism," and libel 133
fair trial, right to 154
fairness 40–41, 103, 105; and libel 134
Fairness and Accuracy in Reporting 99, 108
Fairness Doctrine (1949) 28, 121, 144, 145–146
"fake" fact checks 111
fake news 23–25, 97, 124
"false-light" invasion-of-privacy lawsuits 137–138
Falwell, Jerry 133
family stories 261

FBI 105–106
FCC (Federal Communications Commission) 28, 121, 126, 142, 144, 147
feature obituaries 241, 264–265
feature stories *see* soft-news (feature) stories
Federal Communications Act 1934 144, 145–147, 149
Federal Communications Commission (FCC) 28, 121, 126, 142, 144, 147
Federal Trade Commission 126
fever charts 334, *336*
"fighting words" 117, 119
figures: accuracy 99–100, 101; broadcast media 72, 74; *see also* numbers
finance and business stories 224–228
Financial Times, The: reliability and political bias rating 21
fire stories 223; photo editing 326, *327*, 328
firms 227
First Amendment of the U.S. Constitution 26–27, 114, 115–117, 119, 120, 122, 124, 125, 126, 133–134, 141, 142–143, 144, 149
First Bank Systems of Minneapolis 96–97
First Chicago Corp. 96–97
First, The 29
first-person stories 265
flood stories 223
fluff pieces 87
focus pieces 224, 270
follows/follow-ups 235–236, 265–266
fonts *see* type/typefaces
Food and Drug Administration 126
Food Channel, The 7
food features 266
Forbes: reliability and political bias rating 21
Ford, Harold Jr. 29
formula obits 241
Fox 7, 12
Fox News Channel 6, 19, 28–29, 107; and fake news 23; reliability and political bias rating 21
Fox News Sunday 107
fractions 74; *see also* numbers
fragments 167

France 24 TV 108
Franklin, Benjamin 18, 131
Freedom of Information Act 1966 124
freedom of the press 18, 26–27, 114,
    115–117, 156–157; meaning of
    117–126, *120*; as a right 124
Friends of the Earth 145
fused sentences 167–168
future perfect tense of verbs 176
future tense of verbs 176
futures file 269

Gallup 17
Gates, Bill 109
Gen Z, and social media 17
George, John, *They Never Said It* 94
gerunds 171, 172
Goldberg, Bernard 107
Golf 59
Google 109, 110, 123; Google Search
    Hints 111–112
gore 160
Gorgias of Leontium 31–32, 34
government: censorship 116,
    117; meeting news stories 241;
    publications 59; websites 65–66
grammar 166–190; connecting
    words 186–190; and credibility 13;
    errors *76*; headlines 297; modifiers
    183–186; nouns and pronouns
    170–174; sentence problems
    167–170; verbs 175–183
grants 227
graphic appeal, editing for 315–317
graphic devices in headlines 306
graphics: AP Graphics Bank 55
grief 160
Guardian, The: reliability and political
    bias rating 21
guilt, assumption or implication of:
    accident and disaster stories 223;
    court stories 228–229; crime stories
    231–232; headlines 303
gun stories 236–237
Gutenberg, Johannes 30

Hamilton, Alexander 117
hammers 295
handicap/disability 160; terminology
    163
hangers 331
Hannity, Sean 6, 19, 107
harassment, online 148

hard-news stories: holistic editing
    222–258; leads 81–82, 84–85,
    86–87, 89; style 84, 103; trimming
    92; *see also* stories
Harris Poll 16–17, 26
hate crime/hate speech 117
Hazelwood School District v. Kuhlmeier
    141
headlines 285–313, *286*;
    abbreviations 297–298; accuracy
    102, 301–302; alliteration
    306; balance and contrast 306;
    commanding the reader, avoidance
    of 303–304; creativity in writing
    289–291; decks 295; double
    entendres 300; editorializing,
    avoidance of 304; editors' role 286;
    good quality 305–308; grammar
    297; graphic devices 306; hammers
    295; 'headlinese,' avoidance of
    308; informative 298–300; kickers
    295–296; lessons from magazines,
    tabloids and *USA Today* 307; letting
    the story speak for itself 308; libel
    128–129, 302–303; line breaks
    297; main heads 295; mechanics of
    296–298; mental blocks 308–309;
    misplaced modifiers 301; missing the
    point 304–305; mistakes in 300–305;
    old news 302; orders 294;
    overstatement 303; print 47, 294;
    punch lines 305; punctuation 296;
    puns 306–307; putting a twist on the
    familiar 307; readers not reading
    story 286–292, *291*; rhymes 306;
    second decks 295; sensationalizing,
    avoidance of 304; SEO (search
    engine optimization) 309–311;
    shorter stories 292–293; soft-news
    (feature) stories 91; speaking
    the language of the story 308;
    terminology 295–296; typography
    340, 344–346; typos 300;
    vagueness 300; web 47, 309–311;
    writing process 293–298; writing
    recommendations 298–309
health and medical stories 237–239
Hearst, William Randolph 24
heavy type 341
Hemings, Sally 24
hidden cameras 137
high-tech companies 121;
    government regulation issues 124;

platform-publisher distinction 122; U.S. Code Section 230 121–122
Hill, The: reliability and political bias rating 21
history 104
history pieces 266–267
hoaxes 24–25, 96–97, 267
holistic editing 220–274; accident and disaster stories 222–224; advance pieces 258; business and finance stories 224–228; calendar items 259–260; cause promoting and image-building stories 261; chronological stories 228; color pieces 261–262; columns 273; crime and court stories 228–231; education stories 235; entertainment and celebrity stories 262–263; fact-check stories 263–264; feature stories 258–273; first-person stories 265; follows/follow-ups 235–236, 265–266; food features 266; gun stories 236–237; hard-news stories 222–258; health and medical stories 237–239; history pieces 266–267; how-to articles or service journalism 267; human interest stories 267–268; labor disputes 239–240; meeting stories 240–241; obituaries 241–243, 264–265; opinion pieces 269–270; personal/family stories 261; personality profiles 268; personnel stories 260–261; political stories 243–245; poll stories 246–247; press-release stories 258–259; public-policy stories 247–248; question-and-answer interviews 268; raffles 268–269; religion stories 248–251; science stories 251–254; seasonal features 269; speech stories 254–256; sports stories 270–272; travel pieces 272–273; war stories 256–257; weather stories 257–258
Holmes, Oliver Wendell 27, 144
Host v. Carter (2003) 142
hostage crimes 156
how-to articles or service journalism 267
Huffington Post 108
HuffPost: reliability and political bias rating 21
Human Events 107
human interest stories 267–268
humor, in captions 331

Hustler 133
hyphens 72, 201–202

ICANN 150
idioms, misused 194
image-building stories 261
immediate-ID leads 86, 88, 89
impact 9
impersonal style 41, 103, 105
imprecise/misleading 99
inaccuracies 93–100
inconsistencies 93–95
indecency 147
indefinite pronouns 181
independent clauses 187; punctuation 200, 201
infinitive, pronouns as subject of 171
inflation 226
information graphics 333–335, 334, 335, 336, 337; bar charts 334, 335; fever charts 334, 336; maps 333–334, 334; pie charts 334, 336; process drawings 334, 337; tables 334, 335
information sources: ethical issues 151–158
InfoWars 20
insensitivity, of journalists 26
intellectual property 139–141; and online media 148
intensity density 83–84
interest rates 225–226
interjections 185–186
internal blurbs 312
Internal Revenue (IRS) 94, 95
International Fact-Checking Network 108–109
internet: internet radio 6; journalists' skillset 4; news consumption 4–5, 8, 11; see also online media; web editing; websites
Interpretative Reporting (MacDougall) 39–40
intrusion 137
inverted-pyramid stories 86–87; see also hard-news stories
Investigative Reporters and Editors 38
irregular verbs 176, 179–180
IRS (Internal Revenue) 94, 95
italic type 338, 341, 342, 343

Jackson, Brooks, unSpun 112
Jamieson, Kathleen Hall, unSpun 112

JDart ("joking, deleted, apologized for, responsive tweet") 131–132
Jefferson, Thomas 23–24, 27, 119
job descriptions 206
Jobs, Steve 24–25
jokes, and libel 133
Journal of Correspondence (Adams) 23
journalists: arrogance and insensitivity 26; changing skillsets 4, 8; gifts to 151, 153–154; government licensing of 120; liberal views 19–20; narrative writing 11, 12; "voice" of 11; *see also* ethical issues; reporter-editors; reporters; self-editing
Just the Facts: How "Objectivity" Came to Define American Journalism (Mindich) 32
juvenile offenders 155

Kennedy 107
Kennedy, John 144
Kentucky State University 142
Ketterer, Stan 61–62, 65–66
kickers 295–296
Knight Foundation 17
KOMU- TV 69, 70
Kovach, Bill, *The Elements of Journalism* 12, 35, 36, 105
Krugman, Paul 25

labor disputes 239–240
land 143
law 104
layers, in websites 61–62
Lead Stories 109
leadership, and editors 277, 278
leading 344, *345*
leads 81–85; cliché 82, 88; hard-news 81–82, 84–85, 86–87, 88; meeting stories 240; soft-news (feature) 81–82, 84–85, 87–88, 88–89
Lee, Dave 132
legal issues: anonymous sources 138; broadcast media 142–145; freedom of the press 115–126; legality of stories 51; libel (see libel); macro editing 114–150; negligence (see negligence); obscenity (see obscenity); privacy (see privacy, invasion of); satellite broadcast law 147
legal terminology 99, 229–230, 230–231; legalese, avoidance of 229; problems in 233–234

legends 328
legibility, of type/typefaces 337, 338
Leibling, A.J. 35, 145
Lemon, Don 107
Levinson, Suzanne 310–311
liability 127
libel 114, 116, 117, 126, 127–136; businesses 131; common questions about 129–131; common situations 128–129; headlines 302–303; libel per se 127; online media 148; protection from lawsuits 13–135; U.K. 116–117
liberals: criticism of the media 19; journalists as 19–20; liberal clichés 245; liberal talk radio 28
licensing: broadcast media 120; of journalists 120
Limbaugh, Rush 6, 28, 146
line art 317
line breaks, in headlines 297
line spacing 345
linking verbs 171
links, in websites 61–62, 65–66; intellectual property 139
Lippmann, Walter 36–38
littlegreenfootballs.com 98
Lloyd's of London 228
lobbying, state laws 149
local media: local broadcast television 7; local newspapers, and public trust 31; reliability and political bias rating 21
logical fallacies 112
Los Angeles Times: stylebook 197

MacDougall, Curtis D., *Interpretative Reporting* 39–40
macro editing 48; for big picture 79–113; ethical issues 115, 150–159; legal issues 114–150; overview of 79–80; propriety 115, 159–164; and self-editing 279–280
Macworld 7
Maddow, Rachel 19, 107, 146
Madison, James 26, 117
magazines: changing environment 6–7; editing process 59–61; political leanings 107; redundant editing 76; style 61; title heads 290, 293–298, 309
main heads 295
management, and editors 277, 278

maps 333–334, *334*
Marketplace of Ideas 26–27, 29
Marx, Karl 32
Maximum PC 59
McCarthy Era 118
McCartney, Paul 24–25
means *versus* averages 101, 248
media: changing environment 5–7; convergence 7–8; and credibility 11–14; political attacks on 17; public trust in 16–17; *see also* local media; online media
media attorneys 131
Media Matters 108
Media Research Center (MRC) 99, 108, 123
media watchdogs 108; as biased sources 98–99
MediaBiasChart.com 20–21
MediaBuzz (FNC) 107
Mediamatters 99
median 248
medium type 341
meeting stories: holistic editing 240–241
mental blocks: headlines 308–309
Merz, Charles 37
method, objectivity of 12
Miami Herald 310–311
micro editing 48, 80; grammar 166–190; self-editing 279–280; spelling 196, 207–210; style 196–207, *197*; tightening 196, 210–218; usage 166–167
microaggressions 116, 161–162
military websites 65–66
Millennials, and social media 17
Milton, John 27, 118–119
Mindich, David T.Z., *Just the Facts: How "Objectivity" Came to Define American Journalism* 32
Minnesota Public Radio (MPR) 64
misinformation 118, 122, 151; *see also* fake news
misplaced modifiers 184–185, 301
mistakes: acknowledgement of 13–14; and credibility 24, 25; introduced during editing process 51–52, 100–102; macro and micro 48
misused idioms 194
misused words 190–194
mobile phones 66; news consumption 4–5, 8, 11

Modern News Consumer study (Pew Research Center) 10–11
modifiers 183–186, 193; adjectives *versus* adverbs 183; coordinate *versus* compound 185; form and placement of 183–185; interjections 185–186; and libel 129–130; misplaced 184–185, 301; punctuation 200
Moore, Stephen 247–248
Morning Edition (NPR) 107
mortgages 226
most-important-element-what leads 240
Motherwell, Molly x
Moveon.org 108
MPR (Minnesota Public Radio) 64
MRC (Media Research Center) 99, 108, 123
MSNBC 6, 12, 19, 29; reliability and political bias rating 21
Muckraking Era 27
mugshots 313
multimedia journalism 62
multiple-element-what leads 240
Murdoch, Rupert 28–29
Murrow, Edward R. 7
Musk, Elon 131–132

namelines 313, 328
nameline-underlines 313, 328
names: format in broadcast media 74–75; publication of 154–155, 164; *see also* titles
Napolitano, Andrew 107
narrative writing 11, 12, 41
Nation, The 107
National Association of Broadcasters v. FCC (1984) 147
National Directory of Magazines 60
National Geographic 329
National Public Radio (NPR) 6, 21, 105–106, 107
National Report 25
National Review 107
national security issues 156; U.K. 117
Native Americans 128, 162, 163
NBC 7; criticisms of 19; reliability and political bias rating 21
NBC News 48
NBC v. U.S. (1943) 147
negative news 22–23
negative reviews 267–268
negligence 114, 126, 133, 135–136

neutrality 39, 102–103, 105; and libel 134
New Hour (PBS) 107
New Republic, The 107
New York Times Company v. Sullivan (1964) 133–134
New York Times Company v. United States (1971) (Pentagon Papers case) 119–120, 126, 153
New York Times, The 2, 9, 25, 36–37, 44, 55, 56, 95, 107, 111; criticisms of 18–19; and objectivity 27–28, 29, 33, 104; reliability and political bias rating 21; story length 292–293; style conventions 57; stylebook 197
New York World 37
news: changing nature of 4–5, 9–10, 123; latest 49; *see also* bias
news budget 55–56
news pegs 84
newsletters 59, 76
Newsmax 29, 107
newspapers: acknowledgement of errors 13; bias 13; changing environment 2–3, 5–6, 10, 30; criticisms of 19; declining role of editors 2; editing process *52*, 52–59; political leanings 107; reduction in editors in 275; redundant editing 76; web-first strategy 54
Newsweek magazine: reliability and political bias rating 21
Newsy: reliability and political bias rating 21
Nixon, Richard 144
nonprofit organizations' publications 59
nonstories 81
no-story pictures 332
nouns and pronouns 170–174; collective 181–182; indefinite pronouns 181; possessives and plurals 173–174; and prepositions 187; pronoun case 170–172; pronoun-antecedent agreement 170; relative pronouns 172–173; uncountable nouns 181
novelty 9
NPR (National Public Radio) 6, 21, 105–106, 107
nudity 159
numbers 199–200; accuracy 99–100; broadcast media 72, 74; business

and finance stories 225–227; *see also* figures
Nuremberg Files 149
nut graf 88, 89, 262, 266, 270

O 59
Obama, Barack 110, 112, 161–162
obituaries: feature obituaries 241, 264–265; and hoaxes 24–25; holistic editing 241–243, 264–265; publication of addresses 155, 242
objective pronouns 170, 171
objectivity 12, 51, 102–103, 104–106; demise of 30–32; "impossibility" of 33–34; lost meaning of 36–38; of method 33, 35, 37–38; "new objectivity" in practice 38–41; *and The New York Times* 27–28, 33; principles of 31–32; public expectations of 17; redefinition of 35; re-examination of 32–35; sports stories 271–272
obscenity 114, 126, 138–139, 147, 159; online media 149
Occupy Wall Street 95
official titles *see* titles
off-the-record statements 153
old news, and headlines 302
ombudsmen 13
O'Malley, Martin 161
On the Media *(NPR)* 107
One America News Network 29
Onion, The 97
online media: legal issues 148–150; reduction in editors in 276; U.S. Code Section 230 121–122; *see also* internet; social media; web editing; websites
opinion pieces 269–270
opinions 128
Orwell, George, *1984* 32
overediting 44
overstatement, in headlines 303

pace, of stories 90
page measurements 339
Palin, Sarah 25
parallel construction of verbs 175
parenthetical items 172; punctuation 200
participles: dangling 184–185; past participle 175–177; present participle 171–172, 175

partisanship 28–32; and credibility 18–21, 65; and objectivity 105; pros and cons of 106

Party Press Era (1781–1833) 23–24, 26–27; Second Party Press Era 28–39

passive voice 177; accident and disaster stories 222

past participle 175–177

past perfect tense 176, 177

past tense 175, 176, 177; broadcast media 75; hard-news stories 84

PBS 107, 108

PC Magazine 7

peer editing 283–284

Penny Press Era (1833–1861) 24, 27

Pentagon Papers case (*New York Times Company v. United States* (1971)) 119–120, 126, 153

per capita rates 101

percentages 101

Personal Attack Rule, 1967 145, 146

personal stories 261

personality profiles 268; business and finance stories 224

personnel stories 260–261

pervasive public figures 134

Pew Research Center 19, 108; *Modern News Consumer* study 10–11, 123

philosophy 104

phonetic spelling 70–71

photo editors 317–319, *318*; decisions 320–323, *322*, *324*; taste issues 326, *327*, 328

photographs 314–322, *318*, *322*, *324*, *325*, *327*; AP Graphics Bank 55; captions 324–326, *325*, 328–332; changing technology 326; as copy 324–326, *325*; cropping 321, *322*, *324*; editing decisions 320–323, *322*, *324*; electronic enhancement and manipulation of 323, 326, 329–330; intellectual copyright 139; mugshots 313; photographer-editor relationship 319–320; selection 320–321; sizing 322–323; source checking 110; standalone photos 313; use of 317–319, *318*

picas 339

pictures *see* photographs

pie charts 334, *336*

Pinson, James L. 41

Pinson, Taylor x, 73

place names: broadcast media 75; leads 86; pronunciation 70–71

plagiarism 154

plane crash stories 223

platform-publisher distinction 122

Plato 33, 118

play, of a story 4

plural words 182–183

podcasts 8

points 339

political bias 28–32; and credibility 18–21

political correctness 116, 142, 160, 161

political discourse 31

Political Editorializing Rule, 1967 145, 146

political polarization 11, 17, 29–30

political stories 243–245

Politico 60; reliability and political bias rating 21

PolitiFact 65, 108, 110

polls: as biased sources 98, poll stories 246–247

positive form of modifiers 183

possessive pronouns 170, 171, 174

Postmodern Critical Theory 32, 33, 34

Pound, Ezra 87

Poynter Institute 108

predictive nominative 171

prepositions 186–187

present participles 171–172

present perfect tense: broadcast media 67–68, 75; of verbs 176

present tense: broadcast media 67–68, 75; captions 331; soft-news (feature) stories 84; of verbs 175, 176, 177

presidential election 2020, role of social media in 123

press freedom *see* freedom of the press

press regulation 18

press-release stories: holistic editing 258–259

Prime Time Access Rule, 1970 147

print size: headlines 294

prior restraint 117–118, 119–120

privacy, invasion of 114, 117, 126, 136–138; ethical issues 154; and online media 148–149; right to: 125

process drawings 334, *337*
profanity 159
Progressive, The 107
Project Censored 99, 107, 108
Project for Excellence in Journalism 36–38
prominence 9
pronouns: broadcast media 75; indefinite pronouns 181; object of prepositions 186; possessives and plurals 173–174; pronoun case 170–172; pronoun-antecedent agreement 170; relative 172–173
pronunciation 70–71
proper nouns: and prepositions 187; *see also* nouns and pronouns
property tax 227
propriety 159–164; macro editing 115, 159–164
proximity 9
Psaki, Jen 122
pseudoevents 152
Public Broadcasting System: reliability and political bias rating 21
public interest rule 146–147
public officials, and libel 134
publicity crimes 156
public-policy stories 247–248
Pulitzer, Joseph 24
pull quotes 312
pullouts 312
punch lines 305
punctuation 200–202; broadcast media 72; colons 201; commas 200–201; dashes 201; headlines 296; hyphens 201–202; quotations 204–205; semicolons 201
punitive damages 135
puns, in headlines 306–307
Pyrrho of Ellis 33

qualified privilege 130
question-and-answer interviews 268
quotation marks 205; broadcast media 72
quotations 89; accuracy checking 94; attribution 202–204; capitalization and punctuation 204–205; fact checking 110; false 96; and libel 129, 132; mistakes introduced during editing 100; out of context 152; pull quotes 312

race 160, 161, 162, 163; terminology 163
racism 112, 161; diseases named by place of origin 238
radio: changing environment 6; editing process 53; style 70, *73*; *see also* broadcast media
raffles 126, 268–269
Rand, Ayn 143
Ranly, Don 48
rape cases, publication of addresses of victims 155, 229, 232
Rather, Dan 19, 98
readability measures 211
readable stories 49–50
reader stoppers 168–170
reader-centered stories 48–49, 80
read-in blurbs 312
read-out blurbs 312
Reagan, Ronald 28, 146
Reason 107
recipe writers 266
recording, without permission 137
redundant editing 45, 76
regular type 340
relative pronouns 172–173
reliability and political bias ratings 21
religion stories 248–251
religious affiliation 160, 162, 163
Reno v. ACLU (1997) 149
reporters: foundations of good reporting 279; perspective of 277–281; reporter-editors *3*, 3–4; *see also* journalists; self-editing
Reporters Without Borders 116
Republicans 19, 109; distrust in media 17, 18; and online regulation 122; political use of broadcasting licensing powers 144; poll stories 247
reputation, and libel 130
research reports, as biased sources 98, 109
retouching of photographs 323
retractions, and libel 135
Reuters 55, 95; reliability and political bias rating 21; Reuters Fact Check 109; stylebook 197
reverse type 338
reviews: and libel 133; negative 267–268
rewriting 100–102
rhymes, in headlines 306

Richter scale 223
right stories 50–51
right to know 125
Rivals (www.rivals.com) 9
roman type 338, 341, *342*, 342–343
Rosenstiel, Tom, *The Elements of Journalism* 12, 35, 36, 105
RT TV 108
Ruder, Bill 144
rule of thirds 321
run-on sentences 168
Russian Revolution 1917 28, 36–37

sales tax 226
Salon 60, 108
same-store sales 228
sample blurbs 312
Sanders, Bernie 161
Sandman, Nicholas 128
sans serif 338, 340
Santayana, George 96
satellite broadcast law 147
satellite radio 6
satire sites 97
savings and loans 228
Savitch, Jessica 48
scanning, of photographs 326
scare stories 253
Schmedding, Teresa 311
school newspapers, censorship of 126, 141–142
Schudson, Michael, *Discovering the News* 28
science 104; science stories 251–254
script type 341
search engine optimization (SEO): headlines 309–311
seasonal features 269
second decks 295
second-day stories 49
Section 230 109, 121–122, 149, 355
secrecy 156
Sedition Act 1798 27
selection, of photographs 320–321
self-editing 3, 44, 76–78, 275–284; editor's perspective 280–281; micro editing 279–280; and peer editing 283–284; process of 282–284; reporter's perspective 277–281
semicolons 201

sensationalism 21–22, 27, 28, 152; avoidance of in headlines 304
sensitivity 51, 160–163
sentences: comma-splice 168; fused 167–168; reader stoppers 168–170; run-on 168
SEO (search engine optimization): headlines 309–311
serifs 338, 340
service journalism 267
set width 337–338
"Seven C's Plus One" formula (Ranly) 48
sex/gender 160, 162–163
sexism 112
sexual crimes: publication of names and addresses 155, 229, 232
sexual orientation 162, 163
sexual preference 160
shield laws 125, 138
sidebars 315–316
Simply Sewing 59
single-element-what lead 240
size: photographs 322–323; print 294, 338–339, *343*, 343–344, *344*
skepticism 32–33
slander 127, 130
Slate 60, 108
Snopes.com 97, 109, 110
social media 121; acknowledgement of errors 14; fact checking 109; fake news 124; journalists' skillset 4; and libel 131–132; platform/publisher distinction 122; political bias 29–30, 123–124; public trust in 17; role in presidential election 2020 123; *see also* internet; online media
Society of Professional Journalists, code of journalistic ethics 159
soft-news (feature) stories: editing of 90–91, 258–273; leads 81–82, 84–85, 87–88, 88–89; style 84–85; trimming 92
Somerset Maugham, W. 289
Soros, George 109
Spanish-American War 24
Special Report (FNC) 107
special-interest publications 59, 76
speech codes, college campuses 116
speech stories 254–256
spelling: and credibility 13; micro editing 196, 207–210

spirituality 248
Spiro, Alex 131
Sports Illustrated 59
sports stories 270–272
sports teams: Native Americans names and identities 162
staging, of events 152
Stalin, Joseph 28
standalones 313, 332
Star Tribune 96–97
stereotyping 160–163
sting operations 153
stolen information 153
stories: accident and disaster 128, 222–224; audience-focused 48; business and finance 224–228; cause promoting 261; celebrity 262–263; chronological 228; clear 49–50; climate-change 253–254; color pieces 261–262; columns 273; concise 50; consumer news 224; court 128, 228–231; crime 128, 155–156, 228–229, 231–235; disaster and accident 222–224; earthquake stories 223; editing of 51–53, *52*, 79–113; education 235; ensuring quality of 80–81; entertainment 262–263; ethical issues 151–158; fact-check 263–264; family 261; feature 258–273; fire 223, 326, *327*, 328; first-person 265; focus pieces 224, 270; follows/follow-ups 235–236, 265–266; food features 266; gun 236–237; health and medical 237–239; history pieces 266–267; how-to articles or service journalism 267; human interest 267–268; image-building 261; intensity density 83–84; inverted-pyramid 86–87; killing of 80, 81; labor disputes 239–240; leads 81–85; legality of 51; length of 81, 292–293; letting the story speak for itself in headline writing 308; mixed approach 85, 88; nonstories 81; opinion pieces 269–270; organization and flow 88–90; pace of 90; people-focused 80–81; personal 261; personnel 260–261; political 243–245; polls 246–247; public-policy 247–248; question-and-answer interviews 268; readable 49–50; reader-centered 48–49, 80; religion 248–251; right 50–51; science 251–254; second-day 49; speaking the language of the story in headline writing 308; speech 254–256; sports 270–272; train crash 223; travel pieces 272–273; trimming 91–92; unanswered questions 92–93; undercover 137; war 256–257; weather 257–258; *see also* hard-news stories; soft-news (feature) stories
Stossel, John 149
Student Press Law Center 142
style *52*, 52–53, 61, 76, 99; abbreviations and symbols 198–199; addresses 206; broadcast media 67–68, 69, 70–72, *73*, *74–75*; capitalization 199; datelines 56–57; hard-news stories 84, 103; magazines 61; micro editing 196–207, *197*; *The New York Times* 57; newspapers 56–57; numbers 199–200; punctuation 200–202; quotations 202–204; soft-news (feature) stories 84–85; time-day-place 198, 199, 205; titles 206–207
subheads 316
subjective pronouns 170, 171
subject-verb agreement 178–183
subjunctive mood 178
subordinating conjunctions 188
subsidies 227
subtitles, magazines 309
summary blurbs 312
superlative form of modifiers 184
superlatives, unwanted 95
supplemental wire services 55; *see also* wire services
swearing 159
symbols 198–199
syndicated columnists 13
syndication 55

tables 334, *335*
tablet computers, news consumption 4–5, 8
talk radio 6, 7, 28
taste issues 51, 115, 164; photo editing 326, *327*, 328
tax increases, opposition to 149
Telecommunications Act 1996, Title V 149
television: 24-hour news channels 6; acknowledgement of errors 14; bias

11, 13, 65; changing environment 6, 10–11; local stations 7, 68; see also broadcast media
television videographers 315
tenses: in attributions 203; of verbs 175–177
Thefederalist.com 108
They Never Said It (Boller and George) 94
This Old House 59
Thomas, Richard L. 96–97
Three R's of Copy Editing 48, 60, 80
tightening 196, 210–218; accident and disaster stories 224; business and finance stories 228; court stories 230; crime stories 235; education stories 235; health and medical stories 238–239; micro editing 196, 210–218
time angles: broadcast media 75
time, leads 86
Time magazine 59, 107, 283
time zones 57–58
time-day-place formula 198, 199, 205; calendar items 260
timeliness 9; hard-news stories 87
titles 206; broadcast media 74–75; military 256; religious ministers 249; style 206–207; writing process 293–298; see also names
trade names of drugs 237
trade publications 59
trademark infringements 139–141
tragedy 160
train crash stories 223
travel pieces 272–273
trespass 137
"trigger warnings" 116
trimming 91–92
Troy State College 142
Truman, Harry 46
Trump, Donald 18, 110, 121, 123, 124, 238; and fake news 23
truth 151; getting at 106–112; and journalism 5
Tuchman, Gaye 34
Twitter 14, 123, 246; hoaxes 97; libel case 131–132
type/typefaces 337–344, 338, 339, 341, 342, 343, 345; black 341; body type 337, 338; boldface 340, 341; demibold 341; differentiating

typefaces (fonts) 339, 339–343, 340, 341, 342; display type 337; headlines 340, 344–346; heavy 341; italic 338, 341, 342, 343; leading 344, 345; legibility 337, 338; line spacing 345; measurement of 338–339, 343, 343–344, 344; medium 341; page measurements 339; points 339; regular 340; reverse type 338; roman 338, 341, 342, 342–343; sans serif 338, 340; serifs 338, 340; type style 341–343, 342; weight and width 340–341, 342
typos: in headlines 300; see also accuracy; mistakes

UK, freedom of the press in 116–117
uncountable nouns 181
undercover stories 137
underlines 288, 313, 328
United Press International 54–55, 95; stylebook 197
University of Minnesota 142
university publications, censorship of 141–142
university websites 66
unSpun (Jackson and Jamieson) 112
Unsworth, Vernon 131–132
updates 235
upstyle headlines 296
urban legends 94, 97, 267
URLs, fact checking 65–66, 110
U.S. Code Section 230 121–122, 149–150
U.S. News and World Report: stylebook 197
U.S. Telecommunications Act 1996 7
USA Patriot Act 2001 149
USA Today 107, 110, 307; reliability and political bias rating 21; story length 292–293
usage 166–167; accident and disaster stories 223–224; business and finance stories 227–228; confused words 190–194; court stories 229–230; entertainment and celebrity stories 263; government stories 241; health and medical stories 237–238; misused idioms 194; obituaries 243; public-policy stories 248; science stories 254; speech stories 256

vagueness, avoidance of in headlines 300

Van Anda, Carr 44

verbs 175–183; active and passive voice 177, 222; conjunctions 180–181; irregular 176; linking verbs 171; parallel construction 175; subject-verb agreement 178–183; tenses 175–177

Verification, Discipline 279

video clips 139

videographers 315

Volhk, Eugene 117

Voltaire 96

Vox: reliability and political bias rating 21

Wall Street Journal, The 2, 107; criticisms of 18; reliability and political bias rating 21; *Wall Street Journal* approach 270

war stories 256–257

Washington Examiner, The 107

Washington Post, The 2, 107, 111, 144; criticisms of 18–19; and hoaxes 25; reliability and political bias rating 21; stylebook 197

Washington Times: reliability and political bias rating 21

Washington-examiner.com 108

Watergate stories 144

weapons: gun stories 236–237

Weather Channel, The: reliability and political bias rating 21

weather stories 257–258

web editing: acknowledgement of errors 14; audience engagement 63–64; and credibility 64–66; difference between online and traditional news audiences 62–64; headlines 47; *see also* internet; websites

web-first strategy 54

websites: as biased sources 98; headlines 47, 309–311; *see also* internet; online media

Webster's New World College Dictionary 94, 208

Webster's Third New International Dictionary 94, 208

webzines 60

WEMU-FM 70, *73*

WGN Newsnation 107

White, E.B. 270

Whiteside, Scott 63

widows 331

wire services: broadcast media 68; copy editing process 54–59; phonetic spelling 71

Wired: stylebook 197

Wonkette 20

Woodward, Bob 144

words: common 212–213; confused 190–194; connecting 186–190

World News Daily Report 25

WorldNetDaily 139

Writer's Market 59

www.truthorfiction.com 109

Yellow Journalism Era (1883–1900) 24, 27; Second Yellow Journalism Era 28–39

YouTube 123

Zapple rule 146

zones 60